CHRISTY CAMP[...] [...]rmer defence correspondent and feature writer for the *Sunday Telegraph*, which he j[...]ality of 'fore[...] special supp[...] [...]century histo[...]

His previous book, *The Maharajah's Box*, was an investigation into the strange fate of the last King of Lahore.

Further reviews of **Fenian Fire**:

'Christy Campbell has come up with a genuine historical scoop ... In a superb piece of historical detective work, Campbell has pieced together every element of the conspiracy on both sides of the Atlantic, from the prime minister's house in St James's to the Islington garret where the "dynamitards" were arrested in November 1887 ... It was a classic case of an agent provocateur sting.' ANDREW ROBERTS, *The Times*

'Campbell has uncovered an extraordinary web of personal and political intrigue ... an enthralling tale ... the pace never slackens ... Particularly good is his account of the origins of Irish revolutionary nationalism ... To tell this involved story against the backdrop of bureaucratic bickering, revolutionary intrigue and clandestine meetings between spies and informers is both original and clever. Campbell is making this type of breezy investigative history his own.' ANDREW LYCETT, *Sunday Times*

'The "jubilee plot" is such a bizarre episode that I would regard it as the product of a febrile imagination had Christy Campbell not documented sufficient evidence to remove all reasonable doubt ... From Mexico City to Liverpool and from the House of Commons to Chicago coroner's court, the story moves at the pace of the best sort of adventure story. All the *Boy's Own Paper* ingredients are there ... colourful characters and compelling story ... Its account of Fenian organisation and activity makes a real contribution to nineteenth-century history.' ROY HATTERSLEY, *Observer*

'An extraordinary story ... Campbell has drawn skilfully on recently-released papers from Home Office files and elsewhere, revealing the workings of an extraordinary counter-terrorism operation which penetrated the Irish revolutionary movement in all locations and at all levels. Campbell take us through a fascinating account of how British agents bought the services of veteran Irish-American figures ... The book is history, not fiction. But the reader may sometimes forget that, such is the pace and strong narrative style. It is a scrupulously accurate and detailed piece of research which tells a dramatic tale, but which also provides a valuable insight into little known aspects of the 19th century relationship between Britain and Ireland.'

CONOR BRADY, *Irish Times*

'A real page-turner, *Fenian Fire* shows that Victorian history has a neglected "Intelligence dimension" ... the extraordinary affair of the Diamond Jubilee plot makes *The Day of the Jackal* look placid by comparison.' PROFESSOR J.R. VINCENT

'Excellent ... Campbell has done a marvellous job, reminding us in his enormously entertaining book just how stupid politicians can be.' ANDREW CRUMEY, *Scotland on Sunday*

'A splendidly written piece of research, diverse in location and madly cast ... Terrific!' BRIAN CASS, *Time Out*

'In many ways *Fenian Fire* is a remarkable book; it is populated by a colourful, even bizarre cast of characters ... Campbell's research is prodigious and largely original ... He is to be congratulated on a very worthwhile book.'

C.D.C. ARMSTRONG, *Daily Telegraph*

CHRISTY CAMPBELL

Fenian Fire

The British Government Plot
to Assassinate Queen Victoria

HarperCollins*Publishers*

HarperCollins*Publishers*
77–85 Fulham Palace Road,
Hammersmith, London W6 8JB

www.**fire**and**water**.com

This paperback edition 2003
1 3 5 7 9 8 6 4 2

First published in Great Britain by
HarperCollins*Publishers* 2002

ISBN 0 00 710482 0

Set in PostScript Linotype Galliard
with Photina and Bauer Bodoni display

Printed and bound in Great Britain by
Clays Ltd, St Ives plc

For Mary and Flann
sgd xvn tkc gzu dzo oqn udc

And now I will unclasp a secret book,
And to your quick-conceiving discontents,
I'll read you matter deep and dangerous . . .

Shakespeare, *Henry IV*, Part I

CONTENTS

LIST OF ILLUSTRATIONS

The Clerkenwell explosion, 1867. © *Mary Evans Picture Library*
The Phoenix Park murders. © *Mary Evans Picture Library*
Lady Florence Dixie. © *Mary Evans Picture Library*
Sir Edward George Jenkinson. © *Hulton Archive*
Sir William Vernon Harcourt. © *Mary Evans Picture Library*
Earl Spencer. © *Mary Evans Picture Library*
Charles Stewart Parnell. © *Hulton Archive*
William O'Brien. © *Hulton Archive*
Michael Davitt. © *Hulton Archive*
Attempt to blow up government offices in Westminster, 1883.
© *Mary Evans Picture Library*
Victoria station after the dynamite explosion. © *Mary Evans Picture Library*
The Rising Sun pub. © *Metropolitan Police Historical Museum*
After the Great Scotland Yard explosion. © *Metropolitan Police Historical Museum*
'Dynamite Saturday' – Tower of London and House of Commons. © *The Illustrated London News Picture Library*
Logotype of the Bank of Mexico. © *Public Record Office*
Francis Frederick Millen. © *The Sphere/British Library Newspaper Library*
Millen in Dublin. © *National Library of Ireland*
Despatch from Her Britannic Majesty's Legation in Mexico City. © *Public Record Office*

Victoria R. I. © *Hulton Archive*
Lord Salisbury. © *Hulton Archive*
Arthur Balfour. © *Hulton Archive*
Henry Matthews. © *Mary Evans Picture Library*

James Monro. © *Hulton Archive*
Queen Victoria's Golden Jubilee. © *Hulton Archive*
Robert Anderson. © *Metropolitan Police Historical Museum*
Alexander Sullivan.
Charles Carrol-Tevis.
Thomas Billis Beach, alias Henri le Caron.
Penny Illustrated News, 5.11.87. © *British Library Newspaper Library*
A minute from the *Times* archive. © *Times Newspapers Limited*
Working decrypt by the defence of an intercepted cable from the *Times* agent in New York. © *National Library of Ireland*
The 'Mexico' cable. © *Trinity College Dublin*
Walter and Parnell cartoon from *Fun*. © *British Library*
Sir Richard Webster.
Winston Churchill. © *Mary Evans Picture Library*

CHRONOLOGY

1858   Irish Revolutionary Brotherhood founded in Dublin.
Fenian Brotherhood founded in New York.

1863–5 Fenian recruitment within Union and Confederate armies.
General Francis Millen joins FB.

1865   US Civil War ends. An Anglo-American war is bruited by
some victorious Union commanders.
Abortive IRB coup attempt in Dublin backed by Civil
War veterans.
Fenians in US split – into O'Mahony wing and 'senate'
wing.

1866   Millen offers services as informer to British consul in New
York.
O'Mahony wing of the Fenian Brotherhood raids Campo
Bello island.
Senate wing invades Canada.
Thomas Beach recruited as British informer.
Millen writes secret history of Fenianism for Samuel
Anderson at Dublin Castle.

1867   General Charles Carrol-Tevis recruited as Foreign Office
informer within senate wing.
Fenian rising in Ireland is easily crushed.
Clan-na-Gael founded in New York.
Manchester 'rescue': three hang after attack on prison
van.
Clerkenwell explosion kills thirteen.
Secret Service department created to defend London. It is
closed down after a year.

1870   Second Fenian invasion of Canada betrayed by Beach and
        defeated in a day.

1871   Amnesty and exile for 'Cuba Five' – IRB political
        prisoners (sentenced in Ireland 1866–7). They join and
        reanimate the Clan-na-Gael.

1875   Charles Stewart Parnell elected to Westminster parliament
        as 'home rule' member for Meath.

1876   'Skirmishing' fund established by O'Donovan Rossa to
        attack British power.
        The Clan-na-Gael makes a formal alliance with IRB with
        an international 'revolutionary directory'.
        Catalpa rescue – 'military' prisoners sentenced for mutiny
        in 1866 are snatched from Australian jail.
        Balkan crisis deepens. Clan makes overtures to Russia.
        Holland submarine development funded by skirmishing
        fund.

1877   Criminal Investigation Department founded in
        Metropolitan Police.

1878   General Millen draws up plans for Clan operations in
        Afghanistan, South Africa, Gibraltar and Central America
        and for US invasion of Ireland – contingent on
        Anglo-Russian conflict.
        Michael Davitt tours US with Clan sponsorship. Proposes
        agrarian struggle in Ireland itself.
        Parnell revitalises the Irish Nationalist obstruction
        campaign in Commons.
        Clan makes 'new departure' offer of cooperation to
        Parnell.

1879   Michael Davitt meets Millen in Ireland on military
        reconnaissance.
        Davitt founds Land League of Mayo – he gets funding
        from the Clan.
        Irish National Land League founded in Dublin; Parnell is
        elected president.

1880   Parnell makes triumphant US tour with Clan backing.
        Irish National Land League of America founded.
        W. E. Gladstone forms Liberal government – confronted
        by incipient 'land war' in Ireland.
        Rossa defects from Clan to form hard-line United
        Irishmen.

1881   Rossa's missioners attack Salford barracks.
        Fenian Office set up at Scotland Yard.
        Land war intensifies in Ireland.
        Clan secretly resolves to launch dynamite attacks.
        Tsar Alexander II assassinated in St Petersburg.
        Rossa's men attack the Mansion House in London and
        sites in Liverpool.
        Alexander Sullivan, a Chicago lawyer, is elected president
        of Clan.
        Parnell arrested in Dublin for 'incitement'; Land League
        declared illegal. Agrarian conflict in Ireland reaches near
        revolutionary scale.

1882   Alexander Sullivan gets control of Land League funds.
        Parnell released from jail after 'Kilmainham Treaty'
        agreement with Gladstone's government to rein in the
        land war.
        Phoenix Park murders.
        Edward Jenkinson appointed assistant under-secretary for
        police and crime at Dublin Castle.
        Irish National League supplants semi-revolutionary Land
        League.

1883   'Invincibles' arrested in Dublin for Phoenix Park murders.
        Rossa's missioners attack Glasgow, Whitehall and *Times*
        newspaper offices.
        Edward Jenkinson is 'borrowed' from Ireland to work
        from Whitehall against terror-bombers.
        Special (Irish) Branch formed within CID.
        Bombers apparently backed by Rossa arrested in Liverpool
        and Cork.
        Dr Gallagher bomb team arrests in Birmingham and
        London. They have been sent by Sullivan – but with
        Rossa's secret connivance.

Explosives Act passed making unlicensed possession a criminal offence.

Alexander Sullivan elected president of American Land League.

Thomas Beach (Henri Le Caron) signs $1,200 contract with Robert Anderson to spy on Chicago Clan.

William Mackey Lomasney sent by Clan to make attacks on London underground. Many injuries.

General Millen in Guatemala – makes overtures to Irish Office.

1884   Clan bombing team leave bombs at four London railway stations. One explodes.

Jenkinson is given remit by Liberal Home Secretary Sir William Harcourt to operate from London with extraordinary powers – Robert Anderson is sacked.

John Daly arrested in Birkenhead with Clan-supplied grenades apparently intended for an attack on parliament.

Lomasney (Clan) bomb demolishes detectives' office at Scotland Yard explosion. More bombs around Whitehall.

James Monro appointed assistant commissioner CID.

Sullivan dissolves the Clan link to the Irish Republican Brotherhood because of the IRB's opposition to terror. Forms 'Triangle' leadership of three with himself as head.

Lomasney blows himself up under London Bridge.

1885   Clan launches attacks on Tower of London and House of Commons – press call it 'Dynamite Saturday'.

First overture by Millen in Mexico City to Foreign Office.

13 June: Gladstone loses parliamentary majority. Lord Salisbury becomes Prime Minister with a tiny majority in alliance with Irish Party to effect six-month 'caretaker government'.

Secret meeting between Parnell and Lord Carnarvon to discuss Conservative path to home rule.

Parnell urges Irish voters in Britain to vote Tory in forthcoming election.

November: Election returns Lord Salisbury with tiny majority dependent on Irish support in Commons.

Edward Jenkinson briefs Salisbury in secret on dangers of not backing home rule.

Dissident Clan members led by Dr Patrick Cronin of
Chicago bring charges of financial fraud against Alexander
Sullivan.
Irish Loyal and Patriotic Union formed.

1886   Gladstone signals conversion to home rule.
January: Salisbury government falls when Irish switch
sides in Commons – Gladstone forms administration with
Irish support.
Lord Randolph Churchill declares, 'Ulster will fight,
Ulster will be right.'
Sir Charles Warren appointed commissioner Metropolitan
Police.
Jenkinson's private agents arrested in London by Monro.
Richard Pigott offers incriminating Parnell letters to *The
Times*.
June: Gladstone's Home Rule Bill defeated when Liberals
split – election follows. Lord Salisbury returned to power
with large Conservative–Liberal Unionist majority.
American National League stays loyal to Parnell and
Gladstone. Sullivan secretly prepares to go back to war.
Divisions in Clan deepen.
Ireland gripped by agricultural depression. The land war
is resumed in a new form – the 'Plan of Campaign'.
Parnell stays aloof.
Fenian Brotherhood split: P. S. Cassidy ousts Rossa, who
forms United Irishmen.
Edward Jenkinson sacked.

1887   January:
James Monro takes over 'Secret Department'; Robert
Anderson recalled.
Anglo-Russian war-scare reaches peak.

February:
'Special Section' or 'Special Branch' is formed in
Metropolitan Police.
Breakaway Dillon-Devoy Clan-na-Gael formed in
Brooklyn – it is quickly recognised by the IRB.

March:
Arthur Balfour appointed Chief Secretary for Ireland.
First 'Parnellism and Crime' articles run in *The Times*.
Crimes Act introduced to suppress 'plan of campaign' as
intimidation, rent-strike and evictions again grip Ireland.

April:
Incriminating letters linking Parnell to Phoenix Park
murders are published in *The Times*.

May:
Mikhail Katkov's war party in Russia is politically
destroyed.
'Behind the Scenes in America' articles run in *The Times*.
The last predicts an attack on the Queen Victoria's
Golden Jubilee celebrations.

June:
After more menacing press reports the Jubilee ceremonies
climaxing in Westminster Abbey on 21 June pass
peacefully.
Crimes Act goes into force in Ireland. Several MPs
arrested.

October:
An American named Joseph Cohen is found dead in
south London. Assistant commissioner James Monro uses
the inquest to expose the existence of the Jubilee Plot.

November:
Thomas Callan and Michael Harkins are arrested. At their
pre-trial committal for conspiracy to cause explosions
Millen is named as their leader.

1888   February:
Callan and Harkins are sentenced at the Old Bailey to
fifteen years.

April:
House of Commons select committee takes evidence on
the 'admission of dynamiters'. Monro names Millen as
head of the conspiracy.

June:
Clan-na-Gael in New York appoints 'trial' committee to
investigate charges of fraud against Alexander Sullivan.
Frank Hugh O'Donnell, an Irish ex-MP, sues *The Times*
for libel over 'Behind the Scenes in America' articles and
loses. More incriminating letters are produced at the trial.

July:
Bill passed to establish Special Commission to rake over
Times allegations.

August:
James Monro resigns; continues as head of Secret
Department. Robert Anderson is appointed assistant
commissioner and head of the CID.
Clan 'trial' of Sullivan for corruption begins in New
York.

September:
First Whitechapel murder.
Special Commission preliminary meeting.

October:
Special Commission opens. Millen named as notorious
dynamiter.

November:
Sir Charles Warren resigns as Met commissioner.
Government is warned from several sources that Pigott
letters are forged.
James Monro is appointed Metropolitan Police
commissioner.

December:
Thomas Beach offers to testify at Special Commission for
£10,000.

1889   February:
Beach (Le Caron) testifies and thus reveals himself as a
British agent. His evidence is especially damaging to
Parnell. He reveals accidentally that there are more spies
in the Clan.
Richard Pigott is broken down in the witness box and the

Times letters are exposed as forgeries. He flees to Spain
and commits suicide.
The Sullivan trial clears the Clan leader of fraud.

April:
Francis Millen dies in New York.

May:
Dr Patrick Cronin disappears in Chicago – his body is
found later in a sewer.

June:
Alexander Sullivan is arrested for complicity in Cronin
murder. The charges are later dropped.

October:
Cronin murder trial exposes Sullivan Clan as 'mercenary
junta'.

December:
Divorce petition filed by Captain O'Shea naming Parnell
as co-respondent.

1890   February:
The Times pays Parnell £5,000 for libel.
Special Commission report finds 'respondents obtained
the assistance of the Physical Force party in America'.

June:
James Monro resigns as Metropolitan Police
commissioner.

1891   June: Parnell marries Mrs Katherine O'Shea and dies four
months later.

A NOTE ON SOURCES

The computerised index at the Public Record Office (the national archives of the United Kingdom at Kew, south-west London) blinked frustratingly. 'Document in use' – so the screen responded to multiple requests to access a 114-year-old file. It was listed as the 'Secret Service Papers of Arthur Balfour, Chief Secretary for Ireland 1887', and was marked 'open'. On a return visit a few weeks later, in the summer of 2000, its classification had been changed to 'closed'.

I enquired at the busy delivery desk why this might be so. 'Does it concern the royal family, Ireland or homosexuality?' a helpful staff member responded. I could only guess – Ireland certainly; anything more would be a bonus. 'Then it's going to be secret.'

The papers were 'retained at the Home Office', it emerged. After lengthy supplication the file was partially declassified that autumn: half of it was supplanted by cardboard dummies, more letters were in photostat with certain sentences – occasionally whole paragraphs – carefully inked over. It was so diligently done, it was explained, 'to protect informers'. Anyone named was dead a century ago. Where Ireland is concerned, policy is seamless.

But one name in one letter came through *en clair*. It was 'General Millen', an Irish-American mercenary soldier whose shadowy career I had pursued earlier in a story about a Sikh maharajah and a British intelligence operation in Imperial Russia. 'Millen', the letter from a secret policeman revealed, would be useful in bringing conspiracy charges against certain members of the United Kingdom parliament. The scrap of paper dated from autumn 1887. Why so secret so long?

By their nature, police bureaucracies keep ordered files and their miscreant targets do not. In this instance, however, it was the secret civil servants who put their activities beyond reach. Edward Jenkinson, intelligence chief at Dublin Castle, later attached to the Home Office in London, destroyed his private papers when he was sacked. Those of Sir Julian Pauncefote, permanent under-secretary at the Foreign Office, head of HM Foreign Secret Service, were burned on his death.

James Monro, CB, assistant commissioner of the Metropolitan Police and head of the 'Secret Department' in the period, left no private papers. In Scotland Yard's own museum, housed in a south-east London industrial estate, however, is a transcription of a long letter written in 1903 from Darjeeling to his son Charles, a missionary doctor. The original had been tracked to an Edinburgh cupboard in 1982 by two diligent researchers into the Whitechapel murders of autumn 1888. It is a long, polemic-laden account of his police career, with multiple hints and half-truths but no reference to the 'Ripper' whatsoever. But it had much to say on long-ago manoeuvrings in Whitehall, when three rival intelligence agencies fought with each other to lead, in modern usage, 'the war against terror'. Arthur Balfour, Chief Secretary for Ireland, preferred to call the campaign of bomb attacks waged against Britain in the 1880s 'certain Irish revolutionary difficulties'.

The Public Record Office also catalogues the files of the Metropolitan Police Special Branch under skeletal headings. The accompanying 'administrative history' states: 'From its inception in 1883 the Special Branch has been the lead agency in countering Irish republican terrorism . . . In 1886 consideration was given to its disbandment but it was continued following the receipt of information concerning anarchist [sic] activity which threatened the peaceful celebration of Queen Victoria's jubilee.'

But all files in the MEPO 38 class – its index, even basic descriptions of content, remain closed in perpetuity under section 3.4 of the 1958 Public Records Act.

The Records Management branch of the Metropolitan Police kindly scoured the closed catalogue for any reference to 'activity threatening Queen Victoria's Jubilee'. The result was: 'No records in the series relate to your specific area of interest.' 'All pre-1914 material was pulped during the Second World War,' the most distinguished interrogator of Special Branch history was informed on its centenary.

One department of HMG, however, kept its records in exemplary order. The Foreign Office's 'Fenian Brotherhood' series, twenty-four leather-bound volumes, presents a remarkable sequence of letters, reports and telegrams between the United States (and other surprising places) and Whitehall from 1865 to 1891. But the bureaucratic narratives encrypted within the mass of formal copperplate, scribbled minutes and cipher cables seemed impenetrable without an external crib.

The prime 'crib' was in Dublin – in the papers of the Irish nationalist Michael Davitt. He acted as head intelligence-gatherer for Charles Stewart Parnell, the Irish leader in the British parliament, during the Special Commission of 1888–9 – a legal inquisition into allegations of the Nationalist Party's complicity in terrorism. Writing up his discoveries in a little black book – 'Notes of an Amateur Detective' – Davitt effectively got to the truth. For his own good reasons he chose not to reveal it.

The papers of Davitt's colleague, Timothy Harrington, MP, further contained the decrypts of coded telegrams between *The Times*'s solicitor and his agent in New York. The Times Newspapers Limited archives at Wapping contained revelatory material that was certainly not included in the paper's own official history.

There was plenty more surviving documentation to uncover in the private papers of ministers and courtiers of the period – and in the operational traffic of civil servants, diplomats, policemen, lawyers, journalists, informers and stooges. Particularly revealing were the letters of the 'spymaster-general' Edward Jenkinson (later Sir) to his Liberal patron Earl Spencer, Lord Lieutenant of Ireland, a window into the mind of one of the most curious, devious and contradictory figures ever to be a secret policeman.

The primary sources used for this work are:

The Salisbury Papers (Hatfield House).

The Gladstone Papers, the Cross Papers, the Althorp Papers,

the Balfour Papers, the Carnarvon Papers (British Library, Department of Manuscripts).

The Harcourt Papers, the Clarendon Deposit, the J. S. Sandars Papers (Bodleian Library, Department of Western Manuscripts).

Foreign Office 'Fenian Brotherhood 1865–1891' sequence in FO 5 'America' series; FO letter books and consular archives for New York, Paris, Mexico City, Guatemala City and St Petersburg; Home Office files in the HO 144 series for 'Fenians', 'Explosions' and 'Special (Parnell) Commission'; Colonial Office (Dublin Castle) papers; the Sir Robert Anderson Papers; MEPO (Metropolitan Police) files; the Secret Service papers of Arthur Balfour (Public Record Office, London).

The Devoy Papers, the O'Mahony Papers, the Harrington Papers, the Larcom papers, the Samuel Lee Anderson Papers, the W. H. Joyce papers, the Mayo papers, the Luby papers (National Library of Ireland).

The Fenian Papers (National Archives of Ireland).

The Arthur Fraser Walter Papers (Times Newspapers Limited archives).

The statement of James Monro (Metropolitan Police Museum).

The Monro Ranaghat letters (Church Missionary Society archives, University of Birmingham).

The Davitt Papers (Trinity College, University of Dublin, Department of Manuscripts).

Finally there are the letters and journals of Queen Victoria (held at the Royal Archives, Windsor Castle), material from which is quoted by gracious permission of Her Majesty Queen Elizabeth II.

PART ONE

The Missionary

'Civil servants are human beings ... they have
their private convictions.'

Rt Hon. Arthur Balfour,
Commons Debate, 21 April 1910

I

───────────────

The Fishery, Windsor Great Park, 17 March 1883

In the early spring of 1883 polite English society was gripped by the extraordinary affair of what might or might not have happened in Lady Florence Dixie's shrubbery. It involved an alleged attack by 'men dressed as women' and Hubert, a large St Bernard dog.

The aristocratic Englishwoman, born Florence Douglas, was the youngest daughter of the eighth Marquis of Queensberry. Popular newspapers exulted in her wildness and her habit of espousing deeply unfashionable causes. At the high tide of empire, Lady Florence embraced both the Irish peasantry and the Zulus, heading off to southern Africa at the age of twenty-two as a war correspondent. She met the defeated King Cetewayo in his kraal and persuaded him to come to London.

She cut her tresses short and on her return, at a royal 'drawing room', outraged court protocol by failing to wear lace and ostrich feathers in her hair. She received a polite remonstrance from the Lord Chamberlain for the transgression, a matter which somehow promptly reached the newspapers. Queen Victoria adored her. She lived under royal patronage with her husband, Sir Alexander Beaumont Churchill Dixie, at The Fishery, a rambling house in the Great Park.

The Douglas family was always good newspaper copy. Lady Florence's father blew his head off in a shooting accident when she was three. Her elder brother, the ninth Marquis, drew up the rules of boxing and was later to pursue Oscar Wilde for his liaison with his son, Lord Alfred Douglas. Lady Florence was Bosie's aunt.

On St Patrick's Day 1883 Lady Florence appeared at Windsor

police station in a state of evident distress. Her face was bruised, her clothing mud-spattered and torn, her voluminous dress apparently slashed by a knife right through to the whalebone stays of her corset. The startled desk sergeant took down her deposition.

Lady Florence had been strolling with Hubert, her pet St Bernard, and had ventured into the shrubbery. She had been murderously attacked, she insisted, by two persons who had previously accosted her 'to ask the time' at the wicket gate opening onto the Slough Road. One had thrown her to the ground, slashed at her twice and filled her mouth with earth to stifle her cries. The veiled assailants had dark eyes and dark hair, and in the abhorrent intimacy of the encounter she detected they had shaven but stubbly chins. They were, she insisted, men dressed in women's clothing.

The extraordinary story might have been put down to Lady Florence's eccentricity had it not been for the impassioned Irish politics of the time. After her adventures in Zululand she had headed off in 1881 for another battlefield, County Mayo – the frontline in the bitter 'land war' then raging between semi-feudal Anglo-Irish landlords (or their agents like the hapless Captain Boycott*) and peasant tenants. She took a house, Glenossera, near Ballycastle on the wild Atlantic coast to see for herself. She had formed an opinion and in November 1882 published her findings.

The campaign of rent strikes and 'boycotts' had been inspired by the radical nationalist visionary Michael Davitt, sometimes lieutenant – as often ideological opponent – of the Irish leader in the United Kingdom parliament, Charles Stewart Parnell. The

---

* Captain Charles Boycott, an English-born ex-soldier, was agent for Lord Erne's sprawling estates in County Mayo. In mid 1880 he and his family were cast into what was called 'moral Coventry' by the Mayo Land League, warning off those who might work his farms or supply the needs of Lough Mask House – the baker, the blacksmith, the servant girls. His plight became a cause célèbre in London. Ulster farm workers were drafted in to lift the potato harvest protected by 1000 troops. After six months the captain capitulated.

two men, so removed in social background, so different in their revolutionary methodology, had by the early 1880s together pushed Ireland to the forefront of British domestic politics.

The renewed spectre of mass starvation (the potato crop had partially failed two years running) was only just receding. But rather than emigrate or die, as millions had done in the Great Famine of 1845–9, or rise in doomed armed revolt, the Irish were seeking new means of political resistance.

One lay in Westminster itself. Ireland had supposedly been part of a British unitary state since the Act of Union in 1800. One hundred and three Irish members sat in the United Kingdom House of Commons as Liberals or Conservatives. Catholic emancipation, franchise reform and the secret ballot had by the mid 1870s created a grouping of over fifty MPs, led by the Protestant, Conservative lawyer Isaac Butt, pressing for a modest measure of legislative independence under the British crown. Compared with the upheavals of the previous decade, when an armed rising had been attempted in Ireland, backed by ferocious veterans of the American Civil War, the push for 'home rule' was a polite Tea Room lobbying campaign.

In 1875 a twenty-nine-year-old landowner from Wicklow, a Protestant, was elected member for Meath on a 'home rule' platform. Commandingly handsome, wildly superstitious, sexually charged, Charles Stewart Parnell arrived at Westminster informed by a long family tradition of liberal nationalism. His great-grandfather was a member of the pre-Union Irish parliament. His mother, Delia Parnell, was the daughter of a US navy commodore whose frigate had preyed on English commerce in the war of 1812.

Young Charley seemed set to become an Anglo-Irish gentleman, until his collar was felt by a Cambridge constable after a drunken scuffle. He was sent down from Magdalene. Now he might kick against what he called 'the arbitrary force of England' more directly. Unrepresentative tyranny justified resistance, he argued; the question was where and how to make the stand. The place was the United Kingdom parliament. The weapon was 'obstruction': endless speeches and timetable-wrecking amendments prying into

every aspect of home and colonial affairs – a technique devised
by a Belfast businessman and former 'Fenian',* Joseph Biggar,
MP.

Parnell was equally inventive. Blocked by an exasperated
Speaker from an endless filibuster, he considered declaiming to
the House in fancy dress. Irish woes flowed turgidly through
English political life to the point of constipation. It made Parnell
the most famous Irishman in the world. He was 'a great fact',
declared Lord Salisbury, the Conservative Secretary for India, in
October 1877 when Parnell was elected chairman of the Home
Rule Confederation of Great Britain. 'You can no more shut your
eyes to him than you can to the potato disease or to the Colorado
beetle.' Over the next thirteen years of a very turbulent relationship Mr Parnell would draw the high Tory's most select insults.

The Fenian leaders exiled or imprisoned after the failed rising
of 1867, bound by oath to disown the constitutional processes
of England, had not abandoned the virile purity of armed struggle.
But Parnell's Westminster puppet-theatre of war began to convince some of them at least that they might shackle their lost
revolution to the new rising star of nationalist Ireland.

In the general election of March 1880 William Ewart Gladstone's Liberals won power. Of some sixty Irish MPs returned as
'home rulers', Parnell's boisterous followers numbered twenty-
four. In May he was elected chairman of the whole group, undis-
puted leader of 'the cause'; whether that was constitutional or
revolutionary still remained highly ambiguous.

There was soon a distraction. That summer Parnell met and
fell in love with the wife of a newly elected home rule MP, a
former hussar officer named William O'Shea. They began an affair.

*   *   *

* The Fenian Brotherhood was founded in New York in 1859 by the Gaelic
scholar John O'Mahony, ostensibly as the American wing of the Irish Revolutionary (later Republican) Brotherhood, which had been secretly formed in Dublin
by the veteran revolutionary James Stephens a year earlier with the aim of winning
Irish independence by armed force.

The epithet 'Fenian' (derived by O'Mahony from 'Fianna', mythical warriors
of Irish antiquity) became applied in British demonology, wrongly, to all Irish
revolutionaries.

There was a less gentlemanly outlet for nationalist energies. In 1879 the former Fenian Michael Davitt, having served seven years in Dartmoor for gun-running, had founded the Mayo Land League as a tenant solidarity organisation – with the ultimate ideological aim of dismantling the entire landlord system. At a meeting in Dublin in October 1879 Parnell had become the league's first national president, hugely boosting his radical reputation. The land war, with its sour encounters between barricaded tenants and the bailiff's battering ram, was a propaganda as well as an agrarian battlefield.

Fighting funds flowed from the teeming east-coast cities of America, subscribed by the now grown-up children of the emigrant boats – brought up on stories of Victoria, the wicked Famine Queen. Newspaper engravings of raggedy children in hillside hutments were a gift to the dollar-raisers in New York and Philadelphia. But would the money be used to succour evicted families – or to pay for the exiled revolutionaries' threatened campaign of bomb attacks on British cities? There were nods and winks as dimes went into shamrock-garlanded buckets on the sidewalk.

American money gave Irish nationalism a political leverage it could never flex before. Sir William Harcourt, the Liberal Home Secretary, later noted at the height of the bombing: 'In former Irish rebellions, the Irish were in *Ireland* . . . Now there is an Irish nation in the United States, equally hostile, with plenty of money, absolutely beyond our reach and yet within ten days' sail of our shores.'

To Liberals and Tories alike the Land Leaguers were simian brutes.* Lord Robert Gascoyne-Cecil, the third Marquis of Salisbury, leader of the Conservative Party since 1881, magisterially set out his unionist stall in a famous article called 'Disintegration', published in the *Quarterly Review* as the land war sputtered to a close. 'The highest interests of the Empire as well as the sacred

* The Land League was proscribed as a criminal organisation by the Liberal government in October 1881. A Ladies Land League supplanted it. Twelve months later the Irish National League was formed, with Parnell as chairman – 'a purely parliamentary substitute for what had been a semi-revolutionary organisation', in Michael Davitt's description.

obligations of honour forbid us to solve this question by conced-
ing any species of independence to Ireland,' he declared. 'All that
is Protestant, nay all that is loyal . . . would be at the mercy of
the adventurers who have led the Land League.'

As the land war reached its height – fragmenting into cattle-
maiming, intimidation, abduction and murder – American journalists and free-thinking English ladies descended on Mayo to
see for themselves. Lady Florence was one of them. Ireland's
present ills were not, she concluded, all the fault of villainous
fox-hunting landlords. The league was to blame – it was a socialistic land-grabbing swindle. She commissioned a Dublin journalist
called Richard Pigott to ghost-write a pamphlet called *Ireland
and Her Shadow*. The 'gospel of freedom', it proclaimed, had
been subverted by the 'doctrines of the communist and the infi-
del'. It made her enemies.

On a Leicestershire country walk, a few months before the incident in the shrubbery, a death-threat letter was thrust into Lady
Florence's hand. It was signed simply 'Liberty', but was evidently
of Irish origin. To protect his wife 'Beau' Dixie acquired both a
six-shot Webley revolver and Hubert. According to her account,
at the critical moment of the alleged attack in the shrubbery the
enormous dog had bounded from the trees and had pulled the
knife-wielding assailant backwards. Then she had fainted.

There were good reasons to believe her story. Two days before
the rumble at The Fishery, Whitehall had been rocked by a dynamite bomb evidently planted by Irish-American 'missioners' –
one of a series of explosive attacks that had begun over two years
before. In March 1883 the trial was also proceeding in Dublin
of some of the men who, nine months earlier, had slashed to
death Lord Frederick Cavendish, Chief Secretary for Ireland, and
Thomas Burke, the permanent under-secretary, in Phoenix Park.
The assumption by some (although Lady Florence never said so
herself) was that the assault in the shrubbery was part of a continuing murder conspiracy. It was lapping at the ramparts of Windsor
Castle. The story was a newspaper sensation – IRISH ASSASSINS
ON QUEEN'S DOORSTEP.

Fleet Street reporters rushed to buttonhole the neighbours. There was much conflicting testimony about what had really happened in the shrubbery. Mr Edward Jenkinson, the Dublin-based 'spymaster-general' (his formal title was assistant under-secretary for Police and Crime), who had been urgently summoned to the Home Office in London after the Whitehall bomb, told his patron Earl Spencer, Lord Lieutenant of Ireland: 'They all say here that there is no foundation whatever for any of Dixie's story. If it really is made up and this came out, it will have a very bad effect.'

Sergeant Patrick McIntyre of the Metropolitan Police Special (Irish) Branch, formed the year before to sniff out Fenians in London, was sent to investigate her allegations. He trailed several suspects without success. 'It was all very mysterious,' he concluded. Questions were asked in parliament. Society split over the question: was she or wasn't she making it all up? But for one Windsor resident there was no doubt.

Queen Victoria was convinced her friend had narrowly escaped death at the hands of Irish assassins. She dispatched a stream of courtiers to offer messages of sympathy; finally her 'Highland servant', the faithful John Brown who had bravely fended off assailants before, arrived at The Fishery to examine the scene of outrage for himself.

The kilted ghillie heard Lady Florence's story in her boudoir. He took a liking to Hubert and asked for a reproduction photograph of the outsize hound as a memento. He proceeded to the shrubbery but could find no sign of a struggle amongst the buddleia. He seemed doubtful. A damp March wind was blowing as he departed in an open dog-cart for the castle – where he complained of a chill and took to his bed. Ten days later John Brown was dead. Lady Florence sent the promised picture of Hubert to the grief-stricken Queen with a letter: 'God knows I would infinitely have preferred had my assailants killed me, than that my escape should in a measure have resulted in bringing this sad loss to Her Majesty.'

Lady Florence thereafter turned her political energies to the promotion of rational dress, votes for women and the abolition of blood sports. She was never troubled again by 'Irish assassins'. But her protector, Queen Victoria, most certainly was.

As a function perhaps of the length of her reign (1837–1901) rather than of her attraction for deranged assailants, Queen Victoria was the most shot-at sovereign in British history. There were seven attacks made openly on her person, the first in 1840, the last in 1882. All took place while she was driving, accompanied, in a carriage. All were made at comparatively close range by males using single-shot pistols – except for the fifth attempt in 1850 outside Cambridge House in London, when the Queen was struck momentarily unconscious by an ex-officer of the 10th Hussars wielding a brass-handled cane. None of the assailants was a marksman; none was found to be part of a wider conspiracy. Two of the Queen's attackers were judged insane, three were transported to Australia. Two, whose pistols were afterwards found to be empty, received comparatively short sentences. Two were Irish.

Victoria was brave: she continued to ride out in public after the first wave of attacks and noted in her journal that 'she did not wish to have the kind of security that nervous monarchs throughout Europe insisted upon'. Prince Albert personally designed a chainmail-lined 'parasol' for her protection. She never used it. Her mournful seclusion after her beloved husband's death in 1861 removed the Queen from public gaze and, for the time being, from the reach of firearm-brandishing lunatics. During the Irish revolutionary excitements of six years later she dismissed her ministers' fears that she would be kidnapped by Fenians from Balmoral or Osborne House on the Isle of Wight as 'too foolish'.

The last overt assassination attempt, on 2 March 1882, was made by a Scots-born 'poet' named Roderick Maclean, whose verses addressed to Her Majesty had been returned unread by a brusque courtier. As the Queen's carriage drove out of Windsor railway station a man was seen drawing a pistol. In the mêlée the attacker was beset by two umbrella-wielding Etonians and his weapon was seized by a policeman. Maclean was tried for high treason at Reading Assizes but found 'not guilty on grounds of insanity'. (He had recently been released after fifteen years in an asylum.) The Queen wrote to her eldest daughter: 'It is worth being shot at to see how much one is loved.' Her every escape saw a dip in domestic republican sentiment.

By now, however, in the fifth decade of her reign, the Queen could never feel safe from sudden cataclysmic death – inflicted not by a lone crackpot with a pistol, but by an armed international conspiracy confected by Irish-exile revolutionaries and their sympathisers in America. Their weapon of choice was 'dynamite', the recently developed high-explosive – easy to carry, conceal and prime – used by Russian nihilists to assassinate Tsar Alexander II in St Petersburg in 1881.

Ever since then the so-called 'dynamite press' in America – newspapers such as Patrick Ford's *Irish World* and Jeremiah O'Donovan Rossa's *United Irishman* – had made wildly inflammatory threats. One such title was *Ireland's Liberator and Dynamite Monthly*. Sir Henry Ponsonby, the Queen's private secretary, wrote to Lord Granville, the Foreign Secretary, in April 1881: 'It is stated in "The Observer" today that there is a newspaper in New York which advocates the assassination of the Queen. Her Majesty asks if this is true?' It was.

The Queen, much to her distaste, was shadowed by armed bodyguards. Special 'pilot' locomotives were run before the royal train bearing her to Balmoral, the bridges and culverts scoured for dynamite, the line guarded by an army of railway platelayers.

Although many threats on her life were made, both openly and secretly, there were no politically motivated assassination attempts on the Queen and her family in the period from 1881, when two rival Irish-American revolutionary groups made terror attacks on British cities. The targets remained largely symbolic and inanimate – London Bridge, *The Times* newspaper's offices, Scotland Yard, the Tower of London, Victoria Station, the House of Commons. In early 1885 the bombings halted.

Then, on 1 June 1887, with the great service of thanksgiving in Westminster Abbey to mark Victoria's Golden Jubilee three weeks away, *The Times* published evidently well-sourced information from New York of a threatened series of bomb attacks.

Scotland Yard had meanwhile received information that a bombing team was about to cross the Atlantic, with the Queen Empress as the apparent target.

The newspapers called it the 'Jubilee Plot'.

2

---

487 West 57th Street, New York, 10 April 1889

It was Kitty Millen who found the general's body. She had heard
the distant rattle of the last Ninth Avenue 'L' heading uptown
late the night before – and her father's footfall as he padded in
from his shift at the *New York Herald*. As was his habit lately,
the night editor had gone straight to his study in the Manhattan
brownstone, taking a decanter of whiskey and his firecracker
Guatemalan cheroots with him to pore over old papers almost
till dawn. She did not like to disturb him. He had been sick
lately – the old stomach complaint – but still he would not stop
working.

Her father's name had been in the newspapers again, mentioned in the London 'trial' of Mr Parnell for political conspiracy.
All those Irish members of the English parliament – Pop's old
friends, some of them – charged with associating with criminals
and terrorists. Her father had been named as one of the miscreants: he was listed on the prosecution schedule as 'General Millen
– Dynamitard'.

Kitty Millen knocked and knocked again. When she finally
went in, she found her father slumped in his leather club chair.
His heart had stopped. The desk was strewn with old letters and
recent telegrams. She called her mother and sister urgently. Their
tears flowed.

The Millen girls had rarely been allowed in this room. It was
decked with martial trophies in that way still beloved by the
retired American fighting man – a Russian cavalry sabre, a French
regimental eagle from the battle of Guadalajara, a Salvadorean
musket – along with his framed commission as brigadier-general

of artillery in the army of the Mexican republic, signed by President Benito Juárez.

Two flags lay carefully furled behind the desk: the Stars and Stripes, and one he had designed himself – a tricolour, green, white and yellow, the green on the fly, the white in the centre bearing a golden sunburst. It was supposed to be the war flag of the 'Irish Army of Liberation': in 1878, having crossed the Atlantic in command of a piratical fleet of American ships, he had planned to sail up the Shannon to seize the city of Limerick.

Frank Millen was that not uncommon thing in late nineteenth-century America, a respectable journalist and professional revolutionary. He served the *New York Herald*, whose millionaire proprietor James Gordon Bennett, while himself cruising the world in a yacht so luxurious it had a Guernsey cow aboard to provide milk for his guests' coffee, delighted in hiring notorious felons and revolutionists to fill his pages. The newspaper's foreign editor had served ten years in Dartmoor for shooting a policeman. The drama critic set out to capture the Rock of Gibraltar; the night editor drew up the operational plan. The paper's weather forecaster, Jerome Collins, before perishing in 1882 on a disastrous expedition to arctic Siberia, had plotted to kidnap Queen Victoria's son.

The *Herald*'s unconventional meteorologist had in 1867 co-founded the Clan-na-Gael, the most significant of the Irish-American revolutionary societies that emerged after the failure of the 'Fenian' rising. By 1881 the Clan had suborned the old Fenian Brotherhood and had itself resolved to launch dynamite attacks.

The newspaper gave its own man a rumbustious obituary:

> General Francis Frederick Millen, an old *Herald* correspondent and a well known journalist, died yesterday. He was born in 1836 in Tyrone, Ireland, and received a liberal education. He came to America when a very young man and went at once to Mexico where he entered the army as a lieutenant of artillery . . .
>
> About 1864 he entered into correspondence with James Stephens whose Fenian conspiracy was then reach-

ing its most formidable proportions in Ireland and America and in 1865 he went to Ireland to take a high command in the army which Stephens led his followers to believe he was about to put into the field for the overthrow of the English dominion.

But the raid which the [Dublin] Castle authorities made upon the ranks of the Fenian Brotherhood toward the close of that year completely upset all the revolutionary projects . . . Millen, seeing that there was no chance for him to do any service in the field, returned to Mexico . . .

Here he fought against the forces of Maximilian, but when the country settled into tranquility after the execution of that unhappy monarch, Millen came to New York, where he became the executive officer of the American branch of the Fenian Brotherhood . . .

The *Herald* threw a discreet veil over certain aspects of its night editor's career. It chose not to report, as did the rival *New York Times*, that 'When 19 years old he joined the British Army and served through the Crimean war.' And neither paper mentioned Frank Millen's fifteen-year membership of the Clan-na-Gael. But there was this: 'About two years ago he visited Europe as the agent of the inventors of a new explosive shell, and his presence there was made the theme of many slanderous stories in the English press,' said the *Herald*. 'It was alleged that he visited England in the promotion of a dynamite conspiracy . . .'

Quite so – eighteen months before Millen had been named with maximum publicity in London by James Monro, assistant commissioner of the Metropolitan Police, as the head of the 'Jubilee dynamite gang'. The New York papers had been full of it. 'General Millen took every opportunity, public and private,' said the *Herald*, 'to deny the truth of these stories and there can be no doubt but they were malicious libels of the Pigott stamp . . .'

In that early spring of 1889 the name Pigott needed no further exposition to newspaper readers on either side of the Atlantic. It was uttered with derision in the British parliament whenever a

Tory minister rose to speak. It was a curse on all traitors, growled
in New York-Irish saloon bars. Richard Pigott, Lady Florence
Dixie's one-time literary collaborator, had been the chief prosecution witness in an extraordinary legal process that in April
1889 was still unfolding in London. The 'Special Commission'
was set up to examine allegations first made in *The Times* almost
two years earlier, in the months preceding the Queen's Jubilee.
In a series of articles the staunchly unionist newspaper had accused
Charles Stewart Parnell, with his followers, of colluding in crime.
Letters evidently signed by Parnell had been published in 'facsimile' as damning proof. Pigott had procured them.

The newspaper also published three convincing but anonymous articles headlined BEHIND THE SCENES IN AMERICA –
linking the parliamentary movement with the Clan-na-Gael and
dynamite. The concluding article of the American exposé, published on 1 June 1887, sensationally revealed a plot brewing in
New York to mount what its author called

> a series of pyrotechnical displays in honour of the
> Queen's Jubilee, or in other words, a series of dynamite
> and incendiary outrages to startle the nation amid the
> peaceful rejoicings of the month which opens today.
>
> Whether these schemes are destined to fail or to suc-
> ceed the near future will declare: The fact remains that
> they are being hatched by the very men who hail Mr
> Parnell as their 'esteemed and honoured leader'.

The *Times* leader-writer had claimed that

> The more this Irish conspiracy is investigated in all its
> departments, the more clear does it become that . . . from
> top to bottom it is an organization of the meanest and
> most squalid vices . . . directed by the very scum of
> humanity . . . Yet it is to the service of this conspiracy
> that an historic English party has prostituted its proud
> traditions and its prescriptive authority.

Parnell refrained from a libel suit but an eccentric Irish former
MP called Frank Hugh O'Donnell claimed personal libel in the

'Behind the Scenes' articles and went to law. Further damning letters were produced during the action – defended by Sir Richard Webster, MP, the English attorney-general and a member of the Government. O'Donnell lost. The *Times* charges had been vindicated in a court of law.

The Irish leader demanded that a parliamentary select committee investigate; instead the failed libel case was the trigger for the Special Commission, set up at the instigation of Lord Salisbury. It was politically as ruthless as it was clever: it would deliver a drip-drip of allegations and grisly exposures under a quasi-legal glare which, whatever the outcome, must strip Irish nationalism of its constitutional pretensions.

The commission opened in October 1888. Three months into the proceedings the Home Office official Robert Anderson, who had personally run a deep penetration agent called Thomas Billis Beach within the Clan-na-Gael, advanced his spy to the witness box to give sensationally damning evidence on what was called 'the American part of the case' – the personal, moral and financial links between the Irish Party and the Clan.

After Beach came Pigott. Under withering cross-examination he admitted he had forged the facsimile letters. It was the biggest shambles in the history of political journalism, then or since.

3

Dayabari Medical Mission, Ranaghat, Nadiya District, Lower Bengal, British India, September 1896

The missionary stood as he did each morning, Bible in hand, waiting for the corrugated-iron gates of the Dayabari mission to open and the wretched of the earth to come in their multitudes to seek redemption in the name of the Lord Jesus.

Dressed in a dusty frock-coat, with the stern moustache of a high Victorian patriarch, the missionary directed the women and children to one side, the men to another – to sit patiently beneath palm-leaf awnings as the morning heat began to rise.

An hour of evangelising would take place before the dispensary opened and earthly wounds were dressed. He read Luke. He was especially fond of quoting the physician-apostle's gospel to those millenarist Anglicans in England who thought that saving souls was God's only work.* 'And Jesus sent them forth to preach the Kingdom of God and heal the sick.'

He knew in his heart they came for the medicine, not the Word – but they came in their thousands to the Dayabari. He had chosen the name himself from the Hindu scriptures. It meant 'Abode of Mercy'.

By 8 a.m. Miss Brown, the catechist, was pumping up the harmonium in the mission's mud-brick chapel. The missionary's wife Mrs Ruth Monro, with her attendant native Bible-women, began eagerly reading the Word to the chattering throng of

---

* The Ranaghat mission was independent. The Church Missionary Society, founded by evangelising Anglicans in 1799, did not organise a medical department or recognise women missionaries until 1894–5.

Hindu mothers. His son Charles and daughter-in-law Elizabeth bustled about in the dispensary doing what they could with zinc ointment and quinine. Since they had arrived here three years ago, news of the good man and his family at Ranaghat had spread far and wide. The multitude had been on the move since before dawn, those who could walking with raggedy children from their villages in the malarial flood plain of the Hooghly river. The monsoon had passed; now, in September, the dun-coloured waters lingered. The sickness came.

The missionary recorded such a day at Ranaghat: 'From early morning the crowd poured in – fifty-six hackeries [native ox-carts] with sick people lined the road and every approach to the tents, and the Gospel was preached to 1,146 patients until darkness.' The missionary quoted a native proverb: 'We have a hundred sick people and one pomegranate to feed them.' Yet the work must go on: 'The time will surely come,' he informed the Lord Bishop of Calcutta, 'in His way, when some of the people will find in Him something more – the Physician for their souls.'

The missionary was Mr James Monro, CB, former head of the Criminal Investigation Department at Scotland Yard, latterly commissioner of the Metropolitan Police. Binding the wounds of Bengal may have seemed an unusual career move for someone who, a lifetime before, it seemed, had been known in very confidential London circles as the 'Secret Agent of State'.

But Mr Monro was an unusual man who pursued his unbending precepts of public duty in extraordinary times. Religious devotion was no bar to position in late Victorian Britain. But, to secure advancement and honours it was better, perhaps, that one's beliefs should not entirely inform one's behaviour.

Monro's zeal had made him powerful enemies. He had fearlessly pursued some well-connected individuals in the Cleveland Street telegraph-boy vice scandal. Flushing out a nest of youthful toffs from the baccarat tables of the Field Club brought him, in his words, 'the enmity of certain aristocrats and conservative newspaper editors'. The Whitechapel killer, so later conspiracy theorists would claim, also had friends in very high places. Monro had resigned as assistant commissioner during that autumn of

1888, on the eve of the first murder – and been reinstated and promoted after the last.*

James Monro had also, so it had been sensationally reported, confounded an assassination plot aimed at Queen Victoria in the year of her Golden Jubilee. He had given evidence to a parliamentary select committee of its mysterious leader's connections with prominent followers of Charles Stewart Parnell. He had enjoyed a fine government-provided house in Eaton Square, a phaeton and carriage-horses in the mews, and a direct telegraph to Scotland Yard. Then, in June 1890, quite suddenly, he had abandoned it all. The reason, he would tell his son Charlie, was 'because he had refused to do what he considered to be wrong'.

James Monro's predecessor was ennobled following his 'retirement'. His successor in the 'secret work' also got a knighthood and a lifetime annuity (on his *appointment* to office), cooked up by Lord Salisbury against the 'prospect of the abolition of Secret Service money by a rival government'. But there were no worldly honours for the missionary, no gratuity from a grateful nation. He had forfeited his pension by resigning. His family followed him into impoverished exile without demur.

Monro's self-immolation in the swamps of Lower Bengal was a matter of considerable relief to figures still in authority in Whitehall. There had been far too much talking to newspapers by policemen. Please God, Mr Monro, always a very discreet man, should never do that – or, worse, write his memoirs.

New Scotland Yard, London SW, 28 December 1951

It was over fifty years since Queen Victoria had died, but as fog crept up the granite flanks of the most famous police headquarters in the world, it could have been 1901. The modernist spires of the Festival of Britain across the river were lost in murk. In the

---

* Eleven victims are included in the Metropolitan Police 'Whitechapel Murders' file, spanning April 1888 to February 1891 – but most researchers ascribe the deaths of the so-called 'canonical five' to a single unknown killer, acting between 31 August and 9 November 1888, when Monro was not officially at Scotland Yard. The one archival hint of some oversight is a note from Henry Matthews,

first-floor turret office of the commissioner of the Metropolitan Police Sir Harold Scott had cause to consider the man who in his last months of office had caused New Scotland Yard to be built.

That morning a letter had come from a Scottish doctor, Ian Monro, medical officer of Moray and Nairn county councils. He was compiling a short biography of his grandfather, Mr James Monro, CB, for the clan Monro magazine. There was little beyond family folklore to draw on. Would the commissioner be kind enough to consult the official files? 'I know that, when he died in 1920, the usual notice was inserted in *The Times*,' Dr Monro wrote.

The obituary notice of 30 January 1920 was unrevealing. It ran briskly through his career. He was the son of a lawyer, educated at Edinburgh University and Berlin. He passed the new, competitive exams for the Indian Civil Service and departed, aged nineteen, to Lower Bengal. In 1877 he became inspector-general of police. In 1884 he came to London with his Indian-born family to take charge of the Criminal Investigation Department of the Metropolitan Police.

> The times needed someone of his stamp for Fenian outrages were occurring [the newspaper stated tersely]. In 1888 Mr Monro was decorated with the CB and appointed Chief Commissioner in succession to Sir Charles Warren who had resigned. He held the office for only eighteen months for on 12 June 1890 he resigned because the Home Secretary refused to adopt certain procedural alterations in administration and the system of pensions . . . He married in 1863, Ruth, daughter of Mr Littlejohn, an Aberdeen banker . . .

Dr Monro's letter continued: 'I find that my eldest sister, who has some of grandfather's papers, has left them in her house in

---

the Home Secretary, to his private secretary, Evelyn Ruggles-Brise: 'Stimulate the police about the Whitechapel murders. Monro might be willing to give a hint to the CID people if necessary.'

Edinburgh which she has let until May. In the meantime she is
living with another sister at Beckenham, and so cannot go and
collect the papers . . .'

Sir Harold did his best to help. Mr Heron, the Scotland Yard
registrar, dug away, but he could find nothing. The commissioner
memoed internally:

> It appears that we have no correspondence whatsoever
> in Registry bearing on the inner story of Mr Monro's
> appointment and retirement. This seems extraordinary,
> but apart from the serious reduction of records at the
> time of the move to New Scotland Yard in 1890, some
> responsible member of the staff directed far too drastic
> and ill-judged salvaging of historical documents during
> the late war. I am in touch with the Home Office who
> will make their files available to us if required.

They did not.

The career of James Monro had, it seemed, been expunged
from Scotland Yard's records. There were a few contemporary
press cuttings on file: 'Mr J. Monro late Commissioner of the
Metropolitan Police is now acting as a missionary at Nadiya,'
said the *Police Review* of August 1893. 'In this capacity he has
contributed to the organ of the Anglo-Indian Temperance Association a striking article on the pernicious nature and deadly effects
of Ganja – a preparation of Indian hemp.'

An interview in *Cassell's Magazine* in February 1890, given
a few months before the commissioner's resignation, was more
revealing. It began with a deferential analysis of the great detective's methods. Mr Monro believed absolutely in the primacy of
the professional policeman, trained to observe by pounding the
beat in regulation boots, their measured tread bringing comfort
to the law-abiding. There was no place for dilettantes padding
around the streets of London in 'noiseless shoes or other devices',
the commissioner insisted. 'We have a population of five million
to deal with including much of the scum of other nations as well
as our own.'

The Whitechapel murders were touched upon. The nine weeks

of terror in the East End of London were barely a year in the past: the radical press (and Queen Victoria herself) were still lambasting the Home Office and the police for failing to catch the killer. Could not an outsider be brought in, in the manner of the fictional sleuths then becoming so modish? Prince Bismarck was known to read nothing but detective novels, and the former German Chancellor was no fool.

'The amateur detective is about as much use as these novelists would be if the task were set to them of solving a criminal problem that their own art had not built up,' Monro replied. He loathed 'outsiders' – the Home Office was always trying to foist its place-men into senior police positions. And look at the trouble 'ama-teurs' had caused during the hunt for Irish dynamiters – let alone engaging one to help identify the Whitechapel killer.

'I presume you have framed some theory,' asked the reporter.

'Decidedly I have,' the commissioner replied, 'but I can hardly take you into my confidence.'

'Are you in possession of any clue at all?'

'Nothing positive . . . crimes of this kind, when we consider the class of victims selected – are the most easy of all crimes to commit. The person entrapped is as anxious to secure secrecy as the murderer himself.'

'You are in daily touch with the Home Office?' the reporter asked.

'Certainly. I am in speaking connection with it as you see' – pointing to a nest of tubes – 'and whenever necessary I have interviews with the Home Secretary on matters of urgency.'

There had been trouble with striking dockers and turbulent gas-workers, socialists, anarchists, foreigners, free-thinkers, sod-omites, rakehell gamblers – but nothing the 'genial' commissioner with 'bronzed face and sun-dimmed eyes' in his cheerful office, coal-fire glowing, could not handle with his efficient battery of trans-Whitehall speaking tubes.

Then there were the Irish. There was always trouble with the Irish. 'The clash between law and disorder will I hope grow less every year,' said the commissioner, 'but these things are small com-pared with the anxious work one had to do in the Jubilee year.'

'Ah, as chief of the Criminal Investigation Department, you mean?' asked the reporter.

'Yes. It was a period of intense strain. We were aware of the existence of a desperate conspiracy of destruction, and our task was to break it down before it got into operation . . . little by little, by slow but certain steps we drove the conspirators into the net and completely demolished their plottings. You remember that arrests were made in connection with that business?'

'Yes.'

'But you have no conception of the long, anxious and unwearying effort that was required to bring those arrests about,' said the commissioner. 'Those are not the things that come to the surface, you see . . .'

Nor were they ever meant to. In mid twentieth-century London Commissioner Sir Harold Scott found no enthusiasm at the Home Office for dredging up the sixty-year-old files on the resignation of Mr James Monro. And Dr Ian Monro, it seemed, never did get his grandfather's papers from his sister. But there *was* something in Edinburgh. The missionary had indeed been indiscreet enough to compile his own memoirs. Investigators on the trail of Jack the Ripper would uncover them thirty-five years after Dr Ian Monro's enquiry revealed the extraordinary archival lacuna.

After almost a century of sensationalist speculation on the Whitechapel murders, by the mid 1980s researchers had begun drilling into the official Home Office files, then on the cusp of release after a hundred-year closure. There had been plenty of conspiracy theories of a cover-up – directed by masons, by civil servants, by doctors, by the police, by ministers, by the monarchy, by all of them combined – to conceal the Ripper's true identity. One account had even claimed that Monro himself was the killer.*

James Monro had been the most important operational police-

* *Jack the Ripper: Summing Up and Verdict* by Colin Wilson and Robin Odell (1985) advanced a theory offered by an anonymous 'retired company secretary in Australia' that Monro performed the killings in 'a controlled psychopathic state . . . in order to draw attention to the inadequacies of Scotland Yard'.

man in London in the second half of the 1880s. He was head of
the Criminal Investigation Department from 1884. From February 1887 he was also head of Section D, the prime defence against
Irish terror.

He resigned as head of the CID in August 1888, ostensibly
after a row with his martinet superior, Sir Charles Warren, when
the ex-soldier blocked the appointment to Scotland Yard of an
old friend of Monro's from India. It was not a complete dis-
appearing act: Monro was attached to the Home Office to continue the 'secret work' for a shadowy four-month period. Then,
when Warren resigned, on 24 November 1888 Monro was
appointed commissioner.

His resignation had always excited the conspiracy theorists.*
However, when the 'Ripper files' were fully opened in 1988,
while gruesome in their description of the killings, they contained
only the scantest references to James Monro.

Two prominent researchers, Paul Beggs and Martin Fido,
ploughed on. In 1985, after a twelve-year hunt for Monro's surviving descendants, they found what they described as 'James
Monro's handwritten memoirs, written for the benefit of his
children, safely tucked away at the back of a cupboard in an
Edinburgh suburb, unseen by anyone outside the immediate
family'. The document should have been a golden key to solving
the greatest mystery in criminal investigation, but its discoverers
were disappointed: 'When we read the papers we found not a
single mention of Jack the Ripper or any associated murder
investigation.' But the missionary had a great deal to say on other
'matters that do not come to the surface'.

---

* And had done so from the start – but contemporary journalists saw Irish politics
behind the resignation before any Ripper link. Asking 'where is Monro?' at the
height of the Whitechapel terror, the radical *Star* newspaper advanced this theory:
'Mr Monro devoted too much time to Irish business in support of *The Times*
case. Sir Charles Warren complained in person to Lord Salisbury that Monro was
neglecting home detective duties . . . Salisbury agreed. Monro at once resigned.'

On his appointment as commissioner, the *Star* called the move 'thoroughly
bad . . . it is notorious that Mr Monro when assistant commissioner was constantly
intriguing against his chief and is associated in a peculiar degree with the anti-Irish
policy of this government. He has been at the bottom of half the dynamite scares
which came so opportunely at the eve of elections . . .'

4

Darjeeling, India, April 1903

Ten years after its founding the Abode of Mercy was overflowing.
A four-year famine still stalked India; an earthquake had struck
the mission in 1897, just as the first cases of bubonic plague
reached Lower Bengal. In 1902 a new mission was built a mile
away from Ranaghat, with a dispensary and tin-roofed sheds to
accommodate a thousand, a school and a small mud-walled
church. A trickle of funds arrived from well-wishers in the Church
Missionary Society to buy medicines and termite-proof Bibles.

As the hot season bore down, James Monro knew his own
frailty enough to seek a therapeutic stay at the Darjeeling hill-
station. It was here, in 1898, that he had written his one published
work of millenarist theology called *Preparing for the Second
Coming.*

The Reverend Doctor Charles Monro, still dispensing medicine in the heat of the plains, read a much-travelled copy of *The
Times* for 5 March 1903. The retirement of the Metropolitan
Police commissioner, Sir Edward Bradford, gave the newspaper
cause to rake up the circumstances of the resignation of his predecessor, James Monro. He posted the cutting to his father in
the hills. The response was immediate.

> My dear Charlie [his father replied]. The notice in *The
> Times* received by this mail makes me think of doing
> what has often been in my mind, but which for various
> reasons I have refrained from carrying out. I think it is
> right that you and my children should know something
> more of the life which I led while in the Metropolitan

Police and of the reasons which made me resign my office as Commissioner.

The newspaper had given its own rationale for his sudden departure the day after he left office: 'We understand that Mr Monro has taken this step on account of differences of opinion between himself and Mr Matthews [the Conservative Home Secretary] in connection with the question of superannuation and with other matters affecting gravely the welfare of the police force.'

Now, thirteen years on, James Monro

wished his children to know that their father had resigned not on account of any quarrel with the Home Secretary, but because he had refused to do what he considered to be *wrong* and because, by government grace, he was able to sacrifice his own worldly interests on behalf of those of the men, which as their Commissioner he was bound in honour to uphold, even at the sacrifice of his own.

There it was again, that moralistic cloud-dwelling which had caused so much anguish in the temporal slough of Whitehall. Charles Monro must have been as baffled as he was when his father announced they were all leaving their grand London life to return to India. His father wrote on and on, filling over a hundred hand-written pages with an account obsessively concerned with bruising bureaucratic in-fighting in Whitehall over who was fit to lead the fight against Irish-American revolutionaries.

He seemed driven by the idea of 'discretion' – the word comes up over and over again, as if it was his moral duty to keep his mouth shut. In the letter to his son he made this strange sideswipe at the newspaper whose report had triggered his outpourings: 'But says *The Times*, "Mr Monro, a strong man was not always discreet" . . . what does *The Times* mean by being discreet? . . . I suppose it means that I did not always do as *The Times* thought I should have done.' The remark was laden with significance.

Even spiritually refreshed in the cool hills of Darjeeling, James Monro could still lash out at his former colleagues in a most worldly fashion. One Home Secretary, Sir William Harcourt, 'went off his head whenever dynamite was mentioned'; another, Hugh Childers, 'was as weak as he was obstinate'. Monro's special opprobrium, however, was reserved for Sir Edward Jenkinson, KCB, his predecessor as director of anti-Irish revolutionary operations in London – until he too was suddenly defenestrated from the Home Office in January 1887. Examples of Jenkinson's 'outrageous interference' were detailed in 'printed papers which are among my papers in England', Monro told his son. Copies were made public by the Home Office in the 1990s. In one secret minute Monro accused Jenkinson of making 'suggestions involving illegal action . . . which, had they been listened to, would have involved the police in well-earned disgrace'.

But not once in his memoir did Monro mention the figure who was his closest Whitehall colleague in the 'secret work'. This was Robert Anderson, a Dublin-born barrister and veteran Fenian-finder at the Home Office. Anderson had been booted out by his bitter enemy Jenkinson, then brought back into the secret fold by Monro. When Anderson himself, on Monro's urging, became head of the Criminal Investigation Department on 31 August 1888, Edward Jenkinson was horrified by the appointment. Monro and Anderson were 'close personal friends', according to an official investigation of their relationship conducted years later, yet Anderson was utterly erased from Monro's account.

Monro and Anderson had ostensibly together defeated the fiendish plot to blow up Westminster Abbey with the Queen inside. Sir Robert (he was knighted in 1901) wrote years later in his serialised memoirs: 'I remember as though it happened yesterday my visit to Monro on that eventful day, after the Queen had reached the Palace and the Abbey guests had scattered. The intense anxiety of many days was at an end, and we gripped each other by the hand without a word from either of us.'

The affair remained mysterious. If Monro had indeed saved

the lives of the Queen and her ministers, why had he received no honour? Why had the Monro family all vanished to India in a puff of smoke?

The tone of the memoir changed. The self-justification and *ad hominem* sniping gave way to a police procedural. The missionary wanted the operational details of the Jubilee Plot to be set down on paper. From the hills of Darjeeling, this is what he thought his son should know:

This was the Jubilee year and I had undeniable information that every effort was to be made to bring off a dynamite outrage in the Jubilee week.

In the beginning of the year two noted Fenians left London for America. One of these was a man, General Millen, who had been a General in the Mexican War, and who had a good deal to do with the earlier Fenian risings in Ireland.

This man Millen took his departure from America, after being authorised by the Dynamite leaders there to carry on the war in those parts of the world called the British Isles. Of his commission so to do, I had the fullest information and Millen was closely supervised.

He came to Europe, stayed in Paris for a short time, and then proceeded to Boulogne . . . He remained there for some time and came to be on friendly terms with a resident in the Hotel, an elderly man who had taken up his quarters there with his wife, and who was suffering from gout. This interesting invalid was Supt Thomson of the Metropolitan Police, whom I had deputed for the purpose. He carried out his instructions admirably and so did his wife . . .

The Jubilee time was now drawing on, and with Millen at Boulogne evidently in expectation of someone, I felt rather uneasy. I therefore resolved to cripple Millen by letting him see that the London Police was aware of him being at Boulogne for no good purpose. I therefore sent Chief Supt Williamson, my second in command, to Boulogne with instructions to interview Millen and frighten him . . .

The Jubilee came and passed without outrage. I learned that there had been some hitch in the operations of the conspirators, but that they had not given up their intention of bringing off an outrage, if not in Jubilee week, at all events in Jubilee year. So we waited, watching . . .

There would be plenty more detailed reportage of the affair in his long letter before Monro concluded: 'It will be of some satisfaction to my children to read the above account – for the truth of which I pledge my word – and to know that the Jubilee dynamite scheme was frustrated by their father.'

5

Sodbury House, Great Clacton, Essex, 21 February 1910

In a fine red-brick house in Great Clacton, a Domesday village not yet quite engulfed by the noisy seaside resort nibbling at its boundaries, a policeman's widow read a staid society journal in the gloom of a late winter's afternoon. At first sight the serialised memoirs of a retired civil servant, entitled *The Lighter Side of My Official Life*, looked thumpingly dull. For Mrs Martha Alice Thomson, companion to the widow of a wealthy builder, it was an invitation to attempt a little discreet blackmail.

The article in the February edition of *Blackwood's Magazine* was by Sir Robert Anderson, KCB, James Monro's one-time colleague and successor as head of the Criminal Investigation Department of the Metropolitan Police. He mentioned Mrs Thomson by name; he mentioned her beloved late husband – and their strange secret adventures together more than two decades earlier. They had been known then, while pursuing the most delicate of international inquiries, by the curious code-name 'Ladybird'.

The pompous memoir was not an easy read, but it revealed extraordinary goings-on in the Whitehall intelligence establishment. As she read on, Martha Thomson's eyes lit up.

> There was a hellish plot to bring about a dynamite explosion in Westminster Abbey during the historic ceremony of Queen Victoria's Jubilee [wrote Sir Robert], and one of the principal agents in that plot was taken into pay on behalf of our Government.
>
> But the shameful scheme was discovered and thwarted by Mr Monro, then Assistant Commissioner of Police,

who most fortunately had at that time been placed in
charge of the secret service work.

The arrangement had been made during a disastrous
interval before his appointment; and he had no knowledge of it until a prominent Fenian – I will here call him
'Jenks'* – arrived at Boulogne to carry out his twofold
mission on behalf of the American Clan-na-Gael and the
British Government.

'Jenks' was clearly the mysterious General Millen, late of the
Mexican army, mentioned in James Monro's Darjeeling memorandum – but although the retired policeman had insisted to his
children that he was telling the truth, he had certainly not told
them that the 'principal agent' in the plot was somehow acting on
behalf of Her Majesty's government. Mrs Thomson knew exactly
who 'Jenks' was – she and her husband had spent some considerable
time in his company both in France and in New York.

Mrs Sarah Grant could thump on the ceiling demanding her
attention as much as she liked – the lady's companion ignored
her and read on greedily: the next bit was all about her. 'He
['Jenks'] brought his wife to Europe with him, and posed as a
tourist. Ex-Superintendent Thomson of Bow Street, who had
formerly served in the detective department at Scotland Yard, was
at once sent to Boulogne and he put up at the hotel where Jenks
was staying,' Sir Robert wrote. 'He too had his wife with him.'
The two wives had become friendly – so did their husbands.

'When Mr Monro had gained full knowledge of the plot he
sent Superintendent (afterwards Chief Constable) Williamson to
Boulogne to deal with "Jenks"; the man was notified that the
bargain made with him was now repudiated, and he was warned
against crossing the Channel . . .'

Mrs Thomson 'fulfilled her part admirably' by keeping her
mouth shut, 'and Jenks went back to America in ignorance of
the counterplot of which he had been the victim'.

* The Fenian emissary was called 'Jenks' in Anderson's original article, an obvious
dig at Sir Edward Jenkinson. When the article re-appeared in book form, the
Jubilee plotter was transformed into 'Jinks'.

Armed with a typewritten memoir of her husband's secret services to the state, Mrs Thomson drafted a long letter to the newly appointed Liberal Home Secretary, the Rt Hon. Mr Winston Churchill, MP.

> Sir – The article written by Sir Robert Anderson and published in Feb number of *Blackwood's Magazine*, has caused me much annoyance – and really some injury [she wrote]. I have received letters from friends . . . asking if I have given this gentleman authority so to use my name.
>
> Certainly I have not . . . I always understood, no police officer – especially if he had a pension, however high his rank – dared expose secrets of state.
>
> My late husband, Supt James J. Thomson, after his retirement could have written most thrilling tales of his experiences during his long service, but honour held him silent. Now, as Sir Robert has written, I feel free to appeal for help . . .

She had been a left a pensionless, childless widow, she informed Mr Churchill. Aged sixty-three, she was 'too old for her duties and must leave next month' – and now wanted nothing more than to retire 'to a very old cottage in Debenham, Suffolk, my birthplace. What I now ask is – can you grant me a small civil list pension?'

Martha Thomson outlined her late husband's exotic CV, in particular a conspiratorial trip to Russia on behalf of the 'Privy Council' in 1878 – which nearly ended in a sentence to Siberia, she claimed – and a counter-offer by the Imperial government to form 'a secret intelligence system here in London and Paris – which naturally he declined'.

'He returned to his division and in '86, utterly broken down in health, by the Trafalgar Square riots, the unending Fenian troubles and frequent bad attacks of gout, he resigned,' she wrote. 'He was given his pension and left in May '86.'*

All this hocus-pocus about Russian spies and the Privy Council

* Home Office records post Superintendent Thomson's retirement as May 1887.

would be enough to extract a little reward, she must have hoped.
But much more sensitive was what she had to say of strange
goings-on in the Jubilee summer of 1887:

> Later, as my husband was thoroughly conversant with
> every part of the Fenian movements from the year '66 –
> he was employed privately by the Home Office and Mr
> Monro in many cases – amongst these the Jubilee Plot . . .
>
> Having severe gout in the right hand and time
> pressing, I went with him to Boulogne to help, as I had
> done in several other cases. He received two guineas a
> day, as I believe my expenses were paid too. I received
> nothing else.
>
> We went through an awful three weeks at Boulogne.
> Never for five minutes relaxing our watch over General
> and Mrs Millen, Sir Roberts' 'Jenks' day or night . . . and
> *I* really found out the daughters of General Millen who
> were in London and through getting them watched too,
> and arrested on their way to the Abbey prevented a ter-
> rible disaster.
>
> The following year I joined my husband on the *Times*
> Commission case, and spent five most exciting months
> in America resulting in the crushing of Parnell . . .

The lady's companion posted her rambling, handwritten letter
to Mr Winston Churchill and returned to Sodbury House to wait
for a reply.

6

Home Office, Whitehall, London SW, April 1910

Winston Churchill had been Home Secretary for two months. He had advanced from journalist-hero of the Boer War to Conservative MP at the age of twenty-five – then had tempestuously crossed the House to join Mr Herbert Asquith's Liberals. The safety of the metropolis was his responsibility. American dynamiters were long gone from London; now the bogey-men were eastern European anarchists. Within a few months the top-hatted Churchill would be in action directing the Scots Guards at the Siege of Sidney Street – to the derision of the Tory press.

In April 1910 there were more humdrum duties to attend to. A delegation of Japanese detectives were in London to inspect the efficient workings of Scotland Yard. Mr Churchill made his excuses – there was pressing ministerial business: Sir Robert Anderson had gone into print again.

Having so excited Mrs Martha Thomson two months before with his magazine revelations of 'hellish plots', the retired civil servant exploded his latest journalistic bombshell almost casually: 'To the present hour I do not know whether the Home Secretary was then aware of my authorship of the *Times* articles of 1887 on "Parnellism and Crime",' he confided in the April instalment of his *Blackwood's* serial, 'for in relation to this matter I acted with strict propriety in dealing with Mr Monro and not with the Secretary of State.'

In two lines he had solved a two-decade-old political mystery: it was he who had written the string of articles for *The Times* newspaper called 'Behind the Scenes in America', which had branded Parnell and his party as fellow-travellers in terror.

It was the split over Parnell's naming as co-respondent in a divorce case in 1890 which had emasculated the Irish Party. Now, two decades on, it had barely regained its cohesion, its leaders ageing and Anglicised. But with nothing better to do, like old generals skirmishing with the mess-table silver, the Irish Party leaders could not resist re-staging the long-ago battles of the Special Commission. It had been their Rorke's Drift in The Strand, the plucky little nationalist garrison assailed by Conservative impis and their Whitehall levies. In February 1889 Anderson had almost dished them all with his secret weapon, the spy Thomas Beach. Now the hated Irish-born civil servant had offered himself up for retribution.

Ministers braced themselves for parliamentary unpleasantness to come. Mr Asquith's three-month-old administration, committed in principle to a third attempt at home rule, depended on the support of the eighty-two Irish members. The Liberal Prime Minister, who as a rising young barrister had acted for the defence in the Special Commission, might just give them Anderson's head.

Martha Thomson's letter meanwhile lay unanswered in a Home Office in-tray. On 28 March she had written again: 'More than a month has passed since my appeal – do please bring it to the notice of the Honble Home Sec. I have heard how good he is to the poor and widows ... I have been active many years in public life – now when I can do no more I am alone and very poor ...' Her timing was opportune: the Anderson storm was about to erupt in the Commons.

Civil servants woke up. Who were Thomson and Thomson? What were these bizarre husband-and-wife spying adventures in France and America she referred to? She seemed to want money to go away. A file was opened on the Clacton correspondent. Perhaps Scotland Yard knew something.

Commissioner Sir Edward Henry minuted on the file: 'Mr Thomson retired from the force in May '87, and did no work for the Police subsequent to retirement. In June '87 apparently he was employed by Sir R. Anderson to make some inquiry, Sir

R. Anderson at that time being at the HO.' The Thomson file began a hopeful voyage round the secret crevices of Whitehall.

By Friday 7 April the Anderson affair was in the newspapers. The radical *Daily News*, which had been a constant goad to the Conservative government during the Parnell upheavals, woke up to the political significance of the outburst. Under the banner AMAZING CONFESSION it publicised Sir Robert's apparent admission that he had, while acting as 'Political Adviser at the Home Office' in 1887, written the *Times* articles – 'the same Sir Robert Anderson who was head of the Criminal Investigation Department when its services were availed of by *The Times*'.

The veteran Parnellite John Redmond, leader of the Irish Nationalist Party at Westminster since 1900, put down an indignant parliamentary question: Had the Prime Minister seen Sir Robert's admission? Were there records to show the party of the day were involved? A pending debate on Civil Service funding, so lobby correspondents were informed, would be used to annul Sir Robert's £900 pension. The Irish Party scented a sweet revenge – the long sought-for proof that Lord Salisbury's Conservative government had colluded in 1887–9 in the attempted political destruction of Parnell by *The Times*. A full-scale inquiry was demanded.

Pursued by reporters, the elderly Viscount Llandaff, who, as Mr Henry Matthews, had been Home Secretary that Jubilee summer, refused to comment. Anderson seemed prepared to say anything. This was getting dangerous.

Reporters flocked to Sir Robert's house at 39 Linden Gardens, Kensington, scene of all sorts of secretive shuttlings in the past, to doorstep the singing policeman. He gave a blustering interview to the *Morning Post*, insisting:

> 'I disclaim any connection with any move in a political game. My only object was to let light in on a dangerous conspiracy. During the whole time when the Commission was mooted and during the course of the Commission I absolutely refused to have any communication

whatever with *The Times* . . . I said to them: "In ordinary circumstances I should, as a matter of course, give you the help of my Department. You must go to the Government." The Government would not lift a finger to help them. I felt at the time this was a scandal, but there it was.'

'How does it come, Sir Robert, that you, a civil servant, were allowed to write for the Press?'

'Are you not aware that a great number of civil servants are journalists?'

Sir Robert revealed the utility of journalism in counter-revolutionary warfare: 'If there are several people in a conspiracy . . . the publication of some obviously inside-detail sets the conspirators watching one another, and generally breaks it up. If you will read the articles you will see throughout that element.'

Who gave permission to write the articles?

'I acted quite correctly,' said Sir Robert, 'in going to Mr Monro . . . I told him of my intention, and said: "Will this embarrass you?" He said: "I think it very important."'

'Mr Monro's judgement was that it would be a very important step in the anti-Fenian conspiracy, if I may put it in that way. That is why the articles were written.'

An anti-Fenian conspiracy? That was not Mr Monro's recollection of his years of public service.

The seventy-one-year-old missionary had returned. He had left the Abode of Mercy in 1905, when the 'burden had become too great', handed its running to the Church Missionary Society and retired to a terraced house in Aberdeen. Monro had a key confidant in Whitehall, Sir Melville Macnaghten – an old friend from India whom he could trust absolutely and who was now head of the CID.

Macnaghten had alerted his old friend to the drama unfolding in London. Monro replied on 9 April:

The alleged statement of Anderson to an interviewer that it was arranged between him and me that he should write the letters and that they should be offered to *The Times* as the best medium for their publication is absolutely incorrect . . .

Anderson's statement as to his being Political Adviser to the Home Office at any time when I was at Scotland Yard is, so far as I am aware, unfounded.

My principle throughout has ever been that in police matters, politics have no place – and this principle I followed during the whole time I was at Scotland Yard, under four different Secretaries of State . . . whether the Government was Liberal or Conservative . . .

The unbending copper had lost none of his moral probity, but he was also shrewd enough to seek political protection. His brother-in-law Mr David Littlejohn sounded out a Scottish Liberal MP, Mr Eugene Wason, as a direct go-between to the Prime Minister. 'Mr Monro is desirous that the Home Office should be made aware that should they desire to "interview" him, any account which he might be able to give of certain past events (*and which might not agree with some things which have appeared*), he is at their disposal,' he wrote.

'Certain past events' – what could he mean? The Littlejohn letter, with its hint of something nasty in the Whitehall woodshed, was passed to Herbert Asquith.

The matter was now being treated with the utmost urgency. First it had to be established what exact position Mr Anderson held in the summer of 1887. Civil servants worked through that weekend digging out sensitive files. Some were very sensitive indeed.

Sir Edward Troup, permanent under-secretary at the Home Office, prepared a memo for the Prime Minister:

Mr Anderson, now Sir Robert Anderson, was, I believe, originally employed in secret service work by the Irish Government . . .

Mr Anderson's work was, to a considerable extent, superseded when Mr now Sir E. G. Jenkinson [took] charge of the secret Irish work in the Home Office, and as they did not work well together, it was arranged that Mr Anderson's appointment as Home Office secret agent should come to an end.

He still continued to communicate with certain informers who were known only to him, and in this way assisted Mr Monro, who was at this time head of the Criminal Investigation Department and who was a close personal friend . . .

When the differences between Mr Monro and Mr Jenkinson came to a head, and Mr Jenkinson retired [he was sacked], Mr Monro took over the whole of the secret service work from the 1st of January 1887. He at once recommended the employment of Mr Anderson at a salary of £400 a year . . .

As a thirty-seven-year-old senior clerk at the Home Office in the Jubilee summer, Troup had witnessed the long-ago game of police musical chairs for himself. His account continued with brisk authority:

In August 1888 the troubles between Sir Charles Warren and Mr Monro came to a head, and Mr Monro resigned his post as Assistant Commissioner, but came over to the Home Office and continued from there to direct the Irish secret work . . .

In the end on Sir Charles Warren's resignation, Mr Monro returned to Scotland Yard as Chief Commissioner, and Mr Anderson retained permanently his appointment in the Criminal Investigation Department . . .

The briefing paper went to Downing Street for Herbert Asquith's urgent attention.

7

The benches of the Lower House heaved with frock-coated indignation; Irish members were knowing and boisterous. To Mr John Redmond, the arcane manoeuvrings of so long ago were a matter of 'extreme gravity'. Had the Prime Minister seen Sir Robert's admission? he asked. Were there any records to show the government of the day were party to this action? Asquith depended on the Irish Party's support to stay in power – he must give them something.

The Prime Minister delivered the bones of Sir Edward Troup's memo, adding the permanent under-secretary's drafted words: 'If Sir Robert Anderson wrote The *Times* articles – if he did – or any part of them, his action was contrary to the rules and traditions of the Civil Service . . .'

But Sir Edward Troup was clearly anxious that should be the end of it. 'I am informed that the papers in the Home Office bearing upon the Parnell Commission are few and unimportant,' Asquith added, 'and that there are none which could properly be laid on the table of the House.'

Certainly not Mrs Thomson's ramblings from Clacton about 'exciting months in America which resulted in the crushing of Parnell'.

As the Prime Minister sat down, the leader of the opposition, Mr Arthur Balfour, who in 1887 had been the Chief Secretary for Ireland in his uncle Lord Salisbury's administration, entered the Chamber. The Irish benches erupted gleefully: 'Pigott!' they shouted. 'Where is Anderson?'

Sir Robert was in his club reading Asquith's words on the tickertape wire. He rushed a spluttering statement by messenger to his old redoubt, *The Times*, set up in hot-metal type that night. The last line caused jaws to drop in Whitehall when they read the letters page the next morning: 'If only the Government would release me from my honourable obligations to reticence respecting my Secret Service work my defence will be complete,' said Sir Robert. Had he not revealed enough already? Here he was in *The Times*'s letter pages again, banging away about a conspiracy to kill the Queen . . .

> The story of the Jubilee dynamite plot is now public property. That plot was hatched at the Chicago Convention of August 1886, which . . . Mr Redmond attended as Mr Parnell's representative . . .
>
> The secret Fenian report of the Convention announced the intention to have a pyrotechnic display in honour of the Queen's Jubilee, or in other words, as events proved, to bring about a dynamite explosion in Westminster Abbey at the great function of June 1887.
>
> Proofs abounded that this exposure in the columns of *The Times* hindered a plot of far more terrible gravity even than that which was detected and thwarted by police action . . .

Sir Robert's idea of 'reticence' seemed the very opposite. What might Monro reveal? That same day Sir Edward Troup got in touch by letter with remote Aberdeenshire, and probed, in the most helpful language, what Anderson's 'close personal friend' was prepared to admit. Would he wire back urgently by 11 a.m. the following day?

The Scottish mail was efficient. James Monro got Sir Edward Troup's communication at 10 a.m. on the 13th. One hour was not enough to compose and rush to the telegraph office a statement to Parliament in which he might lay down the burden he had carried to Ranaghat. Instead he composed a carefully worded letter.

Irish members scented blood. That same afternoon of 13 April the debate resumed and it was Winston Churchill's turn to face the Nationalist barrage. This time they were after Monro: had he made a statement? 'I have communicated with Mr Monro, who resides in Scotland, and whose state of health prevents his attendance in London,' the Home Secretary declared. 'I have not yet had his reply, and can only say at present [Churchill had seen the Macnaghten letter] that he certainly does not admit the accuracy of the statements made by or attributed to Sir Robert Anderson.'

The Home Office got Monro's reply by letter on the 14th. Sir Edward read it with concern. 'Mr Monro did *not* sanction Sir Robert Anderson's conduct "in acting as an agent for *The Times* newspaper",' the retired policeman insisted. There was more. If 'relieved of his obligation to secrecy', he offered to reveal new evidence on the events of the Jubilee summer. Oh dear. Mr Churchill could not possibly read this to the House of Commons . . .

Home Office file A499962 was opened that morning and the Monro letter secured within for discreet circulation. Opinions must be sought. Perhaps the storm would pass.

House of Commons, 14 April 1910

The Home Secretary went unbriefed into the conference chamber for that evening's resumption of the debate. A persistent Irish member, Jeremiah McVeagh, probed the circumstances of Monro's mysterious resignation. 'Why is it that Sir Robert Anderson had an increase of salary, a pension and a knighthood whilst his superior official receives neither a pension nor a knighthood?' he asked. Churchill extemporised: 'I am afraid I cannot give any explanation of the freaks of fortune in this world.'

T. M. Healy (veteran Nationalist MP, later first governor-general of the Irish Free State) shifted the Irish fire from Anderson's Jubilee year employment by Printing House Square to his bizarre letter published in *The Times* two days previously. 'Has the Right Hon. Gentleman seen an extraordinary statement by this gentleman that the Home Office had at the time of the Jubilee of Her Majesty Queen Victoria received complete information as to an alleged plot to blow up Westminster Abbey, and whether there are any records at the Home Office which support that statement?'

Churchill replied: 'I must have notice of that. I do not think there are any records at all . . .'

Westminster, 14–20 April

The Irish Party, with its elephantine memory for perceived English injustices, was poking into every cranny of alleged collusion between *The Times* and the government during the Parnell Commission. They hammered away with parliamentary questions through 19–20 April. Civil servants dug frantically in fusty, two-decade-old secret files to brief ministerial replies.

Had a man named William Henry Joyce, an Irish Office official, been employed by *The Times*? No. Had a Royal Naval officer called Captain Malcolm McNeile visited America on behalf of the newspaper? No. Had any part of the £50,000 which was offered by *The Times* to an Irishman in America named P. J. Sheridan to give evidence against Parnell come from the Secret Service fund? No. Had large sums of Secret Service money been paid to *agents provocateurs* for plots which they themselves were organising? No. Had an Inspector Littlechild of the CID interviewed a convicted dynamiter in prison to collect evidence for *The Times*? No. The Liberal government of the day denied every arcane allegation made against its Tory antecedent.

McVeagh would not let go. Had the Home Secretary yet received any statement from Mr Monro? The question was tabled on the 14th, the day the letter from Aberdeen arrived at the Home Office. It would take an uncomfortable six days to answer.

Sir Edward Troup pored over Monro's letter with informed interest. The first part read:

> In 1887 I was Assistant Commissioner, Metropolitan Police under the Home Office, in charge of secret work. Mr Anderson was an agent of mine . . . chiefly as being a channel of information received from a man in America, who corresponded directly with him, and whose name I

did not know. [This was Thomas Beach – alias Henri le Caron.]

When the *Times*'s earlier articles appeared, they certainly caused a sensation in London . . . and I can quite imagine that I may have welcomed public interest being directed to the existence of a dangerous conspiracy.

But such an expression of opinion was a very different thing from authorising an agent of mine to give information to the public . . . no such authority was asked by Mr Anderson, and none was given to him by me. When subsequently articles appeared in *The Times*, I was unaware of the name of the author, and naturally I made no report on the subject to the Home Office.

A long time afterwards Mr Anderson informed me that he had written one or more of the articles, and I felt much annoyed . . .

That seemed harmless enough. But the second half of the letter hinted at darker goings-on. It read:

In these anxious months, I had on my shoulders the burden of the safety of life and property in London threatened especially by the Jubilee Plot – which involved the question of the connection of members of the Irish party with the conspirators . . .

How real this was may be gathered from the report from the select committee of the House of Commons . . . To this report I refer the Secretary of State – it contains much of, but not all the evidence, and if the obligation to secrecy in such official matters is withdrawn as regards me, I can now very effectively supplement it.

The all but forgotten Commons report of April 1888 had roundly concluded that two men, one of whom was later convicted at the Old Bailey for conspiracy to cause explosions, had indeed visited the House in the Jubilee summer on the invitation of an Irish MP called Joseph Nolan, a prominent supporter of Mr Parnell. They had done so while acting for 'their chief', a

man named as General Millen. Quite enough had been said at the
time. No reason to bring all that up again. Sir Edward Troup
reached for a blue crayon to bracket off the opening paragraphs of
Monro's statement. The reference to the 'Jubilee Plot' was excised.

The Monro file shuffled round the Home Office collecting
opinions. On 15 April Sir Edward Troup noted: 'I think that in
reply to this question the Secretary of State should read the passage between brackets in Mr Monro's letter.' He should say: 'I
have received a statement from Mr Monro of which I will read
the material part.' Material part? Irish members would realise that
the letter had been cut.

Three days later Churchill scribbled: 'Let me see in type.'

On the 20th Sir Edward hurriedly advised Mr Sidney Harris,
Churchill's private secretary, 'Please point out to S of S that if he
reads the extract from Mr Monro's letter he may possibly be
called on to lay the whole correspondence on the table. I see no
objection to this: But if he does, in view of the reference to the
Jubilee plot, it would be possible to give the substance only of
Mr Monro's remarks.'

Mr Harris* concurred. The next day he minuted: 'The heading
should be: "I have received the following statement from Mr
Monro." I think this will safeguard us.'

House of Commons, 21 April 1910, 3.45 p.m.

The climax to the Anderson affair had almost come. Jeremiah
McVeagh tabled his question. The youthful Home Secretary rose
– and delivered his private secretary's exquisite textual elision.
There was no mention of 'material part', no mention of the
'Jubilee Plot'. Indeed there were no records at the Home Office
on such a thing, he had already informed the House. Propelled
by his civil servants, Winston Churchill lied to Parliament.

The Irish Party bought it. 'I take it that the statement of Sir

---

* Mr Sidney West Harris (1876–1964), private secretary to a number of Home
Secretaries, pursued a career in making cuts. From 1947–60 he was director of
the British Board of Film Censors.

Robert Anderson that he had the permission of his official superior to write these articles for *The Times*,' quipped Mr McVeagh, 'may be treated as another of "Anderson's Fairy Tales".'

'I could not have put it better myself,' said Mr Churchill winningly.

The debate lurched on between grave solemnity and uproar. After an interminable speech picking over the old bones of Pigott, Parnell, le Caron et al, Mr T. P. O'Connor at last moved the vote to curtail the delinquent civil servant's pension. The Home Secretary rose to reply. Mr Churchill lashed Sir Robert for his 'gross boastfulness', excused only by the 'garrulous and inaccurate [he was keen to stress] indiscretion of advancing years . . . I have thought it my duty to call on Sir Robert Anderson to restore documents which are the property of the public,' he said.

Mr Churchill had himself read the *Blackwood's* articles with obvious distaste: 'It was my duty to do so – I do not think I would otherwise have been drawn into their perusal,' he told the House. But, other than Sir Robert's admission of authorship of the *Times* articles, he could find 'no revelations of confidential matters which are other than trivial or unimportant'.

The Home Secretary was therefore 'not minded to immediate financial punishment – although the power to forfeit Sir Robert's pension remained if he should err further in the future'.* The Irish benches groaned.

Arthur Balfour, sole parliamentary survivor of the administration of 1887–9, spoke next. The leader of the opposition found nothing to say in mitigation of Anderson's actions: 'Civil servants should seal their lips,' he said drily.†

---

* A week after the debate the May issue of *Blackwood's* appeared in which Sir Robert boasted he had routinely issued warrants to steam open cross-Channel mail at the Folkestone post office in pursuit of 'literary filth'. In response Sir Edward Troup told Churchill: 'If you wish to stop his pension, he has now delivered himself into your hands . . .'

† After Balfour cut him loose in the Commons, Anderson wrote another cringing letter to *The Times*. He called the Tory leader's remarks in the debate 'strange' and Mr Monro's statement 'amazing'. 'To me it is an echo of a most painful incident which, on the eve of his resigning the Chief Commissionership of Police, broke up a close friendship of several years.'

The Prime Minister rose. He had *not* read the articles – but added his 'strongest condemnation'. Would Mr Asquith admit collusion between the State and *The Times* newspaper in their campaign against Parnell? The Irish Party tensed for the turning moment of the debate. He would not. Instead he made great play of exonerating ministers past from having 'any participation in or having had anything to do with such matters as are now known to have taken place'.

The vote was moved at last. Sir Robert's reputation had been soundly kicked around the Commons but on the government-whipped division, the policeman's pension survived.

The next day the Home Secretary, as was his ministerial duty, wrote a report of the parliamentary proceedings to his sovereign: 'Sir Robert has behaved very badly,' he confided. 'Mr Churchill has not however been able to bring himself to deprive this old policeman of his sole means of support.' The debate thereafter had descended into chaos, he explained to the King. A former minister had made an equivocal remark about Parnell's alleged complicity in the Phoenix Park murders. 'Uproar reigned and threatened to develop a dangerous excitement.'

The articles in *Blackwood's* which had triggered the whole furore were 'interlarded with disagreeable remarks', Mr Churchill could report, their content was 'both scrappy and dull'.

That was his opinion. If King Edward VII, who had just two weeks to live, had cared to peruse February's instalment of Sir Robert's otherwise stodgy memoir, he would have read about a plot abetted by the British government to kill his mother.

The Irish members had chased the wrong fox. Clattering after Anderson's admission – that he was the author of the *Times* articles – his astonishing revelations about General Millen's relationship with Her Majesty's government went unchallenged. The outraged Jeremiah McVeagh had thundered during the debate: 'The only defence made by Anderson is that, by the publication of these articles, he averted a serious plot for the blowing up of Westminster Abbey by the use of dynamite . . . The Home Secretary has told us there are absolutely no papers at the Home Office. There is no confirmation whatever of this theory, except the statement of Anderson himself . . .'

Mr McVeagh thought he was making it all up to save his pension. The trouble was, for once, Sir Robert Anderson was telling the truth.

Poor Mrs Thomson. Her begging letter was receiving decreasing sympathy on its journey round Whitehall. At first things looked hopeful. When the Anderson rumpus broke in Parliament, Sir Edward Troup noted on her file: 'It is a public scandal that a man in Sir R. Anderson's position should reveal the names of the persons whom he employed on secret service duty.'

The next day, 22 April, an official agreed to 'Write to the PM asking whether £10 a year can be granted.' A snooty reply came from Downing Street: 'There does not appear to me to be any claim on the First Lord's funds, unless some light can be thrown on Mrs Thomson's assertion that her husband was sent on a secret mission to Russia . . . the whole story seems very romantic, if not mythical.' By 9 May the Anderson parliamentary storm had blown over. Mrs Thomson's hopes of governmental succour were dashed. The Foreign Office could find 'no reference in our archives to Thomson'.

The impoverished lady's companion stayed in Clacton, dreaming of her little cottage in Suffolk and, so the archives would indicate, never troubled Winston Churchill again with her curious claims about 'General Millen' – whoever he might have been.

PART TWO

The General

'The Fenians made only one mistake – they
never should have fought.'
Charles Stewart Parnell

8

The life and times of Francis Frederick Millen were long known
to certain secret organs of the British government. Almost forty-
five years before Martha Thomson troubled Whitehall with her
curious claims, the general had composed a handwritten auto-
biography. It was begun in Austin, Texas, in the summer of 1866
and completed in New York five months later, to be dispatched
across the Atlantic and carefully bound in leather. The writer was
paid £250 for his services. It was filed away at Dublin Castle by
an ambitious young legal official named Robert Anderson. He
called its author 'Informant M'.

Acapulco, Mexico, January 1860

Millen's account began at the outset of his revolutionary career,
when he was waiting for movement orders in the sand-blown
Mexican port of Acapulco. As he read an old copy of the *San
Francisco Times* – passed on by a fellow Irish-born soldier in the
service of the Mexican republic – an advertisement from something called the Friends of Ireland Club caught his eye. He was
a Catholic from County Tyrone. He thought himself a patriot.
Millen sent a few dollars to the 'post-box' in California.

His family were prosperous farmers – he had been educated to
be a gentleman. Like many Ulstermen, before and since, Millen had
chosen the profession of arms. At the age of twenty-nine he was a
lieutenant-colonel in the 'liberal' army of Benito Juárez, fighting
the 'church' party of conservative landowners and priests. He had
been a soldier all his adult life; in just whose service he had first
picked up a musket would later become a matter of contention.

A reply reached him: a revolutionary organisation called the
Fenian Brotherhood was being formed, with branches across
America. Its leader was an Irish exile in New York called John
O'Mahony. Millen was dispatched on a curious mission to raise
from its Californian ranks 'an American military colony for the
state of Jalisco'. At the 'San Francisco fire engine rooms'* Millen
found 'eighty men armed with flintlocks and bayonets performing
precise military drills'. They were good soldiers, Millen thought;
'most of them were deserters from the Crimea'.

He returned to Mexico to find the Juaristas in retreat. British,
French and Spanish expeditionary forces had landed to 'restore
order'. The imperial French army stayed and Millen fought
Napoleon III's troops at the bloody siege of Puebla in March
1863. The Austrian Archduke Maximilian, backed by the French,
was proclaimed Emperor. On 12 June 1864, the day of the
unhappy Habsburg's triumphant arrival, Millen left Mexico City.
Secretive diplomatic missions to the United States on behalf of
Juárez followed (he also seemed to be acting as an undercover
agent of the US State Department) until, in New York, Brigadier-
General of Artillery F. F. Millen met a new revolutionary chieftain
and found a new cause.

Fenian Brotherhood Headquarters, 22 Duane Street, New York City, October 1864

John O'Mahony, the 'head centre' of the Fenian Brotherhood,
was hardly a martial figure. Millen arrived at his Manhattan headquarters to find his chaotic office cluttered with works of Gaelic
scholarship rather than dissertations on the military arts. The
veteran of the failed 'Young Ireland' rising of 1848 looked, said
Millen, 'like a ruffian who, if I had met him on the street, I might
readily have mistaken for an overworked assistant book-keeper
... his tall gaunt frame clothed in the shabbiest threadbare suit
of blue.'

---

* The volunteer fire brigades of American cities were favoured hang-outs of Irish
Americans throughout the nineteenth century.

The Civil War had torn the nation apart, but no matter. The imminence of the Irish revolution had been proclaimed and the warring ranks, Blue and Gray, were eagerly proselytised. The brotherhood's recruits were the children of the famine emigrants of the 'forties. They had grown up and been taught how to fight.

The war was juddering to its end. Nearly 190,000 battle-hardened men of Irish parentage were being demobilised from the armies of Grant and Lee. Scores of ex-soldiers were heading for New York and the steamship to Queenstown to join the promised revolution. O'Mahony had a mission for the Mexican general. Its aim was ambitious: to stage a rising in Dublin and proclaim the civil authority of the Irish republic. American recognition and protecting federal gunboats would surely follow. Better still, the rising would turn the diplomatic frostiness engendered by Britain's perceived support for the defeated Confederacy into war. The irony was, of all the doomed attempts to stage an Irish national rising with foreign military aid,* this one had a whisker of a chance. On 12 February 1865 Queen Victoria noted in her journal: 'She had been talking that day of America and the danger, which seems approaching, of our having a war with her as soon as she makes peace; of the impossibility of our being able to hold Canada.'

Millen had his price. 'My General's pay was $400 monthly in greenbacks . . . I offered to accept the pay of a colonel in the US Army, $222 per month,' he wrote.

But piratical American raiders alone could not slip Ireland from the lion's paw. The Fenian Brotherhood was supposedly the trans-atlantic money-box of the wider movement, the Irish Revolutionary Brotherhood, founded in a Dublin timber yard on St Patrick's Day 1858 by another '48 veteran named James Stephens.

Bustling, combative, monstrously egotistical, Stephens dominated the movement – even while living in impoverished exile in Second Empire Paris. His co-revolutionaries dubbed him 'the Captain' – Millen would call him 'the Boss'. A propaganda

---

* French in 1796 and 1803–4, American in 1865–7, Russian in 1856, 1877 and 1887, German in 1914–16 and in 1939–41.

pamphlet described him as 'thick-set, wiry, five foot three inches
tall, florid complexion, quite bald'. A phrenologist added: 'I read a
firm, calm, indomitable iron will, unshaken confidence in ultimate
success.' But when it came to a real fight, Stephens was the
opposite.

In spring 1864 James Stephens had visited sundered America
under the alias 'Mr Daly' to swear in recruits from both warring
armies. He clandestinely returned to Ireland in August. Inflated
by his hero's progress through the battle-fronts, always talking
up imminent revolution, the 'Chief Organiser Irish Republic'
(COIR) boldly proclaimed: 'Next year is the year of action.' He
assured a young IRB volunteer from Kildare called John Devoy:
'We'll get all the arms we need from America – and 3,000 officers
from Chicago alone.' Devoy's task was to subvert the British army
garrison.

Dublin, spring–summer 1865

Millen accepted O'Mahony's mission: go to Ireland, find
Stephens and report. Could an armed rising succeed? Would
Stephens fight? On 14 April he sailed on the SS *Etna* for Liverpool, slipping into Dublin two weeks later 'after fourteen years
of absence from my native land', as he recorded. His cover-name
was 'Mr Robinson'.

West British provincial calm bathed the city. The Prince of
Wales was on a visit; loyal crowds cheered his passing. Millen
watched them from his hotel-room balcony. He also watched the
Royal Horse Artillery and 10th Hussars at the royal review in
Phoenix Park, remarking with his soldierly eye on the 'perfection
of their evolutions'. 'Ireland would be as loyal to the throne of
England as Middlesex if there were reforms,' he observed.

Millen went to work. He met John O'Leary, editor of the *Irish
People*, the newspaper funded by the IRB. He met Thomas Clarke
Luby, its brilliant, Protestant-born polemicist, its leader-writer,
Charles J. Kickham, and a thirty-four-year-old firebrand from
Rosscarbery, Cork, called Jeremiah O'Donovan Rossa. Where was
James Stephens? At last, on 25 May, he appeared in person. 'I

was disappointed in the person of the "Boss",' wrote Millen. 'He was not the beau-ideal of a revolutionary leader. Apart from O'Leary and Luby, I had yet to meet anyone among the Fenians that one could call a gentleman . . .'

Time was passing. There was a jolly outing to Powerscourt in the Wicklow mountains, a dray-load of bearded revolutionaries discussing over a picnic of wild duck whether they could hold the passes against a British counter-attack. Millen took Mrs Mary O'Donovan Rossa to the magazine-fort in Phoenix Park. Posing as a 'Canadian visitor' Millen approached the guard room. His lady companion 'would like to see the view from the battlements', he explained. They were ushered within by a talkative sergeant keen to show off the impregnability of his fortress. While his companion admired the chestnut trees, Millen eyed the grassy slope at the Kilmainham end. The fort could be taken in a *coup de main* from the south, he concluded.

The guard ship at Kingstown, HMS *Royal George*, a Trafalgar-era hulk, could be captured by a raiding party from the sea, he estimated. The Pigeon House Fort guarding Dublin harbour had a weak point 'fifteen yards west of the privy'. A storming party 'could take it by escalade from Sandymount Strand at low-water'. Little by little the Fenian tourist was forming a plan.

Stephens was unimpressed by this obsession with detail. 'When I complained of my inactivity he gave me an order to make him a drawing of a *corps d'armée* of 50,000 men formed in line of battle, with their ammunition and baggage, every man in his place,' Millen wrote. 'A military man will readily see the absurdity of such an order . . .'

At last, in early July, Millen was 'shown through' the ranks of the Irish Revolutionary Brotherhood, drilling in the hills with pikes. He reported 50,000 men ready to fight, whose 'centres' swore to 6,000 stands of arms – not enough. He proposed arming the rebellion by seizing the arsenals he had so diligently surveyed. His final plans for the coup were as polished as those of any twentieth-century putschist. Seize the military targets first, then the political ones – especially Dublin Castle and the Bank of Ireland, the neo-classical temple on College Green symbolic as being the seat of Ireland's last parliament, prorogued by the Act of Union sixty-five years before.

Then, so he promised, the US government would recognise the republic. Millen pleaded for an immediate call to arms. American ex-soldiers were flooding into the city. 'Between June and September barely a steamer arrived . . . that did not bring fifteen of these fighting Irishmen,' he recorded. 'Some were really good, others had lived loafing round the bar-rooms and engine-houses of New York – equally ready to cut a pack of cards or a throat.' Stephens refused the general's demand: all that he could offer was 'action this year'.

On 15 July the American-made plans for the rising, lists of names and letters of credit were 'lost' by a drunken emissary at Kingstown railway station. A boy found them – he could make out the words 'New York' on the envelope. He gave them to the telegraph girl, who gave them to her father. Soon they would arrive on the desk of Superintendent Daniel Ryan, head of the G or Detective Division of the Dublin Metropolitan Police.

Millen's report was taken to O'Mahony in New York by Jeremiah O'Donovan Rossa. John Devoy meanwhile estimated that, of the 6,000 men in the Dublin garrison, line infantry and cavalry, 1,600 were sworn Fenians and would defect to the rebels. In a room above a pub in Clare Lane a ferocious ex-Confederate guerrilla leader named John MacCafferty seditiously lectured British army troopers on the advantages of the pistol over the sabre in hit-and-run cavalry operations. In New York on 5 August O'Mahony proclaimed 'the final call' and announced the sale of bonds of the Irish republic as an independent state.

It was Dublin Castle which moved first. Superintendent Ryan had an informer within the *Irish People* newspaper – a part-time 'folder' named Pierce Nagle, used by Stephens as a courier. Around 12 September Nagle gave the detective sight of an 'action this year' message on its way to an IRB unit in Tipperary. It was enough. On the evening of Thursday 15 September the G men came through the newspaper's door in Parliament Street with sledgehammers. The floorboards were ripped up, the printing press dragged on a cart to be dumped in the courtyard of Dublin

Castle. The paper's files were bundled off to be pored through for seditious evidence. Arrests followed overnight: John O'Leary, Thomas Luby and O'Donovan Rossa were lifted in their bed-clothes; Stephens went to cover in leafy Sandymount in a safe house he had rented under the alias 'Mr Herbert'. Two thousand pounds were offered for his capture. Charles Kickham was caught after a month on the run.

None of the Americans in Ireland had yet been arrested. What might citizens of the United States be charged with? Ryan's men had orders to shadow over 120 of them mooching round the city, readily distinguishable, according to the police briefing, by their 'felt hats, double-breasted vests and square-toed shoes'. Millen dodged between lodging houses, his footsteps followed, as he said in his memoir, by 'queer sort of men' who seemed to take careful note of his visitors. After a week of leaderless in-decision, in a billiard saloon on Lower Grafton Street, the Ameri-can Fenians elected Millen 'chairman of the military council, Irish Republican Army'.*

On 11 November James Stephens was spotted by a disguised policeman while tending his suburban vegetable patch and arrested. Frank Millen's moment of destiny had come.

James Haybyrne's Barber's Saloon, 25 Wicklow Street, Dublin, 15 November 1865

The room above a central Dublin hairdresser's was full of wild-eyed men. The rebel barber's son, Patrick Haybyrne, stood watch at the street door, waiting for the imminent arrival of the peelers. Those Dublin IRB 'centres' who were still at liberty were all on Superintendent Ryan's arrest list. John Devoy was there, a warrant out on him for attempting to subvert Irish soldiers in the British army garrison. There were five Americans in the room: Millen, Thomas J. Kelly, Michael Kerwin, Denis F. Burke and William G. Halpin, ex-Confederate army. It was clear to the gathering

---

* The style 'army' was a deliberate indication of the IRB's legitimacy as a national force; this was the first time it was used.

that they must elect a leader to supplant James Stephens, now under armed guard in Richmond Bridewell.

The Dublin representatives insisted that a military man should lead them – the Mexican general was the ranking officer. Devoy dutifully proposed Millen; the Americans demurred. According to Devoy's memoirs, 'they had no confidence in him'. The Dublin will prevailed and Millen was elected 'Provisional Chief Organiser Irish Republic'.

The meeting adjourned with the understanding another would be called as soon as Stephens was contacted in prison. That happened far sooner than Frank Millen could have imagined. An accusing pencil-written note was smuggled out of Stephens's cell ordering Millen 'to return to America immediately and not to return to Ireland until the first expedition'. The general objected in a counter-letter – the centres had approved his appointment; he was about to start for Belgium to purchase weapons; all available funds should be turned over to him. Colonel Kelly hinted that Millen was going to abscond with the money.

The general was also condemned for his behaviour in a romantic liaison:

> We found Millen at tea with a lady [Devoy recorded], to whom he did not introduce us ... I did not recall who she was until later I heard that he had married a Miss Power of Tipperary, then engaged to Dennis Dowling Mulcahy [a journalist arrested in the *Irish People* raid, later a mourner at Millen's funeral].
>
> There was strong feeling – against her for breaking her engagement, him for taking advantage of an imprisoned man.

Millen's flimsy authority lasted nine days. On the night of 24 November 1865 Stephens was broken out of his cell by a hospital orderly named John Breslin and a night watchman named Daniel Byrne using a beeswax-impressed duplicate key. Devoy and Kelly were waiting at the wall by the Circular Road. Millen stayed out of it: 'It was too dangerous to risk my capture,' he wrote. The escape was a propaganda triumph. The unfortunate prison governor was dismissed for criminal negligence. As Stephens flitted between Dublin safe houses, more wild claims were sent to America of an imminent 'Christmas rising'.

The Americans Kerwin and Halpin pleaded for an immediate fight – otherwise they would surely all be arrested. Stephens sat on his hands: he was in charge; the time was not yet come. Waiting in vain for an order, gaggles of stranded Americans drifted to the US consulate at 1 Lower Merrion Street to implore Consul William West for help. But 'Seeing the thing was run by numskulls they went home,' Millen wrote.

The west coast ports were closely watched. A squadron of Royal Navy frigates was dispatched to Cork to intercept Cunarders off the Fastnet Rock. The Government had intelligence that Stephens would try to escape on one dressed as a 'Frenchman'. Frank Millen got out in his own way. On 30 November he boarded the SS *City of Boston* at Queenstown, heading for New York with fantastical orders to conjure up a rescue mission. Dublin Castle was already taking a special interest in the barber's shop chieftain. On 25 November Sir Thomas Larcom, permanent under-secretary for Ireland, wrote to the British consul in New York requesting information on a 'General Mellon'.

The shambles in Dublin rocked the organisation in America. Soon after the raid on the *Irish People* offices a noisy convention in Philadelphia shunted the autocratic O'Mahony into the position of elected 'president' of the Fenian Brotherhood, with a 'senate' to advise and consent.

O'Mahony resisted and on 2 December he was deposed. The brotherhood split. The Canada-bound senate wing was now under the control of William Roberts, a wealthy New York dry-goods merchant, with a one-armed Union general named Thomas W. Sweeny as 'Secretary of War'. The scene was set for even greater disaster.

9

Headquarters' Expeditionary Bureau, 32 East 17th Street, New York, winter 1865–6

Frank Millen arrived back in New York in mid December 1865 and found the revolutionary cabal that had sent him to Dublin at war with each other. Which of the bitterly divided branches of the unfraternal brotherhood would now advance his strange career? He would shortly marry Miss Power of Tipperary, the girl he had met over tea in Dublin. It was time to join a winning side.

After his overthrow by the senate John O'Mahony had retreated with most the cash to the Moffat Mansion, a kind of grand Fenian capitol on Union Square, to declare 'War in Ireland and nowhere else'. His rivals were heading in the opposite direction with their very unsecret plans for a raid on Canada. Recriminations were flying. O'Mahony was accused of fraud, having issued the promised Irish republic bonds over his own signature. He accused his rivals of being in British pay. O'Mahony paraded Millen at a patriotic convention on 6 January, where he was greeted as a hero returned from the war. The general stayed loyal.

The cosiness did not last. From his Dublin hiding place James Stephens had meanwhile smuggled a letter to O'Mahony in New York accusing the general of 'subverting the power of Ireland and placing himself at the head of the movement'. Millen answered portentously on 16 January in a letter to O'Mahony:

> I have just got your note that charges are made against me by the COIR [Stephens] and you call on me to resign. I do hereby resign my position as chief of the

expeditionary bureau which you may declare abolished.
As a soldier I obey your order. I would wish to go immediately to Ireland, there to confront my accuser and vin-
dicate my character as a patriot, officer and gentleman . . .

O'Mahony climbed down. Millen stayed in New York on half
pay, shuffling plans for a fantasy rescue fleet round his grandly
titled Headquarters' Expeditionary Bureau on East 17th Street.
'O'Mahony could not even afford to charter a ship,' he recorded.
'I therefore proposed by means of using different agents to purchase 500 passage tickets aboard one of the Inman or Cunard
steamers – when at sea to take possession of the ship, wreck the
vessel in some Irish cove and take to the hills . . . If caught, I
would accept the pirate's doom.' This was desperate stuff.

Meanwhile in Pittsburgh William Roberts's senate wing held
a conference proclaiming to the world their intention to invade
Canada. 'Secretary of War' General Thomas Sweeny had been
banging his confident drum since the *Irish People* arrests in Dublin
had aborted the plan for a Dublin rising. Money and volunteers
flowed into the senate's headquarters at 706 Broadway. General
John O'Neill, an Irish-born veteran Indian fighter, was to command. Sweeny appointed a former Union cavalry officer, Brigadier-General Charles Carrol-Tevis, 'adjutant-general of the Irish
Republican Army'. It was all very grand. Fancy uniforms were
ordered from a Broadway tailor. The commanders decked themselves out in blue frock-coats with emerald-green facings and
'IRA' embossed buttons.

President Andrew Johnson and William H. Seward, Secretary
of State, seemed blithely indifferent to a freelance little war on
the United States' border – it would certainly pull the Irish vote.
There was talk among some fire-breathing federal generals of a
march by a remobilised army on 'Montreal and Mexico City' –
to boot the British and the French empires off the north American
continent.

But the men stranded in Dublin could not wait that long.

*   *   *

Dublin, Saturday 18 February 1866

The wreck in Ireland was all but complete. A special commission to try the *Irish People* arrestees had sentenced five of them to long terms for treason-felony* in the first week of December 1865. Rossa got life. There would be no more Dublin jail-break fiascos. The convicts were smartly shipped in chains under the guard of Royal Marines to Pentonville prison in London.

The Americans skulking round the city still remained untouched. Stephens and Devoy had yet to be found. On 17 February the Cabinet met in London to resolve a tough new line. Habeas corpus was suspended, allowing arrest of any suspect simply on the Lord Lieutenant's warrant. At 6 a.m. the next morning, a Saturday, Inspector Daniel Ryan gathered forty-six detectives at the Exchange Court police headquarters in Dublin.

They had names and addresses for Irish Americans in 'a complete circle round the city'. Most were taken as they blinked awake.

> Colonel Byron was arrested in bed in a brothel at No 7 Lower Gloucester St [Inspector Ryan reported] . . . They are all without exception fine, athletic-looking men. They paid for everything liberally and in advance . . . their clothing was very fashionable. The generals on their way to the police station said they would cause a bloody fine row with the American Government and they would not submit to John Bull . . .

By nightfall almost a hundred were in Mountjoy and Kilmainham prisons. The arrestees, many born in Ireland and taken as children to America, claimed they were US citizens. Magistrates sternly insisted they were subjects of Her Majesty and must face the full penalty of the law.

---

* A charge devised by the Crown and Government Security Act of 1848 against 'any person who, within the United Kingdom or without, shall compass, invent, devise, or intend to deprive or depose our Most Gracious Lady the Queen, or to levy war against her'. Conviction meant penal servitude or transportation – no longer hanging, drawing and quartering, still nominally the penalty for high treason.

On the night of the 20th the remnants of the military council met at James Stephens's hiding place, a room above Mrs Butler's dressmaker's shop on Kildare Street. The 'Captain', shuffling round the room in slippers, insisted there was still a chance. John MacCafferty had been sent to New York to get the contents of the O'Mahony treasury. They needed more money, more guns; they must wait again, Stephens insisted. On the evening of the 22nd John Devoy was arrested. Kelly and Halpin went underground.

HM Consulate, 161 West 4th Street, New York, 10 March 1866

Edward Archibald, Her Majesty's consul in New York City, was Britain's intelligence chief in the heart of Irish America. Watching Fenians was not that difficult. Reports flowed from consuls in other Irish centres – Philadelphia, Boston, Chicago, San Francisco. Supposedly an oath-bound secret society, the sundered brotherhood was fighting out its squabbles in turbulent meetings and raucous journalism. All sorts of men earned a few dollars by seeking out Mr Archibald to peddle the latest saloon bar rumours.

The consul would entertain them behind closed doors in the library, his daughter Edith convinced that, any day now, one furtive arrival would pull out a pistol and shoot her father dead. The consul already had a high-level asset – one Colonel Rudolph Fitzpatrick, who had followed the senate in the split and was now 'Assistant Secretary of War'. A flow of well-rewarded information had been reaching the Foreign Office and Dublin Castle almost since the Canada invasion's inception.

On 10 March a new visitor was announced. He doffed his hat, parked his sword in the umbrella stand, took tea in the consulate's elegant first-floor library, fiddled with the shamrock locket on his watch-chain, and offered his services. He would 'proceed to England, and even to Ireland, if required, to furnish the fullest information, and lend his assistance towards the extinction of the conspiracy – provided his name and communications were kept secret . . .' He suggested he should be referred to as 'Frank Martin'.

The consul recognised his visitor as someone who had
approached him the previous year 'to seek information as to the
means by which if practical, he could obtain a commission in Her
Majesty's Army'. It was Millen.

They met again a week later, on St Patrick's Day, at a 'distant
point' far from prying eyes. New Yorkers were otherwise engaged
as the great parade of marching bands and floats bearing patriotic
tableaux sailed down Broadway. 'The city is alive with a monster
demonstration of the Irish population who practically govern
here,' the consul informed the Earl of Clarendon, the Liberal
Foreign Secretary.

Mr Archibald might have allowed himself an ironic smile. He
had just been handed a complete breakdown of the Irish Revolutionary Brotherhood's readiness for battle, names of 'centres',
numbers of men, level of discipline, estimates of weapons hidden
away in Ireland, England and Scotland. Also attached were the
'active service muster rolls' of every Fenian Brotherhood circle in
the United States. The consul relayed to London more details of
his visitor:

> He is a native of the County Tyrone – about thirty-one
> years of age – and has passed some five or six years in
> Mexico where he held, for a time, a military command
> under Juárez . . . He explained to me that Stephens had
> become jealous of him, and had preferred charges which
> O'Mahony was unwilling to investigate, being desirous
> of obtaining Millen's co-operation.

The general meanwhile was once again in a position to provide
up-to-date information from the heart of the Fenian organisation
from where it mattered, on the ground in Ireland. James Stephens
had forgiven the barber's shop usurper. As Mr Archibald further
explained: 'Millen acquainted me that an envoy had arrived from
Stephens who had withdrawn his charges and wished M to remain
here and accompany the expeditionary force which O'Mahony
proposed to send at once to Ireland.'

On 20 March Millen and the consul met again. He was getting
greedy. 'He has today furnished me with a further report with

the condition that if his information should lead to Stephens's re-arrest, this sum shall be in addition to any amount by way of reward to which HMG may consider him entitled . . .' the consul messaged.

The betrayal was absolute. Millen disclosed four of Stephens's hiding places. He named the prison warder, Byrne, instrumental in Stephens's escape from Richmond Bridewell. Millen reeled off a list of named Irish Americans still on the run – 'Herne in Dungarvan, O'Connor in Cahirveen who should be looked after'; Colonel Halpin was living at Number 19 Grantham Street under the cover-name 'Mr Bird'; Captain Kelly was at the same address under the name 'Mr Freeman'.

> [Their] apprehension will place in the hands of the Government every Irish American officer in the island worth notice [Millen wrote]. That done, the conspirators will be without leaders and entirely incapable of doing anything until O'Mahony and his expedition get to their help, which it will be seen, they shall not be permitted to do.

Miss O'Leary and Mrs O'Donovan Rossa were functioning as 'female pay-masters', he revealed, 'making frequent visits to Paris to bring back funds for the payment of men and the purchase of arms'. Sir Thomas Larcom, permanent under-secretary at Dublin Castle, was given the information with the instructions: 'The greatest precautions should be taken to keep the name of the informant secret . . . Copy out the information as to the individuals yourself and give them to the police not saying how you got it. We cannot be too secret . . .'

The same week as the Millen intelligence arrived in Dublin, another potential informer came live in America. The letter that arrived on 29 March addressed to the Foreign Secretary looked unpromising; it came from an obscure 'Poor Rate Collector' in Colchester, Essex, named John Billis Beach. It was the beginning of British intelligence's deepest penetration of the Irish American revolutionary movement and would have sensational

consequences for Frank Millen and Robert Anderson over twenty
years later.

> I have a son who is a first Lieutenant in the Army of
> the United States stationed at Nashville, Tennessee [Mr
> Beach informed Lord Clarendon].
>   My son is surrounded by fenians – and is intimate
> with Capt. [sic] O'Neill . . . from whom he received the
> following information, that the fenians are determined
> to invade Canada and there establish a navy to prey on
> British shipping . . .
>   There are fenian hats, coats, songs and plays with a
> prominacy of green . . . designed to inflame these
> ungrateful, fanatical, bloodthirsty fenians.

Mr Beach of Colchester received a polite reply from London:
Would his patriotic son care to relay further information?

Millen was right about O'Mahony's 'expedition not being permitted to' help. O'Mahony had emptied the Fenian Brotherhood's treasury to buy an ex-Confederate blockade-runner and
fit out a desperate raiding party, not to crash-land in some Irish
cove, but to seize 'in the name of the United States' the obscure
British island of Campo Bello in the Bay of Fundy opposite Eastport, Maine. The British were forewarned (but not this time by
Millen): a detachment of line infantry was waiting on the rocky
outcrop and a squadron of Royal Navy frigates took up station
in the St Croix river. Eastport's one hotel was filled with US
marshals and excitable Irishmen. General George Meade, the
most senior officer in the US army, arrived aboard a warship
with a detachment of troops to confiscate the Fenian gunboat.
O'Mahony was ruined.

James Stephens and Thomas Kelly had meanwhile dodged Mil-
len's betrayal. On 15 March they had been smuggled out of
Dublin down the Liffey in a rowing boat and onto a sail collier.
Stephens arrived in New York via England and France on 10 May
– and grumpily took over what was left of the Fenian rump.
O'Mahony was dismissed in disgrace the next day for failing,

according to Stephens, 'the holiest duty of the Fenian Brotherhood, direct assistance to the men in the gap'.

Frank Millen and his new wife were not anxious to stick
around. They were heading in a leisurely fashion back across the
Rio Grande. On 9 May 1866 Millen wrote to Mr Archibald from
Austin, Texas:

> I arrived here a few days ago and propose remaining
> for some time. I am busily engaged in writing the his-
> tory of my fenian experiences. This little work will cover
> from 30 to 100 pages, more or less of post-paper. When
> finished you can have it for the use of the Irish Govern-
> ment if you wish.
>
> Of course I shall expect some remuneration for my
> trouble, either by receiving an appointment or some
> pecuniary consideration from Government. I need hardly
> tell you that every reliance may be placed in the state-
> ments which I shall make in this pamphlet.
>
> Please address me in this City (Austin) or if you should
> direct to Galveston let it be to PO Box 219 – always in
> my own name. Respectfully Yours, James Thompson.*

US–Canada border, June 1866

Goaded by O'Mahony's doomed excursion to Maine, the
Sweeny-Roberts senate wing had lurched into action. Throughout May thousands of volunteers headed north to muster points
along the border. Stephens declared an invasion of Canada was
about as useful as an Irish attack on Japan. In the early hours of
1 June 800 men, led by O'Neill, crossed the Niagara river. The
next day they captured Fort Erie. On 3 June there was a skirmish
with Canadian militia near the little town of Ridgeway; twenty
were killed on both sides. A federal revenue cutter was dispatched
to the Niagara river and General Meade arrived in upper New
York State with troops and artillery. On 6 June President Johnson

---

* Millen's choice of name coincides uncannily with that of Inspector James J.
Thomson of the Metropolitan Police – this seems a bizarre coincidence.

issued a proclamation forbidding 'the unlawful expedition and enterprise'.

General Sweeny was arrested in St Albans; O'Neill and his force were rounded up while trying to retreat back to Buffalo. Seventy were dead, about 200 made prisoners. The Irish Republican Army was disarmed by federal soldiers and put on trains home. The mayor of New York paid for the tickets.

Stephens was jubilant at the senate's Canadian fiasco. Within a week of his arrival a huge New York crowd turned out to hear him proclaim the vision of an 'Irish flag floating in the Irish breeze by New Year's Day, 1867'. His rivals had dished themselves with their military bombast. He was still going to make the Irish revolution in his image.

On 9 June the COIR had an audience with a sympathetic US Secretary of State. On 28 October he proclaimed to a huge rally that his next appearance would be in Ireland, leading the liberating army. The audience went wild. Those unwise enough to wear round-toed shoes were threatened with lynching, the *New York Herald* reported. Such footwear was a sure sign of being an English spy.

Dublin Castle, Ireland, August 1866

Dublin was an armed camp. The garrison had been reinforced from Britain, its ranks combed for mutineers by a brisk military intelligence team. Grim drumhead courts-martial were enacted through the summer. The sentence for mutiny was death (this was transmuted to transportation). John Devoy accounted for eighty Fenians he had personally sworn in the 10th Hussars, the regiment whose elegant evolutions Frank Millen had so admired in Phoenix Park.

On 27 June there was a change of government in London. The Conservative Earl of Derby took office, with a new Chief Secretary for Ireland, Lord Naas (soon to be Earl Mayo). His lordship demanded much more effective use of intelligence from America. Sub-Inspector Thomas Doyle of the Dublin Metropolitan Police had operated undercover in and out of New York since 1858, but his alarmist dispatches were little more than press-cuttings. Mr Archibald's intelligence sources seemed exemplary, but were meaningless without collation and analysis. The crown solicitor at Dublin Castle, Samuel Lee Anderson, had an eager legal assistant who seemed ideal for the work – his own younger brother Robert.

The young lawyer's first job was to collate reports from America 'deemed so secret they were put away without even being registered . . . all the documents lay in a cupboard', as Anderson himself recalled. The Rudolph Fitzpatrick material was neatly transcribed in a special ledger. The New York consul, however, seemed to have struck a true intelligence gold-seam – lists of names, hiding places, aliases of men on the run in Ireland itself. Anderson carefully inked over all references in covering documents to what he called 'this most important source'.* They were filed away separately, their origin referred to by Anderson simply as 'Informant M'.

HM Consulate, New York, November 1866

More news reached the consulate that November. An English-born reporter from the *New York Herald* – 'who had been a close attendant on James Stephens . . . ever since that gentleman came to this country' revealed Stephens's latest plan for a rising. The information was sent by the next steamer to the Foreign Secretary in London.

> The first blow will be struck in Dublin [the *Herald* man reported]. They have there between twenty and thirty thousand men . . . they are to seize Dublin Castle, and if possible get possession of the person of the Lord Lieutenant. They will hold him and all other English officials as hostages. James Stephens is confident of having the whole country in his possession by the middle of January.

* Clearly retrievable in the originals, held in the National Archives of Ireland, as 'Millen'.

Who better to assist the Boss in his revived ambitions than the professional coup-maker? Stephens had forgiven Millen for his pretensions to the revolutionary crown. On 27 November Edwards messaged the Foreign Office: 'I have the honour to report that [my] informant, a few days since, arrived in this place from Mexico, whence he had been summoned by an order from James Stephens to aid that leader in his promised expedition to Ireland.'

Frank Millen had come back. The French army had withdrawn from Mexico, leaving the Emperor Maximilian to his fate. Juárez was squabbling with his rivals. Working for the Boss again could be no worse – there was plenty of British money in it. Millen had completed the memoir he had begun in Texas: 'A History of Fenianism from April 1865 to April 1866 by one of the Head Centres for Ireland', he called it. He wanted £500 for his work; he got £250 from the British consul. It was dispatched by steamer from New York on 1 December into the eager hands of the brothers Anderson at Dublin Castle.

Millen had live information on men still underground in Ireland. Along with his memoir he delivered a new and intimately informed intelligence brief: 'Edward Duffy, a delicate young man, is now the Boss's deputy in Dublin and carries on the business of the IRB,' he revealed. 'He can be found at Mrs O'Donovan Rossa's house, 17 Middle Mountjoy St. or at the house of the tailor Joseph Denieffe, No 32 South Anne St.' The report was acted upon. Duffy, who was in an advanced state of consumption, was arrested and died in Millbank prison a year later aged twenty-eight.

The promised new 'expedition' was a confidence trick, Millen stated:

> Stephens has no present intention of going to Ireland. He has at his command about 150,000 dollars and he believes that he will retire with his gains to some secluded part of the Continent. If Stephens succeeds in landing about the New Year it will be a signal for a new uprising . . . but I am at present inclined to believe that Stephens himself will be the means of throwing obstacles in the

way of a landing that he will endeavour to escape . . . we will try and check-mate the Boss at his own game but must go very cautious.

Further details will be given as they occur even to the time of embarkation of our interesting friend and the name of the vessel which may contain so precious a load of villainy . . .

A week later Millen and the Boss had a final bust-up. On 5 December the general wrote to the *New York Times*. The newspaper printed his lengthy outburst two days later: 'Stephens declared for battle and I ask why, in God's name, did he not take the field last year as he swore he would . . . He did not do it, he has never given an explanation . . . he is a political humbug, a knave and a rascal.'

Millen wrote at the same time to the British consul, fearful that the public quarrel 'would interfere with his future opportunities for obtaining information of a nature likely to be of use to Her Majesty's Government'. No matter. The time would come round again.

On 29 December, in a last-chance meeting at Stephens's lodgings on West 11th Street, the hard-men of the military council at last deposed their prevaricating chieftain: he was still telling them to wait – there was not enough money, not enough weapons; the rising would be crushed. He was right. MacCafferty pulled a gun and Stephens disappeared to a Brooklyn boarding house. Colonel Thomas Kelly was proclaimed COIR and promptly headed for England, where many American refugees from Inspector Ryan's round-up had fled. The revolution flickered on.

A week later Sir Frederick Bruce, Her Majesty's minister in Washington, received a letter postmarked Philadelphia. It was signed 'John Smith' and offered to supply information from within the senate wing of the Fenian Brotherhood – sulking in New York after their Canadian adventure and preparing for a second round.

The number of serviceable arms of all kinds is about 12,500 [the mysterious correspondent wrote]. The

disposition is not to hurry matters and to use every effort
to bring about some troubles with England – the Fenian
vote has been sold for that purpose to the Republican
party.

You will now know as much as does even their President Roberts – their fondness for whiskey and a good
dinner has made the task of pumping an easy one . . .

In his covering letter to the Foreign Secretary the ambassador
revealed Mr Smith's identity: 'The writer is Tevis . . . He has
quarrelled with the Fenian leaders and is ready to harm them as
much as possible. He is anxious to be employed as an agent of
HMG. He asks one hundred pounds per month, perhaps I could
reduce his terms,' wrote Sir Frederick.

Better to pay in full: the Foreign Office had just recruited as
a spy General Charles Carrol-Tevis, adjutant-general of the Irish
Republican Army.

Frank Millen's timing was curious. Perhaps he was bored; perhaps
his wife was homesick. Prospects of further Mexican employment
were thin. The Emperor Maximilian was shot by firing squad on
19 June 1867 and Benito Juárez entered Mexico City on 14 July.
Two days later Millen made a renewed overture to Mr Archibald
in New York – an offer to return to England or Ireland. Samuel
Anderson commented:

He incurs considerable risk of violence at the hand of his
former associates, in case, by any chance, it should happen
to be known that he gave information.' It almost sounded
like a threat. Millen clearly thought the risk worthwhile.
On 27 September 1867 Anderson wrote to the Irish
Secretary from the Charing Cross Hotel in London: 'I
have arranged to bring "M" who is to meet me
tomorrow to Sir Richard Mayne [commissioner of the
Metropolitan Police].'

The meeting was hugely secret. The timing was opportune.

IO

Woburn Square, London WC, 20 November 1867

Detective Inspector James Thomson was that uncommon thing in the mid Victorian police service, a gentleman-copper. He spoke four languages from childhood. His Scots-born father was a merchant of Smyrna in the Ottoman Levant. His mother filled the house with exotic savants. Young Thomson had studied the new science of electricity, been private secretary to a maharajah – then in 1856, on the spur of the moment, he had joined the London Metropolitan Police. He did so, he said, 'without the knowledge of my family'. In polite society it was rather like running off to the circus. He had married an understanding girl from Suffolk – Martha Alice. There were no children.

In a decade of detecting the inspector had handled several delicate matters with discretion. There had been the affair of the Russian banknote frauds and the case of the missing Countess of Queensberry. Now, on this foggy autumn evening, Inspector Thomson was in pursuit of an American gun-runner wanted for treason-felony.

Thomson shadowed the suspect, a tall man of military bearing, loping along in the company of an unknown companion from the Euston Road into the squares of Bloomsbury. He fingered the revolver in his overcoat pocket (the police were routinely armed for 'Irish duties'), a jittery New York Fenian-turned-informer called John Devaney skulking behind. The informer recognised the mark, lit for a second in a pool of gaslight. It was Colonel Ricard O'Sullivan Burke, late Fenian organiser for the army of the Potomac and an escapee from the fiasco in Dublin of autumn two years earlier.

Burke was the suspected chief Fenian arms agent in England. He went under the alias Colonel Edward C. Winslow and had ordered quantities of bullet-moulds, percussion caps, fearsome Lemaître & Girard ten-shot revolvers and rifles from a Birmingham arms-dealer. The intelligence had come from an informer, John J. Corydon, who had been in Burke's federal army regiment and was a courier for O'Mahony in and out of Dublin through the dramas of 1865. Corydon had turned informer in Ireland in September 1866. Robert Anderson was his paymaster.

Flitting through Tavistock Square Thomson collected a patrolling constable as reinforcement. They turned into Woburn Square, keeping pace. Devaney held back in the shadows. Thomson touched the suspect on the shoulder. He protested his innocence: he was, he insisted, 'Mr Bowry, a medical student'. His companion Joseph Casey (the Kilkenny-born cousin of James Stephens) laid into the detective. Burke ran.

Thomson drew his revolver, shouting: 'By God, Burke, if you attempt to go away I will fire.' The suspect stopped. A little crowd gathered. Burke waved an umbrella feebly. He was bundled into a cab and taken to Bow Street police station. Casey followed in a second cab and was arrested for obstruction. Devaney confirmed the identification. The arrests were kept secret. On the 23rd the two men were remanded to the Middlesex House of Detention in Clerkenwell, a working-class district on the edge of the City of London.

Burke was a prize captive. His arrest was the culmination of an eight-month police and intelligence operation to snuff out the dying spasms of the lost Irish revolution. Colonel Burke had witnessed most of them at first hand.

Demobilised from the Union army Burke, like Millen, had offered his services to O'Mahony in New York. He was dispatched to Dublin in the late autumn of 1865; here he sought out Stephens and Kelly in hiding and was promptly sent to England to buy guns. He had returned to America and was one of the firebrands who had toppled the prevaricating Stephens in December 1866.

The hard-men had not given up. With Stephens out of the

way, in January 1867 MacCafferty, Kelly and Burke headed for England. MacCafferty proposed an attack on Chester Castle to seize weapons. It was betrayed and troops were waiting. Colonel Thomas Kelly meanwhile holed up in a London rooming house, planning a rising in Ireland in which countryside 'musters' would see the flag flying long enough for America to intervene – that, at least, was the strategy. The rising was called for 5 March. The planned climactic gathering at Tallaght Hill some nine miles south of Dublin was routed by a dozen constables armed with rifles. The risings in the countryside were snuffed out as easily.

Thomas Kelly had gone underground, eluding informers and the police until, on 11 September 1867, he was picked up in Manchester on a charge of vagrancy. Corydon was sent to identify him – and picked out another fugitive American caught in the trawl, Captain Timothy Deasy.

The elusive Burke, who had again managed to escape the debacle in Ireland, went to Manchester to plan their 'rescue'. On the 18th the horse-drawn prison van taking Kelly and Deasy from the court house was attacked under a railway bridge by fifteen armed men. A pistol shot fired through the lock killed the unarmed police guard as he tried to peer out through the keyhole. A woman prisoner got hold of the keys and pushed them through the ventilator slats. The two handcuffed captives were broken out to disappear into the crowd. Burke slipped away southwards; Kelly and Deasy reached New York hidden in a compartment on a Liverpool emigrant ship.

Five of the IRB break-out gang were convicted of murder. One was reprieved, four were sentenced to hang; one, an American, Patrick O'Meagher Condon, had the sentence commuted to life on the intervention of President Johnson. On Saturday 23 November the condemned three were publicly executed on a scaffold erected on the prison walls facing New Bailey Street before an enormous crowd. 'The mob were quiet and orderly,' reported *The Times*. Ireland drenched itself in martyred indignation.

Middlesex House of Detention, Clerkenwell, London,
12–13 December 1867

It was a policeman's instinct. Having arrested Ricard Burke in
Woburn Square, Inspector Thomson was convinced that Thomas
Kelly, sprung from the Manchester prison van, would come to
London to return the favour for his liberator – who was now
himself banged up in Clerkenwell along with Casey.

For several wintry nights in the first week of December Thomson prowled around the prison's looming walls, dragging Corydon, the universal informer, with him to make the identification.
After a few nights the watch was stood down as Corydon was
'overworked'.

It was not Kelly, however, but another fugitive from the Manchester break-out team, Captain James Murphy, late 20th Massachusetts Infantry, who planned the escape with a party of around
fifteen London IRB men. The plan was simple enough: to blow
a hole in the prison's twenty-five-foot-high north-west outer wall
opposite Corporation Lane while Burke was circling the exercise
yard between the prescribed hours of 3 and 4.30 p.m.

Large quantities of gunpowder were bought from a London
supplier, Messrs Curtis and Harvey, and secreted in a kerosene
barrel. Burke himself, a former federal engineer officer who had
been in command of the miles of earthworks during the siege of
Confederate-held Petersburg, smuggled out instructions on how
to place the charge. It was enough to demolish a fortress.

On the afternoon of the 12th, as the winter light began to
fade, a London IRB man called Jeremiah O'Sullivan wheeled the
monster petard on a barrow to a point where recent brickwork
replaced masonry. John Abbot, aged thirteen, saw a 'man with a
brown overcoat and black hat holding a squib'. The man gave
one to the boy to play with.

A little white ball went over the wall as a signal. Burke saw it
and prepared for the bang – crouching low as if tying a bootlace.
A warder pocketed the ball for his children. The fuse was lit and
fizzled out. The kerosene barrel was wheeled away for another
try.

Just before lunchtime the same day an urgent message arrived at the Home Office. It was from Inspector Daniel Ryan in Dublin and described the break-out plan in every detail – even down to the little white ball. The message was passed by Sir Adolphus Liddell, the permanent under-secretary, to the Middlesex chief magistrate Henry Pownall and to Scotland Yard. (Robert Anderson would later claim he got the intelligence from a casual informer in Dublin.)

The guards were armed that night on Mr Pownall's warning. The next morning, Friday 13 December, on the orders of Captain Codd, the governor, prisoners' exercise was switched to the morning. Burke took his alone in the 'Female Airing Court' after breakfast. That afternoon O'Sullivan tried again, with the barrel concealed under a white sheet. An unfortunate policeman passed it but he had been ordered to look for evidence of mining under the wall – nothing about barrels.

At around 3.45 p.m. another white ball went over – into an empty exercise yard. The fuse was lit: thirty seconds later 548 pounds of high-grade gunpowder erupted. A sixty-foot section of wall was demolished. The blast wave sliced through the ramshackle tenements of Corporation Lane. Inspector Adolphus Frederick ('Dolly') Williamson of the Metropolitan Police Detective Branch described the scene as like 'so many doll's houses with the kettles still singing on their hobs'. Six Londoners lay dead in the rubble.*

O'Sullivan escaped by clubbing a drunken drayman (who died) and running from armed policemen across London for five miles. He reached New York under an assumed name. Investigations went on for months. The trial of six accused in April 1868 was a shambles of conflicting testimony. Two IRB men turned Queen's evidence. They and three more of the accused were acquitted of

---

* 'Six persons were killed outright, six more died from the effects,' according to the coroner's inquests, reported *The Times* on 29 April 1868; '. . . one young woman is in a madhouse, 40 mothers were prematurely confined, 20 of their babies died from the effects of the explosion, others of the children are dwarfed and unhealthy. One mother is now raving a maniac, 120 persons were wounded . . . 15 are permanently injured with loss of eyes, legs, arms etc . . .'

murder but found guilty of lesser charges. One, a Glasgow Fenian named Michael Barrett, was convicted of wilful murder. He was hanged at the Old Bailey on 26 May 1868, the last public execution in England. A month earlier Ricard O'Sullivan Burke had been sentenced to fifteen years' penal servitude for treason-felony. Joseph Casey was discharged and headed for Paris with his younger brother Patrick.

Whitehall, December 1867

Fenian fire* had fallen on London, but the government had its own crisis: the Earl of Derby, the Prime Minister, had retired to his country estate stricken with gout, leaving Benjamin Disraeli in charge. The Chancellor of the Exchequer, suffering from the same affliction, had to staunch the panic from his own London sickbed. Gathorne Hardy, the hapless Home Secretary, visited the Clerkenwell casualties in St Bartholomew's hospital the day after the explosion, then headed sheepishly to Disraeli's bedside to explain personally how Inspector Ryan's warning from Dublin had been ignored by the Metropolitan Police.

The Home Secretary arrived to find an expert in sedition urgently summoned from Dublin already in attendance at Number 1 Grosvenor Gate: it was Lieutenant-Colonel William Fielding, who had made a name in Ireland rooting out and court-martialling the 'military Fenians' – the soldiers John Devoy had worked so hard to subvert. The colonel reckoned Clerkenwell to be no misfired swashbuckling prank but the precursor to sustained attack.

Benjamin Disraeli meanwhile had received his own wild intelligence (it came from the Emperor Napoleon III) of an international conspiracy to assassinate all the monarchs of Europe. There were rumours of plots to blow up the Houses of Parliament, to seize the Bank of England, to demolish St Paul's; that a boat-

---

* The name given in Home Office circulars in the great panic that followed the Clerkenwell explosion to the incendiary phosphorus-based composition known in warfare since ancient times as 'Greek fire'.

load of Americans were on their way aboard a Dutch brigantine to assassinate Her Majesty.

In the face of such threatened mayhem the London police seemed useless. 'With a force of 8,000 men, it seems to me absurd we have but three educated officers,' the Home Secretary told Disraeli; more resolute sleuths were required. Where better to get them than from the existing counter-revolutionary machine in Dublin Castle?

The Earl of Mayo, the Chief Secretary for Ireland, arrived from Dublin close on Fielding's spurred heels late on the night of the 14th. With him was the ambitious young lawyer who had worked so effectively at the castle, running informers and preparing crown prosecutions – Robert Anderson. The little group got down to business the next morning, a Sunday, at the Irish Office near St James's Park. Sir Adolphus Liddell chaired the meeting for the Home Office.

It was agreed that Fielding was to head a new counter-revolutionary intelligence operation accountable directly to the Home Secretary. The original plan, according to Anderson, was to 'set up in an anonymous house and operate in complete secrecy. This was not practical.' Instead the fledgling secret service was installed in the rambling law rooms of the Irish Office.

Captain Whelan, a royal artilleryman who had also proved effective in rooting out sedition in the Dublin garrison, would be Fielding's deputy and Robert Anderson would function as legal adviser and secretary. Their expenses would be met from 'Secret Service' funds. The new department was to operate quite separately from the Metropolitan Police – although Inspectors Thomson and Williamson would be deputed to it.

The seventy-one-year-old commissioner, Sir Richard Mayne, kicked against the intrusion. Derby wrote to the Home Secretary on 17 December: 'If Mayne will not have a "rival near the throne" and cannot conduct "detective" duties . . . he must give way.' Disraeli was blunter: 'Let him resign if he does not like it.' The commissioner was barged aside.

Wild intelligence operations in Italy and Paris were launched by the new unit to uncover the great international assassination conspiracy. Mayne's men were set to searching sewers and guarding gasworks. Fifty-two thousand gallant citizens enrolled as special constables to patrol the metropolis. Troops guarded Balmoral and Osborne, where the Queen complained she was 'little better than a State prisoner'.

'What is the use of trying to stop these outrages without strong measures to enable us to punish these horrible people . . .' she wrote to Gathorne Hardy. But the great Clerkenwell scare faded. After five months the prototype Secret Service was disbanded. Inspectors James Thomson and Dolly Williamson went back to Scotland Yard; Robert Anderson stayed at the Home Office – an Irish intelligence expert in waiting.

The curious Colchester connection was bearing fruit. As London was gripped by gunpowder panic, the Tennessee informant arrived in Essex to see his parents. Mr John Rebow, the local Liberal MP, had connections with the Home Office. Would Mr Beach's patriotic son care to meet certain gentlemen? Overtures were made.

'In a few days I received an official communication requesting me to attend at 50 Harley Street,' Thomas Beach wrote in his memoirs, 'and there met two officials, by whom a proposition was made that I should become a paid agent, and that on my return to the United States, I should ally myself to the Fenian organisation, in order to play the role of spy.'

A year later, control of agent Beach was passed to Robert Anderson. He referred to him in correspondence as 'Informant B'. He was collecting a little set.

PART THREE

The Clan

'You will note with pleasure that the informer
is foredoomed, that no man can betray and
live, no corner of the earth too obscure or too
far to hide . . .'

Clan-na-Gael circular, September 1883

II

New York harbour, 19 January 1871

The elegant three-masted Cunarder RMS *Cuba* nosed into the approaches of New York harbour. Thousands of Irish emigrants had come this way; not many, especially late unwilling guests of Her Majesty, had arrived to be fêted as the most famous five Irishmen in the world. The 'Cuba Five', as they would soon be called, were the men arrested at the *Irish People* offices in 1865 and thereafter, amnestied by Gladstone, the Liberal Prime Minister, on condition they left British territory until their long prison terms were spent. They included two of Frank Millen's old comrades, Jeremiah O'Donovan Rossa and John Devoy.

As the ship neared quarantine on the evening of 19 January, three steam launches raced from the shoreline to grab the exiles and the political kudos for their own. The first bore a delegation from the Knights of St Patrick, an Irish-American benevolent society with no pretensions to being revolutionaries. The second party arrived aboard a federal revenue cutter, the *Bronx*, the Stars and Stripes flying presidentially from its jack staff. The ambitious (and later exposed as spectacularly corrupt) Republican politician Thomas Murphy, collector for the port of New York, barged his way to the front, waving a letter of welcome from President Ulysses S. Grant.

Behind him trotted his political acolyte Francis Millen, eagerly glad-handing old comrades as he stepped aboard. John Devoy had last seen the general in Haybyrne's barber's shop in Wicklow Street. He still had certain suspicions.

Collector Murphy invited the 'Irish exiles' to board his government vessel and be borne in pomp to Manhattan, but they

assumed the presidential greeting was a hoax. Then a third delegation arrived from the Democrat citadel of Tammany Hall seeking, in the name of the City of New York, to corral the celebrity
felons aboard their own steamboat. Dr Carnochan, the city health
commissioner, ordered his burly quarantine officials to grab
Millen. Fists flew on the *Cuba*'s foredeck.

The dispute went on until two in the morning, when the
squabbling delegations returned to sulk on the shoreline. The
Cuba Five remained aboard to draft a letter that night: 'You may
look upon us as representing the cause of Ireland, for the interests
of which cause we desire that all Irishmen should be united . . .
It is painful for us to see so much disunion among yourselves . . .
we will not decide on anything until the arrival of our brothers'
(nine more felon exiles were a week behind, New York-bound
aboard the faster, newer Cunarder the RMS *Russia*).

They were finally borne downtown by a green throng to
Sweeney's Hotel, a favourite Fenian watering-hole on Chatham
Street, for two weeks of roistering. A resolution of welcome was
moved on the floor of Congress. On 22 February the exiles were
greeted on the steps of the White House by President Grant –
who passed down the line of former jailbirds grunting: 'Glad to
see you.' The London newspapers foamed with indignation.

And that was it. The Irish revolution had caught up with
American politics. Things had moved on since the wild days of
spring 1865. Republican and Democrat politicians queued up to
press the flesh with celebrity revolutionaries, but they wanted
votes – certainly not war with the British empire. The exiles,
appalled by the blatant vote-grubbing, formed an 'Irish Confederation', which they high-mindedly announced would stay aloof
from US domestic politics. Realities would prove different.

The original O'Mahony faction of the Fenian Brotherhood
remained moribund but intact, effectively led since 1868 by a
volatile poet-journalist, an ex-soldier called John Savage. Millen
remained its executive secretary and commanding officer of its
military organisation, the grand-sounding 'Legion of St Patrick'.

In August 1871 an alliance was brokered in New York with

the idealistic Irish Confederates. Frank Millen was at the meeting, sitting down with men he had betrayed. James Stephens, having fled to exile in Paris, turned up, unable to stay away from the revolutionary adulation that had once been all his. The exiles growled with suspicion but some comrades turned up at his New York hotel to see the old rogue. Stephens wrote pathetically to his wife: 'You would marvel at some of the visitors' names . . . General Millen! What do you think of us actually being friends again . . . I *wronged* Millen sweetheart . . . he declared with feeling that only a great man could act towards him as I did yesterday.' The general was as adept a flatterer as he was a betrayer.

John O'Neill meanwhile had remained fatally committed to Canada. He had seen off his rival Roberts and laboriously rebuilt the senate's financial and military structure. Meanwhile an eager young Chicago Fenian, a medical attendant in the Illinois penitentiary, had been appointed 'inspector-general' of O'Neill's freelance army. He was Thomas Beach, Anderson's agent, posing as 'Major Henri le Caron' an Anglophobic Frenchman. After two years of posturing O'Neill had embarked on a second doomed invasion of Canada. The military preparations had all been relayed by Beach to the Canadian authorities in intimate operational detail. Late on the morning of Wednesday 25 April the Irish Republican Army had crossed the Canadian frontier for the second time. It was a fiasco.

That was the end of the great Canadian diversion. It was the effective end, too, of the old Fenian Brotherhood – at least in its flag-waving, squabbling, self-deluding, post-American Civil War phase. The O'Mahony wing would linger on for a few years yet, but the future belonged to a small, highly secretive organisation which sought to achieve the Irish republic by other means than 'warfare in the open field'. It was called the Clan-na-Gael – the family of the Gaels.

The secret society had begun modestly enough with a meeting on 20 June 1867 in the New York house of Jerome Collins, the unconventional meteorologist of the *New York Herald*. The initiation fee was one dollar; weekly subscription ten cents. The

Clan's first success was at the end of 1869, when a New York Fenian
Brotherhood circle seceded *en masse*. The organisation, which
more commonly styled itself the United Brotherhood, admitted to
its ranks only 'Those of Irish birth or descent, or partial Irish
descent'. It borrowed much of its mummery from the Masons, with
an elaborate initiation ceremony (which John Devoy called
'grotesque') in which the blindfolded candidate had to declare his
commitment to the winning of Irish independence by physical
force. Much play was made of hailing and warning signs, tickly
handshakes, cheek-stroking, nose-rubbing, button-twiddling and
artful hat-doffing – by which the agents of the English crown might
be confounded. Its communications used a simple letter-shift
cipher in which the United Brotherhood became the 'VC', the
executive body the 'FC', Ireland became 'Jsfmboe', and so on.

Like the Fenian Brotherhood it was organised on a cell structure – with 'camps' instead of circles – but the degree of operational secrecy was supposedly much tighter. Frank Millen and
Thomas Beach would become adepts of the Clan's cabbalistic
rituals. But making fearsome oaths to gain the Irish republic by
physical force was one thing; achieving it was another.

The same year that the Irish exiles arrived in New York, the
Swedish chemist Alfred Nobel opened a factory in Scotland to
manufacture his new invention, a fusion of liquid nitroglycerine
with an unusually absorbent earth, the remains of fossilised
diatoms, called kieselguhr. The new explosive was patented under
the name 'Dynamite'.

The Repaunos Chemical Company of Philadelphia took out a
licence for its manufacture in the United States. Henry Du Pont,
who had made a fortune manufacturing propellants during the
Civil War, bought a controlling share and boosted output. A
range of products was offered to railway and canal builders with
varying blast effects – Atlas Powder A, with a nitroglycerine content of 75 per cent, being the most destructive.

It was not only civil engineers who were interested in the
new explosive's power to remove obstacles. The anti-politics of
post-First International Europe had made the assassination of a

repressive ruler legitimate. Tsar Alexander II was killed by a dynamite bomb in St Petersburg on 13 March 1881 and Balkan secret
societies became adepts of the obliteration cult. The stalking
bomber, ready to hurl an 'infernal machine' from under his cloak,
became a figure of popular demonology. A new word was coined
– 'Dynamitard'.

Russian nihilists had nothing to lose. Tsar-killing was the
legitimate route to wholesale revolution. For the Irish in America
it was different. What might political murder achieve except
repression in Ireland, anti-Catholic pogroms in Britain and the
alienation of mainstream America? The IRB spurned dynamite.
The Clan-na-Gael, however, a fraternity of respectable pro-
fessionals rather than Dostoyevskian students, had already begun
its long journey from 'civilised warfare' to outright terror. They
could argue that terror worked.*

The question was how far to go. Blowing up statues of Prince
Albert (always a favourite target) was one thing; killing the Queen
a step into revolutionary blackness.

The British consulate in New York had started picking up
rumours of American plots against the lives of the royal family soon
after the Clerkenwell explosion. The letters containing them were
inky and eccentric but demanded attention. The panic in London
that the city was about to be levelled by gunpowder had scarcely
abated when Mr Archibald forwarded to the Foreign Office an
oddly worded note from a Mr W. F. Gray of Washington:

> There are Americans in England now, and yet going that
> are employed by the Fenians. I know them, & I can
> fathom and find out [the informant reported].
>
> They mean revolution, they mean to murder the
> Queen and the Prince of Wales if necessary. You can send
> this to the Queen as I have written her directly . . .

* When Gladstone moved in 1869 to disestablish the Protestant Church in Ireland, he admitted he had been led to it by a 'new outlook on Irish affairs due to
the intensity of Fenianism'. John Devoy wrote over fifty years later: 'His remarks
proved a stronger argument in favour of physical force – and even of Terrorism
– on the part of Ireland to secure justice and freedom, than any Irishman ever
made.'

A year later, a Mr Richard Smith, an elderly British-born sheet-music salesman down on his luck, wrote a rambling letter to the Foreign Office about his employment on mysterious services in New York. He had, he said, thwarted a plot to assassinate the Duke of Edinburgh.* He had approached the Queen for a reward and received an 'unkind reply' – which he now threatened to send to the newspapers. Lord Stanley, the Foreign Secretary, recommended a 'payment of £5 out of SS funds' to keep him quiet.

Sir Edward Thornton, HM minister at Washington, expressed the dilemma thus when he was warned in July 1869 of the plot hatched by the Herald's weather forecaster Jerome Collins to kidnap the Queen's son, Prince Arthur of Connaught, on a visit to Canada – a snatch squad of New Yorkers was reportedly heading north on 'a hunting expedition': 'Plots for such purposes may easily exist in this extensive country without my being able to obtain any clue to them,' he wrote. 'The expressions stated . . . are like those constantly in the mouths of blustering Americans and still more blustering Irishmen in this country, but I do not think they mean much.'

The Irish revolution would rumble on like this through the early 1870s – saloon-bar bravado in New York, and the gentle decay of the still well-armed IRB in Ireland. Threats against the lives of the Queen and her family could be considered the ravings of drunken crackpots. The amnestied rebels had been sent into American exile. The empire and its sovereign were secure from enemies within and without. That was about to change.

Northern Hotel, Cortland Street, New York, March 1874

The exiles found that their celebrity status in New York soon faded. Money had to be earned. John Devoy, an austere bachelor, got a position as a clerk on Wall Street. O'Donovan Rossa had opened the European Steamship and Railroad Ticket Agency at

---

* The Queen's son had been shot and wounded in New South Wales in March 1868 by a Fenian sympathiser.

263 Broadway, the offices of the *Irish World* newspaper. He was drinking heavily and had demanding children in abundance. Devoy roomed at Rossa's new venture, a broken-down boarding house opposite the Jersey City ferry terminal. It was not prospering.

In March 1874 a Fenian ghost arrived at the Northern Hotel. It was Captain John MacCafferty, the former Confederate guerrilla who had been sentenced to be hung, beheaded and his body quartered for high treason after the Chester Castle raid. The sentence had been commuted to penal servitude for life. He had been released and shipped to America under the amnesty in June 1871. John Devoy had been shackled to him on the stone-cutting gang at Portland prison. When they met again nine years later, the 'cold, quiet voice' had not changed – nor had the ferocity.

MacCafferty had an astounding plan. He was going to kidnap the Prince of Wales. He had clandestinely visited Liverpool under the name 'Mr Pattison' to sound out some IRB die-hards. The Prince was to be bundled onto a sailing vessel, 'treated with every consideration' (MacCafferty 'had drawn up a list of the Prince's favourite amusements') and held captive against the release of remaining prisoners – Michael Davitt (sentenced to fifteen years for attempted gun-running in 1870), O'Meagher Condon (serving life for the Manchester 'rescue') and, in particular, the 'military prisoners', the soldiers of the Dublin garrison found guilty of mutiny in 1865, now held in Western Australia. Six of them had been excepted from Gladstone's amnesty on the intervention of the commander-in-chief, the Duke of Cambridge, the Queen's cousin. They were expected never to be freed.

MacCafferty had evidently discussed the Prince of Wales kidnap operation with Charles J. Kickham, now president of the supreme council of the IRB. The veteran rebel, amnestied in 1869, half-blind and profoundly deaf, waved his ear-trumpet in horror. Queen Victoria's son was not a legitimate target. Now, back in New York, MacCafferty wanted $5,000 to finance the operation from the Clan-na-Gael, of which John Devoy was a senior member. Devoy was sceptical; MacCafferty was threatening –

there had been some talk of his alleged 'cowardice' in the Chester
Castle affair. Rossa was much more keen: the turgid life of a
hotel-keeper was not advancing the cause. Ultimately the plot
was not sanctioned. There would be another, spectacular and far
more 'civilised' way of rescuing the military prisoners than by
holding royal princes to ransom.

Devoy had received letters smuggled out of Fremantle prison
in Western Australia – pleas from the six Fenians he had personally
sworn to help escape their 'living tomb'. Devoy broodingly circulated them at a Clan convention in Baltimore in July 1874. Money
was raised, enough to buy an old whaling barque, the *Catalpa*,
with a teetotal Nantucket master and a highly cosmopolitan crew.
They were going to sail across the world and snatch the prisoners
from a jail from which the sharks and the desert were supposed
to make escape impossible. The mission succeeded brilliantly. The
Perth Inquirer said: 'It seems humiliating that a Yankee with half
a dozen coloured men should come into our waters and carry off
six of the most determined Fenian convicts . . . and then laugh
at us without an effort to secure them.'

The *Catalpa* operation electrified Irish America. On 6 June
news of the 'rescue' reached Dublin, where a huge crowd burned
effigies of Benjamin Disraeli and the Duke of Cambridge. The
Clan-na-Gael leaders in America exulted at the show of militancy
– and at the discomfort of Isaac Butt's weak-kneed parliamentary
home rulers. There had been no bungling this time; no dead
policemen or bloodied Londoners pulled out of tenement rubble.
The little barque's arrival in New York harbour saw another
water-borne green exultation and the inevitable reception at
Sweeney's Hotel. The Clan, whose very existence was meant to
be secret, had stamped its authority on the Irish revolution. In
fact the shenanigans in the western Australian bush had reminded
the world there was such a thing at all. One man, Jeremiah
O'Donovan Rossa, the intransigent of intransigents, was determined that no one should ever forget. He would not call it terrorism – it was 'skirmishing'.

Offices of the Irish World, *263 Broadway, New York, March 1876*

Rossa's letter announcing his extraordinary new venture appeared in the *Irish World* on 4 March 1876. He invited subscriptions for a 'Skirmishing Fund' set at $5,000 – to 'strike England year after year'. The paper was soon filled with letters from eager subscribers pledging their dollars to bring fire and ruin on England.

The Clan was being outmanoeuvred. John Devoy wrote in response: 'Skirmishing, by allusions to capturing princes, rescuing prisoners etc., in a sufficiently direct way [would] give a British lawyer ample proof against any man who should fall into their hands . . . I go in for what Rossa calls skirmishing, but I want to do something each time that will bring us something in return.'

Dr William Carroll, a former federal army surgeon, the newly elected chairman of the Clan executive, wrote a month later: 'If things go on as at present we shall have the hot-spirits on the other side up in arms in desultory warfare . . . all this simply confirms the general opinion of our American friends, that while we are capable of brilliant, desperate disconnected personal effort, there is no hope of our ever rising to the level of successful revolutionaries.'

Discipline must be imposed. Clan money was in danger of leaching away to Rossa. In August 1876, at its Philadelphia convention, the Clan voted for the establishment of a 'revolutionary directory' with the power, in Dr Carroll's words, 'To declare war and draw the last dollar'. It would have executive control over both the Clan and the Irish Republican Brotherhood but would take a further year of negotiations to establish. The Clan was committed to 'civilised warfare'. It would be a few years at least before its members primed bombs on the London underground railway.

12

Frank Millen's career as a spy had gone into decline. There was little intelligence from the moribund Fenian Brotherhood which might be considered worth $500 by HM consul in New York. The reports from 'Informant M' disappear from the Foreign Office files after the 'I wish to come home' overture of 1867, to which Samuel Anderson had applied his gentlemanly arm lock.

The star of Millen's mentor, Collector Thomas Murphy of New York, had exploded in spectacular corruption. Millen's wife had borne him two daughters, Kitty and Florence. It was time to earn a proper living. He tried journalism. The *New York Herald* employed him as a correspondent at the suggestion of a young Dublin-born IRB man called James J. O'Kelly.

A Fenian at fifteen, O'Kelly had fought as a French foreign legionnaire in Mexico; he went underground with the London IRB after March 1867, and rejoined the French army as the Prussians advanced on Paris. He got to New York and found a job on the *Herald*. In 1873 O'Kelly suggested that he and his Spanish-speaking colleague should head for Cuba to report on the rebellion. Here Millen committed the greatest crime in journalism: while O'Kelly plunged off into the jungle with the insurgents, he stayed in his Havana hotel, turning round his colleague's rebel-relayed dispatches – and transmitted them to the *Herald* as his own. O'Kelly was captured by the Spanish and sentenced to be shot; Millen escaped Havana on a Miami-bound steamer. Perhaps he was better at making revolutions than at reporting on them.

The Clan came to his rescue with its new martial ambitions.

In 1876 he was appointed chairman of the general military board, United Brotherhood. The looming Anglo-Russian war kept him busy.

Imperial Russia had supplanted the United States as England's potential foe. War was coming in the Balkans. A Slav rising in Bosnia-Herzegovina had spread to Bulgaria, where it was suppressed with great cruelty by the Ottoman Turk overlords. Russia was stirring. In London Benjamin Disraeli's Conservative government held that 'Constantinople was the key to India', of which he had just theatrically declared his sovereign to be Empress. The Prime Minister held no sympathy for Slav or any other inconvenient nationalism. 'Fancy autonomy for Bosnia with a mixed population,' Disraeli wrote to a lady confidante; 'autonomy for Ireland would be less absurd.' A fleet of elderly Royal Navy warships was dispatched to prop up the Turks.

Coney Island, New York, September 1876

The boating lake of an amusement park was a curious place to embark on a scheme to rock the British empire. With some solemnity John P. Holland, schoolteacher and Fenian, placed his model boat in the water. It was hefty – thirty inches long, a solderedtinplate cigar. Its inventor adjusted its fins, topped up two small fore and aft buoyancy tanks with water and pinged its clockwork motor. The little bronze propeller whirred cheerfully. The strange craft disappeared beneath the surface, its wake showing its progress across the pond.

Holland, a Clare-born self-taught scientist, had followed his brother, an IRB member, to Boston in 1873. In his baggage were unusual proposals for submarine navigation. He offered his work to the US navy, which was not interested. In July 1876 he was introduced to the belligerent Rossa, who adored the idea of British ironclads being suddenly blown out of the water by an unseen hand. 'Skirmishing' money was advanced to build a pedalpowered prototype, effectively a manned torpedo, at the Albany Iron Works, New York. The Clan was going to take the Irish revolution underwater.

Thus it was that a group of respectable American citizens were able to offer England's latest enemy a very unusual deal. On 1 November 1876 a Clan delegation arrived at the Imperial Russian legation in Washington. Millen strutted about its marble saloons, his Mexican medals gleaming. Monsieur Shishkin, the ambassador, received them politely. He had heard such appeals before while he was minister at Belgrade, he explained – from Serbs seeking the Tsar's aid in overthrowing their Ottoman over-lords. Aiding the Irish was certainly a novel idea. He had read with interest the 'memorial' prepared on the advantages of an understanding between the Clan-na-Gael and the Russian govern-ment. It talked of 10,000 American soldiers ready to appear in Ireland as 'friends returning to relatives'. Moreover, Irish regi-ments garrisoned India: they would be raised in revolt. The inti-mations of a 'salt-water enterprise' (the submarine) would be of particular interest to the Imperial Admiralty.

But the ambassador pointed out that 'war between England and Russia was improbable, and that only in the case of war could his government enter into direct negotiations with Irish revolutionaries'. He would, however, 'forward it to St Petersburg with an assurance that it came from representative men'.

Rossa had been shut out of the conference. He later turned up at the legation with a rival Fenian Brotherhood delegation. They did not get past the first secretary. This served to convince Shishkin that the Irish revolution was hopelessly split. It was clear to the Clan leaders that Rossa must be stamped on. Two days before Russia declared war on Turkey, an 'Address to the Irish People' published in the *Irish World* of 21 April 1877 gave notice of the Clan's move to oust Rossa: 'Since the "skirmishing" project was first announced, circumstances have greatly altered,' it said. 'Europe is threatened with a general convulsion. War on the most tremendous scale cannot much longer be staved off.' A Special National Fund under Clan control would supplant it (Rossa would nominally stay its secretary). There was $23,000 on deposit. The *Catalpa* mission had demonstrated the Clan's reach. For a strategic enthusiast like Millen, global possibilities opened up.

Edward Archibald sent London a stream of reports of rumoured piratical attacks – on Bermuda; on New South Wales; there was talk of an Irish-American raiding party about to leave San Francisco to capture the Falkland Islands. Mr J. Callaghan, the colony's alarmed governor, demanded a Royal Navy gunboat be sent to protect his 'most isolated and defenceless settlement'. He was concerned that a mysterious American, a 'Mr Noel', was using a peat-digging project as cover. But Port Stanley remained untroubled.

James O'Kelly, whose Cuban adventures with Frank Millen had ended not with his execution but with a spell in a Spanish jail, had been talking to his former captors. In the summer of 1877 he had quit the *New York Herald* in good foreign correspondent fashion amidst a divorce scandal, and gone to Europe to report on the Turkish war. He had swung through London to meet 'literary swells' and to offer, without success, his services to the *Telegraph* newspaper.

In Paris O'Kelly met a rising politician called Charles Stewart Parnell, making a name with his noisy performances in the English parliament. He thought him 'cool – extremely so, and resolute'. Now, in October, the would-be war correspondent found himself broke in Madrid – a very long way from the siege of Plevna. No matter – he would bring the war to him. He wrote to Devoy, saying that the 'young, ambitious' King Alfonso was squaring up to join Russia in a war with Britain. 'I think it would be well to make advances to the King in reference to the aid we might be able to render him in getting hold of Gibraltar by treachery.' It would be great story – AMERICANS CAPTURE ROCK.

Frank Millen meanwhile was stirring up his own far-flung mischief. 'I have lately read articles on India wherein it was clear that the native rulers of Afghanistan, and other places in the East, are going to take decided action against the common enemy,' he wrote to the Clan chairman, Dr William Carroll. The general seemed willing to go himself; in the dusty bazaars of Central Asia he might broker his New York-funded Fenian alliance with the Emir of Kabul.

*   *   *

It was the central issue of a rising in Ireland, however, that pre-occupied the Clan through the second half of 1877. The Russo-Turkish war had become a bloody slugging match. The Russian armies lumbered towards Constantinople to halt, exhausted, before its walls. On 13 February 1878 six British ironclads passed the Dardanelles. Millen's plans for a 10,000 strong American volunteer army to act in Ireland itself dramatically gathered pace. On 23 December he posted a portentous eve-of-battle notice to the Irish Republican Brotherhood:

> Brothers. Not since the time of the Crimean war and the Indian Mutiny has there been so propitious a juncture in the affairs of our country. England will drift into war with Russia upon the question of patching up a peace between the Tsar and the Sultan . . . [he proclaimed].
>
> In 1865, we saw with regret that large sums of money which ought to have been invested in arms, were expended in sending numbers of useless 'officers' from this country . . . We believe, however, that a rising in Ireland could be combined simultaneously with the landing of an expedition from this side . . .
>
> For obvious reasons we abstain from entering upon any details of the work, which might require the names of men and places that had better not be trusted to paper.

The last time Millen had drafted the Irish order of battle a copy reached Her Majesty's government. It would do so again.

The Skirmishers' Ball, Philadelphia, 17 March 1878

Irish America was experiencing a new spasm of patriotic fervour. On 5 March the victorious Russians had pinned the Turks to a humiliating peace treaty at Adrianople. Britain would not wear it. A huge Anglo-Russian conflict fought from the Balkans to the Hindu Kush seemed inevitable. O'Donovan Rossa caught the war fever by going on a week-long drinking spree in New York.

On this most auspicious St Patrick's Day the luminaries of the

Clan gathered in Philadelphia for a fund-raising ball. HM Foreign Secret Service managed to crash the party. Mr George Crump, the British consul in Philadelphia, had recruited an informer he referred to as agent 'Desmond', who worked the ballroom eagerly. One reveller was very forthcoming:

> General F. F. Millen, believed to be the Chairman of the Military Board, affirmed to my informant that there is a great desire on the part of the Russian government to aid the Irish nationalists [the consul relayed]. The report that a Russian naval officer was in New York for the purpose of purchasing steamers for the Russian Govt to be used as transport was founded on truth.

The gossipy general had further revealed that Dr William Carroll and an 'Australian representative' were now being entertained in St Petersburg as emissaries of the 'Provisional Government of Ireland'. Millen was giving away the crown jewels to a stranger at a party. The Russian contacts were meant to be a deadly secret. Dr Carroll had indeed been to Dublin to stamp the Clan's authority on the IRB and was now in London, but had certainly not gone to Russia. Whether Millen was mixing fact and fiction for money or bravado the archives do not reveal.

In late April agent Desmond went to New York and learned a great deal more of the Clan's plans. Most of it seems to have come straight from Millen – 'in whose company he was several times'. Consul Crump told Whitehall on 16 May:

> A rising of the Fenians in Ireland is positively intended ... it will be precipitated by an outbreak of hostilities between England and Russia ... Every Irish militia regiment has its Fenian officers elected who have a full knowledge of the proposed scheme.
>
> General F. F. Millen is to be the commander in Ireland. Limerick will be the point for concentration as the River Shannon penetrates to the heart of the country. General Millen will plan an expedition from this country ... which will be formed into 'skeleton' regiments of

NCOs and officers, the ranks to be filled by the Fenians
in Ireland.

Whitehall was not over-alarmed. British dominion in Ireland
was not to be shaken by the threat of American legionaries landing
in Limerick. The Foreign Office now had Millen's war-plan safely
on file. Details of the proposed Gibraltar raid would shortly reach
them via another Millen indiscretion. What they did not have
sight of was much more significant – Carroll's revolutionary
diplomacy in Europe. The doctor was extremely busy – but not
engaged in conspiring with Russian admirals. On 15 January 1878
he had sat down in Dublin with the man that James O'Kelly had
described so glowingly. After breakfast at the Hibernian Hotel
Dr Carroll asked Charles Stewart Parnell if he was in favour of
the absolute independence of Ireland.

'He replied that he was and that as soon as the people so
declared he would go with them.'

Carroll answered on behalf of the Clan: 'We would be his
friends and would . . . support him in all he did to that end.' The
revolutionary doctor and the constitutional politician could do
business together. This was going to be far more dangerous to
British rule in Ireland than any clockwork submarine.

13

New York, autumn 1878

The most important move in Irish nationalist politics in a generation was made in New York almost by accident. Some American
revolutionaries were growing tired of 'saloon conspiracy' without
end. Parnell's robust parliamentary behaviour gave them a glimmer of an alternative. The catalyst for change was the arrival in
America in August 1878 of Michael Davitt. He had carried a
bundle of bullets to Chester Castle, waiting in vain for the bold
Captain John MacCafferty to turn up. Released from Dartmoor
in December 1877 on 'ticket of leave' after seven years of a
fifteen-year sentence for gun-running, he had come in search of
his mother and sister in Manayunk, Philadelphia.*

On a dusty Sunday afternoon Davitt sought out at the New
York Herald office one of the few people he knew in the city,
James O'Kelly, veteran of the IRB arms agency in England –
dabbling in which had got Davitt his own sentence for treason-
felony. John Devoy was there, mooching about the office. The
visitor had a new agenda: Davitt preached *land*, 'making English
rule impossible' on the ground. Devoy sent Davitt on a gruelling
propaganda lecture tour with Clan backing, bringing the stale
whiff of blighted Connaught to draughty Masonic halls across
America. His audiences adored it. A new battlefield had opened
on which support from the Tsar of Russia was not needed.

* The family had fled famine-struck Mayo to find work in Lancashire cotton
mills, where Davitt's right arm was torn off in a machinery accident. Politically way
to the left of Parnell, he nevertheless supported the eventual Liberal–Nationalist
coalition in Parliament and would act as the party's intelligence chief during the
Special Commission. He became a Westminster MP in 1892.

On 25 October 1878, without outside consultation, five senior members of the Clan sent a cablegram to Parnell. It was routed with due revolutionary protocol via Charles J. Kickham, president of the supreme council of the IRB. 'Nationalists here will support you,' it stated, if he delivered 'vigorous declaration for self-government . . . agitation for peasant proprietorship . . . avoidance of sectarian issues . . . disciplined action at Westminster', and the 'support of struggling nationalities in the British empire and elsewhere'. F. F. Millen ('a well-known revolutionist', according to Davitt) was one of the signatories.

The text appeared in the *New York Herald* under the headline A NEW DEPARTURE FOR IRELAND. The New York press assumed the 'proposed alliance' was as good as made. Closely questioned by the attorney-general at the Special Commission in 1889, Parnell denied he ever received the cable.

The Irish Republican Brotherhood were horrified. Any kind of cooperation with the British parliament was against their very oath. Devoy set off for Europe, closely followed by Davitt, to sell the new policy to the supreme council. Through the third week of January 1879 a series of gritty sessions in Paris (the amnestied Devoy's term of exile from British soil had not expired), with Kickham waving his obfuscating ebonite ear-trumpet, reduced Davitt to tears. The council assumed that physical force was being abandoned outright. There was no agreement. Devoy insisted on going to Ireland to test opinion of the new policy even though he risked arrest. He travelled under the cover-name 'Mr Jones'.

But as if to prove his militancy Devoy proposed sending Millen on a parallel military mission. Davitt wrote from Mayo to his new political ally: 'I fear your proposal in ref Morgan [Millen] will not, if carried into effect, do anything like pay the expenses he will entail . . . The state of trade is in no way favourable to Morgan's employment. Recent events would inflame him for "glory". Under Heaven I don't know how he could do anything at present . . .'

But Frank Millen was already inflamed for glory. He proposed a Clan operation mounted from Mexico against the obscure British colony of Belize. 'I feel certain that President Diaz would be glad

to work with us in a secret manner,' he informed Dr Carroll in
September 1878. Nothing happened. Four months later there
was new excitement: the general was keen to be sent to Africa to
aid Britain's latest implacable foes, the Zulus. On 21 January
1879 King Cetewayo's army had wiped out a 1,200-strong British
force at Isandhlwana. James O'Kelly was very animated: 'I say
that one million cartridges placed in the hands of the Zulus would
help the Irish cause more than an equivalent amount of arms
landed in Ireland,' he wrote to Devoy in Paris on 17 February.
He further proposed a scheme to incite the 'Kaffir tribes' of Cape
Colony to revolt. Millen unsurprisingly had volunteered to lead
the expedition. In France, meanwhile, war by other means was
on the agenda.

Parc de la Gare Maritime, Boulogne-sur-Mer, France, 7 March 1879

John Devoy, Michael Davitt and John O'Leary (brought from
Paris as a 'witness' for the ultra-suspicious IRB supreme council)
met a well-muffled gentleman codenamed 'Mr Emerson' in the
French port of Boulogne. He and a colleague had crossed the
Channel on Davitt's overture.

The travellers were Parnell and Joseph Biggar. The 'physical
force' revolutionaries and the constitutional obstructionists talked
affably about the prospect of an alliance in a 'little park by the
quayside', before retiring to the Hôtel Brighton. But 'while we
were unable to make an agreement binding in the two bodies,
Parnell was prepared to go more than halfway to meet us,' Devoy
recorded much later. It was the first of three meetings between
Parnell and the Clan that spring/summer.

617 South 16th Street, Philadelphia, 9 March 1879

The Clan leaders met at Dr Carroll's surgery two days later.
Constitutional means to Irish independence were not on the
agenda. It was agreed the executive body and the National
Fund trustees would merge. Rossa was excluded 'because of his

truculence, not to say treason'. Millen and O'Kelly presented
their detailed 'South Africa' plan – to be effected at a cost of
$15,000. The meeting was impressed. Dr Carroll messaged
Devoy in Paris to take the whole strategic construct – South
Africa, Afghanistan, sea-borne raiders and a rising in Ireland – to
the Russian minister as a bargaining ticket to get to St Petersburg;
meanwhile it was up to the IRB supreme council in Paris to decide
where and how to employ Millen.

'It is proper to state here that Morgan [Millen] has two proposals for his services in his especial line. One in Honduras and
the other Colombia, South America, but prefers service with Elder
[the code-name for the IRB] to any other,' the doctor messaged.

There was no reply from the supreme council. Carroll dispatched Millen to Ireland without further notice. He would travel
as 'an agricultural instructor'. It was a replay of O'Mahony's 1865
commission to assess the military strength of the IRB. Advance
payment of $1,000 was agreed and on 24 April the general
embarked on an Antwerp-bound steamer to cross the Atlantic
under the cover name 'G. G. Robinson'. He would be in Europe
for three months.

Millen's thirty-page report was delivered to the Clan convention at Wilkes-Barre, Pennsylvania, on 9 August 1879. A copy
reached the Foreign Office soon afterwards. How it got there is
not revealed: it sits in the file without comment or covering letter.

Millen went first to the city of 'M', 'noted for its arms factories'.* 'Fortunately I was able to do this in the character of a
military man, who was desirous of learning the price of arms and
forwarding the same to the President of the Republic of Honduras
who is a friend of mine.'

The general travelled next to Paris, where the IRB supreme

---

* Reading Millen's report, annotated by HM Foreign Secret Service, alongside
his expenses sheet presented to the Clan treasurer reveals what the FO did *not*
know about the mission. For example, the FO assumed 'M' was Birmingham; it
was in fact Liège, Belgium.

Like a good journalist Millen lived well, was a big tipper and charged for plenty
of 'dinners with friends', especially in Belfast (these were presumably members of
his family).

council was hugely suspicious of the visitor. The general mooched round the city for a fortnight while Dr Carroll sent messages from Philadelphia explaining that his presence was a token that 'talk was at an end . . . and that a strict preparation for the bloody work ahead can only interest us here'. Millen next travelled via London to Dublin, arriving on the night of the 15th; here he met 'Mr Black'. It was Michael Davitt.

Millen went on to Belfast, Glasgow, Galway, Ennis, Limerick, Tipperary and Cork, to embark on the Queenstown steamer and arrive back in New York on 6 August – writing his long situation report on the way. His findings were not about to make the occupants of Dublin Castle come out with their hands up. At one clandestine muster he observed:

> The men were very earnest, but apparently not overly
> able to supply themselves with arms and few of them
> seemed to know much about military matters. No exer-
> cises were attempted . . . I suggested the propriety of
> opening a bowling alley and shooting gallery which could
> be made profitable and at the same time afford the men
> an opportunity of acquiring a knowledge of rifle practice.

The general had yet another wild scheme. Soon after his return to New York he sought an audience with Señor de Uriarte, the Spanish consul-general in the city, and presented a plan stamped with the seal of the 'Irish Liberation Army' for the capture of Gibraltar. It was much more detailed than James O'Kelly's presentation made in Madrid eighteen months earlier.

'A system of time torpedoes, working by machinery, could be very effectively employed . . . They might be so arranged as to explode any minute of any day within thirty days from the time of setting them,' Millen suggested. Bomb-fusing technology had come a long way since the Clerkenwell 'squib'.

The baffled Spanish diplomat promptly took the Gibraltar plan to Mr Archibald. The consul relayed it to London with the com- ment: 'It is signed by General F. F. Millen, who, it will be remembered, was in former years one of my informants . . . Mr de Uriarte has kindly offered to keep Millen "in hand" . . . and will furnish me with any information in reference to Fenian movements which he may obtain by conferences with Millen.' By whatever route his plans reached Whitehall (he seemed to be using the Spanish consul as a conduit), the general was proving very bad at keeping a secret.

Davitt and Devoy were distinctly unhappy at Millen's arrival in Ireland. Having himself suggested the general be sent, Devoy messaged to the Clan executive in Philadelphia that Millen's unheralded appearance was an 'insult'. Dr Carroll replied on 17 June: '[You are] as wrong as possible in now doubting Morgan's [Millen's] coolness, caution, thoroughness, etc, which you praised so highly . . .' Michael Davitt also expressed his own reservations in letters in which he cryptically referred to Millen's manoeuvres as another 'Gentle Torpedo' affair – his own curious code-name for the general.

Perhaps the general's global strategic scheming was beginning to seem like yesterday's politics. By summer 1879 the great Anglo-Russian war scare had blown itself out. The Zulu impis had been crushed at Ulundi and the turbulent Emir Sher Ali had been deposed by a British invasion of Afghanistan. It was in Ireland itself that liberation politics would move on dramatically. It began in the west.

PART FOUR

Dynamite

'The Queen has now reigned nearly thirty
years, is forty-eight years old, has lived in
troubled times . . . she has been shot at three
times, once knocked on the head, threatening
letters have over and over again been received
and *yet* we *never* changed our mode of living
or going on . . .'
Queen Victoria, 8 January 1868

14

Daly's Hotel, Castlebar, Mayo, 16 August 1879

It rained over Ireland throughout the spring of 1879. It rained without cease throughout the early summer. In the west the potato crop blackened in the sodden lazy-beds. Mayo, depopulated and cowed since the Famine, erupted in raggedy mass meetings. On Saturday 16 August, at Daly's Hotel in Castlebar, Michael Davitt proclaimed that 'the land of Ireland belongs to the people of Ireland' and the Mayo Land League was born. Rent strikes would be the weapon.

Parnell agreed to become president of a national movement. He set off for New York at the end of the year to raise money for the campaign. The Clan hired Madison Square Gardens for his first speech, heard by an adulatory crowd of 5,000, armed 'honour-guards' flanking the stage. Parnell spoke in sixty-two cities and addressed the House of Representatives. On 11 March 1880, the day Parnell boarded the steamer home (a British general election had been called),* the Land League of America was formed.

New York, 27 June 1880

The Clan's romance with Parnell was short. 'Moral persuasion' was winning – the American Land League soaking up green sentiment and its campaigning dollars. Rossa breathed fire on its other

---

* William Gladstone defeated Lord Beaconsfield (Disraeli) to form his second ministry. Sir William Vernon Harcourt was Home Secretary, the Earl of Granville Foreign Secretary and William Edward Forster Chief Secretary for Ireland.

flank. There were defectors. James O'Kelly went to Ireland in
early 1880 on a Millen-inspired mission to import guns. Instead
he disavowed his Clan oath and successfully stood as a Parnellite
MP for North Roscommon in the general election of 28 April
1880.

It was William Carroll who broke off the engagement. The
Clan must stay wedded to armed force or it was nothing, he
declared; Parnell was 'a political adventurer posing as a liberator'.
On 27 June there was a Clan–IRB plenary meeting in New York.
By an eight-to-five majority the executive voted down a resolution
that would have banned Clan members from being Land League
officers. The overt and covert organisations might still cross-
pollinate – to the special outrage seven years later of *The Times*
newspaper.

But the meeting also passed a motion that reminded Clansmen
they should 'not neglect the work of revolution'. The following
day Carroll resigned as chairman (he remained on the revolutionary directory), to be replaced by James Reynolds, a brass founder
from New Haven. Frank Millen was at the turbulent meeting.
He too resigned 'as chairman of the military board'. Central
America offered attractions anew: he promptly went off to Panama
on a *New York Herald* mission to meet Ferdinand de Lesseps,
the famous constructor of the Suez Canal – now intent on blasting
another out of the malarial jungle.

There remained Rossa – or Jeremiah 'O'Dynamite', as his
weary co-revolutionists had now dubbed him. Squeezed out from
the skirmishing fund which did no skirmishing,* Rossa found
that his ravings had become too much even for the *Irish World*
newspaper, which barred him from its columns. In April he was
at last suspended from the Clan for calling a schismatic conference
at Philadelphia.

At a much-mocked *salon des refusés* held in June 1880 Rossa
founded the 'United Irishmen of America – the Party of the Men
of Action'. He launched his own newspaper, the *United Irishman*,

---

* Its resources were invested in subtler plans, such as the submarine; £2,000 was
used to pay Davitt's living costs while he struggled to launch the Land League.

called by John Devoy 'the queerest Irish paper ever published'. Its rantings were extraordinary. When the Queen's indisposition due to a sprained ankle was announced, Rossa claimed it was the work of his agents disguised as cleaning ladies – 'who had soaped the stairs at Windsor Castle'.

It was not all make-believe. At the end of 1880 the first little band of Rossa's 'skirmishers' set off to blow up what they might of England.

Salford, Manchester, 14 January 1881

The first casualty of Rossa's terror war was a seven-year-old boy called Richard Clarke. On a January afternoon in the grimy coke town two men removed a ventilating grid from the outer wall of Salford Infantry Barracks in Tatton Street and placed a crude bomb inside. It exploded at around 5.20 p.m., demolishing the garrison butcher's shed, fatally injuring the little 'workman's son' (he died three days later) and injuring three others. The inquest returned a verdict of murder by person or persons unknown. But it was clear who did it – the bloody Irish.

The Queen's Speech to the new session of parliament, delivered a few days before the explosion, contained both legislation for land reform and a 'coercion act'* to smash what was called the 'extended system of terror' that the land war had unleashed in Ireland. On 16 January John Devoy made a blood-curdling speech in New York attacking the crack-down. 'For every Irishman murdered we will take in reprisal the life of a British minister,' he raged. 'For a wholesale massacre of the Irish people we will make England a smouldering ruin of ashes and blood.' The American green shoot of the new departure had turned black.†

---

* General term for measures under various names passed throughout Irish history to deal with outbreaks of disorder – giving central authority powers to impose curfew, hold trials without jury, ban subversive organisations and other measures. The 1881 Protection of Life and Property Act, for example, introduced the offence of 'incitement' and temporarily allowed detention of suspects without trial.
† Michael Davitt was appalled. In his speech to the Special Commission eight years later he described Devoy as 'an avowed personal and implacable enemy'.

There was uproar when Devoy's speech was reported in London. Sir William Harcourt, the Liberal Home Secretary, spoke in parliament of the need to 'stamp out this vile conspiracy'. Robert Anderson's sleepy role at the Home Office was reactivated. Howard Vincent, head of the still comparatively novel Criminal Investigation Department (it had been established in 1877 after a corruption scandal had rocked the detective bureau), was ordered 'to devote himself exclusively to Irish business'. A 'Fenian Office' was established at Scotland Yard – which was to cooperate with Anderson, Colonel Vivian Majendie, the Home Office's resident explosives expert, and the Irish and regional British police. Harcourt asked for and got £300 over and above the existing £500 'Secret Service fund'.

It was the Clerkenwell panic revisited. The Palace of Westminster, the Tower, the Royal Mint and Buckingham Palace were heavily guarded. On 3 February Harcourt announced the arrest of Michael Davitt for incitement. Amidst scenes of 'indescribable confusion' thirty-six Irish members were ejected from the House. Parnell and former IRB-man Patrick Egan, the Land League treasurer, rushed to Paris to transfer the league's funds out of British legal reach. Ireland was moving to its greatest revolutionary crisis since 1867. It seemed, at this turning moment, that the Irish leader must fly to America and raise the standard of outright rebellion.

The Clan, meanwhile, was not going to be outmanoeuvred by Rossa's bombers. A volunteer was sought to go to Europe and make a reconnaissance for a terror campaign, to be launched as and when the Revolutionary Directory chose. He was William Mackey Lomasney, known as the 'Little Captain', a quiet-spoken Detroit bookseller, later described by Devoy as 'a fanatic of the deepest dye'. He insisted on travelling alone and suspected that 'British spies in the Department at Washington were on his track'.

Before his departure Lomasney conducted secret experiments on a lonely Lake Michigan strand with 'the manufacture and preparation of certain goods'. They were dynamite bombs. He was obviously impressed with their effects. He described Rossa's attempts 'to scare and scatter an empire with common blasting powder' as a 'burlesque'.

Around 11 February 1881 Lomasney arrived in Paris to consult with what he called the 'firm'. It would be the Irish Republican Brotherhood's job to track down Rossa's bombers in England and terminate their 'folly and bungling'. In the French capital the terror technician met the semi-fugitive Parnell. Lomasney reported the meeting to New York: 'I feel he is greatly deserving of our support . . . He means to go as far as we do in pushing the business.'

As Lomasney suspected, the intelligence operation in America had indeed cranked up again, but Edward Archibald was not aware of the Clan's 'lone volunteer'. The first wave of reports from the New York consulate after the Salford bomb spoke of fearsome conspiracies.

'The lives of your Queen, the Prince of Wales and his sons, indeed of the whole royal family are in jeopardy,' an anonymous correspondent had informed the consul. Five hundred 'revolutionists' in America had formed an assassination society called the Knights of Hassan-ben-Sabbah-el-Homari, sworn to wipe out the entire British establishment, it was claimed. The 'Knights', named after the eleventh-century founder of the Persian 'assassination' cult, were just waiting 'until everything is ripe for revolution, while Parnell and the rest will undoubtedly profit through the convulsion and terror their assassinations would produce'. One of them was at that very moment stalking the Strangers' Gallery of the Commons, armed with a 'French air-cane'.

A report relayed from Chicago soon afterwards stated: 'Dynamite will be deposited in the coffins in Windsor Chapel and blown up with an electric battery when the Queen is staying there.' Such stories soon found their way to the newspapers. The great dynamite scare flapped over London like a shroud. Russia had been transfixed by muffed assassination attempts for months. Then on 13 March Tsar Alexander II was blown to bits by the nihilist group, the People's Will, as he drove out in a carriage in St Petersburg.

Mansion House, City of London, 16 March 1881

The Rossa team which struck Salford had slipped away south. Late on the foggy evening of 16 March two men placed a wooden box beneath the window of the Egyptian Hall at the Mansion House, the Lord Mayor's residence in the City of London. However, the sumptuous banquet due to be held that night was cancelled as a mark of respect to the Russian Emperor.

The bomb was discovered by a patrolling constable with its fuse smouldering and taken to Bow Lane police station. The wooden box, bound with metal hoops, contained five pounds of crude blasting powder packed in newspapers. Two days later Sir Henry Ponsonby arrived at the Home Office to convey Queen Victoria's fears that Buckingham Palace was about to be blown up.

A week later Captain Robert Clipperton, HM consul in Philadelphia, reported a bizarre new threat: 'I am informed that explosives have been made and delivered in England by the O'Donovan Rossa party in the form of coal loaded with dynamite to be thrown into the bunkers of ships of war – transatlantic and other steamers . . .' They had been offered to the 'Boer agent' in New York, who seemed baffled about what he was to do with them. The consul gave warning of more direct danger: 'Another scheme is to leave dynamite explosives at sundry places in handbags with a clockwork arrangement set to explode at a certain time. Banks or public institutions will be the objective points.' On 10 April he messaged again: 'I hear from different secret sources that it is contemplated to blow up public buildings in Liverpool.' He sent a detailed list of the intended targets.

House of Commons, May 1881

Robert Anderson's years of sonorous activity at the Home Office were about to be rewarded. His jealously guarded agent in the Clan, Thomas Beach, came to Europe in late April 1881. Beach made two trips to London (with a visit to Paris in between); on both occasions he met Charles Stewart Parnell at the House of Commons. The first meeting, which took place 'by the lobby refreshment stand', was brief – Patrick Egan introduced the visitor as 'one of our friends from America'. The second, a month later, was far more conspiratorial. This time James O'Kelly, MP, was the interlocutor. In his evidence to the Special Commission Beach recalled Parnell's words, 'delivered in low tones' while they padded down the Pugin-gothic corridor leading to the Commons library: 'You furnish the sinews of war, you have them in your hands,' the Irish leader told the Clansman from Illinois. 'I have long ceased to believe that anything but force of arms will bring about the independence of Ireland.'

They talked alone for forty-five minutes; Beach returned later briefly to 'say goodbye'. In the tea room he was handed a photograph signed: 'Yours truly, C. S. Parnell.'*

That night, 23 May, Beach went to Robert Anderson's house at 39 Linden Gardens and reported the Parnell meeting in detail. His host took notes almost until dawn. Parnell was the coping stone in the universal conspiracy. He would prove it when the time was propitious.

Liverpool, May–June 1881

The Philadelphia consul had been right about Liverpool. Just as he predicted almost a month before, around midnight on 16 May 1881 two men deposited an iron-pipe bomb crudely filled with gunpowder in the doorway of Liverpool's main police station on Dale Street. It blew out the ground-floor windows but caused no casualties. On 10 June they tried again, dragging a much heavier gas-pipe bomb, loaded this time with commercial American dynamite, towards Liverpool town hall. Rossa's missioners were surprised when priming the fuse by a policeman, who dragged the bomb away before it erupted. The bombers were pursued and caught.

---

* Beach produced the photograph triumphantly at the Special Commission eight years later. In his examination Parnell stated 'that conversation is entirely untrue'. Of the 'force of arms' line he said: 'I never said that and never even thought it.' Letters that Beach wrote to Clan figures after the meeting, revealed in the 1950s, confirm that the thrust of the spy's testimony was accurate.

The consul had also been right about the fuses. Two weeks later Liverpool customs discovered six more Rossa-dispatched bombs in barrels marked CEMENT aboard the Cunarder RMS *Malta*, newly arrived from New York. They were zinc canisters packed with slabs of Atlas Powder A dynamite, configured to be detonated by a pistol shot activated by clockwork.

Clan-na-Gael Convention, Palmer House Hotel, Chicago, 3–10 August 1881

The Clan met for its tenth 'shareholder's meeting' in Chicago in an atmosphere of crisis. Rossa's bombing offensive, blundering though it might be, had stolen its revolutionary thunder. The American Land League was leaching away its funds. Ireland was in uproar. As the convention began on 3 August, in London the House of Lords threw out a conciliatory land reform measure – but Parnell still insisted he would hold to the 'moral-force' tactics of obstruction and rent strike.

A 'sharp-toothed, thin-lipped' lawyer cruised the saloons and bars of the Palmer House Hotel, glad-handing the delegates. He heard what they were saying: something must be done. His name was Alexander Sullivan; he was an ambitious Clansman who had risen through Republican machine politics in New Mexico and Illinois – with a habit of shooting those who got in his or his equally intimidating wife's way.

Thomas Beach was a delegate. He reported to Robert Anderson at length on the proceedings of what he called 'the Great Dynamite Convention of 1881'. It was to be a set-piece of his testimony to the Special Commission of 1889 – the moment when the Clan, with its clandestine feelers still open to Parnell, resolved to go on the terror offensive. Beach sketched the Chicago gathering disparagingly in his memoirs – burly stewards guarding the doors of cigar-smoke-filled rooms, as 'forty lawyers, two judges, clergymen, merchants, manufacturers and working men' squabbled over whiskey bottles. Millen was also there.

The militants prevailed. To 'ensure greater secrecy' the executive body was reduced to six members. Sullivan was elected president. The Clan's power-base would be effectively transposed from New York to Chicago. The lawyer pushed through a hugely wordy final resolution which ended: 'We mean war upon the enemy, we mean that war to be unsparing and unceasing . . .'

There was a splinter meeting afterwards of 'Irish national representatives', Beach reported to Anderson. To further the cause 'they were prepared to use even dynamite, but repudiated any attack on the royal family . . .' The Irish delegates knew the practicalities. The Clan might match Rossa with symbolic attacks against town halls and barracks, but Queen-killing was still unthinkable. It would surely only trigger a ferocious crack-down. There were some in America beginning to desire nothing less.

Gladstone's Land Act at last received the Royal Assent on 22 August. Its conciliatory 'fair-rent' tribunals might just put a stop to the land war. A conference of the Land League was called in Dublin to decide how to react. Militant telegrams meanwhile poured in from America. Parnell said he was prepared to give the Act a chance – but his crypto-revolutionary reputation was rescued by Gladstone, who tore into him in biblical terms. Parnell made a wildly inflammatory reply. On 13 October he was arrested in Dublin for 'incitement', along with four lieutenants – James O'Kelly, William O'Brien, John Dillon and Thomas Sexton, all of whom were smartly placed in Kilmainham jail (Parnell was comfortably installed in the matron's room). On the 18th a 'no-rent manifesto' was dramatically smuggled from the prison. Two days later William Forster, the Chief Secretary, proscribed the Land League as a criminal association.

Funds to sustain the land war kept flowing from America to Patrick Egan in Paris. With the front organisation now declared illegal, the Ladies Land League was established by Parnell's sister Anna to organise camps for evicted tenants. Society ladies arrived in Mayo to dispense soup. Gladstone agonised.

At the American Land League convention, held in Chicago in November 1881, Aleck Sullivan began his slow-motion coup to gain control of its fast-swelling funds. The moderate chairman,

General P. A. Collins, was deposed – to be replaced by a Clan member, a kindly looking Episcopalian cleric, the Reverend George C. Betts. Thomas Beach referred to him in reports as the 'Reverend Dynamite'.

Robert Anderson in London was earning his money meanwhile. On 4 January 1882 he forwarded a Beach report on the Chicago conference to the Irish Office, commissioned at the special request of William Forster. It was very secret. The league's cash was being 'invested in US bonds, to be used at some future time for a far better purpose than funding [evicted] tenants', the spy reported. 'Coercion' meanwhile had backfired. 'I fail to see any good resulting from action of late on your side,' said Beach; 'it has not tended to stamp out the movement, but on this side has increased it a hundred fold.' The charitable fund-raisers had a new slogan. It was: 'One dollar for bread, nine dollars for lead.'

15

Dublin, Saturday 6 May 1882

Dublin was decked in Union flags. The formal state entry into the city by the new Lord Lieutenant was a theatrical assertion of British dominion. Earl Spencer, known as the 'Red Earl' owing to his luxuriant auburn beard (he was 'Foxy Jack' to those less admiring), chose to ride imperiously on horseback, accompanied by a cavalry escort, from Westland Row station to the castle. The new Chief Secretary for Ireland, Lord Frederick Cavendish, followed by carriage, waving diffidently at the cheering crowds. Puffs of smoke erupted – they were bags of flour lobbed by boisterous students.

Among Spencer's retinue, newly disembarked that morning from the Holyhead steamer, was his private secretary, Mr Edward George Jenkinson, a former Indian civil servant. He had raised a cavalry unit in the Great Mutiny and had lately been divisional commissioner for Oudh. In indifferent health, he had brought Mrs Annabella Jenkinson and the two boys home to England in 1879. His political sentiments were suitably Liberal and the recommendation of his distant cousin, Lord Northbrook, had secured him a position with the Whig grandee of Althorp. Mr Jenkinson blinked through the carriage window at the white-faced colony. Dublin, as Frank Millen had noted on a similar day so long ago, seemed as loyal to the English crown as Middlesex.

After the wearisome ceremonies Lord Frederick was minded to stretch his legs. Indifferent to the many assassination threats against his predecessor, he set off from the castle alone to walk across the city to Phoenix Park. At the gates he was joined by the permanent under-secretary, Thomas Henry Burke.

They strode cheerfully past the cricket pitch and the polo lawn, little plots of England. Evening was falling. Almost opposite the vice-regal lodge a black cab pulled up. Four figures jumped out, slashing at the two men with surgical knives. Burke tried to defend himself, but his hands were hacked at and the knife pierced his throat. Cavendish was stabbed several times around the heart. The attackers left black-bordered visiting cards at Dublin newspaper offices announcing the murderous debut of a previously unheard of organisation, the 'Irish Invincibles'. It was a bloody disaster.

Four days previously Parnell and his lieutenants had been released from Kilmainham. On the afternoon of the murders Davitt was discharged from Portland prison, having served his sentence for incitement. After months of secretive diplomacy, brokered by the radical MP Joseph Chamberlain through his bag-carrier, an ambitious if not over-intelligent former hussar officer named Captain William O'Shea, Gladstone's government had struck a deal with its imprisoned tormentors.* The land war would be curtailed if coercion was abandoned. The secret deal would be referred to as the 'Kilmainham Treaty'. William Forster had resigned in disgust the day Parnell walked free. The murdered Lord Frederick, married to Gladstone's niece, had replaced him. Earl Cowper, the Lord Lieutenant, had resigned a week earlier; Spencer had supplanted him.

In London there was mournful revulsion at the murders. A moral threshold had been crossed. The immediate concern was security in Dublin. The head of the Royal Irish Constabulary was

* The passionate liaison between Parnell and the captain's wife, Mrs Katharine O'Shea (she had borne his child in February 1882) was progressed from behind the bars of Kilmainham through smuggled letters written in 'invisible ink'.

Mrs O'Shea, the very English sister of a distinguished soldier (the future field marshal Sir Evelyn Wood, VC), opened an intimate correspondence with Gladstone relaying Mr Parnell's hopes and fears. By late 1881 the love affair was an open secret in the Liberal Party.

Her husband meanwhile chose to condone or ignore it, relying on his wife's family money and the Irish party leader's influence in advancing his own political career. Two more of Parnell's children (the first died in infancy) were born between 1883 and 1884 and registered in William O'Shea's name.

The devastating results of the Clerkenwell explosion, 13 December 1867. The misfired attempt to spring an Irish-American gun-runner from prison with a monster charge of gunpowder demolished a row of tenements, killed six Londoners, injured scores more and threw the government into panic.

The Phoenix Park murders, Dublin, 6 June 1882. The double assassination of Lord Frederick Cavendish (chief secretary) and Thomas Burke (perma-nent under-secretary) by a breakaway repub-lican terror-faction, the 'Invincibles', poisoned the emerging political dialogue between Gladstone's Liberal government and Charles Stewart Parnell. Five years later *The Times* attempted to prove the Irish leader's collusion in the outrage.

Lady Florence Dixie, aristocrat, war-correspondent, advocate of Irish independence and protégée of Queen Victoria. She published a pamphlet attacking the Land League of Ireland as 'socialistic' – resulting on 17 March 1883 in an alleged assault on her by 'men dressed as women' in the grounds of Windsor Castle.

Above Edward George Jenkinson (KCB, 1888), unofficially dubbed 'spymaster-general' when he was appointed assistant under-secretary for police and crime at Dublin Castle in the wake of the Phoenix Park murders. His clandestine transfer to London led to allegations of 'illegal activities' and bruising rows within Whitehall.

Above Sir William Vernon Harcourt, who as Home Secretary in 1881–85 faced the brunt of the Irish-American terror bombing campaign aimed at Gladstone's Liberal government. He meanwhile accused Lord Salisbury of 'tampering with treason and dynamite'.

Right Earl Spencer, Lord Lieutenant (Viceroy) of Ireland 1881–85, Liberal grandee and reluctant convert to home rule, who was Edward Jenkinson's powerful patron and confidant.

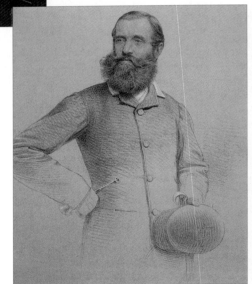

Above Charles Stewart Parnell, leader of the Irish nationalist party in the Westminster parliament through the 1880s. His tortuous balancing act between revolution-ary and constitutional routes to Irish independence served both to alienate hardliners in America and to bring the vengeful scorn of *The Times* newspaper and the Conservative government.

Above right William O'Brien, campaigning journalist and Irish nationalist MP, sent by Parnell to Chicago in 1886 after the defeat of the first home rule bill to presuade the dynamite faction in the Clan-na-Gael to hold to the bombing truce.

Right Michael Davitt, Fenian, paroled-convict, journalist and nationalist visionary. He became a Westminster MP in 1892. Politically far more radical than Parnell, he acted as the Irish party's intelligence chief during the Special Commission. His 'notes of an amateur detective' got to the heart of the Jubilee plot, but for dark political reasons in America the truth remained secret.

Left On the evening of 15 March 1883 a bomb aimed at the Home Office erupted in a street off Whitehall. The explosion was heard in the House of Commons. Irish-American terror had touched the heart of the British government.

Below On 25 February 1884 a clockwork-fused bomb erupted at Victoria station cloakroom. More bombs were found at London termini. The 'devilish scheme' propelled Edward Jenkinson's seemingly irresistible rise.

The Rising Sun, the London public house shattered by the bomb planted on the night of 30 May 1884 in a urinal beneath the nearby headquarters of Special (Irish) Branch. The landlord sold shards of glass as souvenirs.

After the Great Scotland Yard explosion, the venerable site was cleared for the new War Office. James Monro sponsored the building of a magnificent Metropolitan Police headquarters – 'New Scotland Yard' – on the north bank of the Thames.

'Dynamite Saturday': on 25 January 1885 Clan-na-Gael dynamite bombs exploded at the Tower of London and the (empty) chamber of the House of Commons.

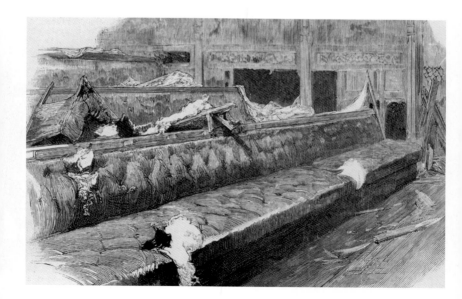

Top Logotype of the Bank of Mexico, London and South America – from the records of HM Legation at Mexico City – through which British govern-ment payments to General Millen were routed.

Above Francis Frederick Millen. This engraving from *The Sphere* magazine was sent by assistant commissioner James Monro to central America as a mugshot in pursuit of the 'head of the Jubilee dynamite gang'.

Right Francis Millen in Dublin, autumn 1865, resplendent in the uniform of a Brigadier-General in the army of the Mexican Republic.

H. B. M.'s Legation
Mexico, October 15th 1885

My Lord

I have the honour to report that I have this day sent a telegram to your Lordship in cypher to the following effect:—

"x x x starts to-night and will probably arrive in Paris about the 5th of November"

I have the honour to be

My Lord

Your Lordship's

most obedient-

humble servant

Lionel Carden

+ Her M:

-arquis of Salisbury K.G.

Foreign Office

Despatch from Her Britannic Majesty's Legation in Mexico City, 15 October 1885, to Lord Salisbury (who was both Prime Minister and Foreign Secretary) stating that 'x x x' (Millen) was about to embark on his first conspiratorial journey in British pay to Paris. Edward Jenkinson went to the French capital to meet him.

compelled to resign. A soldier, Colonel Henry Brackenbury, lately police chief for Cyprus, was plucked from his duties as military attaché at the Paris embassy to become effectively secret police chief in Ireland. After two weeks of bureaucratic tussle over his title, he was called Assistant Under-secretary for Police and Crime.

The hunt for the murderers fell to the Dublin Metropolitan Police. Superintendent John Mallon, the head of G (the Detective) Division, was quickly convinced there was no direct American connection. It looked at first like a faction fight in the Land League, the action of breakaway extremists after Parnell's perceived 'surrender' at Kilmainham. Suspicion grew that a higher London-based executive, led by a fearsome-sounding 'Number One', had inspired the murders – which through supposedly informer-proof cut-outs had recruited a well-funded assassination society, the Invincibles, as an operational arm.

Mallon pursued the Dublin investigation relentlessly. Suspects were arrested, released, then followed for months. Informers were ground down in sequence – finally, in January 1883, a builder named James Carey broke. His evidence sent five men to the gallows and eight more to long jail sentences. But what of the higher directory? The names of Frank Byrne, secretary of the Land League of Great Britain, and the prominent league organisers John Walsh, Thomas Brennan and Patrick Sheridan emerged – plus the league's treasurer, Patrick Egan, a 'rabid revolutionist', according to Superintendent Mallon. All were by now out of judicial reach in France or America.

Colonel Brackenbury went to work drafting a report recommending his intelligence operation be greatly widened from Dublin Castle – dedicated to the vigorous infiltration of secret societies in Ireland, Britain, France and America. The Government agreed to a budget of £25,000 over two years. Robert Anderson was pressed by Harcourt to represent Brackenbury's efforts in London.

Parnell's own statement of outrage at the murders (a reward for catching the killers was posted over his and Davitt's name) was greeted with derision in London – which did him no harm among extremists. American reaction was equivocal: it was a

'landlord plot to discredit Parnell', or an act of 'misguided patriotism', depending on which nationalist newspaper you read. The
Liberal government reacted as it had to with a Crimes Bill, a
renewal of the coercion legislation of the year before in tougher
guise. Parnell, while reviving obstruction in parliament to fight
it, moved in parallel to advance the political dialogue already
opened with his former jailers while he was in Kilmainham. His
go-between to Gladstone was William O'Shea's wife, Katherine.
The land war was shut down; the Ladies Land League was disbanded. In its place was set the parliamentary National League,
the beginning of a tortuous climb towards constitutional legitimacy. Turning Irish America on the same course would not prove
so easy. The bombers had not gone away.

Rossa's missioners had so far been armed with crude rag-fuse and
blasting-powder bombs. On 28 June Mr Pierrepoint Edwards,
acting consul-general in New York (Archibald was in London for
consultations on shaking up intelligence-gathering in America),
sent a report from a Pinkerton's detective who had seen devices
'of polished wood with the appearance of Swiss musical boxes;
while others are covered with silk and have a pin-cushion attached
to the top, being apparently for use on the toilet table'. They
exploded on opening. 'The alleged maker of these machines is
no doubt Patrick Crowe, of Peoria, Illinois,' the consul commented. He was evidently also responsible for the sophisticated
clockwork-fused dynamite devices found the previous summer by
Liverpool customs. Bombs might now come as postal packets
or explode on a lady's dressing table. This was an assassination
campaign.

Alarming reports arrived at the Foreign Office through the
summer: one of a plot to abduct Princess Louise on a visit to
Canada by a gang ostensibly on 'a fishing and shooting excursion';
another from Naples of two Sicilian assassins heading for New
York to receive a commission from a mysterious 'masculine-
looking woman' known as 'Sara'. The target was the Prince of
Wales, who would be shot down from the windows of a specially
hired London house with a *mitrailleuse*, a primitive machine-gun.

Colonel Brackenbury had meanwhile proved a reluctant secret policeman. While supposedly confronting incipient Irish mayhem, he was discovered trying to get himself posted to the expeditionary force embarking in pursuit of the turbulent Egyptian nationalist Arabi Pasha. There was a huge row – the colonel had behaved 'infamously', said Spencer, who huffily asked him to stand down. There was a replacement under his nose: his own private secretary, the talented Mr Jenkinson. On 4 August 1882 Jenkinson travelled to London for consultations. It was agreed he would step into the delinquent Brackenbury's shoes. He would operate from Dublin Castle, with Samuel Lee Anderson as his deputy. It was all supposed to be very secret, but an Irish MP named Frank Hugh O'Donnell found out – and asked pointedly in parliament who was this 'mutiny magistrate trained in the despotic school of Indian officialdom, furnished with all the powers of "spymaster-general" in Ireland'? Others would later have cause to ask the same question.

One of the first reports to be forwarded to the new intelligence chief revealed a Rossa plot to blow up a steamer in New York harbour laden with 500 Missouri mules destined for the British army in Egypt. A detailed description of the bomb and the fusing device was attached – a double-sleeved metal tube, with an insertion point for a timing pencil. Sulphuric acid eating through a layered paper wrapper towards a percussion cap gave a delay of around forty minutes. The mules sailed for Alexandria unmolested – but a few months later they would be followed across the Atlantic by new examples of Patrick Crowe's Illinois-made explosive ingenuity.

Glasgow and London, spring 1883

On 20 January 1883, at around 10 p.m., a large gas-holder at Glasgow Corporation's Lilybank Street gasworks exploded in a sheet of flame. An hour later a coaling shed at Buchanan Street railway station blew up. At 2 a.m. a japanned tin hat-box was found by an off-duty soldier at Possil canal bridge. It appeared to be packed with fine sawdust. It burst into flames on contact, severely burning its discoverer. The bombers slipped away south.

On the evening of 15 March another lady's hat-box was deposited in Playhouse Yard, backing on to *The Times* newspaper's offices in Printing House Square in London. At around 8 p.m. it misfired, pouring out clouds of black smoke, but there was no explosion. The explosive itself was crude, home-made lignin dynamite – sawdust soaked in liquid nitroglycerine – but the fuse was very clever, a brass tube fitted with a tap which could be turned 'like a gascock to let the acid trickle through'.

Parliament was in session that same evening. A handful of members snoozed through a debate on naval reserves; most were at dinner. As Big Ben struck nine, a growling rumble shook the House. The Home Secretary was in the Commons dining room. 'Several at the table said it was an explosion,' Harcourt told Spencer the next day. 'I rejoined I have heard so much of explosions I have long ceased to believe in them.' This one was very real – the bomb had been placed behind a ground-floor balustrade in the government offices in Charles Street. It was the officials of the Local Government Board who were inconvenienced, but the bombers' target was clear. Sir Giles Gilbert Scott's Italianate building also housed the Home Office.

The heart of British government had been touched by American-made terror. Ministers were now to be constantly guarded by armed detectives. A regular infantry battalion was readied to protect public buildings. After months of bureaucratic shuffling between Jenkinson in Dublin, Anderson at the Home Office and Vincent, head of CID at Scotland Yard, it was time for a new departure in Britain's anti-terror apparatus.

Harcourt pushed it through. On Wednesday 20 March 1883 a new 'Irish Bureau' met for the first time at Scotland Yard, superseding the semi-dormant Fenian Office. It was headed by Chief Inspector Dolly Williamson, veteran of the Clerkenwell excitements and a legend among London's criminal classes. He had a habit of prowling the metropolis in an oversize floppy hat with a large flower in his buttonhole.

The inspector was to recruit twelve detectives and report directly to the Home Secretary. The little force would soon be known as the Special (Irish) Branch. Williamson was to liaise daily with Robert Anderson at the Home Office, who was responsible for collating intelligence. The bureau was headquartered in a small, two-storeyed building vacated by the surgeon-general's department in the centre of Great Scotland Yard, a run of red-brick houses leading off Whitehall through an archway towards the Thames. Let into the ground floor was a public urinal frequented by customers of the nearby Rising Sun pub. The layout may have suited thirsty detectives, but was not ideal as the headquarters of a secret police force.

Edward Jenkinson had already arrived clandestinely in the capital three days earlier on Harcourt's summons. He drafted a memorandum with very distinct views of what should be done by a new organisation with national coverage and international reach. It should be permanent and its existence kept secret. At its head should be a 'Head of Political Crime' (himself) with the power to run agents known and responsible only to him. Anderson and Scotland Yard should be cut out of the loop. His proposals were, for now, judged a little too ambitious.

Jenkinson wrote to Earl Spencer from his extemporised office at the Admiralty: 'There seem to be great difficulties about organising a separate department – but something has been done and I hope more may follow . . . the difficulty is to get men and agents. Anderson's brother at the Home Office is a poor fellow (a second class detective Sir W. [Harcourt] calls him!) and except Williamson there is not a man in Scotland Yard worth anything . . .'

16

New York and Chicago, winter 1882–3

The Clan had made its own bloodcurdling declarations of war against England. William Mackey Lomasney had conducted his reconnaissance for a bombing offensive, but thus far it was Rossa's missioners who had been making all the noise. Alexander Sullivan, the swaggering Clan-na-Gael president with his taste for high Western boots and pearl-handed pistols, was not going to hold his hand for long.

His irresistible rise was now greased with cash supposedly subscribed to succour evicted Irish tenants. Early in 1882 he had secured his gold-seam with a secret trip to Paris to see Patrick Egan, the Land League treasurer. He demanded £20,000 and half of all future receipts from America – to finance a bombing offensive. 'Egan expressed strong sympathy about the object of the money but haggled like an Irish farmer selling a pig at a fair,' John Devoy recorded. Sullivan threatened to break off relations and that would be the end of the Land League. He got the money.

In April 1883 Sullivan was elected president of the Irish National League of America (as the American Land League renamed itself) at its convention in Philadelphia. Parnell sent a telegram of congratulations. The Chicago lawyer now had control of the campaigning open movement as well as of the secret one.

He had already resolved months before to put the Clan's fingerprints on 'business' in Britain. The instrument was a thirty-one-year-old Glasgow-born physician, as adept in mixing explosive as medicines. Dr Thomas Gallagher was an American success story. His widowed mother had led a gaggle of children off an emigrant ship. Thomas, aged fifteen, was the eldest. He had laboured to learn medicine at night while working in a foundry. He had qualified and prospered – with his gold-topped cane and long curling hair 'he might have been an actor', according to one of the detectives who shadowed him round London.

With Clan backing, Gallagher made an extended reconnaissance of London in autumn 1882 – paying the obligatory visit to survey the House of Commons. Rossa's men had got close; the doctor was sure he could get closer. He returned to New York to report to the Revolutionary Directory. A bombing team was chosen and a method of operation: explosives would not be imported from America but manufactured in Britain, in a city with a large Irish population in which the arrivals would not be noticed.

In March 1883 a Birmingham chemist notified the police of the purchase of industrial quantities of glycerine (for 'hair-dressing preparations') and nitric acid. A local detective posing as a chimney sweep found a jacket with a 'Brooks Brothers, Gentlemen's Outfitters of Broadway' label in the bomb factory – a 'paint shop' at 128 Ledsam Street in the Ladywood district. It was staked out.

On the morning of 5 April the bombers began to move. Two hundred and fifty pounds of cooked-up liquid nitroglycerine, poured into rubber 'fishing stockings', tied up like giant condoms, were taken by train to London. Birmingham detectives cabled Scotland Yard from New Street station.

The suspects were followed from Euston. One was arrested in a hotel with bags of explosives under the bed. Gallagher was traced to a boarding house in Southwark, and arrested on the morning of 6 April. The London press went into a lather of dynamite excitement. The Home Secretary glowed with satisfaction. He told Earl Spencer: 'Jenks [Jenkinson] has done splendidly – we are indebted to him for what security we possess against these fiends.'

The Gallagher trial began at the Old Bailey on 11 June. The treason-felony charge included 'unlawfully compassing, imagining and devising and intending . . . to levy war upon the Queen . . .' – something, the defence counsel argued, to great

political excitement in Ireland and America, that could only be
done by regular forces. One of the bombers, William Lynch (alias
'Norman'), turned Queen's evidence – and revealed that the mission had a mysterious fellow-traveller. It was not just a Clan affair.
It hinged on a large sum of money – £500 – found on the doctor
which, so Lynch claimed, Gallagher told him he had got 'from
the old man'.

Just who that was the doctor refused to reveal during the trial
or after. It emerged later that O'Donovan Rossa had provided Gallagher with the money. On 14 June at the Old Bailey
Gallagher and his accomplices were sentenced for treason-felony
to penal servitude for the rest of their natural lives. It was intended
that they should die in prison.

Jenkinson meanwhile had apparently confounded a conspiracy
in Ireland itself. The purchase in Cork of quantities of chloride
of potash and powdered sugar, ingredients for incendiary Fenian
fire in compound, had been picked up by local detectives. The
target was Liverpool. The courier, with an apparent link to Rossa,
was arrested in transit and the Cork bomb factory raided. The
suspects were shipped for trial to Liverpool – where the jury might
be more biddable. In August five men were sentenced to life
imprisonment.

Edward Jenkinson was winning. His proposals for a national
counter-terror agency accountable only to the Home Secretary
were being smiled upon. Throughout the summer he had been
in and out of London throwing his weight about. At Harcourt's
suggestion Jenkinson was given a new deputy, Major Nicholas
Gosselin, late Royal Irish Fusiliers and a resident magistrate,*
who would act as his eyes and ears in Britain.

'The Gosling', as Harcourt insisted on calling him, was sent
north to sniff round Glasgow and Newcastle. He would have a
deputy – a Major Blair, described by Spencer as a 'rough sort of
man' – while a confidential clerk was appointed to coordinate
activities from the Home Office. The money came from Irish

* RM – a unique Irish post created in 1822 – permanent law officers resident in
'disturbed areas' reporting directly to the Chief Secretary.

government funds. Jenkinson took a country house, Stocks,* twenty miles north of London. Two bodyguards patrolled the grounds. A parallel political police operation was emerging beyond parliamentary oversight.

Under the new arrangements Chief Inspector Williamson was taken out of all Scotland Yard control to report to Gosselin directly. Anderson was sidelined. He still held a bargaining chip – his shadowy source in the Clan. But Jenkinson was after him, pouncing on a request for a pay-rise that arrived in Whitehall from agent 'Thomas' in Chicago. 'Where is he living now and to what place does he propose to move and what advantage is there in his moving?' he demanded of his colleague. Thomas Beach later claimed in his memoirs that Jenkinson sent a detective to Illinois in an unsuccessful bid to identify him.

There was a new intelligence broom in New York meanwhile. On 1 January 1883 the recently knighted Sir Edward Archibald at last retired. His replacement was a career diplomat named William Robert Hoare. Edward Jenkinson already had his own conspiratorial line open to America. His instrument was a noisy apostle of Rossa's schism from the Clan called James 'Red Jim' McDermott. With his crimson cheeks, ginger moustache and seal-skin waistcoat he looked like a yellow-press cartoon. He had been John O'Mahony's private secretary at the Moffat Mansion, when Frank Millen was military secretary of the Fenian Brotherhood, and seemed well-mannered and plausible enough – except when drunk.

Unlike Anderson, who sat in the Home Office blandly re-cycling his agent's transatlantic flow of Clan circulars, Jenkinson was determined to take his asset onto the offensive. The spymaster-general was already making scant distinction between counter-intelligence and conspiracies that were all his own.

* Later a girls' school, famous in the late 1960s as the home of a party-loving American glamour-magazine publisher.

17

Dublin, February 1883

Michael Davitt was serving another six months in Richmond Bridewell, re-arrested for incitement under the Coercion Act. He was surprised in late February 1883 to be passed a card by the chief warder from a visitor requesting an interview. It was engraved JAMES McDERMOTT, NY, CORRESPONDENT OF THE *BROOKLYN DAILY ARGUS*. Reluctantly Davitt agreed.

The carrot-haired visitor made provocative remarks about the Phoenix Park murders and confided that 'he was on a visit to the boys'. He was observed heading back to Dublin Castle – to 'interview' the normally publicity-shy Edward Jenkinson on behalf of the American press. A few days later Red Jim went on a Dublin pub-crawl and was arrested after a punch-up with a cab-driver. As he snored in the cells of College Street police station, a gossipy desk sergeant showed papers found on him to an inquisitive journalist – a sheaf of letters of introduction from O'Donovan Rossa to sympathisers in Ireland. The journalist copied them and passed them to Davitt. McDermott was released without charge and promptly headed for London.

Davitt sensed acute danger. An American bomber in British pay could blast the constitutional movement to pieces at will. Six years later during the Special Commission, fearful that McDermott would be sprung as a hired-gun witness for *The Times*, Davitt pieced together how Red Jim had been recruited.

In his campaigning newspaper the *Labour World* Davitt claimed the information came from an 'ex-member of the secret service engaged with McDermott in New York and London' whom he declined to name. The anonymous double-agent was in fact a law graduate of Trinity College, Dublin, named Matthew O'Brien. He had failed as a solicitor and been a policeman in Australia before turning up in New York around October 1882 pursuing a 'romantic marriage against the wishes of his wife's relatives'.

According to Davitt's exposé, sometime in October 1882 O'Brien happened to be in Rossa's favourite New York watering hole, J. P. Ryan's Liquor Saloon at 8–10 Chambers Street, when 'he overheard two men plotting to kill Earl Spencer'.* One of them had a bristling ginger moustache. He followed them a short way to Number 12, where there was a door plaque: THE UNITED IRISHMAN, ORGAN OF THE MEN OF ACTION, EDITED BY JEREMIAH O'DONOVAN ROSSA.

O'Brien promptly took the well-beaten path to HM consulate – where Sir Edward Archibald, with a few weeks to go before a keenly sought retirement, thought his proposal workable enough. Matt O'Brien would recruit James McDermott as a spy within the Rossa camp. Red Jim, indeed, was an old friend of the consul – he had been peddling him secrets for years. He had given warning of John O'Mahony's Campo Bello expedition of 1867. Why not employ him again if he still had some credibility left as a 'missioner'? Money was needed – a down payment to prove solidarity in the cause of wrecking London from end to end.

The deal was struck. Telegrams went to Dublin Castle for approval. McDermott and O'Brien presented themselves to Rossa as ready for work. Sir Edward provided Irish government-sanctioned funds to buy Rossa's confidence: a down payment of £100 – £500 more to follow. Davitt's accusation was clear – Edward Jenkinson was bankrolling the very operations he was supposed to be terminating.

The details that Matthew O'Brien supplied Davitt of Red Jim's conspiratorial odyssey became very precise. In late January 1883 McDermott had sailed from New York to Liverpool, travelling as 'Peter Quigley'. He put up at the Birkenhead Railway Hotel

* Jenkinson messaged Dublin Castle on 27 December: 'I have had a cypher telegram today from my New York agent, who is not at all an alarmist, to the effect that Lord Spencer is to be attacked. Air guns to be among future weapons . . .'

to await the arrival of his shadowy paymaster, a 'Mr George Jones'. It was Edward George Jenkinson. They seemed to have got on splendidly. Red Jim then headed for London to confer with his co-conspirator from Chambers Street, who had also crossed the Atlantic. Someone was supplying plenty of cash.

Edward Jenkinson's career-advancing coup of 28–30 March against the Cork–Liverpool bombers had ostensibly begun with a local police operation: they had been informed of the purchase of incendiary ingredients from a Cork chemist on Easter Monday 1883. Davitt's exposé told a very different story. It was entrapment. From London, James McDermott had gone to Dublin to make his bizarre visit to Davitt in prison, conduct his 'interview' with Jenkinson at the castle for the *Brooklyn Argus* – and spend his brief night in police cells. Red Jim had then headed south-west for Cork to seek out potential bombers and ensnare them with the New York consul's cash – leaving a trail of cooked-up evidence. It fooled them at the time but might not again.

In mid May McDermott promptly disappeared to Paris.

Paris, May 1883

Irish revolutionary politics in the French capital had atrophied since the dramatic days of January 1879, when Michael Davitt and John Devoy had met the supreme council of the Irish Revolutionary Brotherhood to hammer out the 'new departure'. Charles Kickham was dead, James Stephens a burned-out case. Patrick Egan tended the Land League money-box at Monroe's bank in the rue Scribe; Aleck Sullivan, the Clan-na-Gael president, was now greedily dipping into it.

Three Irish exiles in Paris, however, were making lots of revolutionary noise – they were Joseph Casey (who sixteen years earlier had grappled with Inspector Thomson during the arrest of Ricard Burke in Woburn Square), his younger brother Patrick (one of the bombers at the Clerkenwell house of detention) and a would-be poet called Eugene Davis. The Casey brothers worked as newspaper compositors; Davis was Paris correspondent for Rossa's *United Irishman*.

Red Jim arrived to seek out the notoriously militant Casey brothers. They seemed to believe his revolutionary credentials.

There was a curious development: the Hon. Francis Plunkett, second secretary at the British embassy, received an approach from a Paris resident, an 'American General', with an offer to supply information. News of the overture was forwarded to London and passed to Jenkinson for comment. He was 'very amused', the spymaster told the Home Secretary on 31 May. He had 'heard all about the distinguished American General and his interview with the three Fenians before . . . he little knows that I know his name and have been told of all that passed at the interview.' He even knew the address of the potential informer's mistress – '61 Avenue Friedland'. Red Jim McDermott had clearly told him all about the source of the offer. It came from that old friend of the Foreign Office, General Charles Carrol-Tevis.

Red Jim arrived back in New York on 6 June. Rossa greeted him with suspicion. McDermott claimed that one of the Corkmen who had escaped indictment for the Liverpool trial was the informer. For now he seems to have been believed. Two days later William Hoare, the new British acting consul, learned in a telegram from Jenkinson that two men were on their way from Cork to kill McDermott. Red Jim was smartly dispatched across the Canadian border.

A cable later reached Davitt, now released from prison, from the editor of the *Montreal Evening Post*. 'One James McDermott of Brooklyn' was in the city, it stated, 'trying to organise dynamite clubs'. The loud-mouthed visitor had made free use of the nationalist's name in support of a transparently bogus plot to blow up public buildings. Davitt cabled back: McDermott was the 'organiser of bogus dynamite conspiracies in Cork, Liverpool and London'. McDermott put out feelers by letter to Rossa, who assured him that the allegations were not believed – they were British Secret Service mischief-making; why not get the train south?

J. P. Ryan's Liquor Saloon, 8–10 Chambers Street, New York, 21 July 1883

It was a sweet set-up for an assassination. Red Jim was well into a boozy lunch with Rossa when, at around 2.30, two men strode diffidently into Ryan's bar. One ordered a drink. He turned, pulled out a seven-shot Bulldog revolver and fired a single bullet at a red-faced diner from short range: he missed. The assailants ran out – one escaped on a Third Avenue trolley-car, the second was caught by a patrolman.

A 'calling card' was found outside the bar – obviously intended to be left on the slain Red Jim's sealskin waistcoat: 'This is the body of James McDermott the English spy who left New York for Ireland last January in the pay of the British Government . . . who now dies at the hands of an Irish avenger who has followed him 3,000 miles.' It was signed 'Captain Daylight'.

The man running down Pearl Street arrested by Patrolman Adamson was identified as a twenty-three-year-old named James Geaney; he gave no evidence at his court appearance two days later – nor would anyone else. The barman had 'seen nothing'. The case was dismissed. The New York press meanwhile published lurid accounts of Red Jim's apparent career as the universal informer, including an intimation that he had visited Lynch (alias Norman) of the Gallagher team in Millbank prison – and that he had made the inducement to turn Queen's evidence.

Edward Jenkinson was in near panic. He told Earl Spencer: 'Jim McDermott was safe in Montreal and was enticed over to New York by Pat Joyce, O'Donovan Rossa's secretary, who worked upon his credulity and led him to believe he was no longer suspected . . . when they got him to New York they tried to shoot him. I have the correspondence in my hands.' He formed a wild plan to save his agent's revolutionary credibility: get him to England and stage a show trial. On 25 July, with a ticket paid for by Consul Hoare, McDermott boarded the Liverpool-bound SS *City of Montreal* under his old alias, Peter Quigley. Gold spectacles provided a pantomime disguise.

While Red Jim was in mid Atlantic, James Carey, the Phoenix

Park informer, was shot dead by a veteran of the 1867 rising named Patrick O'Donnell aboard a steamer supposedly bearing him to safety in South Africa. It began with a chance encounter at a poker game – but the warning was soon given to informers: 'Remember Carey.'*

The steamer bearing Red Jim docked a week later. Head Constable Ryan of the RIC went aboard and arrested 'Mr Quigley'. He was confined in Walton jail. Jenkinson explained to Spencer on 7 August: 'I have had James McDermott arrested . . . on a charge of conspiracy. It is the best way of dealing with him – and it *may* remove suspicions from him for there are many still who do not believe that he was an informer . . .'

He was put up at the Liverpool police court on a charge of conspiracy to murder. Whiskery 'Fenian' evidence was found on him – including the Paris address of 'Head Centre James Stephens'. The prosecuting magistrate became suspicious; the local press asked uncomfortable questions. The phoney trial plan had to be dropped. On 17 September Red Jim was released without trial, spirited out of Walton jail in the middle of the night dressed as a coal porter. Gosselin, under the alias 'Mr Nicholson', escorted him across the German Ocean to Hamburg. But his strange career was by no means over.

* O'Donnell was brought to England, tried and executed for murder on 17 December 1883. Jenkinson thereafter took pains to send other informers by a circuitous route via the Middle East to Australia.

18

Guatemala City, Central America, summer 1883

New York had become increasingly uncomfortable for Frank Millen. There had been a row with John Devoy, who had raised prickly questions on the general's origins. He was 'an adventurer', the stern nationalist alleged in his shortlived newspaper the *Irish Nation* – that was undeniable. But much more damaging to his revolutionary credentials, Millen had once been 'a sergeant in the British Army'. The veteran Fenian John O'Leary wrote in response from Paris: 'I have never seen anything in General Millen, or heard anything about him, which was in any way incompatible with the belief that he is an honourable and brave man and a good Irishman.'

In March 1883 the good Irishman's whereabouts were indicated to the Foreign Office by Sir St John Spenser, the British envoy extraordinary to Central America. Millen was in Guatemala – the tiny central American republic in a constant state of border conflict with its neighbours. One of them was the obscure British colony of Belize.

Millen had turned up in the dusty Palacio Nacional in Guatemala City six months earlier and offered his services to President Justo Rufino Barrios. The dictator was an old friend – as young men they had fought together in the bloody war of 1863 against hated El Salvador. The ambitions of the turbulent 'El Reformador' were unbounded: he sought now to conjoin a 'United States of Central America' – through conquest if necessary – with himself as a kind of jungle Bismarck. It was not a scheme smiled upon by HM Foreign Office or the US State Department. Millen offered to reform the republic's army – he would place flattering articles in American newspapers, he would promote immigration schemes. He had influential friends in New York . . . and London.

A few months later more news arrived in Whitehall. Millen had struck a deal to furnish 10,000 Irish immigrants to start a new life amongst the Mayan ruins. Sir St John Spenser sent details to the Foreign Office – it was 'one of the many expedients resorted to by this bankrupt government', he reported. 'A colony of Italians' had been similarly seduced and left stranded, starving, in the jungle. A terse reply was sent on 6 September: 'General Millen's antecedents are not such as would induce the Irish Government to entertain any scheme promoted by him, even if it had in it elements of promise . . .'

The curious Guatemala correspondence crossed Edward Jenkinson's desk. It followed a similar report in May from Mexico City that 'The head of the Irish assassination committee, known as "No. 1" [head of the Phoenix Park 'Invincibles']', was there. There was no extradition treaty – the huge country was a haven for all sorts of exotic fugitives. The spymaster began to take an interest in the Mexican republic. It would eventually take him on a very strange personal odyssey.

New York and Chicago, September 1883

The Clan-na-Gael was about to experience its own Central American-style pronunciamento. The failure of the Gallagher mission was the excuse. At their parallel meeting on the occasion of the Irish National League convention in April the Clan had resolved under Aleck Sullivan's urging to slash the number of delegates to future conventions – to 'keep out spies'. A new secrecy oath was to be sworn; informers were to be summarily dealt with. Thomas Beach took a train with Sullivan from Chicago to Milwaukee; on the way the ruthless new style of operating was outlined. Bombers would be sent in the utmost secrecy to London without reference to the 'home organisation'. The IRB had shown a 'lack of courage', the lawyer said. There would be no more attempts to cook up explosives in England.

In September Sullivan staged a further bid for power. Amidst self-serving paranoia about informers, the executive body was reduced from seven to three. It adopted a triangle as its cabbalistic seal – with Sullivan at the apex.

Jenkinson had told Spencer in June 1883: 'The [Clan] leaders now think the idea of legitimate (by which is meant open) warfare must be abandoned *and* other resources adopted . . . This is the danger we now have to meet. I know for certain they have commenced operations in England again and am watching them – but this you must keep very secret.' He was well-informed. The Clan had indeed resolved to go on the offensive but there would be no more muffed missions to topple Big Ben. The target would be the ordinary people of London and William Mackey Lomasney the instrument.

London, 30 October 1883

On the evening of 30 October, at around 7.50 p.m., a bomb erupted on a Metropolitan Railway train pulling out of Praed Street (now Paddington) Station. The cramped third-class carriages at the back of the train were full – seventy-two passengers were seriously injured. Eleven minutes later an explosion rumbled out of the eastern mouth of the tunnel at Westminster Bridge Station, engulfing the last two coaches of a District Railway train. No one was hurt.

The Home Secretary and his wife Lady Lily Harcourt visited the injured in St Mary's hospital. The tunnels were combed for evidence; rewards were offered but no one was caught. Jenkinson wrote animatedly to Earl Spencer: 'I gave Harcourt warning in the spring they meant to attack the Underground railway.' But how to bring the bombers to retribution? 'It is impossible to get legal *proof* before. We can get information – but not evidence,' he added with a secret policeman's eternal frustration. 'It is clear to me that we will have to treat these scoundrels before long in a much more summary way.'

Edward Jenkinson was about to demonstrate what he meant.

Birmingham Concert Hall, 20 December 1883

It was a curious assignment for a detective – sitting uncomfortably in the circle of a music hall watching a performer get the bird.

'D. O'Brien, the Famous Irish Story Teller' was a very bad act indeed – a couple of croaky songs, then a sentimental monologue about the evils of the Irish land tenure system. There was whistling and booing. After twenty-five minutes of this torture Detective Inspector James Black of the Birmingham police thought it 'very dry'. The performer was an Irish-American who had been followed from the moment he got off the boat from New York in early October 1883.

Jenkinson thought this turn was dynamite. He had information that the artiste was on 'business' in England for the Clan. He wrote urgently to Earl Spencer on 17 October: '. . . there is something big afoot. The man we were watching at Birmingham told our informant that, if he failed this time, the organisation was dead for at least ten years.'

The monologue artiste was a Limerick-born member of the Clan-na-Gael called John Daly. The music-hall appearance was for 'one night only' – a bizarre diversion from the business in hand: he had been sent across the Atlantic by Aleck Sullivan to blow up the English parliament. Mr Daly lived quietly enough, lodging with a man named James Egan and his wife.

The informant was a Liverpool Irishman called Daniel ('Big Dan') O'Neill, who had been recruited by the busy Major Gosselin. Jenkinson's biggest worry was the usual one – would the local police move in too soon and arrest just one man? Would there be enough evidence for a conviction?

The Birmingham police were ordered to watch and wait.

London, spring 1884

Jenkinson's Whitehall advance tracked Aleck Sullivan's rise measure for measure. Spy paranoia had placed the Chicago lawyer at the apex of the 'triangle'; dynamite hysteria had caused the spymaster to 'blossom into the most important individual at the

Home Office', according to Detective Sergeant McIntyre. 'Jenks'
was spreading his wings as he shuttled to and fro across the Irish
Sea, sending pompous memoranda to the Foreign Office on how
things could be conducted better in the United States. But even
the talented Mr Jenkinson could not stage manage everything.
In early 1884, unheralded this time, American bombers put their
mark on London again. On 12 January dynamite was found in the
Primrose Hill railway tunnel of the London and North-western
Railway. Late on the evening of 26 February a handbag exploded
in the left-luggage cloakroom at Victoria Station. Perhaps the
target was symbolic. The Queen immediately sent the Home
Secretary a telegram of concern.

Searches of the London termini found explosive-packed handbags at Charing Cross, Paddington and Ludgate Hill. The detonating device was an American-made alarm clock, mechanically
linked to a small-calibre pistol. One 'Peep o'Day' clock had
stopped; two had tripped but failed to trigger the small-calibre
cartridges aimed so as to detonate the slab charges of Atlas Powder
A dynamite found in the bags under newspapers and clothing.*
One contained a coat, apparently ripped in half, with 'unusual
quartz buttons'.

A reward offer of £1,000 for information was circulated on
handbills throughout London. It was suspected that the clockwork bombs had been infiltrated from France, or so the press
were informed.

Consul Clipperton sent a blood-curdling report from Philadelphia on 3 March. An informant reported a conversation with a
Rossa partisan in New York named McNamara: 'We have several
plans on hand to get an Infernal Machine into the Houses of
Parliament, machines in all shapes and forms, some as books
which explode when opened, others as handbags,' he said. 'An
attempt was to be made on all the bridges of London at one and
the same time.'

---

* On 4 March Consul Clipperton was sent to interview the director of the
Repaunos Chemical Company of 305 Walnut Street, Philadelphia, Mr Lammot
Du Pont – who promised every assistance. His product was being used extensively
in blasting out rock foundations in Manhattan, he explained – from where it

Paris was not the springboard for the Victoria Station bomb, so the Philadelphia source intimated – it was Antwerp, where the 'men sent over could be met with at the brothels known as the "Rag" and chiefly at the "Grotto"'.

Two more men were on their way to Europe, according to the report. Their aim was to 'explode a little dynamite near to Her, not to harm Her but to get the whole detective force to watch Her, then to make our flank movement in London', the mysterious Mr McNamara threatened. 'We have the support of Parnell and every one of his followers are in our favour but they cannot come out openly . . .'

Room 56, The Home Office, Whitehall, London SW, 7 March 1884

Edward Jenkinson's apotheosis was drawing near. The threat to the Queen herself was apparent. The Home Secretary implored Earl Spencer to let his Dublin Castle spymaster operate full-time from Whitehall. 'We must bury this horrible business with one hand and under one mind which will be able to gather together the information from all quarters and draw on all resources whether in Ireland or England,' he said. Jenkinson drafted his own job description: 'Great Britain and Ireland must be treated as one,' he wrote on 6 March. 'The officer who holds the threads of what is going on in Ireland must also have access to all information obtained in England or coming to England from abroad.'

He wanted a 'recognized official position in the Home Office' and insurance against 'a break in the chain of the work which would almost certainly take place on a change of Ministry'. This was a shrewder request than he could yet know.

'All information and all dispatches from the Foreign or other offices relating to Fenian organizations, or the operations or movements of dynamiters would be sent direct to me,' he insisted, 'and it would be my duty after issuing orders in matters of urgency

---

might be easily stolen. Mr Du Pont was himself killed in an accidental explosion shortly thereafter.

or of ordinary detail to lay them before the Secretary of State . . .'
He should further spend Secret Service money 'according to my
own discretion and judgement . . .'

Not bad for a former obscure divisional commissioner for
Oudh. He was asking for powers to act and to finance operations
beyond political oversight. Ministers would be consulted *afterwards*. The Home Secretary had no choice: that night he agreed
– but there would be no 'official position'. Jenkinson's memorandum was put on file but not countersigned. Parliament was
not yet ready to debate the appointment of a secret policeman
accountable only to himself.

The next day, 7 March 1884, the spymaster departed Dublin
'on leave of absence'. He was set up on the first floor of the
Home Office in London, with direct access to the Secretary of
State and a telephone line to Dolly Williamson at Scotland Yard.
How could they fail with such modern marvels? Harcourt formally
introduced the new intelligence chief to police officials – they
were to 'do his bidding'. There were nods and grunts of welcoming approval – the new arrival, amateur detective though he might
be, certainly seemed to get results.

It would have all been most agreeable apart from the American
dynamiters. Jenkinson's wife and mother were settled at Stocks;
his boys were down for Sandhurst and Dartmouth. He looked
through the window of Room 56, observing the great and the
good, milling from their carriages into Palace Yard – without his
attentions they might be atomised at any moment. Mr Strickland,
his confidential secretary, brought him the latest Foreign Office
telegrams.

There was more news from Philadelphia. Consul Clipperton
reported an informer's conversation with O'Donovan Rossa: after
the London station attacks 'the English people might rise against
the Irish people residing in England if they continued such
operations'.

Rossa had replied: 'That is exactly what we desire . . .'

Birkenhead, Merseyside, April 1884

After four months of constant shadowing, on the evening of Tuesday 8 April, John Daly somehow slipped his Birmingham police minders. Early the next morning he was spotted at Wolver-hampton station by a railway detective, who observed him buying a ticket for Birkenhead. Daly took the ferry to Liverpool and shook off his pursuer. Gosselin was informed.

Two days later Daly reappeared at Birkenhead station. Gosselin was waiting with a plain-clothes posse. The suspect was collared with his overcoat bulging. Three parcels, each containing several small brass cylinders charged with high-concentrate nitroglycerine dynamite, were revealed. A fourth package contained clever sul-phuric acid-filled glass detonators with free-moving lead weights inside. The bombs were clearly designed to be thrown like a grenade – the weights would break the glass tube on impact.* The story soon emerged from the Birmingham police that Daly planned to hurl the grenades from the Strangers' Gallery into the Chamber of the House of Commons.

James Egan, with whom Daly was staying, was arrested when a bottle of nitroglycerine and seditious pamphlets were found buried in his garden. The two men were tried at Warwick Assizes in early August 1884. No evidence was given as to how or from

---

* In October 1883 Consul Clipperton had sent a report from a New York source reporting a conversation with John Devoy, who said: 'They had the most perfect hand grenades ever used and which would play an important part in the near future. He described them as being made of type-metal and charged with nitro-glycerine and certain to explode "even should they fall on a feather bed".'

whom Daly obtained the explosives at Birkenhead. Daly received life, Egan twenty years.

Daly said in his defence: 'Gentlemen, I am no assassin. There is a mystery. God give me fortitude to preserve that mystery.'

There was indeed a mystery. Why were plain-clothes police waiting the moment the suspect walked into a railway ticket office encumbered with parcels of dynamite grenades? A sequence of Jenkinson letters to Earl Spencer preserved in the Althorp papers solves it.

'Daly is still in Birmingham expecting some small bombs from America which we have news of and are on the look out for,' he wrote on 3 April.

'Yesterday I heard of the arrest of Daly by telegraph "with the things on him",' he wrote nine days later.

> These things are three hand bombs which came over about three days ago in the *City of Chester*. They were brought over by a fireman who managed to elude the vigilance of the customs. Our difficulty was to get the things passed to Daly and then to arrest him with the things on him, without throwing suspicion on our own informant.
>
> Two plans missed fire – Daly was too suspicious – but the third plan succeeded . . . the bombs are of first-rate workmanship and were made in America. Daly intended to go up to London and throw one of these three bombs into a nest of Cabinet ministers . . . from the gallery of the House of Commons. He was quite prepared to sacrifice his own life.
>
> All that Sir Wm Harcourt knows is that Daly was being closely watched . . . he was arrested and the things found on him . . . I hope Your Excellency will not give any of these details . . .

He added a postscript: 'London. 4 p.m. Daly's arrest. Nothing could have worked out better . . . our own informant is not suspected . . . I have been looking at the bombs with Col Majendie – they are terrible but of most excellent workmanship, brass and turned . . .'

Jenkinson 'had news of' the grenades as they left New York: he knew about the fireman courier. He admitted plainly to his patron that three times the packages were 'passed' to Daly in the period he was conveniently lost in Liverpool. Results were what mattered. The Home Secretary should not be troubled with the details of how they were achieved.

The bombs were removed to Woolwich Arsenal. In an explosive *coup de théâtre* Sir William Harcourt arranged for a stage to be set up in one of the sheds, roughly simulating the Cabinet Room at Number 10 Downing Street. A single four-inch-high gleaming brass grenade was placed on a wooden table surrounded by twelve dressmaker's mannequins set on chairs. A bombardier nervously shook the device to break the acid-phial fuse. It hissed and smoked angrily – then erupted.

The cabinet of dummies was slashed to pieces. Lewis Harcourt, the Home Secretary's son, recorded in his diary for 27 April: 'The bomb only had a drop of 2 ft. but there were wounds in every figure, the smallest number being 17 and the largest 49!'

Room 56, The Home Office, April–May 1884

The American end needed attention. Red Jim was blown, now living it up on the continent. Matthew O'Brien, after a curious interlude running an entrapment operation at the New York Post Office with a Scotland Yard detective named Jarvis (they would write enticing letters from a poste restante – then note who came to collect them), had also been rumbled. Jenkinson sent O'Brien to South Africa to save his skin.

Jenkinson's confiding letters to Earl Spencer give tantalising glimpses of his developing game, way out of sight of Scotland Yard, of black operations in New York. On 3 April he indicated he had 'a little game going on in America with P. J. Sheridan [one of the alleged Phoenix Park conspirators] . . . any false step here might spoil it.'

'I am very hopeful about the Victoria explosion case,' he added. 'One man has been told specially to work the clues without any

restrictions in England and another goes over on Saturday to
America to work the case with Pinkerton's – this is very secret
. . . I am rather afraid of Howard Vincent to whom Mr Williamson
tells too much . . .'

Everything was to be cloaked in the deepest secrecy. He was
'afraid' of the Metropolitan Police commissioner – but uncon-
cerned enough to reveal his developing political sympathies to
his patron. 'Hand in hand' with fighting dynamiters 'should go
the work of removing the causes of Irish disaffection', he said in
a letter that spring; 'it is only the hope that it will be done that
reconciles me to the work . . . for you know I am a Home Ruler
at heart . . .'

Edward Jenkinson's tenure of Room 56 would all have been
quite splendid if there were not already in the capital an entirely
constitutional anti-terror apparatus – the Special (Irish) Branch.
Bruising rows had already started. A speculative story appeared
in the *Standard* on 11 April naming Jenkinson as head of some
undeclared new national detective force. He was furious at the
leak: 'It was all due to the blathering of the Scotland Yard people.
They cannot hold their tongues,' he raged.

But Robert Anderson remained the target of Jenkinson's
special scorn. The spymaster had been trying to get rid of him
for months, first scheming and failing to take control of agent
'Thomas', then chipping away at his rival's salary, paid from the
budget he now controlled. On 9 May Anderson was at last formally 'relieved of all duties relative to Fenianism in London'.
He lingered in bureaucratic twilight as secretary to the prison
commissioners.

The following month the volatile spymaster might have been
allowed some perverse pleasure in the Clan's latest choice of
target.

Detectives' Office, Special (Irish) Branch, Scotland Yard,
London SW, 30 May 1884

Detective Sergeant John Sweeney had had a long fruitless day
shadowing a London-Irish suspect. At around 9.05 p.m. on the
evening of 30 May he finished his report and put it in Dolly
Williamson's in-basket at the detectives' office, uncomfortably
housed in the old surgeon-general's office in Scotland Yard.

He locked up and headed for home, grunting goodnight to the
constable at his guard post outside. A few minutes later explosions
rumbled round central London. Bombs erupted outside the
Junior Carlton Club and a politician's house (the wrong target),
both in St James's Square. No one was killed. But most injurious
to the pride of the forces of order was the clockwork-fused bomb
left in the public urinal beneath their very own stronghold.

The device detonated at 9.20 p.m., hurling the toilet's guard-
ian, PC 417 Clark, thirty feet through the air. The Rising Sun,
a glittering gin-palace across the way, became a chandelier of
mirror-glass splinters. One bomb which failed to go off was found
the next morning placed next to a Landseer lion in Trafalgar
Square.

Jenkinson told Spencer with ill-suppressed glee: 'You cannot
imagine what confusion there was at Scotland Yard. There is not
a man there with a head on his shoulders . . .'

Sir Howard Vincent had had enough. He had been trying to
resign as head of the CID for over a year. Harcourt would not
let him go. The urinal-bomb fiasco propelled him in early June
out of Scotland Yard into a new career as a Tory member of
parliament. Who might replace him? Edward Jenkinson was far
too grand. A candidate emerged – an obscure colonial administrator on leave from Bengal, where, so the Home Secretary informed
the Queen, much of his work as inspector-general of police was
'to deal with secret societies'. He had shown great zeal in pursuing
the Wahabi conspiracy. The Irish should be no more vexatious to
handle than Muhammadan fanatics. His name was James Monro.

The dour, sun-burnished Scot settled into his new offices in
Whitehall Place. He would, it was to be hoped, cooperate affably

with Mr Jenkinson on the 'Irish work'. He sized up the Harrow- and Haileybury-educated secret policeman, like him a former Indian administrator. Jenkinson, tight-laced, slightly hysterical, fawning on his political masters, seemed better attuned to the jungles of Whitehall than to those of Oudh. For now at least the policeman kept his opinions to himself. Jenkinson gave Spencer his view. The new arrival, he said, showed 'little energy or originality . . .' It was not the start of a beautiful friendship.

PART FIVE

Spymaster-General

'Hitherto I have regarded [detective work] as
of all dirty, sneaking and ungentlemanly trades
– the meanest and lowest . . .'
Robert Louis Stevenson, *The Dynamiter*, 1885

Whitehall, June 1884

Among those very few in London who knew of his official existence, it might have been said that Edward Jenkinson's behaviour
was becoming distinctly peculiar. By the summer of 1884 he
had begun to affect a wig and false beard to make sudden noc-
turnal tours around the metropolis and furtive descents on the
continent. After his climb into the secretive clouds of Room 56,
armed with his (as yet unsigned) executive memorandum, not
even the Home Secretary had full sight of the spymaster-general's
actions. That was the bargain struck after the Scotland Yard
bomb.

James Monro plodded through the scant files that he was
allowed to see. Most had been lost in the detectives' office
explosion, he was loftily informed. Sir Edmund Henderson, the
ageing, ineffectual commissioner of the Metropolitan Police, gave
him little support. He had not the faintest idea what his shadowy
colleague was doing – although he would make every effort to
find out. Before long the bumbling sleuths of Scotland Yard
would be dispatched round the world – to chase not Fenians, but
Jenkinson.

The spymaster's growing circus of personally recruited agents
had embarked in the summer of 1884 on some very curious
intelligence operations. In the first week of July an 'attractive
widow' turned up at the Gresham Hotel, Dublin, under the name
'Mrs Tyler'. She expressed 'extreme revolutionary views' while
entertaining in her sitting room, over plentiful champagne, 'conspirator after conspirator of the standing corps of Dublin's
practical jokers', in Michael Davitt's words. The fragrant visitor

was especially eager to know more about Mr Parnell's views on dynamite. He was a secret sympathiser surely. The 'Lady Dynamiter' was rumbled. Reconstituted scraps of a Home Office telegram retrieved from her fireplace were sent to Sir George Trevelyan, Chief Secretary for Ireland since the murder of Sir Frederick Cavendish in 1882, with the accusation 'that the Government were employing *agents provocateurs* to promote crime'. Mrs Tyler promptly vanished from Dublin. Questions were raised in Parliament. She was a Jenkinson spook.*

Sir Robert Hamilton, permanent under-secretary at Dublin Castle, was furious. 'I hoped that when Jenkinson had gone to England that we were safe from some scandal of this sort, of which I lived in daily dread when he was here,' he told Earl Spencer. 'Jenkinson is dangerous.'

Shamrock Bar, rue Duras, Paris, July 1884

A Jenkinson operation run out of Paris in summer 1884 was even stranger. The spymaster had recruited a Captain Darnley Stewart Stephens, late police chief for Lagos (where he was said to have hung a miscreant Ashanti with his own hands), into his little band of Room 56 irregulars. The captain arrived in the French capital in mid March, bearing a letter of introduction to Patrick Casey from a Nationalist Irish MP. 'This gentleman was supposed to enlist the sympathies of Frenchmen in the Congo question,' reported a journalist who pursued the affair.

Captain Stephens explained this was a cover – he was a secret bearer of the revolutionary flame. Casey, who had been inveigled into a phoney dynamite plot by Jim McDermott the previous summer, went along. As they mooched about the exile watering-holes – the Shamrock on the rue Duras and Reynolds' Irish-American Bar on the rue Royale – wild plots to attack the Palace of Westminster and Windsor Castle were confected by Casey,

---

* The identity of Mrs Tyler remains impenetrable. She was described in one account as the 'wife of a high official of Scotland Yard'. The 'attractive widow', however, seems not to have been Mrs Martha Thomson.

Eugene Davis and the confiding Captain Stephens – details of which soon found their way to the news editors of London papers and their indignant leader-writers. Jenkinson appeared anxious to fan the dynamite excitement, writing excited memos to Earl Spencer about 'a scare on a grand scale' being cooked-up in Paris. He seemed to be confecting it himself.

There were more mysterious arrivals in the French capital. A certain John P. Hayes of Philadelphia (Consul Clipperton's well-sourced informer) and a woman claiming to be the 'illegitimate daughter of Prince Albert' ('one of Mr Jenkinson's corps of female detectives – aged about forty – not good looking' in Davitt's description) joined the Casey–Stephens drinking firm to boozily proclaim dynamite vengeance. Brooding in a corner of the Shamrock Bar, Inspector Maurice Moser, dispatched in parallel by Monro, observed the farcical Jenkinson-inspired proceedings with disgust. He reported the true state of affairs to his chief.

The captain proposed a scheme to rescue his reputation as a man of action. According to Michael Davitt, who uncovered the story during his counter-investigations for the Special Commission, Stephens and Casey went to London, ostensibly to ensnare Irish members in a scheme to break John Daly out of jail. At Dover station the captain deposited an old pot with a 'fuse' attached on the railway line – proclaimed by the local papers when it was discovered the next day to be evidence of a 'diabolical plot'.

At the House of Commons no Nationalist member could be found to express interest in a crackpot scheme to break John Daly out of Winson Green prison – certainly not Mr Parnell. They retired to a pub near Scotland Yard and Casey sent in a card inviting their old Parisian acquaintance Inspector Maurice Moser to join them. He did so in a fury. What was the detective to do? Jenkinson's agent was swaggering drunkenly around London with a notorious dynamiter in tow. Moser agreed to stunt up a 'wild chase', as the story eventually appeared in print, to preserve Stephens's revolutionary reputation. In fact the pair decamped to the respectable South Kensington house of the captain's mother before 'dramatically escaping' back to Paris.

Jenkinson had had enough. Stephens was sacked. 'He behaved so badly – drank so hard and was so indiscreet that I was obliged to get rid of him,' he told Harcourt. That was not the end of his undercover career, nor of Maurice Moser's. The detective would also leave Home Office employ and, like the captain, find new patrons.

What was Jenkinson doing, ostensibly sponsoring a plot to break out of prison the man he and Gosselin had laboured so mightily to arrest? Perhaps it was guilt. His letters to his patron that summer and autumn took on a confessional air. The Daly bomb-passing stunt was justified because 'obtaining a conviction would have more effect on the public mind than the prevention of an outrage', he told Earl Spencer. 'The Daly arrest had an immediate effect on the promoters of such outrages and makes them afraid of us and leads them to believe we get information of all their plans from traitors in their camps.'

Jenkinson's well-poisoning in America was indeed producing results. The Irish National League convention of August 1884 was held in Boston. At a splinter meeting of the Clan the Triangle (Sullivan and two stooges called Denis Feeley and Michael Boland – both 'shyster lawyers', according to John Devoy) formally dissolved the link with the IRB because of its sputtering opposition to the bombing campaign. There was uproar. The totemic ideal of Ireland freeing itself had been abandoned in favour of American-imported terror. Clan clubs which expressed opposition were summarily suspended.

On 4 September Jenkinson confided this curious opinion to his patron:

> In England and also, I am told, among very many of the most influential Fenians in America, there is a strong feeling against the dynamite policy . . .
>
> A very serious outrage causing much destruction of property and much loss of life might change the feeling towards them to one of active hostility and they might have to retire from the field altogether . . .

It sounded like an invitation for sanction to terminate the dynamite war by bringing down some fiery cataclysm. On his record of fancy disguises and bogus conspiracies, Edward Jenkinson might be thought just the person to engender it himself.

London, winter 1884–5

A kind of cataclysm *was* coming, but it was instigated, as far as the records show, by the ruling Triangle of the Clan-na-Gael. In the gathering dusk of a winter's evening, shortly before 6 p.m. on 10 December 1884, three men set off in a rowing boat from the Surrey side of the river Thames. They paddled under the brooding granite of London Bridge. A charge was attached to a newly fixed drain-hole grating just above the waterline of one of its rusticated arches,* the fuse was set – and a blinding flash instantly erupted. The tide took the dismembered bodies down-river. Nothing was ever found. After his propaganda coups in smiting Scotland Yard and the London Underground, William Mackey Lomasney's dynamite career had blown itself out.†

More Clan bombers were on their way. On 2 January 1885 a device detonated in the tunnel between King's Cross and Gower Street stations on the Metropolitan Railway. There were minor casualties. 'A contemptible affair,' so Jenkinson described it to Spencer; 'if the railway people had had their wits about them, they would have shut the gates on the arrival of the train at Gower Street and waited until the police came.'

On Saturday the 24th, at around 2 p.m., a bomb detonated

---

* Jenkinson had ordered the gratings to be installed after the London bridges attack warning from Philadelphia the previous March.

† A Thames waterman named Carter gave a description matching Lomasney's as the man who hired the boat for the doomed excursion. His brother and a man named John Fleming were also atomised in the explosion. In February 1885 a cache of Safety Nitro Company of San Francisco dynamite was found in a vacated house in the Harrow Road, north-west London. The occupant's description matched Lomasney's.

beneath a stand of venerable muskets at the armoury of the Tower of London. Four young people on a sightseeing trip were injured. This time the outer gate was briskly shut and no one allowed to leave. James Monro was summoned from Whitehall Place by telegraph; he rushed to the Tower to find more than 200 people milling about in shock. Trestle tables were set up and Inspector Abberline of H Division briskly questioned the shuffling line until he encountered someone with an American accent. He said his name was 'James Gilbert'.

House of Commons, 24 January 1885, 2.10 p.m.

Ten minutes after the Tower explosion a parcel burst into flames in the medieval crypt of Westminster Hall. Weekend sightseers scurried out in panic. It exploded feebly, injuring a policeman trying to carry it upstairs. It seems to have been set as a diversion and it worked – guards rushed towards the smoke and commotion. Moments later a second bomb erupted in the Commons Chamber, detonating with great force close to the Treasury Bench. It was the weekend – the Chamber was empty; no one was killed. The attackers escaped in the chaos. The press called it 'Dynamite Saturday'.

Jenkinson had told the plodding boobies at Scotland Yard a month before that a spectacular outrage was brewing. A 'very reliable source' (almost certainly John P. Hayes) had predicted an attack on the House of Commons. Jenkinson had warned Monro in late December that increased security had to be mounted quickly and quietly so as 'to protect his informant'. But all policemen were beneath contempt.

A few weeks later a report arrived in Room 56 from the British consul in San Francisco warning of a new conspiracy. A man named Burkham arrived from California in late March wanting £3,000 to betray it. Jenkinson installed him in a grand hotel on ample expenses and waited for the plotters to show up. Monro meanwhile was not informed.

Londoners knew nothing of the war in Whitehall. All they wanted was the real bombers caught. Scotland Yard did it the old-fashioned way. A detonator was found at Gilbert's lodging house. His real name, found on letters (from his mother in Skibereen, County Cork), seemed to be Cunningham. His landlady mentioned an 'American trunk', now missing. A cab-man recalled moving such a trunk to an address in the East End, where a young man was found – another American called Burton. He professed his innocence.

Evidence was accumulated. Both men pleaded not guilty at their trial, but Cunningham got life for the Tower and Gower Street explosions, Burton the same sentence for the left-luggage bombs of February the previous year. A playground squabble developed between Jenkinson and Monro on who had acted first on intelligence received from Southampton port-watchers that a man named Burton wearing 'glass buttons' (like those on the torn coat found in the Charing Cross Station left-luggage bomb) had landed from a German steamer. Jenkinson was accused by Monro of 'coaching witnesses' to get a story showing himself in a good light.

No charge was brought for the Palace of Westminster attack. The man who had placed the short-fused parcel of Atlas Powder A dynamite in the Chamber had disappeared.

New York, April 1885

Commander Malcolm McNeile, RN, was an unlikely spy. He was, indeed, a total amateur. Mr Jenkinson's eve-of-departure briefing at the Home Office had all been rather hurried. Was he expected to impersonate an Irishman? He was not. He was to go to America, tour the consulates and ensure that all intelligence on Irish revolutionary matters flowed seamlessly to Room 56. The commander would, he must understand, be operating undercover.

Since he had slipped ashore from the SS *Adriatic* on 28 March 1885, the commander had found himself followed by hostile eyes. For a British secret agent in the international power politics of 1885, downtown Manhattan glistened with as many dangers as the souks of Bukhara – although to gain entry to J. P. Ryan's Liquor Saloon, at least he did not have to dress up as a Pathan.

Playing the green great game in the jungles of New York could be life-endangering. On 8 January Jenkinson's agent Joseph Phelan had been almost fatally stabbed in the *United Irishman* office by a Cork man named Short (one of the original avengers who had set out to shoot Red Jim McDermott). 'I am dreadfully upset,' Jenkinson told Earl Spencer on 10 January 1885. 'It makes me feel as if I could not go on with this horrible work. [Phelan] was a quiet, steady man with a wife and large family and came over here in 1883 to assist me solely because he disapproved of dynamite work and wanted to stop it.'

Britain was once more squaring up to war with Russia. It was the Balkans again, an interminable row over Bulgaria – that and the advance of the ambitious generals across central Asia towards the borders of Afghanistan. A scrap over a few fly-blown oases seemed set to trigger a world war. Reports arrived in the Foreign Office that the Imperial Russian consulate in New York was doling out cash to fit out a fleet of piratical 'cruizers' in New England fishing ports 'loaded with all the necessary apparatus . . . crewed by men of the lakes service'. In May 1885 the Prime Minister's nephew, Lieutenant Charles Gladstone of HMS *Northampton*, was dispatched by the Admiralty on an undercover intelligence mission, but could find no trace of the phantom fleet.*

If Commander McNeile needed an instant introduction to the Russo-Irish-American enemy during his undercover week prowling Manhattan, he would have found the proceedings of the 'Irish revolutionary meeting', held in a concert hall on 3 April, revealing. It was more pantomimic than terrifying. The appearance on the platform of 'Professor Mezzeroff' brought a storm of applause from the excitable audience. Jeremiah O'Donovan Rossa introduced his dramatically black-cloaked guest as 'England's invisible enemy' – whose pyrotechnic genius would soon reduce London to ashes. The professor had, so he claimed, already

---

* In his short memoir of Parnell, William O'Brien, MP, recounted his own meeting in London in spring 1885 with an Imperial emissary who wanted the Irish leader's signet ring to take back to St Petersburg as a token of good will for a 'Russian Volunteer Fleet' to bear 5,000 American troops across the Atlantic. Parnell refused, saying, 'The Russian may escape hanging – but you and I won't.'

dispatched volunteer dynamiters to the Sudan and Russia to aid England's foes. The professor, with his stage-prop safe full of 'Skirmishers' Receipts' – explosive chemical formulae – was an elderly, New York-born Irishman named Wilson.

But Rossa, still accounting anything that blew down or caught fire within the bounds of the British empire as evidence of his vengeful long arm, needed such theatrics. Spurned by the Clan but claiming their outrages as his own, in February 1885 he had announced the rebirth of the long extinct Fenian Brotherhood. A handful of old believers had turned up to his opening convention a month later. On this April evening some interesting figures joined him on the rickety stage at Chickering Hall.

One was John F. Kearney, the Caledonian Railway signalman, who had confessed his role in the Glasgow bombings of two years earlier to Superintendent Williamson – to whom he continued to send undercover reports. Kearney had turned again. His re-admission ticket to the party of the men of action was evidently exposing Joseph Phelan as Jenkinson's spy.

The next speaker was General Francis Frederick Millen. He gave a stirring account of the role of Irish soldiers in the American War of Independence – 'George Washington was a naturalised Irishman,' he claimed. The meeting ended with noisy resolutions for the striking down, should he proceed with an imminent royal visit to Dublin, of 'Albert Edward Guelph', the Prince of Wales.

What was Frank Millen doing appearing with pantomime professors and would-be regicides on a Rossa dynamite platform in New York City?

Chualchapa, El Salvador, Central America, March–April 1885

Things had not quite worked out as planned in Guatemala. The dreams of Millen's patron, Justo Rufino Barrios, to proclaim a United States of Central America with himself as dictator had led to a unique diplomatic feat – war with three of his neighbours at once. On 31 March the Guatemalan army burned down some ranchos on its own side as a pretext and invaded El Salvador, winning the frontier battle of El Coco. Honduras and Mexico declared hostilities and sent troops to the border.

Three days later, astride a white stallion, Barrios urged his 14,000-strong army forward towards a scrubby village called Chualchapa. El Reformador was instantly struck dead by a Salvadorean bullet. The Guatemalan army broke, its soldiers cut down with machetes as they fled.

Displaying his talent for tactical retreat, Millen, having planned the invasion, had escaped the jungle wreck two weeks earlier and headed for New York. The feuding Clan had no employment for him, although Aleck Sullivan in Chicago remained trusting enough. The United Brotherhood's bombing campaign had paused after the House of Commons attack. Perhaps the general needed to be seen alongside those making the loudest revolutionary noise. He had a new plan.

Very soon the strange careers of Edward Jenkinson and Francis Frederick Millen would conjoin. The point of intersection was Mexico City.

22

HM Legation, 11 Calle de Gante, Mexico City,
23 April 1885

Lionel Carden's career in the Foreign Service was progressing.
The Eton-educated diplomat with his elegant New York-born
wife had followed his mentor, Sir St John Spenser, the previous August on a most sensitive mission – to re-open relations
between HM government and the Republic of Mexico. They
had been sundered during the revolutionary upheavals of twenty
years earlier in which Frank Millen had played his soldierly part.
There had been anti-British riots in the enormous city perched
in the bowl of an extinct volcano when the government of
President Porfirio Diaz agreed to recognise English debt. Now,
seven months on, things were sweeter – Mr Carden had just
hosted a masked ball at the legation in honour of Señora
Diaz.

On this late April morning the legation, housed in a poplar-
shaded Spanish colonial mansion, was agreeably cool. Mr Carden
was still not acclimatised to the altitude.

A visitor was announced. He wore well-cut American clothes
and affected a sword. He had a New York accent with traces of
a sibilant Ulster whistle. Mr Carden, the son of a Church of
Ireland clergyman from Tipperary, recognised his origins. But
what was his curious offer? On 24 April the acting chargé d'affaires
wrote a long dispatch addressed to Earl Granville, the Liberal
Foreign Secretary:

> My Lord, I received a visit yesterday from an Irish Ameri-
> can, who stated himself to be one of the chiefs of the

executive of the secret Fenian organization in the United
States, and who expressed his desire to give information
to Her Majesty's government respecting the personnel
and plans of this association, with which he has been
connected for upwards of twenty years.

His name, which I withhold for the present at his
special request, is well known as that of an Irish American
agitator of the advanced class . . .

He has moreover shown me letters from O'Donovan
Rossa, proving him to be on terms of confidential inter-
course with that individual.

The visitor had much to offer. For 'a suitable remuneration'
he would 'prove the name and identity of No. 1', leader of the
Phoenix Park murderers. He would 'furnish the names and
addresses of all the members of the present Executive of the
Organisation', and 'describe the connection of this body with the
corresponding one in Ireland'. The visitor was keen to stress 'that
he has never taken any actual part in any outrages, and that he
disapproves of them, for which reason he is willing to give information'.

'Should Your Lordship desire it, I could telegraph his name
and description . . .' Carden messaged.

The dispatch sat on the desk of Sir Julian Pauncefote, head of
HM Foreign Secret Service, for a fortnight. At last, on 16 May,
it was passed to Sir William Harcourt with a copy to 'Mr J'.
The spymaster rushed to the Foreign Office, eyes gleaming with
excitement. The resident clerk was warned to expect overnight
cipher telegrams – it was all to be very secret. 'Inform the chief
clerk privately, not to be recorded,' Sir Julian minuted. Carden
was cabled that night: 'Secret and urgent. Please send name and
description of person referred to in your dispatch . . . liberal
remuneration would be given for information of the kind
mentioned . . .'

The consul telegraphed Sir Julian by return. 'Name of person General F. F. Millen. Age about 50 – height about 5ft 10,
rather thin. Hair brown, somewhat curly, military visage – clean

shaven except long moustache – pearly grey eyes of peculiar appearance . . .'

After twenty years the general was back.

HM Legation, Tokyo, Japan, 2 May 1885

Another Fenian ghost was stirring. As Sir Julian Pauncefote pondered the wisdom of informing the Home Secretary of the Mexico contact, the Foreign Office was about to reactivate another sleeper. On the morning of 2 May the Hon. Francis Plunkett, HM's envoy extraordinary to Japan, observed with alarm the crew of a Russian cruiser in Tokyo harbour, the *Vladi-mir*, beat to quarters and run out their guns on the arrival of a Royal Navy frigate. Perhaps the Anglo-Russian war would start here.

There was some secret business to conduct. He had received a cipher telegram that morning from Sir Philip Currie, Pauncefote's deputy. It read: 'Private. Should you mind writing [to] Tevis reminding him of conversation with you of May 'eighty three and ask if, of the same mind he would allow agent to call on him? Strictest secrecy guaranteed.'

It referred to General Charles Carrol-Tevis, whose offer to re-enter business as an informer two years earlier had caused Jenkinson such self-congratulatory amusement. The time had come to take it up. On 11 May a seductive letter was sent from Japan via the American mail to the former adjutant-general of the Irish Republican Army, now living a comfortable life as a military correspondent for the *New York Times* in Paris. He had been made *chevalier* of the *Légion d'honneur* for his gallantry in fighting the Prussians in 1870–71. Mr Jenkinson was passed the 'very secret' Tevis correspondence on 16 May – the same day the Home Office was notified of the Millen contact. His global intelligence cup was overflowing.

Room 56, The Home Office, 21 May 1885

Edward Jenkinson was winning his Whitehall war. His system of 'plot and counterplot' was prospering – what was there for Monro to complain of? The spymaster had made this extraordinary statement to Earl Spencer on 12 March:

> I have been taking advantage lately of the split between the IRB in England and the VC [United Brotherhood] in America – and the feeling that exists among the Irish in England against the dynamite policy as at present carried out – to utilise the men of the IRB as detectives on our own side.
>
> In the IRB nothing of importance can be done we should not know of, and in some places the organisation is almost under our management and control . . .

Monro had had enough. After yet another scuffle over withheld intelligence he threatened to resign. On 21 May Sir William Harcourt summoned Jenkinson to his office for an apoplectic dressing down. 'It is monstrous that the London detectives should not know of these things . . . it is all jealousy, nothing but jealousy, you are like a dog with [a] bone who goes into a corner and growls at anyone who comes near him,' he thundered.

But the next day Harcourt apologised. He was 'very sorry'.

Foreign Office, London SW, 22 May 1885

Of course the Home Secretary climbed down. Mr Jenkinson was about to pull off his Mexican coup. The Foreign Office cables were flying to Mr Carden. Would the informant 'come to France or Germany secretly? . . . His expenses will be paid . . . What remuneration does he expect?' Sir Julian Pauncefote messaged on 18 May. The answer came by reply – he wanted £2,500.

Jenkinson put his own mark on the next cable. 'Secret. If he comes to continent he would be met by someone from Home Office [i.e. himself], not by anybody belonging to detective service. Payment in advance out of the question. Information will be liberally paid for, but must first be substantiated.' The sum demanded, double his own salary, seemed bearable.

The informant wanted an additional £200 expenses 'to fetch papers from New York and visit other places in United States in order to refresh memory in regard to certain details'. On the 22nd he was offered £100. The deal was struck.

HM Legation, Mexico City, 23 May 1885

'I have the honour to report that the name of the person referred to . . . is General F. F. Millen,' the consul informed Earl Granville, the Foreign Secretary, directly on the 23rd (so far only Pauncefote, Jenkinson and Harcourt knew the name *en clair*). 'He has for many years been connected with the *New York Herald* having at one time been employed as assistant night editor . . . His social relations are good,' said Carden, 'and I was surprised to find his name proposed as a visitor to the principal club here by a gentleman of the highest social standing . . .'

But it emerged that Millen was not yet ready to go to Europe – it would, he explained, take him 'away from his literary pursuits' – he was after Mexican government money to write a biography of General Diaz: flattering dictators had not failed Millen before, as a journalist or spy. He would, however, 'not be unwilling later on to enter into an arrangement with Her Majesty's Government to keep them regularly informed as to the proceedings of the extreme party of the Irish nationalists'.

Carden wrote the general a draft on the legation chequebook for £100, payable on the Bank of London, Mexico and South America. On the morning of 28 May Millen caught the sleeper at the Buena Vista Station for the eight-day journey via El Paso to New York for his 'memory refreshing' trip. He would return to Mexico City and write a full statement of his revolutionary life and times for a payment of £2,500. Business was getting better – almost twenty years earlier he had pulled the same stunt for $500.

Edward Jenkinson would have new political masters by the time Millen returned. After five years grappling with Ireland,

Gladstone was exhausted and outmanoeuvred. On one flank, from within the Liberal Party, the Birmingham radical Joseph Chamberlain was advancing his own limited self-government scheme for Ireland – using his go-between, William O'Shea, to negotiate with Parnell. On 9 May the Cabinet rejected the Chamberlain plan. Four days later Gladstone announced that a renewal of coercion was inevitable.

On the other flank, the mercurial Conservative Lord Randolph Churchill was also deep in conspiratorial negotiations with the Irish leader. Churchill, popular among Nationalists since his championing of the 1884 franchise reform which trebled the Irish electorate, indicated that a Conservative government would drop coercion. Once in power all sorts of further understandings might be reached. Churchill's motives were to get the Liberals out, whatever it took. Parnell in turn fully realised that only the Tories with their standing majority in the House of Lords could pass home rule into law. On the night of 8–9 June thirty-nine Parnellites voted with the opposition on a fractious budget item. Seventy Liberals, followers of Joseph Chamberlain, abstained. The Government was defeated. Four days later Gladstone resigned.

Lord Salisbury set to forming a minority government pending a general election which must fall that autumn. The Tory caretaking interregnum would last barely seven months.

Whitehall, London SW, June 1885

Sir William Harcourt had just days left in office. It was all ending in tears. In the first weeks of June the great Clan plot run out of San Francisco (according to Jenkinson's informer Mr Burkham) had caused the Metropolitan Police to scurry all over London on the orders of the spymaster. It was a money-extorting hoax. Monro accused his enemy of incompetence and worse in a stream of coruscating memoranda. On the 17th the Home Secretary made a last bid to get them to cooperate. The meeting was terse. When Jenkinson was ordered by Harcourt 'to supply the information and the Met to work it out' – he 'simply declined'. He would take his chances with the new men. On the 24th Sir Richard

Assheton Cross took over at the Home Office. The bespectacled, bewhiskered Conservative took brisk account of the state of the war against Irish revolutionaries. All seemed in good hands: no bomb had gone off since the House of Commons explosion. The two principals in the fight should, he suggested cheerfully, carry on as a 'cabinet of equals'. They could barely stand being in the same room.

Monro and Jenkinson went back to their Whitehall corners to consider the next move in their war against each other.

23

London, June 1885

The intelligence strands of the dynamite war were held in Edward Jenkinson's hands. How much should he impart to his new Conservative masters engaged in their tenuous parliamentary alliance with Mr Parnell? His own position was vulnerable – tenant of a post which was meant not to exist, his salary and operational funds still routed circuitously via Dublin Castle. Monro kept up his sniping. The Mexico contact must be used to the full.

A week before Gladstone's Commons defeat Jenkinson drafted a 'very secret' memorandum on just what General Millen should provide to earn his promised £2,500. It was sent on 30 May by special bag via New York to Mexico City.

It was clear, whatever the informant might have to say about Rossa's organisation, that the approach came from a high-ranking member of the Clan-na-Gael. Jenkinson wanted to know who had bombed London – and who on the Revolutionary Directory had sanctioned and funded the missions. 'The General will not be entitled to the full remuneration ... until some of these persons shall have been arrested and returned for trial,' he insisted. 'It is not part of the stipulation that a conviction should be obtained.'

He wanted warning of 'outrages which are contemplated should war break out between England and Russia'.

He also wanted the name and whereabouts of the elusive 'Number One' and actionable proof of his complicity in the Phoenix Park murders.

This was operational intelligence against enemies without. Much more sensitive was what the informant might deliver on enemies within. Jenkinson wanted intimate details of the land war of 1879–82, including the 'names of many well known men belonging to the Parliamentary Party, and the part which any of them took in the agitation and outrages'. He wanted details of 'The negotiations which have taken place from time to time between the parliamentary party in England and the leaders of the Organisation [the Clan-na-Gael], and to name those of the parliamentary party who have taken the greatest share in such negotiations.'

Proof of an operational link between Parnell and the London bombers would send the Irish leader to prison for life. His party held the balance of power in parliament. The former divisional commissioner would be the most powerful man in England.

> Should the statement as taken in Mexico not be suf-
> ficiently full, further questions as regards details will be
> sent out [said Jenkinson]. It may even be necessary that
> the general should meet some person from the Home
> Office in order to explain to him more fully matters which
> might not be clearly understood.
>
> This person would not belong to the Detective service,
> and arrangements would be made under which the Gen-
> eral could meet him somewhere in Europe with perfect
> safety and secrecy . . .

The memo arrived in Mr Carden's hands around 10 June. Lord Salisbury, meanwhile, was forming his administration. On the 24th he took office as both Prime Minister and Foreign Secretary.

HM Legation, Mexico City, July 1885

Frank Millen had not stayed long in New York. He had arrived back in the Mexican capital by the Central Railroad on 1 July. The huge city shimmered in heat. In the shade of the legation garden Mr Carden entertained his secretive visitor for a week of 'daily interviews'. On 11 July the consul wrote to his new political master in London with the intelligence 'take'. It was disappointing.

Secret. My Lord ... I have the honour to report that xxx returned here from New York about ten days ago ... I may say that his knowledge in regard to the dynamite outrages appears to be more general than particular ... [he messaged].

He has always been opposed to the policy of terrorising by individual outrages or assassinations, and this fact, in spite of his having been and of his still being in the confidence of many of the originators of these schemes, prevents him from being able to supply as much detail as would be desirable.

There was some harder information, however. The dreaded Number One of the Invincible conspiracy was John MacCafferty – a fact which according to accompanying minutes was already known in London. Millen had no direct written evidence, but he had a proposal as to how the long sought for principal of the Phoenix Park murders, now in Chicago, 'might be induced to go to England'.

Salisbury passed the correspondence via Sir Julian Pauncefote to Edward Jenkinson. The spymaster was crestfallen. 'The information now sent is chiefly ancient history and is very imperfect and incomplete and we are not yet in possession of the full statement which was promised,' he minuted on 12 August. He was prepared to wait. There was better news that day: his son Eddy had passed twenty-seventh in his class into the Royal Military Academy at Sandhurst.

London, August 1885

The timing of Frank Millen's overture was fortuitous. He was *opposed* to terror, so Mr Carden had reported, and had little operational information about outrage to offer. But no matter – it was political intelligence that was now at a premium. Lord Salisbury perforce now had to do business with the man whose separatist agenda he had hitherto pronounced to be contemptible.

The uncomfortable bargains brokered with Parnell by Lord

Randolph Churchill were kept by the new government. Coercion legislation was not renewed. A 'soft' Chief Secretary, Sir William Hart Dyke, was appointed. A peasant-proprietor land purchase scheme was rushed through the new parliament. The record of Liberal 'misrule' in Ireland was raked over when Parnell, spurred on by Churchill, disinterred a notoriously gruesome murder case – the massacre of a family at a remote farm near Maamstrasna in Connemara. Three men had gone to the gallows in 1882 on dubious evidence. Earl Spencer had sternly dismissed pleas for clemency. A retrospective motion of censure on the Lord Lieutenant was moved. The Tories, it seemed, would support it.

The Queen was horrified: 'The Parnellites were not to be trusted,' she warned her new Prime Minister. Lord Salisbury could not but agree: 'any bargain with them would be full of danger,' he replied. It was the price of power.

Outraged at being winkled out of office by the perverse Tory–Irish compact, Sir William Harcourt opened a royal counter-offensive in a letter to Sir Henry Ponsonby, Queen Victoria's private secretary. The non-renewal of the Crimes Bill 'would hand over Ireland to anarchy . . . it would be the Irish Tories and their friends who would be murdered in their beds,' he dramatically told the Queen's most confidential counsellor on 1 July. Salisbury had made a 'great blunder', he insisted – how could Liberal doubters defect to a party which had 'sacrificed the peace of Ireland and perhaps the integrity of the empire for the sake of four months in office'?

'In a month or two – after thus tampering with treason and dynamite – all decent folks will wish heartily for our return.'

After five years enduring the abhorrent Mr Gladstone, Her Majesty had welcomed Lord Salisbury to office with tears of relief. That he might tamper with treason and dynamite? It was inconceivable.

Salisbury's choice of Lord Lieutenant was especially significant – the Earl of Carnarvon, a former constitutionally innovative colonial secretary and newly enthusiastic 'green'. As a bridge to Parnell it was a shrewd move. As the general election loomed, the continuing Tory–Irish liaison was played out in shadowy trysts by intermediaries. The most controversial encounter was when Carnarvon, with the Prime Minister's sanction, met Charles Stewart Parnell for an 'interchange of opinion'.

The secret meeting took place on 1 August at the shuttered and dustsheet-draped house of Lord Carnarvon's recently deceased mother. An assembly in Dublin was discussed, and safeguards for the Protestant minority. An 'actual alliance might be sealed in time for the general election', Carnarvon noted. Parnell meanwhile 'was holding in check for the time being both Davitt and the American extremists'.

The Prime Minister would later loudly deny he had any knowledge of the Mayfair meeting – at the same time binding Carnarvon to silence. There was a hidden agenda behind the overtures. If news leaked (as it was bound to do through Parnell's intermediary to Gladstone – Mrs Katherine O'Shea) then the Liberal leader could be bounced into a counter-bid, an outright offer of home rule. The move could be presented as a craven surrender to the dynamiters.

Lord Salisbury's game was 'risky and devious', according to the marquis's most recent biographer: 'to lure the Liberal leadership into a trap from which it could not escape, thereby emasculating it whilst protecting the Union which he always believed Britain had a debt of honour to defend . . .'

24

Room 56, The Home Office, September 1885

There was an obstacle to both Frank Millen's and Edward Jenkinson's hopes of future reward from HM government. The bombing had stopped. Things were so quiet that summer the spymaster even took a break 'at the seaside'. Would there be a job on his return? On 2 September he told the Home Secretary: 'At present the situation is this – nationalists and fenians of all sections have fallen into line with Parnell – they are all determined to wait and watch the result of the general election . . .' He argued, naturally enough, that now was not the time for his post to be abolished.

Jenkinson had opened his own charm offensive on Lord Carnarvon, meanwhile – sending him titbits of secret information. The Lord Lieutenant, already stage-managed by Salisbury in his own backstairs diplomacy with Parnell, was clearly seduced by the spookery. 'When you write to me on these very private matters use double envelopes – it is an additional security,' he replied.

Jenkinson's month-long wait for Millen's 'full statement' paid off when Carden sent a report with 'ten sub-enclosures' on 3 September. The report addressed to Salisbury and the supporting documents are missing from the Foreign Office 'Fenian Brotherhood' file. Carden's covering letter and Jenkinson's comments survive, however – enough to make a partial reconstruction. The report remained 'deficient in the detail which I apprehend would be of most interest to Her Majesty's government . . .' said the consul – but he felt sure this would be redressed, given 'sufficient encouragement'.

The general was clearly angling for money. He had 'debts in Mexico City'; he wanted to leave a 'trifle for his family'. Mr Carden suggested a monthly salary and mined this conversational nugget on his visitor's origins. 'He has given me to understand that at one time he held a commission in the English army . . .'

But Jenkinson, who was in a position to know, seemed enraptured by the disclosures. 'This report is exceedingly clear and great pains have evidently been taken to extract from X all that he knows,' he told Sir Julian Pauncefote. It would, he said, 'form the basis of future useful work . . .' What might that be?

Meanwhile he had made no attempts to hide his own conversion to home rule. 'If the hopes of the nationalists are realised, as I hope they will be, you will not have any further need for my services,' he had boldly told Sir Richard Cross, the Conservative Home Secretary, in his first weeks of office. What use might an avowedly Parnellite spymaster be to Lord Salisbury?

He had one key sympathiser in the Cabinet – Carnarvon. Jenkinson fed the Mexico intelligence into a very long handwritten situation report, completed on 25 September, addressed to the Lord Lieutenant.

> It is therefore clear that we have arrived at a most critical time in Irish history [the document stated]. It is a most serious consideration that the peace of Ireland depends upon the influence and position of Mr Parnell . . .
>
> Any words which may lessen Mr Parnell's influence, or dash the hopes which at the present time fill the hearts of the Irish people, might lead to an outbreak of crime and to the renewal of dynamite outrages.

The document also contained an exhaustive structural argument for home rule. An undercover agent had been sent to Ulster and concluded: 'The Orangemen are joining the nationalists everywhere.'

There were curious details. The document mentioned a 'secret dinner' in Dublin for P. S. Cassidy, 'a member of O'Donovan

Rossa's council and a leading Clan-na-Gael man'.* Two Irish MPs
were present, who urged Cassidy to go back to New York and 'use
his influence with all parties to stop all further explosions'. Cassidy
would 'see what can be done in next Parliament . . . If we cannot
succeed legitimately it must be war to the bitter end.' Jenkinson
had proof of Cassidy's promise 'in a letter before me'.

However many attempts had been made to link Parnell and
his followers to the Phoenix Park murders and other outrages,
'we have no proof that they were a party to them,' Jenkinson
concluded. 'We have now to deal with a united party under the
leadership of a man who deserves the name of a statesman who
is looked up to and followed by the Irish people in Ireland and
in all parts of the world . . .'

Lord Salisbury would not have agreed. Nevertheless the Prime
Minister was hooked on the new intelligence seam running from
Mexico City – scribbling his red 'S' monogram on every cryptic
communication issuing from the Foreign Office. From 9–12
October cables flew back and forth across the Atlantic:

> FO to Carden. What monthly payment do you suggest?
> Remuneration for statement, and terms of future service
> must be settled personally with Govt official. Will he
> come secretly to some place in Europe?

> Carden to FO. I would suggest forty pounds a month
> for a term of three months – XXX is willing to go to
> Paris secretly.

> FO to Carden. Secret. Start X at once, advancing expenses
> for journey. Let him on arrival send assumed name and
> address in Paris to G. Whitfield,† poste restante Charing
> Cross, London.

---

* Patrick Sarsfield Cassidy, born in Sligo in 1851, was another journalist-
revolutionary – he was city editor of the *New York Sunday Mercury*. Jenkinson
indicated he was a member of both the Clan and the Fenian Brotherhood.
O'Donovan Rossa later claimed that Jenkinson recruited Cassidy as an informer
on his trip to Dublin.
† No 'G. Whitfield' is listed in Home or Foreign Office directories for the period.
It must be assumed to be a cover-name.

Frank Millen was back on the British payroll. On 14 October he turned up at the legation to accept the contract in person. Carden wrote him a banker's draft for £180 on the embassy account and provided a special recognition cipher. His contact in Paris would bear a counterfoil.

It was agreed that he would travel via Chicago to consult with Alexander Sullivan. The next day Carden cabled Lord Salisbury: 'XXX starts tonight and will probably arrive in Paris about the 5th of November . . .'

The Mexico contact was now running on Foreign Office money. Sir Thomas Lister, assistant under-secretary at the FO, cabled Lionel Carden approving the Millen payments already made on Lord Salisbury's behalf. The general caught the Atchison Topeka and Sante Fe sleeper northwards a second time, trundling across Texas and the Mid West to Chicago, and thence to New York and the transatlantic steamer to the French Atlantic port of Le Havre. His long conspiratorial journey would be matched by another's. Who might be the 'Govt official' who would meet him in Paris?

It was Edward Jenkinson. That he did meet Millen is clear from a sequence of letters to Lord Carnarvon. 'I may have to go over to Paris on the business I told you of – any day after the 5th – so I should like if possible to see Lord Salisbury before that date,' he told the Lord Lieutenant on 2 November. He stayed at his club, the East India in St James's Square, waiting for the Charing Cross poste restante to bear a message from the traveller. He was running late.

The spymaster did indeed see Lord Salisbury – four days later at his Arlington Street house in London. The meeting was uncomfortable. The 'gloomy' Prime Minister had read Mr Jenkinson's memorandum.* He most assuredly did not agree with its

---

* Jenkinson had had his long report of 25 September set in type and six copies produced by the Foreign Office secure printers. On 2 November he sent one each to Carnarvon and Salisbury and, on his own volition, sent copies to the Liberal opposition leaders Lords Spencer and Rosebery. Carnarvon found out and was appalled: 'I had no idea you would send it to anyone but the Prime Minister,' he wrote. Jenkinson's cringing reply indicates he thought he was acting with Carnarvon's tacit approval.

The document was reprinted in 1889 by Arthur Balfour, the Conservative

conclusions. 'Home Rule could not come from the Conservatives,' Salisbury stated bluntly; 'opinion in England about Ireland
would not allow it.'

'He thinks it must come to a head in the way we most dread,'
Jenkinson reported to Carnarvon. 'I'm afraid it must be so – but
it is so terrible and lamentable I do not like to think about it . . .'

What did the spymaster and the 'green' Lord Lieutenant dread?
What was the 'terrible' outcome which the Prime Minister now
seemed to think inevitable? Jenkinson's warnings could not have
been blunter. 'We may be quite sure of this: That unless Mr
Parnell succeeds in obtaining during this next year Home Rule,
or a promise of Home Rule . . . he will either fall from power
and lose all control over the Irish people or he will have to place
himself at the head of a revolutionary movement,' his report had
stated. Indeed, according to 'leading Fenians in New York and
Chicago', the Irish leader had already secretly given his word to
do just that.

The Prime Minister seemed completely indifferent to whether
Parnell continued the unsavoury liaison with his own party at
Westminster or fled to America to raise the flag of outright
rebellion. At least then the Irish enemy might be confronted in
his true colours. The utility of General F. F. Millen in the higher
scheme of things was yet to be determined.

At last a message came via the Charing Cross dead letter box.
On 11 November Jenkinson confided to Carnarvon:

> The man from America has arrived and I go to the conti-
> nent tomorrow to meet him – and shall be away four or
> five days.
>
> Saturday I handed to Sir R. Cross the report of Com-
> mander McNeile RN who went to America in the spring
> to visit the consuls . . . I hope to be able to pass it on to
> Your Excellency next week on my return from France.

Chief Secretary for Ireland, unchanged, as a briefing paper for ministers during
the Special Commission. It contained the 'no link to outrage' line, the opposite
of what the attorney-general was at the time trying to prove in court.

Edward Jenkinson caught the Newhaven boat-train armed with his match of the Mexico recognition cipher. Frank Millen was waiting, living in style on his foreign office cash.* In autumnal Paris the spymaster-apostle of home rule and the turncoat-Irish revolutionary would get down to some very curious business indeed.

* Millen presented his estimate of travelling expenses:

Railway to New York via El Paso	$137.64
8 days' sleeping cars	24.00
Baggage	15.00
8 days' meals	32.00
Porters – gratuities	5.00
Stay in Chicago (1 day)	15.00
Stay in New York (1 day)	10.00
New York to Havre –	
(steamer direct or via Liverpool)	120.00
Miscellaneous expenses on board	15.00
Havre to Paris	7.50
Miscellaneous expenses till	
arrival in Paris	20.00
Total	**$401.14**

PART SIX

The Fall

'All that's very well. But your idea of secrecy
over there is to keep the Home Secretary
in the dark.'

Author's Note, Joseph Conrad,
The Secret Agent (1920 edition)

25

London, winter 1885–6

The swing-door of British politics turned again. A general election was called for 23 November 1885. Salisbury's risky game played with the Carnarvon overture paid off when, two days before the poll, Parnell urged Irish-sympathising voters in British constituencies to vote Tory.* His tactical aim was to produce a hung parliament and it succeeded. When after three anxious weeks the results were at last all in and counted, the home rule majority in Ireland itself was overwhelming. Salisbury stayed in power with a majority of two – counting in eighty-six newly elected Nationalists. Parnell could make or break the British government.

Edward Jenkinson plunged on with his ecumenical mission to capture both parties for home rule. He now had a special asset. Where he and 'the man from America' had met in Paris in the

---

* Captain O'Shea was rejected by his home rule constituency association in Clare for his refusal to take the party oath binding members to joint action. After failing to find a new Irish seat he stood in the general election as a Liberal in Liverpool and was defeated (although Parnell broke his own 'vote Tory' manifesto by campaigning for him).

Of his rejection in Ireland, O'Shea wrote a curious letter to his wife from Dublin on 2 November 1885: 'I . . . mean to hit back a stunner. I have everything ready . . . I have packed my shell with dynamite.

'It cannot hurt my friend [Chamberlain] and it will send a blackguard's [Parnell's] reputation with his deluded countrymen into smithereens.' Just what he meant would be interrogated later during the Special Commission.

At a subsequent election in Galway in February 1886 (the general election victor T. P. O'Connor had also won a seat in England), Parnell 'imposed' O'Shea as the Nationalist candidate against fierce party opposition – ostensibly in a (doomed) move to keep the captain's mentor Joseph Chamberlain on-side. It was clear, however, that he was buying the continuing silence of the husband of his mistress.

second week of November 1885 – what agenda they considered
– is not recorded in any recoverable archive. But a supposition
can be made. Millen had gone from Mexico City on his Foreign
Office-funded journey to Chicago to consult with Alexander
Sullivan himself. The spymaster was now at just one remove from
the apex of the Triangle. The Clan bombing was on hold and
Millen had the influence to help keep it there – or to turn it on
again.

Armed with the original Mexico intelligence, Jenkinson had
produced not an operational blueprint for the defeat of armed
Irish nationalism but a rationale for its appeasement. He had
presented it to Lord Salisbury and got no thanks. He had gone
to Paris to meet the general in person. With Millen on the hook
the spymaster had the power, should it ever prove necessary, to
turn paper threats into real ones.

There was one more leading actor in the unfolding drama to try
and convince – William Gladstone. In a most un-civil-servant-like
move, on 11 December Jenkinson sent the leader of Her Majesty's
loyal opposition a handwritten update of his doom-laden memorandum. It was newly informed by his debrief of Millen in Paris
the month before.

> Secret and Private. I have to intimate knowledge of what
> is going on behind the scenes both in Ireland and
> America . . .
>
> The C-n-G is by far the more powerful than any other
> organisation and has at its command large resources both
> in money and men . . . at the present time this organisa-
> tion and all the other Irish organisations in America are
> determined to hold their hand and to give Parnell as they
> say, 'a chance' . . .

Should Parnell fail, however: 'The outrages and murders of 1882
will be repeated. There will be dynamite explosions – the murder
of statesmen and officials, all are determined and preparing for
it . . .

'The refusal of Home Rule now would much more probably lead
to the disintegration of the Empire than would its granting . . .'

Gladstone replied the next day: 'Secret. I agree very emphatically – but these are not abstractions, they call for immediate
action. I must ask in what capacity you address me? – and what
use I can make of your letter?' That would become clear.

'The face of British politics was about to alter for a generation,'
in the words of a conservative historian, 'due to the most momen-
tous political announcement in four decades.' It did not look like
it at the time. The great upheaval was signalled by a short letter
published in *The Times* of 12 December from Gladstone's son
Herbert, postmarked Hawarden Castle, the Liberal leader's
country seat. 'If five-sixths of the Irish people wish to have a
Parliament in Dublin . . . in the name of justice and wisdom, let
them have it,' he wrote. Westminster antennae twitched: Gladstone had been converted. His own fractious Cabinet colleagues
had not been consulted. Lord Salisbury called it the 'Hawarden
kite', flown to test the sentiments of the Liberal leader's own
party, its home rule fault-lines already creaking open.

The spymaster was touching the secret core of politics. A
scrappy memo in the *Times* archive, written during the Parnell
Commission four years later, gives a clue to Jenkinson's background string-pulling: 'GOM ['Grand Old Man', i.e. Gladstone]
had a conversation with A. Balfour at Eaton Hall sometime in
1885 or early in '86. G wanted B to use his influence to get the
Tory Party to take up Home Rule. The reason he gave was that
murder and outrage would follow wholesale unless the demand
was acceded to.' At the bottom of the note is scribbled: 'Jenkinson
– said to be Managing Director of Manchester Canal.'*

On 15 December, three days after receiving Jenkinson's apoca-
lyptic report, Gladstone did indeed meet Arthur Balfour at the
Duke of Westminster's seat, Eaton Hall in Cheshire, to urge a
Conservative home rule settlement for Ireland. Like some grave
foreign policy question, the issue was too serious to be battled
out on party lines, Gladstone argued. He 'had evidence of the
urgency of this matter . . . based on information recently received',
he informed the Prime Minister's nephew. It was not just Parnell's

---

* He became a director of the Manchester Ship Canal in February 1888.

bumper harvest of votes that had changed Gladstone's mind. He had read Jenkinson's warnings.

So had Lord Salisbury. He would not sunder the Conservative Party by buckling to blackmail – even if the threats were coming via his own security chief. He could afford to wait. The Liberals would surely split. Lord Carnarvon meanwhile had a last try, presenting draft proposals for a separatist Irish constitution to Cabinet on 14–15 December. They were soundly rejected.

Lord Randolph Churchill, having intrigued with the Nationalists the previous summer to get the Liberals out, saw the opportunity plainly. Home rule had become a trap. 'We have got Gladstone pinned to it,' he told Harcourt outright at the end of the year, 'we will make him expose his scheme in the House of Commons. Let him defeat us with the aid of the Parnellites, and then let us dissolve and go to the country with the cry "of the Empire in danger".' He was already drafting his shock troops, the loyalists of Ulster – making no secret of his intention to agitate them 'even to resistance beyond constitutional limits'.

Salisbury's government limped into the new year. On 17 January Carnarvon resigned, citing 'ill health'. Jenkinson told Spencer that day: 'I am very much disturbed in my mind about what may be the policy of the present Govt towards Ireland. I hope it won't be many days before the Govt is defeated . . .'

Indications that the Government intended to introduce a draconian new coercion bill leaked from the Cabinet Room the next day. With a wafer-thin majority such a move would be an act of parliamentary self-immolation but Lord Salisbury was indifferent. It was the Liberals who were falling apart.

Queen Victoria opened Parliament on the 21st, the last time she would ever do so in person. There was scant reference to Ireland in her speech – a sparse statement that the Union would be preserved; nothing specific on coercion. Four days later, however, the Government announced the introduction of a bill to suppress the National League itself. The Irish, soaring on the thermals of the Hawarden kite, pulled the plug on the night of 26–7 by voting with the opposition on an obscure agricultural amendment. As a portent of the storms to come, eighteen anti-home rule Liberals voted with the Government; seventy-six abstained. The Tories were out – the Irish cheered their fall – but Gladstone was hardly jubilant.

The next morning Salisbury's Cabinet resolved to resign. A disbelieving Queen Victoria summoned her Prime Minister to Osborne. His defeat struck her like a bereavement. On 1 February William Gladstone was received by his sovereign, kissed hands and expressed his intention of introducing a measure of home rule for Ireland. Her Majesty was appalled.

So were some powerful Liberals. Lord Hartington, leader of the 'Whig' faction of aristocratic landowners, whose younger brother Lord Frederick Cavendish had been murdered in Phoenix Park, refused to serve in the new administration. Joseph Chamberlain, appointed president of the Board of Trade, urged the utmost caution. Earl Spencer, with great distaste, bowed to the seemingly inevitable. 'How odious (and maybe wicked) it is to think that Parnell and his crew are to govern Ireland,' he wrote.

Disencumbered at last of the loathsome necessity of fawning on the Irish, the Conservatives in opposition might now defend the Union by whatever means it took.

The home rule charge, aided so eagerly in secret by Edward Jenkinson, had engendered a counter-operation. It was funded by a so-called 'committee of three – two peers and a commoner', according to Michael Davitt, who investigated the affair in the run-up to the Special Commission, recording everything in his 'Notes by an Amateur Detective'. The committee (whose members he did not name) hired an American-Irish journalist named Philip Bagenal, a veteran anti-Land League polemicist, to enlist recruits for the black-propaganda campaign.

Someone uniquely well qualified was hanging round London. After Jenkinson had dismissed him for drunkenness, the volatile Captain Darnley Stewart Stephens had appealed for help to the prominent Conservative Sir Stafford Northcote. He steered him towards Mr Bagenal.

The amply-financed captain set up headquarters in a room above the Golden Lion in Wardour Street, Soho, a notorious hang-out for 'Fenians', real and otherwise. There, through the autumn of 1885, he read volumes of revolutionary literature and entertained a stream of visitors. They included, so Davitt discovered, Philip Callan, a former Irish MP, expelled from the party by Parnell for intransigence and drinking; Joseph Hayes, the Philadelphia informer and veteran of the Casey drinking firm in Paris; Captain William O'Shea, the cuckolded husband of Parnell's mistress – and his bag-carrier, a London-based 'nationalist' (and long-time informer for Anderson and Monro) named George Mulqueeny, who worked as a clerk in the docks. Boozing and conspiring in the Golden Lion was all well and good – but the committee wanted results. The captain set to compiling a pamphlet that would sensationally reveal Mr Parnell's links to terror.

Another Soho caller that autumn was a debt-ridden, middle-aged Dublin journalist named Richard Pigott. It was Pigott who, having sold his failing newspapers to Parnell and Patrick Egan during the upheavals of four years earlier, had aided Lady Florence Dixie in her anti-Land League outbursts. He had made a living thereafter as a 'dynamite revelationist', writing blood-curdling stories about non-existent plots for London newspapers. He had a side-line in high-class French erotica. His career was about to progress dramatically.

Dublin and Paris, winter–spring 1885–6

Richard Pigott had already found parallel employment in the anti-Parnellite cause. In Dublin in the autumn of 1885 the Irish Loyal and Patriotic Union had been formed – a group of journalists, academics and businessmen committed to the defence of the Union. It was the Liberal chief whip, Lord Richard Grosvenor, who introduced Pigott to the ILPU's secretary, a twenty-four-year-old Dublin-born journalist named Edward Houston who had made a campaigning reputation with graphic reports of the Phoenix Park murder investigations. They struck a deal.

Pigott was paid for a pamphlet called 'Parnellism Unmasked', a plodding inquiry into the Nationalist Party's finances. Stronger stuff was required. He mentioned to his employers rumours of the existence of revelatory 'letters' dating from the days of the land war and the Phoenix Park outrage; these would damn Parnell. An Irish exile called Eugene Davis, now living in Lausanne, seemed to know all about them, he indicated. Off he went in February 1886 to Switzerland at the start of his paper-chase. Houston paid him a guinea a day.

There are famously two versions of Pigott's manoeuvrings: the one given under oath at the Special Commission – and the one given in his ultimate confession. The following is the story that Houston chose to believe. From his Swiss fastness, Eugene Davis indicated to his visitor that 'Clan-na-Gael' emissaries in Paris might be prepared to do business.

Pigott went to the French capital, where in March 1886 he was accosted in the street by a 'Mr Maurice Murphy' – who revealed that a mysterious black bag had been left in Paris three years earlier by the fugitive Invincible Frank Byrne. It contained a bundle of letters implicating Parnell and others in the Phoenix Park murders. Murphy wanted £1,000 for them. Pigott was invited to draw up a memorandum of their contents – which he passed to Houston in London.

The youthful journalist sought a meeting with George Earle Buckle, the editor of the staunchly anti-home rule *Times* newspaper. He cautiously expressed interest – but would only proceed to publication if the originals could be produced. Money was not a problem. Pigott told his mentors he must make an expenses-paid trip to New York to obtain, so he claimed, the permission of a high-ranking Clan-na-Gael member in the city for the 'documents' to be handed over.

Pueblo, Colorado, March 1886

As Richard Pigott was supposedly on the track of evidence left in Paris by a 'fugitive Invincible', HM Foreign Office was about to be approached by a real live one. A letter arrived at the British legation in Washington. Datelined 13 March, Pueblo, Colorado, it was from Patrick Sheridan, the former Land Leaguer who had been fingered in the Phoenix Park trial by the informer James

Carey as one of the key plotters. He had fled to America, defied attempts at extradition – and joined the Clan-na-Gael in New York. Edward Jenkinson had mentioned he had 'a little game going on with him' in a report to Earl Spencer two years earlier.

Now Patrick Sheridan had set up as a wool rancher in the uplands of Colorado with a herd of a thousand Merino sheep. Business was booming but, he informed the ambassador, he now wanted his 'liberty guaranteed' to return to Ireland to get back some property in Roscommon of which 'he had been robbed'. The hoped for reply should be addressed in 'a non-official envelope' to 'Henry', he insisted.

The ambassador was intrigued. This was clearly a delicate approach to turn informer. 'No one was better acquainted with fenian and Invincible matters prior to 1883 and he has no doubt still a good knowledge of what is going on,' he messaged. 'I think that even now Government might be glad to get him over as he could give valuable information.' The approach by 'Henry' was put on Foreign Office file.*

London, spring–summer 1886

The otherwise all-seeing Mr Jenkinson seemed blithely unaware of the political intrigues bubbling during that spring of 1886. His own little efforts had worked out splendidly. Lord Salisbury had fallen, as he had so earnestly hoped. The back-Parnell-or-expect-the-deluge memorandum he had copied to Spencer and Gladstone was now the Liberal government's lodestone in navigating the dynamite-primed shoals of Ireland.

His ambitions were soaring – but within a few months home rule would have crashed into ruin and his career with it. It would be his own fault – he had made too many enemies. 'Like all

* An anonymous article published in the Republican newspaper *An Phoblacht* in 1930 claimed that Parnell took the IRB oath administered by an unnamed Land League organiser in the library of Trinity College, Dublin, sometime in early 1882. In 1995 the Irish historian Patrick Maume identified him as Patrick Joseph Sheridan. He thought the evidence was inconclusive but possible – showing 'the lengths to which Parnell was prepared to go in order to keep separatist support . . .'

"Indians", he doesn't understand politics,' Spencer had once perceptively told Harcourt. Nor did he understand how relentless a foe was James Monro – even less the shifting sympathies of HM Foreign Office in the Whitehall intelligence war.

The opening skirmish was in February. The New York consul sent Room 56 curious intelligence that 'men from Kansas City' were on their way to Europe 'to assassinate the Prince of Wales'. It was all nonsense – the Prince proceeded unmolested on a planned trip to Cannes under the discreet protection of the French Sûreté – but Monro found out about the tip-off and was furious. He insisted such American cables were copied to him. Hugh Childers, the Liberal Home Secretary, concurred – information must be shared, he said, and a meeting was called.

Jenkinson lied. For months past he 'simply had not received any foreign telegrams', he said; he certainly wasn't going to tell the dullard copper about the Mexico contact.

That same day, 26 February, Sir Edmund Henderson at last tendered his resignation as Metropolitan Police commissioner – hounded by the radical press as 'a living antiquity' after bloody riots by unemployed labourers in Trafalgar Square. Jenkinson unabashedly put himself forward for the top job. Monro was horrified. Instead a soldier was appointed, General Sir Charles Warren, a Royal Engineer and amateur archaeologist – lately the subduer of Bechuanaland. His brisk approach might bring order to the socialistic rioters scandalising London. As he grappled with Irish revolutionaries in his first months of office, Sir Charles seemed to think they were all 'Invincibles' – Mr Jenkinson did not brief him too deeply on the subtleties.

In parliament, meanwhile, Gladstone laboured to hold his party together as the home rule battle inched forward. Lord Hartington now led an openly hostile 'Liberal Unionist' bloc. Joseph Chamberlain resigned from the cabinet on 20 March to propagandise against separation.

Lord Randolph Churchill, just as he had promised, had 'played the Orange card', swooping on Belfast the month before to deliver a wildly inflammatory speech to his newly mobilised loyalist admirers.

The Bill for the Future Government of Ireland had its un-opposed first reading on 8 April. Ireland would have a two-chamber parliament under an imperial crown, reserving customs, internal policing, foreign relations and some other powers. Irish members would withdraw from Westminster. Parnell gave it a cautious welcome. Gladstone became an Irish-American hero. In an interview with the Chicago *Daily News* Alexander Sullivan called it 'a great step in the right direction'.

The second reading was moved on 10 May. Salisbury made a speech equating the Irish with 'hottentots' – twenty years of firm government, he said, was the solution. Chamberlain proposed partition, leaving a three-county Ulster redoubt. Orangemen began to drill with wooden guns in Antrim glens. On 13 May an advertisement appeared in the *Belfast News-Letter*: 'WANTED: a few men thoroughly trained in military drill . . . Apply . . . Loyal-ist.' Jenkinson sent Gosselin to Liverpool to investigate rumours of half a million British loyalists getting ready to cross the Irish Sea in support of an armed rebellion. 'Gas and bunkum – but it's not all froth,' the major reported. Propaganda proliferated – black, white and grey. An oblique paragraph appeared in the Liberal-supporting *Pall Mall Gazette* under the strapline MR PAR-NELL'S SUBURBAN RETREAT, announcing for no apparent reason that the member for Cork was residing in Eltham and might be observed any day 'riding out towards Sidcup'.* It did not say that the leafy village south-east of London was where Katharine O'Shea lived with her aunt.

A curious pamphlet appeared soon afterwards with a much more direct message. 'The Repeal of the Union Conspiracy' por-trayed Parnellism as a front for revolution. Its anonymous author was especially excited by the links of certain Irish members of parliament with the ferocious Paris-based dynamiter Patrick Casey. His exploits were indeed remarkable.

It was Casey who had 'planned the Phoenix Park murders and

---

* The article has been interpreted as a coded message sent by senior Liberals aiming to damage Captain O'Shea's – and thus Chamberlain's – credibility, rather than to expose Parnell's by now semi-permanent co-habitation with the captain's wife. (Parnell's horses were called Dictator and Home Rule.)

some of the most daring dynamite explosions'. It was Casey, so the pamphlet alleged, who had sent John Daly to London to 'hurl bombs from the Gallery of the House of Commons'. The would-be bomber had been twice admitted 'by orders of the members of the [Irish] Parliamentary party'. After Daly's arrest it was Casey who had come to London to plan his rescue from Warwick Assizes – pausing meanwhile 'to take refreshment at the House of Commons with Mr T. P. O'Connor MP'. It was Casey, with the evident help of another Irish MP, Dr J. E. Kenny, who had rented the house in Harrow Road where the remains of Captain Lomasney's dynamite store was discovered.

The pamphlet further revealed the names of the Irish Republican Brotherhood's so-called 'military council'. They included: James J. O'Kelly, MP – an agent apparently both of the Sudanese Mahdi and French intriguers in Egypt; 'General Charles Carrol-Tevis, an American soldier of fortune who has served in the Franco-Prussian War, and in almost every other European and South American struggle of the past fifteen years'; and 'General Macadaras, a Frenchman of Irish extraction, who organised the Foreign Legion in the Franco-Prussian War'.

Nationalist newspapers dubbed the raucous sheet (reviewed glowingly in *The Times*) the 'Black Pamphlet'. Captain Stephens's labours in the Golden Lion had produced a result. The author was well-informed: half of the stunts pinned on Patrick Casey they had confected together. The Black Pamphlet was read at Scotland Yard. As far as James Monro was concerned there seemed no reason to doubt its veracity.

Edward Jenkinson had new concerns. The Prince of Wales had received a threatening letter and, 'assuming him to be head of the secret police in London', sent it to Mr Jenkinson. He set one of his agents, a certain Miss Worth, to entrap the correspondent, a man named 'Magee', with 'a bag of farthings painted gold to represent sovereigns'. The plan was not successful.

James Monro had himself already taken an abiding interest in Miss Worth. Her boarding house at 16 Glasshouse Street was advertised in the newspapers as a place where 'messengers' might

receive employment – 'Irishmen preferred'. One such named
Connolly had come to Scotland Yard to apply for an omnibus
conductor's licence. He gave his employer as a reference, a man
named Dawson, whose actual line of business, however, was
unclear. Mr Monro was alerted to the suspicious Irishman's presence. Instead of a conductor's licence he got a brisk interrogation
by the assistant commissioner. What did Dawson employ him for?
Watching 'Fenians' in public houses, Connolly answered eventually; he and plenty more like him were paid twenty-five shillings
a week. The centre of operations was the Soho boarding house.

Inspector John Pope was sent to apply for lodgings. Miss
Worth conveniently offered the plausible old gentleman a room
belonging to a recently departed Mr Dawson. In a trunk left
behind the inspector found a list of names and addresses – the
muster roll of Jenkinson's unofficial army of informers and
pavement artists.

Early on the morning of 22 May Monro's men fanned out
across London to arrest them. They were a 'school of private
detectives working as rivals and enemies of Scotland Yard', Monro
told Hugh Childers, the pliable Home Secretary. Jenkinson was
informed the next morning. Childers spelled it out: there would
be no more 'special men' on the streets of the capital. Meekly
the spymaster conceded defeat in the metropolis. 'It is my duty
to stifle all personal feelings,' he told Spencer, 'and give the new
plan a full and fair trial . . . perhaps the time will come . . . when
there will be more need for my services and when we may require
stronger measures . . .'

Monro would not let go. The mysterious 'Dawson' was tracked
down by Chief Inspector Littlechild to a house in Norland Square,
Kensington. The inspector kept the suspect under observation
and made further investigations. His real name was 'H. Llewellyn
Winter', a gentleman who, it also emerged, appeared to have two
wives. The first Mrs Winter was found living humbly in Kent
with their three young children. She believed her husband to be
'working in America', from whence occasional remittances
arrived. He had 'divorced' her – without her knowledge – falsely
swearing before a judge that she had committed adultery with

his brother. The second Mrs Winter was a wealthy Welsh widow, the inspector discovered, whom he had 'married' in Bangor two years before.

Monro scented victory. He could arrest Winter for bigamy. Startling revelations about his activities in the employ of Mr Jenkinson might emerge. There was an uncomfortable conference at the Home Office. Jenkinson could only splutter in protest. An arrest warrant was indeed issued, but when Inspector Littlechild called again at Norland Square on 7 June, the duplicitous Mr Winter had flown the love-nest for Paris. Jenkinson had tipped him off.

That same evening the fateful vote was moved on the second reading of the Home Rule Bill in the House of Commons. The Liberals split, a ninety-three-strong combination of Chamberlain's radicals and Lord Hartington's Whigs dissenting. Captain O'Shea, Nationalist member for Galway, abstained. He resigned his seat thereafter. The Government was defeated 341–311. Parliament was dissolved and a snap election was called for 1 July. The results would take almost three weeks to be counted.

26

Hôtel des Deux Mondes, Place de l'Opéra, Paris, July 1886

Richard Pigott returned from his high-rolling transatlantic trip via Dublin, arriving back in Paris on 10 July. According to his account he was summoned late that same night by 'Maurice Murphy', the man who four months before had made the original offer of the black bag, to a café on the rue Faubourg St Honoré. 'Five Irish-Americans; representatives of the Clan-na-Gael were waiting in a private-room,' he would later claim; they made him swear that the source of the letters would not be revealed. He summoned Edward Houston to Paris to be present at the imminent handover; Houston brought with him a learned interlocutor, Dr Maguire, professor of moral philosophy at Trinity College, Dublin, and a prominent champion of the Union.

In a Feydeauesque encounter at the Hôtel des Deux Mondes, Houston and the professor waited in an upstairs room. 'Clan agents' were announced by Pigott to be loitering in the lobby. Sample letters were sent up for the professor to examine. Dr Maguire was satisfied. He produced a money-order on Thomas Cook's for £500 and Pigott scampered downstairs to return with the bag. 'Maurice Murphy' and his companion 'Thomas Brown' disappeared. They were Patrick and Joseph Casey.

Pigott, however, had decided to test the market. Perhaps the Liberals would pay more. On his journey back through Dublin, about to close the deal on the black bag, the mercenary journalist very secretly intimated the explosive nature of its contents to Earl Spencer. He alerted Jenkinson. 'I have no faith whatever in Pigott,' he replied on 10 July, 'and do not believe he has any information which would be of use to us or that he could do us any harm.' But the spymaster expressed relief that nothing had reached the newspapers before the polls had closed ten days before.

'I am afraid we shall have bad work if a Conservative Govt comes in,' Jenkinson added. 'But if no outrages happen they will be bound to settle Home Rule. But should any bad outrages be committed in England, Home Rule would be shelved for a long time . . . No outrages will be committed by any organisation *just yet* . . .' That was not the information Scotland Yard was about to receive.

Reynolds' Irish-American Bar, rue Royale, Paris, July 1886

That same day, 10 July, a report arrived at the Foreign Office from the British embassy in Paris that 'some dynamite plot was being prepared by the Irish-Americans who frequent Reynolds' Bar'.

A youthful informant called 'Smith' had seen 'a suspicious-looking bag, and heard a ticking noise coming from it'. Large numbers of Americans had lately been in the notorious establishment muttering 'phrases like we shall have another earthquake ready soon'. The French police had 'searched one room, inhabited by a housemaid who had threatened to use a revolver . . . more discoveries might be made in the cellar', reported Smith. This time, however, it was Jenkinson rather than Monro who was kept ignorant of the apparent new threat.

The embassy's second secretary gave the informant money to get to London and told him to go to 'Scotland Yard – where he would be expected'. He duly turned up. Monro gleefully spirited the arrival away for interrogation. Was there an Englishman hanging round Reynolds' Bar? There was. Jenkinson was copied in by the Foreign Office on the 'Smith' report two days later. 'I have an agency in Paris,' he crossly memoed Sir Julian Pauncefote in reply; 'the Scotland Yard authorities have really nothing to do with such matters outside London.'

Monro concluded at last that the threatened 'earthquake' was a hoax: 'Reynolds' people have evidently been playing a practical joke on Smith,' he wrote on 17 July. But the policeman had what he wanted – a sighting of his enemy's agent in Paris. It was his old friend Mr H. Llewellyn Winter. Monro sent an inspector across the Channel armed with an extradition warrant. Three days later Winter was arrested by the French police – the charge was falsely swearing to a divorce.

London, July–August 1886

At last, on 20 July, the result of the election was announced. Home rule was defeated. The coalition of Conservatives and Liberal Unionists had a majority of 116. Gladstone resigned. Lord Salisbury took office for the second time and set to making his Cabinet. Lord Iddesleigh (Sir Stafford Northcote) was appointed Foreign Secretary; Lord Randolph Churchill was made both Chancellor and Leader of the House; Sir Michael Hicks Beach, a relative moderate, was the new Chief Secretary for Ireland. Henry Matthews, QC, a sixty-year-old criminal lawyer and protégé of Churchill's, was appointed Home Secretary – the first Roman Catholic in the Cabinet since the Battle of the Boyne.*

The new Home Secretary arrived for his first day in office to find Britain's security chiefs squabbling about the arrest of some obscure bigamist in Paris. James Monro insisted the fugitive Winter be brought back to London for trial. Mr Jenkinson thought such a move most unwise. 'An exposé of my past relations with the detective department of Scotland Yard would create a public scandal and my examination in open court might bring under public notice many things connected with my system of secret work,' he memoed his new master on 22 July. Henry Matthews could only but agree. Winter stayed in Paris, his collar unfelt by Scotland Yard.

*　　*　　*

* As a Catholic, the young Matthews had been debarred from Oxford or Cambridge and been educated at the Sorbonne in Paris. His oratorical style was quaintly continental, earning him the nickname 'the French dancing master'.

His enemy might have captured London but the spymaster still controlled intelligence from the rest of the world. Let Monro bicker over bigamists – a much bigger game was in play. The Irish National League of America, paymasters to the parliamentary party, was due to open its Chicago convention in three weeks' time. Home rule had fallen but the bombing truce held. Would the Clan-na-Gael capture the convention for terror? Parnell himself was invited to attend.

Jenkinson compiled a 'very secret' situation report. But instead of presenting it to his Conservative ministerial master he sent it on 5 August to Earl Spencer. The Liberal grandee had need of such information. His party and the Irish were now battle-worn allies. A convention vote for dynamite would destroy them both.

The intelligence was ominous. 'Secret circulars' that Jenkinson had 'just received' from within the Clan demanded extra funds to be devoted entirely to 'Delusion' – the codename for dynamite – with which to inflict 'silent, mysterious blows against the enemy'. Alexander Sullivan, the Triangle chief, 'had sent out emissaries to Parnell and the Supreme Council of the IRB', Jenkinson reported. 'He and Patrick Egan, the President of the National League, are working together and have the whole machinery of the League at their disposal.' The open and secret movements were one.

The Fenian Brotherhood meanwhile had reduced the 'rabid' Rossa to a figurehead. A new eleven-man council had just met in New York. Both the IRB and the Clan were in contact with Russian agents in the city, the spymaster could report. Where was he getting such high-level intelligence? It could only have come from Millen.

Irish National League of America Convention, Grand Pacific Hotel, Chicago, August 1886

The political stakes could not have been higher. Jenkinson had warned that another American bomb would bury home rule for a generation. Parnell dispatched three parliamentary lieutenants to attend the convention – William O'Brien, John Redmond and

John Deasy – by the fastest steamer on the Atlantic, the Cunarder SS *Servia*. Michael Davitt went with them as evidence of radical solidarity in the cause of holding the bombing truce. As the emissaries chugged out of Liverpool, the Clan had already gone into secret preliminary session in Pittsburgh. Rumours abounded of internal feuds over the Triangle's cash accounting – but more directly that a resolution would be forced through to resume the terror war.

The hard-men headed from Pittsburgh to Chicago, Sullivan's town, to participate in the 'open' proceedings of the league. The Irish MPs paralleled their journey westwards from New York. Their Pullman club car became a rolling news conference. William O'Brien described the journey in his memoirs: 'We were escorted by a group of generals, colonels, judges and journalists, about whose prosperous broadcloth and jolly hospitalities there hovered not the faintest scent of nitro-glycerine.'

Parnell judged it too politically perilous to go in person. A vote for 'Delusion' with him anywhere near the platform would be the end of the parliamentary road. 'Even a victory for dynamite in his absence would be a less dangerous matter,' was O'Brien's judgement.

Portraits of Gladstone, newly anointed hero of all Irish Americans, beamed down at a convention hall heaving with quondam dynamitards. Patrick Egan chaired, but in O'Brien's words, 'From the start one personality overbore and oppressed the council chamber . . . a lawyer and politician of vast, if devious, talents – Alexander Sullivan, about whose bloodless lips and sharp white teeth there played a certain pitilessness which all his softness of voice could not change to anything better than cold self-control.'

In a tense backroom meeting O'Brien and Davitt persuaded Sullivan to hold his tongue. The firebrands were quashed – one was physically grappled from the platform while urging 'unrelenting war on England . . . using the fires of hell if necessary'. At its end the convention resolved, 'We heartily approve the course pursued by Mr Parnell.' The Clan's dynamite war stayed on hold.

House of Commons, September 1886

The propaganda success of the Black Pamphlet had meanwhile won its author some powerful new friends. Captain Stewart Stephens had come a long way since being sacked by Jenkinson. According to Michael Davitt, on 1 September 1886 the captain 'had an interview with four members of the Cabinet in Lord Randolph Churchill's rooms at the House of Commons'. Lord Salisbury was present; so was Henry Matthews.

They seemed far more interested in revelations about Stephens's former employer than in dynamiters. Mr Jenkinson, he told them, had letters implicating Irish MPs in the Phoenix Park murders. One of them was Mr Parnell's secretary – another was a special goad of Salisbury, William O'Brien. The spymaster had chosen to 'suppress' the documents, said the captain. 'Stephens used influence with Matthews to shunt Jenkinson,' Davitt noted. His utility had expired. The Foreign Office would effect his termination.

HM Legation, Stockholm, September 1886

Three days later a bizarre tip-off reached the Foreign Office from the British embassy in Stockholm.

A 'Chicago Fenian' called O'Clery, who conveniently was the 'cousin of a Parnellite MP', was staying in the Swedish capital. He had recently been in St Petersburg, where 'he had met John McCafferty', the Number One of the Phoenix Park conspiracy. The ambassador's informant was another American named Clifford, who accompanied O'Clery on marathon vodka-drinking sessions at which revolvers had been brandished. Jenkinson was sent the report.

The Foreign Office meanwhile provided Scotland Yard with an equally wild story that Russian dynamite was on its way to England. Port police and consuls were alerted. Sensational intelligence began to cross Monro's desk – that a new Irish bombing offensive was about to break on the capital, this time with clandestine Russian backing. It was a complete invention. Sir Julian

Pauncefote's byzantine construct clanked into life when first Room 56, then Scotland Yard launched rival expeditions to wintry Scandinavia.

Monro's detective arrived in Sweden to discover from the local police that two 'supposed dynamitards' were in Stockholm. The British ambassador was 'apparently waiting for information from London respecting them'. But far more infuriating, someone called 'Malcolm' had already been sent from London to snoop around. Monro's man telegraphed the news – it was clear Jenkinson was still up to his old tricks, launching freelance missions without reference to the Metropolitan Police. The assistant commissioner raised a huge row in Whitehall.

Jenkinson blustered. He had indeed sent agent 'Malcolm' (it was Gosselin) to the Swedish capital to investigate – but his agent had concluded the great Baltic dynamite plot was a drunken hoax. There was nothing to tell Monro. 'I don't know why it should be thought that I desire to keep back information from Scotland Yard,' he explained lamely.

It was the end. To save himself, on 28 October Jenkinson wrote a mad letter to Matthews proposing the formation of a 'central political crime intelligence department' with himself as its head.

The Home Secretary simply wanted his head. On 11 December the ominous OHMS envelope arrived in Jenkinson's in-tray. It was not wholly unexpected.

> I regret that today, after much anxious consideration, I have determined to relieve you from your present duties as speedily as possible and I fix the 10th January as a convenient day [wrote Matthews].
>
> I shall probably wish to retain some at least of your informants . . . I shall of course desire all papers containing information to remain in the Home Office . . . I shall take personal charge of them.

There was a terse little meeting in Henry Matthews's office that afternoon. His informants faced mortal danger, Jenkinson explained, if he was not there to protect them. The Home Secretary would not be moved; Scotland Yard was now responsible for all anti-Fenian operations. 'I must bring the present arrangements to an end,' he said – although Gosselin would stay on.

Jenkinson wrote to Spencer that night:

> I believe that from the moment this Govt came in they were determined to get rid of me ... It was that I had served you faithfully and that I was in favour of Home Rule. That is the true sum of my offence ...
>
> I have just got from one of them [informants] the most full and interesting accounts of the convention of the FB or Rossa Party which took place in New York on the 23–24 November [1886]. Rossa was deposed and P. S. Cassidy appointed sec and chief exec. I have two letters in Cassidy's handwriting before me giving the details and saying that they mean to go in for active work at once ...
>
> What could be better than this. His two agents in London and Paris are my agents and I see all his letters to them – and neither of them knows that the other is in my pay.
>
> I not only get the information, but one man is a check on the other. Yet Mr Matthews says Cassidy writes rubbish and that he can't make out that either of these informants have ever done anything!! It is too foolish ...

Captain Stewart Stephens had a new commission. On 19 December there was another meeting in London with Lord Randolph Churchill – who told him, 'You have the ball at your feet – don't let it stop for want of kicking,' Davitt recorded. He was sent to America on a 'mission relating to the supposed connection between two MPs and the Fenian Party in New York'. In his pocket was a letter of commendation from Lord Salisbury.

Room 56, The Home Office, January 1887

The year of the Jubilee dawned. On 7 January Annabella Jenkinson sent Earl Spencer a note:

I see in the papers this morning that there is a vacancy
on the India Council. Mr Jenkinson is away in Paris
(poste restante) winding up some business connected
with his Government work and I am anxious not to let
this chance pass through want of applying – I have therefore written to Lord Cross.*

I feel so anxious about my husband who has been so
terribly worried and overstrained lately – having been so
badly treated by Mr Matthews . . .

Edward Jenkinson was in Paris settling some final secret affair.
On 10 January 1887 he returned to Room 56 for the last time,
opened the safe and stoked up the little coal fire. Piece by piece
he fed his files into the flames.

Two days later Lord Iddesleigh (Sir Stafford Northcote) dropped
dead from a heart attack in an ante-room at Number Ten Downing Street. Lord Salisbury took over the mantle – he was both
Prime Minister and Foreign Secretary, just as he had been in the
Conservative caretaker administration of two years before. Once
again he might now put his stamp on the most intimate business
of HM Foreign Office.

* Secretary of State for India. As Home Secretary in Lord Salisbury's 1885 caretaker administration, he was copied in on the Millen and Tevis correspondence.

27

Whitehall, January–February 1887

James Monro accepted his victory with diffidence. 'I had no wish to succeed Mr Jenkinson,' he told his son Charlie in the Darjeeling letter; 'in the end, at the urgent request of government, I consented to act as chief of the secret department as regards intelligence.' Room 56 was shut down. The war against American bombers, should they ever return, would now be run from the assistant commissioner's office at 21 Whitehall Place.

He was now in charge of both the CID and the Secret Department. In his first role, pursuing the ordinary miscreants of the teeming metropolis, Mr Monro answered to the commissioner. In the 'special work' he would report directly to the Home Secretary. His second remit was given 'verbally'. Sir Charles Warren brooded testily on this most unmilitary arrangement.

The reluctant secret policeman surveyed his empty kingdom. The files were scant. No consular cables crossed his desk. The Foreign Office kept their secrets close and their ciphers opaque. Gosselin, up in the north of England somewhere, maintained his low-level informers within the IRB – but seemed uncomfortably loyal to his fallen boss. Monro would build the nation's defences in a policeman-like manner. On 2 February a completely new section*

---

* It was styled variously Section D, Special Section, the Special Confidential Section, Special (Secret) Branch, Home Office Crime Department and Special Branch. Monro would refer to it as the Secret Department. The new branch, in effect a secret national domestic security service, was responsible to the Home Secretary, not to the Metropolitan Police commissioner. It would act nationally (this was to be kept secret), with a remit to observe anarchists as well as Fenians and was financed out of imperial and not Metropolitan Police funds. It was administratively separate from Section B – the Special (Irish) Branch established

was established within the Criminal Investigation Department, headed by another Scot, Chief Inspector John Littlechild, with three inspectors under him – John Pope, William Melville and Patrick Quinn. They would be substitutes, it was noted, 'for the private anti-fenian agents employed by Mr Jenkinson'.

Monro needed an ally – an intelligence specialist. There was 'an old friend' pottering in a Home Office backwater as secretary to the prison commissioners, an avowed enemy of Jenkinson. In early February 1887 Robert Anderson was invited back into the secret Whitehall fold. He was to be Monro's 'assistant in the secret work'. He did well – his salary of £600 was topped up by a Secret Service subvention of £400, 'to be reviewed in six months'. It was further agreed that Mr Anderson 'need not repay' the £2,000 paid to him in March 1886 as compensation for being booted out by Jenkinson. Anderson had all along retained the loyalty of his informant in Chicago, a Sullivanite. He had been discreetly feeding Mr Monro titbits of information from this source throughout his battle with his disgraced predecessor. Thomas Beach came on line again.

The mandarins conferred. Sir Julian Pauncefote and Sir Godfrey Lushington, permanent under-secretary at the Home Office, considered delicate issues over discreet luncheons. How much should the policeman know of past operations?

'Mr Monro came over . . . a few days ago when it was settled that, for the future, all communications in regard to Irish conspirators which have lately passed directly between this Department and Mr Jenkinson . . . should be carried on with him at 21 Whitehall Place,' Sir Julian minuted Sir Godfrey on 16 February. It was to be 'for the future'. The past, for now, would remain discreetly veiled. There it was. Henceforth the secret agent would be seeing live intelligence from America. There would be some surprises.

That same day William Hoare sent an urgent cable from New

---

at the outset of the Irish bombing campaign in 1883 – which continued in existence under the veteran Frederick Williamson. Section C was the port police.

York for Lord Salisbury's attention. Someone had turned up at the consulate. 'Inform Hicks-Beach [Irish Secretary]. Bagenal's friend says must leave by steamer tomorrow: life in peril: wants fifty pounds cabled: must have it.'

'This telegram was sent at the request of Captain Darnley Stewart Stephens,' Mr Hoare explained by letter two days later, 'who represented that he had been sent to New York on a secret mission for the Irish executive, and that his mission had in some way been discovered by the leaders of the Fenian organisations here, who had threatened his life if he did not leave the country immediately.'

The captain had been sent the previous December after the meeting with Lord Randolph Churchill to find compromising material on Michael Davitt, then in America on a propaganda tour (also to get married). Davitt had exposed him. Monro must have blinked. According to the consul's report the terrified captain – on his 'secret mission for the Irish executive' – bore a personal testimonial from Lord Salisbury himself.

The moralistic policeman thought he might conduct his secret office above the dirty business of politics. It was not to be.

New York and Chicago, January 1887

Monro had lifted Jenkinson's circus of barmaids and bigamists from the streets of London. Putting his stamp on transatlantic operations was not going to be done with a simple policeman's knock. Who was he supposed to be fighting? Anyone reading the New York papers could see that the Irish revolution in America had gone to war on itself.

The Clan-na-Gael was breaking apart. John Devoy had kept up his bitter campaign against the Triangle, bravely aided in the fight by a Cork-born physician named Dr Patrick Cronin of Chicago, a city Sullivan otherwise had under his thumb. Amid the ever louder allegations of money raised for 'active work' lining the Triangle's pockets, there had been more defections – including Luke Dillon of Philadelphia, a Civil War veteran and former Indian-fighter with a legendary reputation.*

The schismatics met in Brooklyn to form a rival organisation. Dillon was elected chairman of its executive committee. The new 'Clan' (they kept the name) was immediately recognised as its legitimate partner by the Irish Republican Brotherhood. The coalition remained opposed to bombing.

The revived Fenian Brotherhood had meanwhile toppled Rossa in favour of Patrick Sarsfield Cassidy, who was now head of the so-called Fenian Council in New York. The Sligo-born journalist with the Jacobite hero's name was ostensibly a fire-breathing militant. But as Jenkinson reported, he had returned to New York from a meeting with Parnell's representatives in Dublin the year before, on a short-fused promise to check explosions. The promise had expired.

O'Donovan Rossa retrenched around a little group of ultras, the United Irishmen, breathing journalistic fire as much against those who had overthrown him as against the iniquities of England.†

There were now four mutually hostile groups in America.

The order of battle was paradoxical. The breakaway Devoy-Dillon Clan kept to a tenuous ceasefire. The Sullivan Clan in Chicago (they called themselves the 'US' – standing for 'TR' or Triangle) stayed publicly committed to Parnell but was secretly preparing to go on the offensive. Cassidy's Fenian Council in New York was openly committed to dynamite, but through some fix of Jenkinson's it was so far keeping the peace. Rossa raved at the margins. Each accused the other of being a 'Scotland Yard' stooge. It needed someone very devious to put all that together. Deviousness was not one of Mr Monro's qualities.

*   *   *

* It was Dillon, born in Leeds and taken to America by his emigrant parents, who had struck the Chamber of the House of Commons in January 1885 and been one of the few American dynamiters to escape back across the Atlantic.
† After Cassidy's takeover of November 1886 Rossa invented a character called 'Rody the Rover' in his increasingly eccentric newspaper – a mysterious British spy in New York who was 'in the Council of the Fenian Brotherhood – carrying out his contract with the English – to kill out the dynamite movement in America'. Plentiful clues were dropped as to the informer's identity – Cassidy himself. In April 1890 Cassidy sued for libel. Rossa gave rambling evidence that his enemy had gone to Europe in 1885 with letters of introduction from 'the police chief of New York' to 'the chiefs of police in Ireland and England'. The jury found against Rossa.

Locating Frank Millen in the splits and twists of 1886 is problematic. References to the general vanish abruptly from the Foreign Office 'Fenian Brotherhood' record soon after his departure from Mexico City in November 1885 (they would reappear three years later). The New York consulate's own 'Secret Dispatch Book' for the period contains nothing on Millen.

There are no more references to him in Jenkinson's surviving correspondence (although he clearly had a high-level informer in the Sullivan faction during the year of home rule's fall) – nor any direct evidence that the payment seam from the Bank of Mexico, London and South America was continuous. But someone was still directing the general's multiple undercover career.

He faced the same venal dilemma as he had on his escape from the failed coup in Dublin two decades earlier. Which of the squabbling groups might reward him best? He stayed loyal to Sullivan and the Triangle.

The Chicago lawyer had a commission. His enemies in the Devoy-Cronin faction were reforging the link with the Irish Republican Brotherhood – claiming the mantle of legitimacy – lick-spittling Parnell and his busted 'moral force' route to Irish independence. Millen would go to Europe to broker the Triangle's own agreement with those that Sullivan might present as true bearers of the revolutionary flame, the die-hard Fenian exiles in Paris.* James Stephens was still shuffling around, the Casey brothers and Eugene Davis boozily proclaiming dynamite vengeance to whatever journalist happened to be buying the drinks. Millen accepted. In early December 1886 he boarded the steamer for Europe. He would travel to France via Dublin and London. Strangely, for one embarking on such a conspiratorial journey, he took his wife and daughter with him.

* There was a meeting of the Supreme Council of the IRB in Paris on 4–5 January attended by delegates from Great Britain and Ireland at which 'dynamite and other matters of a similar nature were discussed and unanimously condemned', according to a report by Major Gosselin. The note in Dublin Castle Special Branch files dated 26 January 1887 continues: 'There is no danger of active work of any kind unless some inner circle is formed provided with American funds. This is not at all improbable as we know General Millen when here had command of a large sum.' The report went to the Chief Secretary for Ireland the following day.

17 Thurlow Square, London SW, Christmas 1886

Ambling muffled in a greatcoat through the wintry squares of
South Kensington Frank Millen hardly looked the deadly dynamiter of penny-dreadful legend. The benign military gent and his
daughter Kitty were lodging in Thurlow Square – a good address
on the fashionable side of the park. The oil-painted stucco house
was home to a civil engineer named William Henry Maitland and
his large family. They all enjoyed a jolly Christmas. Miss Kitty
was treated a month later to an informative tour of the Palace
of Westminster. She was admitted to the Ladies' Gallery of the
Commons as the guest of an MP, a Mr Nolan – an acquaintance
of her father's. He had accepted strict instructions that, on the
general's enforced absence on business, only he might 'escort her
round town' – according to evidence James Monro would give
two years later to a parliamentary select committee.

It all seemed most respectable.

In early January 1887, so Mr Monro told the inquisitive MPs,
the general bade Kitty goodbye and went to Paris.

Paris, January 1887

If Frank Millen can be firmly placed in the French capital in the
first days of 1887, so can someone else. Edward Jenkinson was
in Paris 'winding up some business connected to his government
work', so Mrs Annabella Jenkinson told Earl Spencer in her place-
seeking letter of 7 January.*

What business? There is no direct evidence but it might well
be assumed that Millen and Jenkinson met – just as they had
done in Paris thirteen months before. Millen had come to broker
Sullivan's offer of alliance with the old firebrands. It could only
signal the Clan's intended return to war. But what were the

* There was no vacancy on the India Council. Salisbury noted to Lord Cross on
13 January, a week after the loyal wife's supplication: 'It had come to this. If
Jenkinson did not go, Monro would have done so. But nevertheless Jenkinson
has done good work and ought not to be cast adrift . . .'

reasons for Jenkinson's journey? Home rule was the only answer, he had told Lord Salisbury. Another bomb would bury it, he had warned Earl Spencer. His every act since his own conversion to home rule was to keep the bombing truce, not to break it. Was Jenkinson in Paris to bolster the IRB 'peace' negotiations? Any motive for meeting Millen meanwhile seemed impenetrable.

A window on Millen's Parisian dealings at least was given in a letter from Luke Dillon to John Devoy. Written from Philadelphia on 7 February it gave a glimpse of the general's mission – and the first hint of the Jubilee plot:

> General Millen returned [to New York] from his excursion to Paris, and has drawn on his imagination for facts as usual. That grand connecting link in the chain that binds us to the people at home has been found . . .
>
> In Paris he met the representative of the Fenian Brotherhood who of course has done all the General wanted . . .
>
> A council of the Fenians was called on Sunday last under the command of Cassidy . . .
>
> Poor Rossa was left out in the cold, but was caught by one of the council peeping through the keyhole.
>
> The Council refused to have anything to do with the Triangle, but did receive Millen's communication. Millen wanted to form a coalition with the Fenian element [Casey, Stephens et al in Paris], but I have it on the word of one who was present that they will have nothing to do with them.
>
> This member of the Council came to me to request my assistance to raise two thousand dollars to enable them to do some work. They claim that they intend celebrating the Queen's birthday, and that one hundred and fifty men are prepared to work with Greek fire with which they are at present supplying them.
>
> I would not mention this, even to you, if I felt there was a possibility of these men accomplishing anything . . .

The council wanted an interview with Dillon himself, he told Devoy. 'I presume they have learned in some way that I am not entirely ignorant of the manner those things are done.' He would go through with it 'to get at the bottom of Millen's overtures . . .' Their purpose was clear enough – if not quite yet to Luke Dillon. Alexander Sullivan had resolved to go back to war. It was a clever construct: the Triangle's break in the truce would be secret; the bombing would be resumed by a 'Fenian Council' front – or at least those members who would cooperate. They would even pay for it. Millen would propel the operation from a forward base in Paris.

All that was needed was a rumble of revolutionary thunder for Parnell and his American allies, Sullivan's rivals, to be destroyed. The formula might be said to be politically useful elsewhere.

At Sullivan's side in Chicago was a trusted Clansman, Thomas Beach. New arrangements in Whitehall were already moving him to the heart of the matter. They were also advancing a parallel secret career – the man mentioned in Dillon's letters as one of Millen's Paris contacts, 'the representative of the Fenian Brotherhood'. He, for one, seemed to be being most cooperative. It was General Charles Carrol-Tevis, the senate wing informer of twenty years before, the Foreign Office's very own spy in the French capital.

St Petersburg, January 1887

As the year of the Jubilee opened, there was other secret business for HM Foreign Office to conduct. Tevis would be at the heart of it. In icebound St Petersburg a battle was joined between rival factions at the Imperial court for the heart and mind of Tsar Alexander III. Ambitious generals backed by Mikhail Katkov, the ultra-nationalist editor of the *Moscow Gazette*, were urging him to break the alliance with Germany and Austria-Hungary. The Dreikaiserbund, the League of the Three Emperors by which the German Chancellor Bismarck had settled the peace of Europe, was due to expire on 18 June 1887. The treaty was a high secret of state – but Katkov knew all about it.

Let it die unmourned, Katkov argued, and Russia could realise
its pan-Slavist ambitions in the Balkans – thwarted ten years before
when the victories over Turkey won by the Tsar's assassinated
father were rolled back by the shameful Congress of Berlin. Make
a defensive alliance with France – then pursue 'an active policy'.
The editor was winning the argument. Lord Salisbury saw it
plainly. It would be war.

The English Prime Minister had supplanted Bismarck as the
Moscow Gazette's demon-in-chief – spinner of Balkan plots, under-
writer of Russia's humiliations. The railway pushing out across
central Asia would soon be completed to bear the imperial armies
towards the Afghan frontier. British military plans were urgently
reassessed. India could be held if the 'native' regiments stayed
loyal. The Punjab police had reports of subversion in the Sikh
regiments, bastion against an invasion from the north. A 'prophecy' was circulating in the bazaars – that their long-ago dispossessed Maharajah was about to return. The White Tsar had
seen his triumph in a vision.

Nicholas de Giers, the Imperial Foreign Minister, despaired.
Russia would lose. There were those – ultra-nationalists as well
as revolutionaries – who sought a lost war as the only way of
shaking the obscurantist empire from its medieval torpor. Outmanoeuvred and humiliated, de Giers was clinging to office by a
thread. In London the head of HM Foreign Secret Service, Sir
Julian Pauncefote, sought a way to save the apostle of peace.

Paris, January 1887

There were others who dreamed of a great smash-up in Europe.
General Georges Boulanger, the French War Minister with
Napoleonic pretensions, crudely whipped up anti-German fervour. Paris teetered on the brink of a coup. A group of far subtler
conspirators saw a glittering opportunity for revenge on Germany
for the humiliating defeat of 1871. France could never prevail
alone – but conjoined with Russia a triumphant war would
win back the martyr provinces of Alsace-Lorraine. It was called
la revanche. Through the great war-scare winter of 1886–7

conspiratorial agents traversed the continent on frozen trains seeking to bind the atheist republic and holy Russia in a military compact. It was whispered of as *l'alliance Franco-Russe*.

The most exotic go-between was a Jewish-born doctor named Elie de Cyon, Paris correspondent of the *Moscow Gazette*. 'Many Irish fugitives made themselves known to me as a close associate of Katkov's,' he wrote in his memoirs. 'They were offering the services of Irish nationalists, particularly the group established in America.' The contacts began in 1885. Cyon had a good friend in Paris, a trusted member of the little circle of *revanchistes*. He was a retired American general, an Irish patriot, flamboyant veteran of many armies and many battles. It was General Charles Carrol-Tevis, the 'representative of the Fenian Brotherhood' mentioned in Luke Dillon's letter – who had 'done everything [Millen] wanted' on his trip to Paris.

Tevis was strictly a Foreign Office asset. But when Edward Jenkinson was copied in May 1885 with the Tokyo telegrams reactivating the Paris resident's long-dormant undercover career, the Home Office spymaster already seemed to know all about him – even the address of his Parisian mistress. Red Jim McDermott had supplied him with the information back in the high-rolling days that the ginger-moustached *agent provocateur* spent with the Caseys, Eugene Davis, 'Prince Albert's daughter' et al. – cooking up dynamite plots for a fiver a time to terrify London newspaper readers.

Another 'conspirator' had joined the drinking firm in Paris that summer – John Patrick Hayes, the Philadelphia-based informer. Hayes proceeded to London to collude in the production of the Black Pamphlet, portraying Tevis as a die-hard Fenian and Patrick Casey as a dynamite fiend.

Hayes returned to America, to New York this time, with a bold new proposition to sell.

Michael Davitt had good cause to probe his movements thereafter. He published some of his discoveries, heavily coded, in his campaigning newspaper the *Labour World* in autumn 1890:

> Shortly after the conversion of Mr Gladstone to Home
> Rule [early 1886], an agent of Mr Hoare's, high in the

councils of the Fenian Brotherhood in New York, suggested a mission to Katkov in Moscow for the purpose
of enlisting his anti-British feeling on the side of the Irish
revolutionary effort.

It was likewise proposed by this same agent that a
dynamite movement should be inaugurated in London
in order to prevent if possible 'the bartering away of Irish
independence by Gladstone and Parnell for a mess of
Home Rule'.

The proposal was accepted by those to whom it was
made and two emissaries set out from New York to fulfil
the double mission.

One was a British-paid agent, according to the account, the
other seemed not to be – although Davitt inserted a whisper of
suspicion. 'The envoys reached Paris in safety. There they made
out one Patrick Casey,' the strange story continued. 'They likewise called up General Blank whose name, for certain reasons,
cannot be given just yet, and obtained from him a letter of introduction to Katkoff of Moscow.'

'Blank' was clearly Tevis – but who were the envoys? More
revelations were promised but they were never published.* It
looked as if one of them must be Millen pulling his old Russian
stunts – but according to cryptic entries in Davitt's own notebooks 'the agent of Mr Hoare's' was John P. Hayes and Patrick
Sarsfield Cassidy the duped fellow-traveller.† Tevis entertained
the envoys at his elegant apartment on the rue Daru. There was

* The series of articles headlined 'Unionism and Crime' was abruptly halted due
to the Parnell–O'Shea scandal. Davitt's paper folded soon afterwards.
† Davitt's 'Notes of an Amateur Detective' read: 'SC [Sarsfield Cassidy] war over
and called on Z. [Tevis] He and H [Hayes] wanted letters of introduction to
Katkoff of Moscow. They were got from XXX [Cyon]. H paraded these in London
and Dublin. The couple did not go to Russia. Genl demanded return of letters
and they came months after in an open envelope.
    'H brought two Englishmen to see Gen one day and talked dynamite war in
their presence. Lived with whores while here and drank.
    'In end 1886 H went to Dublin and pretended Russian "generals" were
prepared to go in for war in Ireland . . . Stayed about a month. Burst into tears
one night and said he was suspected . . .'

brave talk of the doomed invasion of Canada so long ago. Cassidy was seduced – would the general honour him by agreeing to act as the Fenian Brotherhood's representative in Paris?

If Davitt is to be believed, in the year of home rule's fall HM Foreign Office was privy to, if not yet quite directing, a conspiracy linking Katkov's messianic ambitions in Moscow with a dynamite plot dressed in ultra-nationalist clothes to derail Parnell and Gladstone with him. It was never effected. Neither 'envoy' got to Moscow. Hayes was too bungling or venal a conspirator. Inflated by his revolutionary diplomacy Cassidy went back to New York to stage his Fenian Council coup against Rossa.

By the early spring of 1887 things had moved on. The Conservatives were in power. The inconvenient Mikhail Katkov was alarmingly in the ascendant in St Petersburg. What if Fenian fire could be turned against him?

Paris, February 1887

The instrument was providential. Maharajah Duleep Singh, the dispossessed ex-King of the Punjab in British India, had turned up in Paris in mid 1886 publicly proclaiming his hatred of his former English mentors. Queen Victoria was heartbroken. He had been a special favourite since being brought to London as a 'beautiful and charming boy' almost forty years before – when his kingdom was annexed after two Anglo-Sikh wars.* He had been granted an enormous India Office pension – and a government-mortgaged Suffolk shooting estate where he might advance, it was to be hoped, to become a true Christian gentleman.

He had tired of his gilded imprisonment. Siren voices called from the Punjab. He was the subject of a prophecy. In 1886 the Maharajah abandoned his wife and large family, was rebaptised a Sikh and departed for Paris with his teenage lover, a chambermaid from Kennington. Now plump, middle aged and greedy he pronounced himself 'England's proud implacable foe', threatening to offer his services to Russia. He found a willing English-speaking

* See Christy Campbell, *The Maharajah's Box* (HarperCollins, 2000).

type-setter in Paris who printed up pompous proclamations to 'his people', who were yearning, so he believed, for his return. Duleep sent the inflammatory manifestos to London as evidence of his unbending purpose. The printer's name was Patrick Casey.

The Maharajah had an audience with the Imperial Russian ambassador, who reported the overture to the Foreign Ministry in St Petersburg. Nicholas de Giers had no use for an avowed enemy of England, but others in Russia certainly might.

Queen Victoria was profoundly alarmed. The Maharajah sent her letters at once cringing and abusive. He was set to fly into the welcoming arms of the Tsar, he told her. A huge scandal was threatening. James Monro was sounded out – might Scotland Yard send a detective? The assistant commissioner was extremely reluctant. 'An agent employed to watch is sure to be arrested by the French police and kept in custody until he disclosed his employers,' he told Henry Matthews briskly in November 1886. The Foreign Office took the operation over. Tevis was instructed to make overtures and did so via Casey.

In mid February Tevis met the Maharajah to make a proposition. It was very much not an inducement to return to London. Tevis had connections with Mikhail Katkov. Get to Moscow, and the great man would embrace Duleep's cause, he told him. Tevis lured him with wild proposals, including an American 'military colony' to be established in Afghanistan, which would 'attract 13,000 Irish deserters from the British army'. Tevis had already been in contact with its potential commander, 'one of our most devoted friends', someone uniquely experienced in such ventures. It was Millen.

Tevis would be the Maharajah's confidential secretary and anchor the empire-shaking enterprise from Paris. The plan seemed beyond all reason, but Duleep believed it. As the Maharajah prepared to embark on his bizarre journey, every conspiratorial communication was copied to Whitehall overnight – to Francis Hyde Villiers, private secretary to Sir Julian Pauncefote.

Do not try and stop him, Tevis urged. If Scotland Yard detectives were on Duleep's track (they were not), then withdraw

them immediately, he messaged the Foreign Office. Sir Julian
Pauncefote dusted off reports of the Cassidy-Tevis-Katkov con-
tacts the previous spring. Plant dynamiters in the inconvenient
Moscow editor's lap and Nicholas de Giers might indeed be saved.

New York, March 1887

Millen had returned to New York early the month before with
the fruits of his Sullivan-inspired diplomacy in Paris. The general's
January encounters in the French capital had seemed more to do
with coalition-making than with dynamite, but in New York the
discussions had become more warlike. John Devoy received
another report on 14 March: 'The F[enian] B[rotherhood] are
seeking alliances offensive and defensive, principally the former,
their object being not organisation but the procurement of funds
for the celebration of Mrs Brown's very good health . . .'

The deal was struck. Cassidy commissioned Millen to go to
France and arrange the 'celebrations'. Payment was $500. The
general, typically, touched the *New York Herald* foreign desk for
some advance expenses – he might have a story for them.

Millen was meanwhile secretly reporting to Alexander Sullivan
in Chicago all along. Davitt accused William Hoare, the British
consul, of having a stake in the mission. Millen was being paid
four times over.

It was working out splendidly. Sullivan would get his victory.
A bomb anywhere near 'Mrs Brown' would bury Parnell and his
American allies with him. Cassidy would out-Rossa Rossa with
his militancy. Millen would pocket the cash and retire with his
revolutionary reputation intact. It would have to be exposed, of
course – all that was needed was the biggest scare imaginable.

On 13 March there was a very big scare indeed. Tsar Alexander
III departed the Anichkov Palace by carriage on his way to the
solemn memorial service for his father, assassinated by nihilist
dynamite exactly six years before. Police were forewarned and
waiting – 'a cloud of detectives swarmed from the crowd' to
grapple to the ground a twenty-three-year-old student named
Andreyushkin, a member of the 'terrorist fraction of the People's

Will'. In his hands was a hollowed-out book, a copy of the Russian criminal code. It concealed a short-fused dynamite-shrapnel bomb doused in strychnine. Bismarck had inspired the attack, so Katkov raged, 'to paralyse the foreign policy of France and Russia' in the *Moscow Gazette*. Berlin accused Katkov of plotting a coup.

Paris and St Petersburg, 21 March 1887

Maharajah Duleep Singh departed Paris with his mistress, servant and several spaniels eight days after the St Petersburg *attentat*. The Nord Express rolled at a stately pace across Europe towards the nervous Imperial capital on the Neva. Duleep bore with him a passport, recently obtained on Tevis's intervention from the British embassy on the rue St Honoré. The parchment document – oddly perhaps for an exotic protégé of Queen Victoria – was in the name of one of her most reluctant subjects, 'Patrick Casey' of Kilkenny, *soi-disant* dynamite enthusiast. Casey had also obtained the necessary Russian visas. As he changed trains in Berlin, the passport – plus a large sum in francs and gold coins – was deftly stolen.

At the border crossing the Maharajah, dressed in his oriental finery, insisted he was Monsieur Casey. The frontier gendarmerie were baffled. They thought he was a circus magician and his young female companion a fortune-teller. After a frantic round of telegrams Katkov's agents spirited the passportless traveller and his entourage over the border. They arrived in the Imperial capital, St Petersburg – to be moved smartly on to Moscow, citadel of pan-Slav ambition, tucked up in the Hotel Dussaux on the Bolshoi Lubiyanka. The identity switch seemed pantomimic, apart from the agenda being spun by Tevis in Paris and the Foreign Office in London. For a month thereafter the exotic Sikh clung to his bizarre alter ego. He thought being taken for an Irishman was 'very amusing'. News of Katkov's strange guests began to leak.

Why, it began to be asked in diplomatic circles, should the editor of the *Moscow Gazette* have wished to smuggle the notorious dynamiter Patrick Casey into Russia?

New York and Paris, April 1887

Frank Millen boarded the SS *Gascogne* of the Compagnie Générale Transatlantique in New York harbour on 10 April – bearing the Fenian Council's commission 'to celebrate Mrs Brown's very good health'. In his impresario's astrakhan-collared overcoat he looked more likely do so at the music hall than with dynamite. He travelled as 'Mr Muller'. The crossing, direct to Le Havre this time, took eight days.

According to a report compiled seven months later by James Monro, 'He went at once to Paris where he . . . put himself in communication with well known fenians in Paris, and notably with a man named Tevis who is the principal agent of the Fenian Brotherhood in Europe.'

Monro wrote his report in November 1887 when still in pursuit of the 'Jubilee plot'. He did not know then (but he found out later) that 'a man named Tevis' was also the principal agent of HM Foreign Secret Service in Europe.

PART SEVEN

In the Year of the Jubilee

'Never, ever can I forget this brilliant year . . .
so full of marvellous kindness, loyalty
and devotion . . .'
Queen Victoria's *Journal*, 31 December 1887

28

Dublin and London, spring 1887

Ireland was plunged into new crisis. Agricultural prices had collapsed in the autumn of 1886: tenants could not or would not
pay rent. On 23 October the *United Ireland* newspaper, edited
by William O'Brien, MP, published an article called the 'Plan
of Campaign' by a fellow Irish member, Timothy Harrington,
secretary of the National League. It called for rent money to be
pooled to resist evictions. Mass meetings and rent strikes gripped
Ireland to a measure unseen since the semi-revolutionary period
of 1880–82. This time Parnell stayed aloof.

The Government went on the attack. Four MPs were pros-
ecuted on charges of intimidation – and acquitted by a Dublin
court. Tougher legislation was needed and a stronger hand to
wield it.

Sir Michael Hicks-Beach, the Irish Secretary, bowed out with
failing eyesight. He was replaced on 7 March 1887 by the thirty-
nine-year-old Arthur Balfour, Lord Salisbury's nephew, the rising
Tory politician whom Gladstone, armed with Jenkinson's apoca-
lyptic warnings, had tried to recruit to home rule at Eaton Hall.
Balfour set to drafting a Crimes Bill with the power to declare
any organisation illegal by special proclamation.

On the day of Balfour's elevation a sensational article appeared
in *The Times* newspaper. Headlined PARNELLISM AND CRIME
it heralded a blockbusting series of exposés on the alleged links
of the Irish Party with agrarian outrage and murder. Gladstone
was the real target: the Liberal leader was 'deliberately allying
with the paid agents of an organisation whose ultimate sanction
is murder'.

Two more articles appeared – the work of the paper's leader-writer, John Woulfe Flanagan, the son of an Irish Catholic-Unionist judge – examining grisly episodes of the land war, the Phoenix Park murders and the dynamite campaign.

Printing House Square had barely begun to fight. Leading articles goaded Parnell to sue. Sitting in the safe of the editor George Buckle was political dynamite: the letters – six allegedly by Parnell, five more by Patrick Egan from Pigott's 'black bag' – received from Edward Houston the previous autumn. *The Times* had behaved not entirely incompetently. Extraordinary efforts were made to acquire genuine Parnell signatures for comparison. George Smith Inglis, the eminent handwriting expert, declared the letters genuine. At last, in January 1887, Edward Houston had been paid for his efforts.

The newspaper had originally intended publishing the letters on the opening of the new parliament. W. H. Smith, Leader of the House of Commons, was informed of the intended move on 27 January 1887, but a glimmer of doubt intervened. Houston had earlier sounded out the Liberal Unionist Lord Hartington as a potential purchaser. He consulted the eminent lawyer Sir Henry James, himself a Liberal defector, who warned that the source, if it was Richard Pigott, was tainted. *The Times* was informed. On 12 April Henry Matthews offered to substantiate how an inflammatory letter of January 1882 might have been smuggled out of Kilmainham prison; the investigative task was passed to Robert Anderson.

Still Parnell did not sue for libel. It was time to bring out the battering ram. On the morning of 18 April, the day Balfour's Crimes Bill was to get its second reading in the Commons, *The Times* interrupted its usual six-column typographic torpor with a 'splash' crossing pages eight and nine – MR PARNELL AND THE PHOENIX PARK MURDERS.

'We place before our readers today a document the grave importance of which it would be difficult to overestimate,' the leader-writer thundered. The paper promised 'documentary evidence which has a most serious bearing in the Parnell conspiracy . . .' It was a letter printed in 'facsimile' dated 15 May

1882, supposedly to Patrick Egan, in which Parnell allegedly stated 'Burke got no more than he deserved in Phoenix Park'. Robert Anderson had already taken special notice. Number 39 Linden Gardens was piled high with ten years of Clan-na-Gael circulars dispatched from his closely guarded agent in Chicago. He had a unique contribution to make to what he would call the 'counter-Fenian conspiracy'.

Six days before the *Times* exclusive broke Anderson had approached a potential intermediary, Hugh Oakley Arnold-Forster, adopted son of William Forster and a prominent Liberal-Unionist opponent of home rule. He replied on 14 April: 'Dear Anderson. I find that our people C– [Chamberlain] & Co do not like to undertake anything of so pronounced a nature . . .

'I should myself suggest that you should allow me to open negotiations either with the Loyal Pats or with Buckle of *The Times.*'

Arnold-Forster saw the editor at the Reform Club the day the facsimile letter was published. The deal was struck. On 1 May he wrote to Anderson: 'I have seen Buckle and in accordance with your wishes I have at his behest and according to your instructions communicated your name to him.'* *The Times* had recruited the secret civil servant as their anonymous special correspondent.

Anderson's intervention was timely. When the letters had been published in American newspapers the month before, Patrick Egan, the former Land League treasurer, compared them with old correspondence conducted with Pigott over the sale of his newspapers to the league six years before. The phraseology was strangely similar. A committee was appointed to investigate, reporting in the newspapers in May that the letters were the work of the Dublin journalist. William Hoare, the New York

---

* The very opposite to Sir Robert Anderson's account during the 1910 parliamentary furore: 'Mr Arnold-Forster pressed the matter on me and I went to Mr Monro at Scotland Yard . . . whose judgement was that the articles would play an important part in what may be termed the anti-Fenian conspiracy,' he told *The Times.*

consul, sent the cuttings proclaiming Pigott as the forger to Lord Salisbury.

Any jitters over Pigott were swept away when the first of Anderson's fabrication-free articles called 'Behind the Scenes in America' ran on 13 May. It tore into the 'new departure' of 1879 as an alliance of 'quasi-constitutionalists and revolutionaries'. The second article, published a week later, dwelt on the May 1883 Clan convention at Philadelphia, Sullivan's election as chairman of the National League of America and its role in financing Parnellite MPs. A further article was promised for 1 June.

Rumours of a grave threat to the Queen were already in the papers on both sides of the Atlantic. The *New York Times* had reported on 4 May:

> Extreme nationalists in this country are preparing for another series of dynamite outrages in England, and many signs point to the Queen's Jubilee as the time fixed upon for the beginning of the reign of terror.
>
> Some of the most violent of the members of the Clan-na-Gael have been induced to join in the work, and all the noisy and talkative element has been quietly got rid of.

The *Morning Advertiser* in London had an exclusive on 28 May, an interview with a 'Paris dynamiter' named Michael Flannery. The exiled Fenians had called a bombing truce the year before, Mr Flannery revealed, so that 'Mr Parnell should have no opportunity of throwing the blame upon us in case he failed to obtain Home Rule . . .

'We therefore made certain communications to Mr Parnell through certain channels,' he said. 'We promised to leave the field free to him for his own operations . . .' But time had run out. 'The result has been a complete failure for the Parnellites.'

'The inaction of the extreme party' had also been caused by the Rossa–Cassidy split in New York, Flannery revealed. But 'a month ago' (when Millen was in Paris) 'a general understanding was arrived at between both wings on the Continent'.

'Were any practical steps resolved upon?' asked the reporter.

'Yes, oh, yes!' said Flannery. 'The dynamite movement is assuming dimensions that will bring upon its side men who were formerly with us in everything except the particular plan of action ... It has been felt by some that to levy war upon men, women, and children in the streets of London was not to make war upon England. The new movement will be ... a unanimous movement against English national power ...' The fearsome Professor Mezzeroff was experimenting with a new explosive, melinite, in concert with two French revolutionary chemists.

Was Mr Flannery 'prepared to say anything with regard to the secret relations between the Parliamentary party and the Irish extremists'?

The interviewee was most certainly not – only that 'with regard to the articles, "Parnellism and Crime" ... the dynamiters in Paris know perfectly well who is the principal author ...'

What was their programme? 'One section of the advanced party will operate against the naval and military power of England,' answered Flannery. 'Another section, working under the same leaders and under the same constitution, will be directing its attention to the Afghan frontier ...

'The Maharajah Duleep Singh has come to an understanding with the leading members of the Irish advanced party to work in parallel lines with them ...' he said. 'It is well known now at the British embassies in both Paris and St Petersburg that Duleep Singh actually used Patrick Casey's passport ... the officials at the Paris Embassy appeared to regard the proceeding as ironical ...'

'Will there be any Fenians on the spot to meet him?'

'Yes, a couple of Fenian delegates have been appointed to meet Singh on the Afghan frontier.'

'Might we expect dynamite explosions in England on or about the date of Her Majesty's Jubilee?' Flannery refused to answer.

Robert Anderson's third article was published in *The Times* on 1 June. It recalled the Irish National League of America's 1886 Chicago convention but emphasised the secret Clan congress that had preceded it and had 'approved active work'. The revelations concluded with some very well-sourced intelligence from New York:

> It is definitely known that urgent appeals have been made for funds to enable them to resume the outrage campaign in England and the belief is universal that the passing of the Crimes Bill will be the signal for slipping the leash which now holds the dynamiters in check.
>
> While themselves [the Clan] remaining in the background they have for this purpose sanctioned negotiations in their name with the O'Donovan Rossa faction, who, having deposed Rossa himself as a swindler, have reconstituted 'The Fenian Brotherhood', with a 'Council' in New York.
>
> Under these auspices a circular has been lately issued of which the following is a copy: 'The Council of the Fenian Brotherhood, having determined to resume active operations, appeal for aid from all Irishmen to sustain them in the work. Work must be done this year. Will you help? All moneys and post-office orders to be addressed to John Murphy, Treasurer, P.O. Box 2282, New York City, who will return receipt for same.'*
>
> The 'active operations' intended are described in the cynical jargon of the conspirators as a pyrotechnic display in honour of the Queen's Jubilee or in other words a series of dynamite and incendiary outrages to startle the nation amid the peaceful rejoicings of the month which opens today.

There are no intelligence reports from the New York or other US consulates in the Foreign Office files for the months from March to June, but Monro was meanwhile getting very detailed

---

* John Murphy was the Fenian Brotherhood's accountant. A 'strictly private' letter in the *Times* archives from a 'J. Murphy, Ex-Detective Inspector' of New York, dated 22 September 1888, gives an account of cheques he had personally seen in a mysterious fund, 'paid to a certain man', drawn on the *United Ireland* newspaper account, Hibernian Bank, Dublin. Two of them were signed by its editor William O'Brien and another Parnellite MP, Dr J. E. Kenny, he reported.

information from somewhere. Nine days before the Flannery interview was published, the policeman was magisterially able to inform the Foreign Office of American intentions, rather than the other way round. He memoed Sir Julian Pauncefote on 19 May:

> I send you a note on intended dispatch of explosives from America. I shall feel much obliged if you would send the note to our Consul at Havre by tonight's mail and ask him to make enquiry about the case.
>
> If it is manifested, its progress in transit will not be difficult to trace but, at present, it will be advisable not to reveal character of its alleged contents, in case of danger to the informant.
>
> Information has been received that a case containing 24 tins of explosives in the shape of what is known as Greek fire, has not long ago been sent from America by a steamer of the French line.
>
> It is said that the case was consigned to one Miller, or Muller at Paris.
>
> It is very important to ascertain from the manifests of the steamers which have arrived at Havre from America during the present month, whether any such case arrived and what has become of it . . .
>
> I have a couple of officers at Havre, and their services are very much at your disposal.

Mr Bernal, the British consul at Le Havre, replied on the 25 May: 'There is no trace on the manifests of the five last steamers of the Compagnie Générale Transatlantique which have arrived here from New York of the case referred to.' There was no explosive. Someone seemed anxious to plant a bomb in Mr Monro's imagination.

Where had such detailed American intelligence come from? It seemed that Monro had still not heard of the Mexico City contact. He was not so stupid as to be unable to make the connection between Millen and 'one Miller or Muller at Paris'. And why would explosives be sent under such transparent cover?

The informant was Thomas Beach, Anderson's agent alongside

Alexander Sullivan in Chicago. That is how the civil servant knew
so much about the Triangle's overtures to the Fenian Council.
He fed the information to Monro bit by bit – just as he was
penning his exclusives for *The Times* based on the same source.*

James Monro meanwhile had taken discreet precautions of his
own. He had a closely guarded agent in France, Inspector William
Melville, working undercover as a port watcher at Le Havre.
Sometime soon after Millen's arrival around 18 April the inspector
was discreetly detached to find the traveller in Paris. He found
him at the Hôtel du Palais.†

The pace was quickening. Seven days before the assistant commissioner told the Foreign Office that explosives were being
shipped from America his own man in Paris had reported that
Millen was on the move. He was heading for the channel port
of Boulogne. Monro, for now, chose to keep this information a
strictly Home Office affair.

Thomas Beach himself had also crossed the Atlantic. His journey to London paralleled Millen's to France. He recorded in his
memoirs: 'Nothing of importance came to pass up to the month
of April 1887 when I made another trip to Europe without,
however, any letters or credentials on this occasion.' But someone
had inspired him.

---

* Anderson depicted the two men acting in clubbable collusion – 'inspired by
the confidence and freedom of an intimate relationship – with evenings spent
tête-à-tête over dinner', he wrote in 1910. 'Neither then nor at any other time
did he express to me disapproval of the denunciation of the dynamiters in *The
Times*.' His former friend's denials were a 'failure of memory'.
† Monro wrote in the Darjeeling letter of the general's movements later that
summer: 'We thought that Millen would probably return to the same hotel in
which he had lived before proceeding to Boulogne. And so he did. Here *again*
he met with an Englishman (or rather Irishman) who had been in France for
some time, being none other than Inspector Melville of Scotland Yard.'
William Melville, born in Sneem, County Kerry, began his secret police career
as a sergeant in the S(I)B in 1883. He was later head of the Special Branch and
the War Office Intelligence Department in the critical period before the Great
War – under the title 'M'.

29

The power struggle in Russia was approaching its climax. On 16 April, two days before Frank Millen stepped ashore at Le Havre, Duleep Singh at last met Mikhail Katkov in Moscow. They embraced with a kiss – their victory was surely not far off. Fleet Street correspondents reported wildly meanwhile that the notorious dynamiter Patrick Casey was somehow wandering round Moscow with 'a Hindoo companion'. Lord Salisbury decided: no more dissembling.

On the 27th Sir Robert Morier, HM minister in the Imperial capital, was instructed to reveal to Nicholas de Giers who 'Casey' really was – and, much more damning, just whose agents had smuggled the circus of assassins across the border ten days after the St Petersburg attentat. It was Katkov. The intelligence would be turned to good account.

On 10 May Katkov personally presented the Tsar with a long memorandum from the Maharajah promising to 'wrench India out of the hands of England'. His Imperial Majesty scribbled approving minutes in the margin. On the morning of 29 May Katkov cabled Duleep in Moscow: 'Your Highness, your business is in a good way.' Triumph over the Foreign Ministry doves seemed just days away.

De Giers fought back. The British Foreign Office had already handed him the weapon. Briefed very discreetly by Sir Robert Morier, the Foreign Minister had been able to reveal to his astonished sovereign later that same day, the 29th, that it was Katkov who had smuggled 'Patrick Casey' into Russia. The man was an assassin. He was intending the death of Queen Victoria. Rumours of a Jubilee dynamite plot were the talk of London. On 30 May Katkov was summoned to the Imperial summer palace at Gatchina outside St Petersburg. Before Tsar Alexander III the editor begged forgiveness on his knees. It was all lies; it was a conspiracy against him . . .

The coup by newspaper had been spiked.

Hôtel Bourgogne, Boulogne-sur-Mer, France, May–June 1887

It was a scene of the utmost respectability – an English couple taking tea with an American gentleman of military bearing and his charming wife in a French seaside hotel. The couple were taking an ozone-blown constitutional on doctor's advice, so the English lady explained, for her newly-retired husband's gout. They all seemed the best of friends. The Thomsons were on the Millen case.

The general, as Inspector William Melville had reported to Monro from Paris, had left for Boulogne on 12 May. He summoned Madame Millen to join him from Dublin. The Thomsons arrived soon afterwards – and 'as the two wives struck up a friendship – so did their husbands'. But who had sent them and why? The evidence is contradictory. Monro said in the Darjeeling letter that *he* 'had deputed Supt Thomson for the purpose'. Mrs Martha Thomson said of her late husband's commission: 'He was employed privately by the Home Office and Mr Monro in many cases – amongst these the Jubilee Plot.'

Sir Edward Henry, commissioner of the Metropolitan Police, when asked in 1910 to find out more about the Clacton claimant, replied: 'Mr Thomson retired from the force in May '87, and did no work for the police subsequent to retirement. In June '87 apparently he was employed by Sir R. Anderson to make some inquiry.'

The commissioner's verdict (he was the only disinterested observer) was that the odd couple were freelancing for Anderson.

Boulogne was getting crowded. Inspector Melville was detached

from Paris to watch the proceedings.* Another interested party
stirred. Michael Davitt later had his own cause to investigate the
seaside ménage. The 'amateur detective' interviewed General
Charles Carrol-Tevis on the subject in Paris in October 1888. He
noted his discoveries in his cryptic little black book:

> Gentle T called on Genl Z. Said he came over 'to operate'
> during Jubilee business. Put up at hotel in Paris. Received
> £500 from SC and £100 from NY Herald.
>
> Said he would make B[oulogne] base of operations.
> Z sent woman to B to watch his movements and asserts
> that he remained at B all the time he was pretending he
> was preparing things in England . . . Why would Z send
> woman?

'Gentle Torpedo' was Davitt's old code-name for Millen. 'Genl
Z' was his interviewee – Carrol-Tevis. The two had colluded in
Paris before Millen's move to Boulogne. 'SC' was Patrick Sarsfield
Cassidy, head of the Fenian Council.

The identity of 'the woman' that Tevis sent to spy on the
general remains impenetrable (it was assuredly not Martha Thomson). But more revealing was that tantalising line – Millen was
'pretending he was preparing things in England'.

James Monro was beginning to have his own doubts. Perhaps
it was Inspector Melville on his discreet watch who told his chief
that the gathering in Boulogne was not what it seemed. Perhaps
the assistant commissioner was alarmed to discover that the
Thomsons were there at all. He and Anderson firmly closed ranks
afterwards on the matter of who had sent the adventurous couple.
There was good reason to keep quiet: undercover policemen were
spying on undercover policemen – while HM Foreign Secret
Service seemed to be spying on all of them. There were all the
makings of a diplomatic scandal.

Perhaps it was an intercepted letter of the general's that

---

* Home Office rewards paid out at the end of the 'Jubilee dynamite case'
included: 'Inspector Melville £25: Watched Millen . . . with the greatest tact at
Boulogne and Paris and conducted numerous inquiries in London.'

prompted Monro to make his next move. 'I had no doubt that he was up to mischief, but it was difficult to watch him at Boulogne without exciting suspicion,' he wrote in the Darjeeling memorandum. 'I found out, however, who the recipient of his correspondence in England was, and this was duly attended to . . .'

There is the strongest indication from subsequent events that the general's English correspondent was Mr Edward Jenkinson.

Hôtel de Poilly, 13 rue Amiral Bruix, Boulogne-sur-Mer, 8 June 1887

The Millens had moved hotels. The Thomsons accompanied their new friends in the change of lodgings. On the morning of 8 June they were all about to set off on a breezy carriage drive. There was a visitor in the lobby of the Hôtel de Poilly, an elderly gentleman in a floppy tweed hat, a flower in his buttonhole and large, black polished boots.

Retired Inspector Thomson knew who he was immediately. They had worked together long ago in Mr Anderson's brave little secret department at the Irish Office after the Clerkenwell explosion. He went through a mummery of non-recognition; so did his charming wife. The cross-Channel arrival was Chief Constable Williamson.* He wanted a word with Monsieur Millen, and spoke to him 'like a Metropolitan Police man'.

The Scotland Yard emissary demanded 'absolute disclosure and abandonment of his mission'. The general refused to say anything.

It was Whitehall's turn to be knocked-up. Monro told the Home Secretary on 14 June:

> As you are aware I have for some time past been watching
> the operations of General F. F. Millen, an emissary from
> the dynamite faction in America.
>   This man is the accredited agent of the Fenian Brother-
> hood under the presidency of the notorious P. S. Cassidy,
> united for the occasion with some of the leaders of the

---

* Monro had arranged Williamson's unofficial promotion to boost his now ailing colleague's salary. Sir Charles Warren refused to recognise it.

Clan-na-Gael. Of this I have undoubted proof which
cannot however be produced in any court of law, as its
production would compromise informants . . .

I received information that a case of explosives had
been consigned to him at Paris via Havre, but this has
not been traced.

I have had him seen and warned – he admits and denies
nothing, but the visit has suddenly much disconcerted
him . . .

Monro had bigger game in his sights. He was going to rattle
the Foreign Office and see what fell out. He insisted in his letter
to the Home Secretary not just that the Boulogne police be
alerted to the presence of an apparent dynamiter – but 'the French
Government should similarly be applied to by our Ambassador
to give assistance in this matter'.

'His correspondence should be noted, and if the addresses of
the letters which he posts are given to me I shall be able soon to
ascertain who the people are in this country whom he is tempting
to commit outrage at the time of the Jubilee of Her Majesty,'
Monro added with a strong hint of knowingness.

Millen's addressees were indeed noted. He was corresponding
with some most unusual people.

Monro added a footnote to his letter to the Home Secretary.

It is also reported* that a General MacAdaras who lives
in Paris in some style, and who is intimate with Patrick

---

* Monro had been alerted by a curious report in the *New York Times* on 14
June, an intercepted letter from a British agent in St Louis, Missouri: 'If any
attempt is to be made it will be by the Fenians and it will be on 21 June,' it said.

'Your information that Duleep Singh had been taken off by the Irish is, I
believe, true. It is said here that "Gen" MacAdaras as he is called, is the father
of that brilliant scheme. He seems to have unlimited command of money and his
connection with the IRB is no longer a matter of doubt. We have enough here
to justify his arrest if he ever sets foot in England.'

MacAdaras, named in the Black Pamphlet as a member of the IRB Military
Council, was a former officer in the East India Company's army, a Fenian sympathiser who had married an extremely wealthy St Louis widow. He owned a château
in the Médoc and a Paris mansion. Patrick Casey had been his secretary – but other
than entertaining rebels to dinner MacAdaras had no connection with dynamite.

Casey and his associates is sending emissaries to this
country to commit outrage now ... and his name has
been reported to me more than once recently.

He is a freelance – not connected either with the FB
or the Clan-na-Gael – but he has some money and his
associates are undoubtedly suspects ...

Henry Matthews sought an urgent meeting with Sir Julian
Pauncefote. The mandarin must have been bemused. Scotland
Yard wanted the French government's aid in pursuing the
agent whose recruitment in Mexico City he and Lord Salisbury
had personally supervised. Now, eighteen months later, his
mission seemed to be the assassination of Queen Victoria with
dynamite.

'In view of the 21st June [the Jubilee] this is most urgent,'
the Home Secretary minuted.

The head of HM Foreign Secret Service could only agree.
'Patrick Casey' had served his purpose in St Petersburg. It was
well past time to shut down the Jubilee plot.

Aboard SS City of Chester, *New York harbour,* 11 June 1887

Three men sat forlornly on their steamer trunks on the New York
dockside. The mission had been bungled: the Liverpool-bound
boat they were supposed to catch had no berths left. Their dispatcher had handed out packets of cash, a few dollars each – there
would be plenty more waiting on the other side, he promised.
Berths were found on the SS *City of Chester* of the International
Steam Shipping Co. in a six-bunk steerage cabin. On 11 June
'Mr Thomas Scott', 'Mr Harry Scott' and 'Mr Joseph Melville'
went aboard. Passage would take ten days – they would arrive on
the 21st, Jubilee day. There was fiddle music and dancing to
while away the middle passage, but, the steward noticed, the three
men seemed to stay in their cabin.

In their trunks were secreted three Smith & Wesson (Russian
pattern) revolvers plus plentiful ammunition. Carefully sewn into

their clothing was over 100 pounds of Philadelphia-made Atlas A dynamite.

Frank Millen, enjoying the seaside air of Boulogne, might have been 'pretending'. As far as Alexander Sullivan in Chicago was concerned the Jubilee plot had become real.

Sous-Préfecture, Boulogne-sur-Mer, 15 June 1887

Monsieur Surplice, British consul in Boulogne, was informed on the night of the 14th: 'I am directed by the Marquis of Salisbury to state to you that from facts which have come to the knowledge of HM Govt it is considered necessary that a careful watch should be kept over the movements of General F. F. Millen, an emissary from the dynamite faction in America.' He was to ask the local police for assistance.

At 11.30 on the morning of the 15th, at the Boulogne *sous-préfecture*, Inspector Williamson and the British consul met M. Louis Tournon, Commissaire Spécial de Police, and M. Catart of the Police des Chemins de Fer. The danger to Her Majesty was spelled out; grave pronouncements were made on the need to cooperate against such international brigandage. Williamson produced his own description of the dynamite fiend:

> Millen. Description: Age 50 to 55, height 5 feet 8 in. visage – red face, blotchy as if from excessive drinking – large nose – hair (wavy) brown, turning grey, moustache white, no whiskers. Very slight build, dressed – dark clothes, dark overcoat with astrakhan collar and cuffs, – hard felt hat. Wears sword scarf pin – has Irish harp and shamrock on locket and watch chain: Had with him a brown leather portmanteau – brown American trunk, and carried dark coloured rug.

Monro had forwarded a description of the mysterious second 'Fenian General': 'MacAdaras. Age 45: height 5 feet 11 in: very strong build. Florid complexion – French style of beard and moustache. This is all the description that is known of him. He associates with Pat Casey and Eugene Davis . . .'

As Monro had insisted, Lord Lyons, the British ambassador in Paris, was alerted. The diplomat thought it best that communication with the French government on such a sensitive affair be conducted 'verbally'. M. Flourens, the Foreign Minister, was very cooperative, he reported. On the 17th the descriptions of the 'Fenian Generals Millen and MacAdaras' were transmitted to the head of the Service du Sûreté.

London, 15–20 June 1887

The Jubilee was just a few days away. The bunting and flags were going up across the capital. Grand hotels and cheap boarding houses were bursting with patriotic visitors. Nerves were on edge. An American arrival was arrested on a Queenstown steamer with a box of fireworks. An unfortunate French governess was apprehended on the Isle of Wight with a suspicious substance in her handbag. It was modelling clay.

On 15 June the Central News Agency put out a dramatic statement from an 'official source at Scotland Yard': 'Information had been received in London which leaves no doubt that dynamiters have arranged to commit an outrage in Jubilee week.' The bomber was even named: 'The movements of Patrick Casey and his associates in Paris have been closely followed by special detectives . . .'

The *Morning Advertiser* had another scoop two days later – an interview with the notorious firebrand himself:

'Have you any special information which leads you to believe that there may soon be grave trouble on the Afghan frontier?' asked the reporter.

'Soon, I won't say; but these troubles are coming, and any trouble there will be backed up by Irishmen of known ability, both as soldiers and organisers.'

'May we touch upon the question of dynamite, Mr Casey?'

'Yes, certainly.'

'Is there anything coming off?'

'In all probability there will be something coming off, and very soon . . .'

The newspaper was sceptical:

> We are assured that for months past, reports as to the
> more prominent members of the conspiracy abroad and
> their probable accomplices at home have been received
> in London almost daily, and that the chief ports of the
> United Kingdom have been watched . . .
>   We venture to think that the lieges may enjoy their
> Jubilee without fear of mines and explosions of bomb-
> shells, infernal machines, or any other 'devilish enginery'
> of the Dynamite Brotherhood.

The Home Secretary thought the opposite. There was a flurry
in Whitehall at the discovery that Irish labourers had been con-
tracted the year before to overhaul the Palace of Westminster's
plumbing. Gothic-revival water closets were intimately inspected.
Tickets for the ceremony, reserved for the great and the good,
were advertised in a newspaper for public sale at a vast price. There
was an enormous scandal when one was traced to 'Bluemantle' –
a herald at the Royal College of Arms – and another to an
impecunious canon of the abbey itself. 'What an opportunity for
a dynamiter to get a quiet pot-shot at HM,' wrote an apoplectic
Matthews. Colonel Majendie procured electric torches to probe
every inch of the abbey's ancient crypt for dynamite.

The nation was undaunted. Tributes poured in from every
outpost of empire, including a dozen hens' eggs from a poor but
loyal peasant woman in Galway.

In Manhattan black skull-and–crossbone banners inscribed
JUBILEE hung from boarding houses in the Bowery. A huge
Irish rally at the Cooper Union cheered O'Donovan Rossa's
appearance and stamped their feet for dynamite. There was a
requiem mass at the Church of the Holy Innocents for the souls
of a 'million Irish dead'.

The empire fought back. The Union flag was raised over
Tiffany's and Daly's Theatre. Six thousand Anglophiles gathered
at the Metropolitan Opera House for a grand celebration concert
to the un-English strains of Wagner and Meyerbeer. The guest
of honour, Mayor Abram Hewitt, gave the members of the

St George's Society an impromptu speech on the woes of Ireland.
'Let us hope this last slur on the Great British Empire will be
removed . . . in the day of that great woman who has preached
love and friendship for the fifty years of her reign,' he said. The
audience applauded wildly.

Westminster Abbey, London SW, 21 June 1887

Jubilee morning had come. James Monro set off with his wife by
carriage for Whitehall Place in full-dress fig, eyes darting from
beneath a fore-and-aft hat like a general's, ostrich plumes flutter-
ing in the summer breeze. At 11.15 the royal procession departed
Buckingham Palace with an escort of Indian cavalry. Plain-clothes
detectives weaved among the huge crowds, fearful of a crackpot
with a pistol or grenade. Monro chose to remain at his post: he
was expecting a greater catastrophe.

> I did not let my children take seats in Westminster Abbey
> which were reserved for them [he wrote in the Darjeeling
> letter]. On the day of the Jubilee itself, after the royal
> procession had begun to move along the prescribed
> routes, I received a message telling me that conspirators
> had managed to get in some dynamite to the vaults. The
> letter was signed and the writer evidently knew some-
> thing of dynamite matters, but he was unknown and it
> was too late to make inquiries . . .

The Queen entered the abbey for the first time since her coronation on 28 June 1838. She remarked in her journal on not
being able to see Mr Gladstone, who was in attendance (she was
certain) but was evidently concealed by a screen. A tiny figure in
diamond-sprinkled black, she mounted Edward the Confessor's
coronation seat, specially padded for the occasion. James Monro
waited for the growling rumble of a subterranean explosion. What
could he do – send a runner to Sir Charles Warren in his place
of honour as commissioner, imploring his boss to order everybody
out?

'I never was in a more delicate position in my life,' Monro

wrote. Should he risk 'panic amongst those who were in the Abbey, the flower of England's nobility', as he called them? He was certainly not going to inform his blustering chief – 'just the man to behave injudiciously, in some way or other, and cause the very panic which I was so anxious to avoid'.

'There was only one resource, offer a prayer for guidance,' said Monro, 'and so I prayed, and in the end resolved to do nothing, but trust that God, who had ever helped me, would do so now . . .'

There was no explosion. There was never going to be.

PART EIGHT

Delusion

'It's a B-O-M-B, Bomb!
It's a B-O-M-B, Bomb!
It's awfully hard on Scotland Yard
It's a B-O-M-B, Bomb!'
Music-hall song (*c*. 1887)

30

*London Joint Stock Bank, Prince's Street, City of London,
24 June 1887*

The Jubilee bunting still fluttered when an American strolled into
the marble banking hall opposite the Mansion House in the City
of London. Mr George Wicks, the cashier, took notice of the
unusually dressed customer – more so when he produced two
ample drafts drawn on American banks. The first, dated 11 June,
was for £205 6s 9d on Drexel & Co. of Philadelphia; the second,
dated three days earlier, was on Cantoni & Co. of New York – both
were in favour of a 'Mr Joseph Melville'. Mr Wicks unctuously
bundled up 105 white Bank of England fivers in two batches. Was
the gentleman over for the celebrations? Sadly Mr Melville had
missed the great day in London itself – he had arrived in Liverpool
aboard the *City of Chester* on the 21st – but no matter, the festivities
would continue for days yet. The cashier noted down the batch
numbers in the ledger – 18,101 to 18,139 inclusive.

Hôtel de Poilly, Boulogne-sur-Mer, 23–27 June 1887

Frank Millen stayed in his shuttered hotel room. Commissaire
Spécial de Police Louis Tournon prowled the Boulogne post
office noting the addresses of the suspect's 'many letters to
London brought by his woman every day'.

'He told the hotel staff he will depart tomorrow – Friday,' the
commissaire informed Scotland Yard on the 23rd, 'and that he
wants to return to America. I will continue surveillance until he
leaves and warn the English *agent* in good time.'

There was a sudden change of plan. Four days later the Millens

caught the afternoon train to Paris. Lord Lyons messaged Pauncefote from Paris two days later:

> The following information was sent to me quite confi-
> dentially and unofficially yesterday afternoon from the
> Ministère de l'Intérieur here.
>
> Gen Millen arrived at Paris from Boulogne-sur-Mer
> on Monday the 27th of June at 7.40 p.m. and alighted
> at the Hôtel du Palais, 28 Avenue Cours de la Reine.
> He is specially watched . . .
>
> Before his departure from Boulogne, he had addressed
> letters to General Carroll-Jarvis [sic], 3 Rue Daru Paris,
> and to Colonel Farrer, Oriental Club, Hanover Square
> London.* Inquiries are being made respecting General
> Carroll, and the relations he may have with Millen.
>
> It was better not to dig too deep.

Metropolitan Hotel, 797 Broadway, New York, June–July 1887

On 25 June a moustachioed figure with 'very English manners'
checked in at the Metropolitan Hotel on Broadway. His name,
he said, was 'Mr H. L. Walters'. The desk-clerk tipped off a
reporter from the *New York World*. He had seen the visitor's
card: ANGLO-CONTINENTAL INQUIRY AGENCY. PRINCIPAL
MAURICE MOSER – LATE INSPECTOR CRIMINAL INVESTI-
GATION DEPARTMENT, GREAT SCOTLAND YARD. The
reporter stalked the famous London sleuth round Manhattan.
His story, published two months later, was not flattering.

'His mission here was in the interest of *The Times* and a certain
clique of Tory noblemen to obtain forged letters to implicate
Parnell and other prominent nationalists in the Phoenix Park
assassinations,' the *World* alleged.

---

* The club's list of members for 1887 includes a Major Rowland Farrer. The
India List has him as 'unemployed supernumerary . . . in charge of pensions,
Chicacole' in southern India. No direct link can be made to Jenkinson, but the
internal evidence would suggest that the mysterious colonel was somehow a
conduit from Millen.

Moser was the man James Monro had sent to Paris in 1884 to pursue Jenkinson's circus of bogus dynamite plotters. Now, three years later, he was in the service of *The Times*'s solicitor.

On 5 July the detective met 'a man about town', according to the story, someone called 'Roberts' who offered to aid his investigations. The inspector had more encounters – he evidently embarked on a love affair with a woman called 'Golden' living in New Haven, to whose side he frequently repaired.

An address was ascertained – 17 Silver Place in Washington Heights, where Moser had tracked down a fugitive 'Invincible' who had letters for sale. Two more especially damning letters could be obtained, the mysterious inhabitant revealed, from a man named Patrick Sheridan, now a sheep-rancher in Colorado – the price was $800.

Cipher telegrams flew to London between July and August 1887. (Someone in New York was intercepting them – they all ended up in print.) Soames seemed to want the Sheridan letters very much indeed. Moser asked for $1,700 – *The Times*'s solicitor wired it. The detective proposed to Roberts that they split the rest and 'return to England to live in clover', so the *World* story alleged. The letters were bogus.

The Moser episode may have been high farce but it was revealing. *The Times* had plenty of secretly sourced money to pursue more anti-Parnell evidence in America. For a suitable fee Mr Roberts, whoever he was, was keen to lead them to it. Sheridan, the mysterious 'Henry' who had made the overture to the British ambassador in Washington, was a special target for the newspaper. The Western Union cable office on 16 Broad Street was leaking to the nationalist camp. It was a dress rehearsal for a much bigger sting.

Aston Clinton, Buckinghamshire, July 1887

Edward Jenkinson was bored. He had been treated generously enough with an Irish Office pension and decamped to an agreeable house in beechy Buckinghamshire. There were discreet hints of a knighthood. But, he clearly thought, as news of startling letters and threats to the Queen sloshed around the newspapers, his talents might be better used.

There was this conspiratorial communication with Earl Spencer on 28 May about the *Times* revelations: 'Parnell is the leader of a great Irish national movement – and that in the large number of men who follow him there must be those holding extreme views . . . What he can do is keep them under control. This has been done as it would be easy to prove from secret documents in our possession.'

Not everything had been burned the day he left Room 56.

What he did not seem to be doing in the Jubilee summer was directing some great plot of his own. He sent Lord Salisbury tiresome, place-seeking reminders of his own former importance and cleverness: 'The action of secret societies both in the UK and America was frequently paralysed . . . by the measures adopted by me for sowing suspicion and distrust of each other in the minds of the leaders . . .' he wrote on 10 June, enclosing a neatly printed curriculum vitae. The Prime Minister was not minded to re-employ him.

On 12 July a letter arrived at Althorp: 'When I got home this morning I saw *The Times*. I have lost my dear boy. How will my wife be able to bear it? What shall we do?' Earl Spencer had seen the short news item: 'Fatal Accident to Midshipmen, Halifax, July 11. Midshipmen Taylor, Stewart and Jenkinson of HM Ship *Canada* were sailing in a small boat in Bedford Basin – when the boat was struck by a squall and swamped and all three were drowned.' Harry Jenkinson was dead.

17 Thurlow Square, London SW, July 1887

With their father in Paris, Frank Millen's daughters were now occupying James Monro's attention. The ubiquitous Thomsons were deputed to snoop around. It was established by discreet questions that Kitty Millen had been living since the beginning of the year, 'after landing from central America', with Mr and Mrs William Henry Maitland of Thurlow Square.

On 29 January a gentleman had called at the Maitlands' house

near the Victoria and Albert Museum, so the Thomsons discovered. His name was Mr Joseph Nolan, elected Parnellite MP
for North Louth in 1885. He was heavily involved with the Land
League and had been both an elementary teacher in Liverpool
and a seaside showman (he is listed in *Dod's Parliamentary Companion* for 1887 as 'Casino and Aquarium Manager at New
Brighton').

General Millen had also evidently been present to introduce
his daughter to Mr Nolan in person – flitting through London
after his exertions in Paris before departing for New York for his
meeting with the Fenian Council. On 24 February Joseph Nolan
called at Thurlow Square again to escort Miss Kitty to the Palace
of Westminster for a sightseeing trip.

On the morning of 10 June Kitty's sister Florence arrived from
Dublin and Mr Nolan gallantly repeated the favour for the pair
of them. At the end of the month the girls went to Paris, summoned by their father after his tactical retreat from Boulogne.

On 14 and 15 July, according to evidence Monro would give
the select committee six months later, the dynamiter's daughters
were back in London – to be again squired round the Palace of
Westminster. 'They were taken to the Ladies' Gallery – on the
second occasion they were taken by Mr Joseph Nolan to the Bar
of the House of Lords,' Monro could reveal. 'After they left, they
were accompanied by Mr Nolan some little way up the street on
both days. They then left for Paris.' Somebody was following
their movements precisely.

They bore something with them on the second visit to give
their parliamentary host. Someone in London had pressed into
their hands a packet received from their father. It contained three
letters – the contents of which would later greatly animate the
Commons select committee. Mr Monro already knew what was
in them.

31

Hôtel du Palais, 28 Avenue Cours de la Reine, Paris, July 1887

The famille Millen lived in genteel fashion at the Hôtel du Palais under the discreet watch of the French Sûreté. There were several visitors.

One was Thomas Beach. He had come to London the previous April without any 'letters or credentials', according to his memoirs. He clearly met and was briefed by his controller, however. Special Branch Sergeant Patrick McIntyre recalled: 'Mr Anderson suggested it might be as well if he had a few interviews with Irish members. Le Caron [Beach] went in search of "victims" and succeeded in meeting one gentleman at Gatti's restaurant in the Strand.'

The victim was Dr Joseph Fox, a former Land League activist in Troy, New York State, the most Irish city in America – now a Parnellite member of parliament. He was reading a copy of the *Irish World*. Beach approached him as a fellow American in London: hadn't they met before – at a patriotic convention? Beach went through the nose-tapping mummery of the Clan 'hailing sign'. The doctor got up and departed in a huff. As an attempt at entrapment it was laughable. Subtler methods were required.

Anderson sent Beach to Paris. The spy recorded in his memoirs:

> The authorities learned of the presence of General Millen
> . . . and to Paris I was dispatched, in order to find out if
> possible what Millen was doing. I found le brave general
> of the Clan-na-Gael very comfortably settled, accom-
> panied by his wife and two interesting daughters. I called

upon him, representing that I had heard of his being in
Paris through the *Herald* office, and was calling by as an
old friend . . .

The second appearance was of Monro's man. As Monro told
his son in the Darjeeling letter, Inspector Melville was indeed
waiting at the Hôtel du Palais to renew his acquaintance with the
general. 'Millen was joined by his daughters for a while, and as
none of the family knew French well, they were not slow to avail
themselves of the polite services of the Irishman above mentioned
to help their linguistic deficiencies,' he wrote. 'He became in
consequence the tutor of Millen's daughters, being none other
than Inspector Melville of Scotland Yard.'

The general might have invited a procession of competing
agents into the bosom of his family, but neither Thomas Beach
nor inspector Melville (at least in the carefully filtered reports that
survive) mentioned another of Frank Millen's encounters in Paris
that summer.

Michael Davitt discovered it in his Carrol-Tevis interview:
'Gentle [Torpedo] stopped at Hotel St P[etersbourg] while Pig
was there. Asserted he did not know P was in place. He knew P
well as he had often called at *The Irishman* offices in Dublin.'

'Pig' was Richard Pigott. As the Special Commission would
spectacularly discover, the Dublin journalist was still up to his
ears in the lucrative forgery operation that had provided *The Times*
with its shock exclusives that spring. There is evidence of his
continuing activities in a previously unlooked for place – the
private papers of Robert Anderson. They contain a packet – indi-
vidually printed proofs of the *Times* 'facsimile' letters. One of
them was never published – nor raised in any tribunal. Dated
six months after the Phoenix Park murders and addressed to an
anonymous recipient, it is ostensibly in Millen's handwriting:

Private – No. 140 East 43rd Street, New York – Sept
13th 1882
Dear Sir, I am sorry to find that you should entertain
such notions. I have had interviews with Parnell and he
emphatically assured me that he regretted the affair of

the Phoenix Park only because happening at the time it
did it interfered seriously with his plans. Burke he con-
siders well deserved his fate. But he could not say this in
public for obvious reasons.

You cannot know the difficulty with which he has to
contend. It has always seemed to me that he is a thorough
going Revolutionist . . .

The leader . . . agrees with me that the greatest favour
we can do our people at home is to teach them in a secret
way the rudiments of the military art. You are aware there
are thousands of nationalists who are thirsting for this
class of knowledge . . .

I am dear sir very sincerely F. F. Millen.

In the Davitt papers is an assuredly genuine Millen letter. Dated
18 September 1880 it was sent from the same New York address
to Pigott, then editor in Dublin of the *Irishman*, the newspaper
he sold to Parnell and Patrick Egan as a Land League propaganda
vehicle in August 1881. It offers the general's services as a military
correspondent. It was retrieved from Pigott's house after his flight
and suicide. The wording includes: 'People at home should teach
themselves the rudiments of the military art . . . *The Irishman* can
do a good service for many thousands of nationalists who are
thirsting for this class of knowledge . . .'

Millen's 'Parnell is a thorough going Revolutionist' letter was
forged. It was a bomb *The Times* chose not to detonate in print.*

That Richard Pigott was merrily manufacturing 'Millen' letters
in Paris in the summer of 1887 is apparent. Why one should be

---

* There is no parallel evidence that Parnell and Millen ever met as the letter implies
– between the date of the Phoenix Park murders, May 1882, and September 1882.

There is evidence, however, that Robert Anderson was prepared to vouch for
the letter's authenticity. A curious Home Office 'Prison Department' file with
the date clearly altered to '1898' contains a single innocuous letter from Millen
of seventeen years earlier, offering his services as to a Colonel Thomas Tully, a
famous organiser of military pageants. The file is titled 'Suspected Dynamitard –
Gen F. F. Millen', and is minuted: 'Matter is being dealt with by Mr Anderson.'

Another scrappy memo in the *Times* archive, a checklist of nationalist MPs –
samples of whose handwriting the newspaper had on file – reads: 'Letters of Millen
in Scotland Yard for comparison.'

in Robert Anderson's private papers is curious. But much harder to explain is what happened next:

> I think it was in July about the 10th or so – a letter from Millen came into my possession [Monro's account of the Jubilee Plot continued]. It contained instructions to his correspondent to give the enclosures, which the letter contained, to Kitty, to be given by her to the same person as on previous occasions.
>
> The enclosures consisted of three letters addressed to three Irish MPs the first being Mr Joseph Nolan – the second Mr William O'Brien – the third I forget, it might have been Mr Harris.
>
> Each of these letters was in Millen's handwriting, which I knew well as he still maintained a correspondence with the Boulogne invalid.
>
> But none of these letters, although in Millen's handwriting, was signed with Millen's name. The signature in each case was of a different name from Millen, and the name in each of the three letters was different from that adopted in the others.
>
> This was of course most suspicious. The letters so signed were letters of introduction to the addressee on behalf of one Mr Joseph Melville, who was a friend of the writer of the letter, and interested in the work.
>
> Needless to say that their French tutor had also been obliged to leave the Hotel in Paris and continue his travels (in this case to London).
>
> On – I think – the 14th July or thereabouts, Miss Kitty Millen proceeded to the House of Commons and there had a long interview with Mr Joseph Nolan, MP.
>
> What passed at the interview we do not know, but we came to the conclusion that Miss Kitty had, as desired by her father, been entrusted with the letters – one of which was for Joseph Nolan, the others for two other Irish MPs.

Were they genuine or forgeries? Why should Pigott bother to manufacture them when he and Millen (not to mention Thomas

Beach) all appeared to be colluding anyway? None seem to survive. Harder to unravel is how the letters introducing someone called 'Mr Joseph Melville' came to be read by James Monro four days before they were passed to their recipients at the House of Commons.

The policeman dropped a big hint in the testimony to his son at Ranaghat – the 'Boulogne invalid still maintained a correspondence'. Millen had sent the letters to his seaside confidant Inspector James Thomson for transmission via 'Miss Kitty' to the three Nationalist MPs. They were meant to be opened and read. Someone seemed anxious both to incriminate their recipients – and to ensure the mysterious Mr Melville was apprehended.

Monro sent his men to discreetly prowl round the House of Commons – and alert him as soon as anyone called 'Melville' showed up.

Red Lion, Westminster, London SW,
Thursday 4 August 1887

The ornate public house a short stroll from the Palace of Westminster was bustling with politicians and journalists seeking lunchtime refreshment on a thirsty August day. Two men entered, ordering beer and sandwiches in American accents. Two plainclothes detectives lingered by the doorways. They had followed them, as discreetly as their polished policemen's boots might allow, from the House of Commons over the way. Monro's stakeout for 'Melville' had paid off.

An hour or so before, one of the Americans had presented his card to the duty officer at the Strangers' entrance. PC Oram looked at it closely. Mr Monro had alerted him to the name three weeks before. It read MR JOSEPH MELVILLE, ASTOR HOUSE, NEW YORK. It was sent up, as the visitor requested, to Mr Joseph Nolan, MP, who duly received them in the lobby. The speaker's register was signed by 'Melville' and by the second man with a scribble that looked like 'Mr McTin'.

The constable discreetly summoned Inspector William Horsley, who had been padding round the Palace of Westminster on Monro's orders since shortly after 10 July, waiting for 'Melville' to show. Horsley summoned his assistant, Detective Constable William

Foley. The plain-clothes policemen tracked the visitors to the pub.

The two refreshed suspects emerged by separate doors. The man who had signed himself 'McTin' was lost in the crowd. Melville was followed by Constable William Foley across Westminster Bridge towards the Elephant and Castle, an Irish district, to a house – 7 Gladstone Street – near the Bethlehem lunatic asylum. Constable Foley staked it out. He observed Melville the next morning talking to a stranger, a third suspect, 'at the corner of St George's Circus and London Road . . . near the obelisk, they talked for five or six minutes before separating.'

The Commons visit was repeated that afternoon. Joseph Nolan once again brought Melville and McTin into the House, whence they 'disappeared'.

Three days later Inspector Patrick Quinn called at the modest house in Gladstone Street to interview Melville directly. What was Melville's business? he asked. The American answered warily: he was 'investigating frauds on German houses'. He was further the agent for a Mr Philips of the Pennsylvania & Reading Railroad, promoting 'a patent lightning arrester for petroleum wells'.

Monro cabled Pinkerton's Detective Agency to investigate the American end. Their agent could find no trace of a 'Mr Philips' and his lightning conductor in Philadelphia nor, yet, of a 'Mr O'Brien'. The staff of the Astor House, New York, had no knowledge of Mr Melville. The watch continued on 7 Gladstone Street, a humble lodging house next door to the Prince Albert public house.

Monro later told the Commons select committee of his continuing quest for the elusive Melville.

> About the 10th or 11th August he suddenly disappeared from his lodgings and went over to Paris; he was followed there, picked up and again interviewed.*

* By whom is not indicated – but probably by Inspector William Melville. A letter in the Davitt papers from a London IRB man, Maurice Collins of Bethnal Green, indicates that Inspectors Melville, Sweeney and Littlechild attempted to recruit him as a spy in an East End pub on 2 August 1887. 'Dynamitards' were mentioned . . . and 'The Times newspaper', said Collins.

Like Millen calling himself 'James Thompson' in Austin, Texas, 'Melville–Melville' seems a bizarre coincidence.

He gave further references and described where Mr
Philips lived; that was inquired into, with the result that
we found Miles O'Brien and we found Philips, and both
of them denied having any knowledge of Melville.

'Philips' was an Albert Burchell – a 'type-writer in the office of
the Pennsylvania and Reading Railroad'.

Hotel Metropole, Northumberland Avenue, London WC, August 1887

Inspector Littlechild did not have to look too hard for the deadly
dynamiter. 'Captain Melville', suavely dinner-jacketed, flamboy-
antly moustached, made quite a show at the fashionable Hotel
Metropole just round the corner from Scotland Yard. At his side
was a pretty girl.

John Littlechild approached the couple sternly in the lobby.
'He told Melville that his account of himself was false, as ascertained in America, and that police would look after him while in
London,' Monro recorded in the Darjeeling letter. But rather
than flee to America after the inspector's warning, Melville and
his girl – a 'Miss Kennedy, a milliner of Boston, whom he had
picked up in Paris' – embarked on a sightseeing trip to picturesque
Killarney, then returned to London for the police to resume their
watch.

Littlechild followed the suspect doggedly round the capital.
At Baring's bank he was observed turning further drafts into Bank
of England fivers. Littlechild discreetly conferred with the cashiers
and noted the numbers. Monro posted a stop order at the Bank
of England.

So far in James Monro's tortuous investigation there had not
been one glimmer of real dynamite – apart from the apparently
inaccurate intelligence on 19 May that '24 tins of explosive had
been consigned to one Miller or Muller at Paris'.

The grand connecting link were the Paris-sent letters from
Millen to his daughters that Monro had seen in the original on

10 July – introducing 'Melville' to the three Parnellite MPs. Monro seemed to have no idea who Melville really was – or the mysterious McTin, or the third man seen near the St George's obelisk on 5 August by Constable Foley.

On 9 September Joseph Melville and Miss Kennedy departed for Paris yet again – putting up at the Hôtel de Londres et New York in the Place du Havre. This time he was on his way to see the Mexican general.

'Melville did not know that he was under observation, but he was seen to leave his hotel and go to the Hôtel du Palais where he saw Millen. He then left for America, along with Miss Kennedy, on the 17th of September,' according to Monro. The two principals had apparently met at last. But Monro seemed more interested in Miss Kennedy's visits to the *grands magasins* than in dynamite. On her numerous shopping trips 'she invested largely in lace', he noted.

It was a mean little sting but Monro was getting quite Jenkinson-like in his methods. He cabled the New York customs. Miss Kennedy's baggage was inspected on arrival and its lacy contents fingered. A large quantity of underwear was found in her bustle. She was 'arrested for smuggling'. The New York papers were tipped off and further informed that her companion 'Mr Joseph Melville had lately been in London and had been seen frequently in the company of the police.' It worked – the *New York World* of 28 September revealed the real name of Miss Kennedy's companion – he was John J. Moroney of Tenth Avenue, New York.

But Monro had still not found 'McTin'.

32

42 Lambeth Road, London SE, October 17–18, 1887

The American was in the advanced stages of tuberculosis. His body was wasted, the sputum flecked with blood. Mrs Elizabeth Keys, the landlady, told him he must see a doctor, but her lodger, Mr Joseph Cohen, refused. 'I have already seen one – it's bronchitis,' he insisted as always. What about calling his friends? 'I have none in London,' he said. The coughing grew worse.

He had lodged with her since late June, always paid his six shillings a week rent promptly and stayed within doors for the greater part of the day. He had gone, he had told her, 'to Paris' for a few days five weeks before. Mrs Keys did not know his occupation, nor where he came from, but she had heard him speak of 'being in America'.

There had been a lot of coming and going lately – two American gentleman, one of whom had been over every day last week; his name, he had told her, was 'Mr Brown'. The gentleman had called when her lodger first became really ill. It had been quite a to-do. A big tin box had been removed from Mr Cohen's room – it was so heavy the cab-man had to help shift it.

It was clear they had get the sick man to hospital. A local physician was summoned – Dr Johnson of York Road. He explained how it was done: written depositions were needed from two householders and a clergyman for an immediate admission to the Hospital for Consumption at Mount Vernon, Hampstead, on the northern heights above the smokes and fogs of London.

A Catholic priest was found, the Reverend Patrick McKenna of Finsbury Circus. Two Irish builders – Thomas Stack and Thomas O'Malley of De Beauvoir Square, Hackney, whom Mr Brown seemed to know already – wrote their pleading letters. On 18 October Brown and Stack took their depositions to Hampstead for an interview with Dr Bernard O'Connor, the hospital supervisor. The patient would be moved the next day. Mr Brown returned to sit up with his friend until 11 p.m. – then disappeared into the night.

On the morning of the 19th the second American called again at Lambeth Road. He came downstairs and asked Mrs Keys to sit with Mr Cohen while he went out 'for a few minutes'. Around midday she went up alone, entered the room and found her lodger 'dead but still warm'. The visitor never returned. Shortly afterwards 'Mr Brown' reappeared and took some money, it later emerged – bank notes and a quantity of gold sovereigns – from beneath the dead man's pillow and locked it in a cupboard. He took the key and left. The dead man's ring was missing. Elizabeth Keys went to the police.

Monro clearly already knew where to find at least one of the two Americans. He told his son in the Darjeeling letter: 'The police of "H", Whitechapel Division, reported to me the presence within their jurisdiction of a man whom they could not account for. He seemed to have nothing to do and all that he did was visit a man who was very ill and who also seemed a stranger . . . the police were supplanted by the Secret Department who shadowed the visitor of the sick man.' It was 'Mr Brown'.

At 9.30 on the morning of the 19th Inspector Patrick Quinn, on Monro's orders, went to an address near the Angel, Islington – 9 Alfred Street, Colebrooke Row – where he found 'Brown' in bed in a back upstairs room. The consumption hospital order was in his pocket. He was briskly questioned: what was his name? What was his business? He was 'Harry Scott', he said; 'he had a friend in London who was dead.' Scott was followed to the house in Lambeth and the upstairs room, where Cohen still lay dead in bed. 'The man is dead,' he said. 'I must see to the funeral.' 'I must take you into custody,' said Inspector Quinn, 'the funeral will be attended to.'

The suspect was taken to Whitehall Place, where he was interrogated by Littlechild and Monro. He gave his name as 'Michael

Larkins'. He did not know the dead man's identity – he was someone he had met in a pub, he told them. A cheap key was found on him.

'He had in his pocket an extract cut from the "Daily News" announcing the date on which Mr Balfour was going to Birmingham,' Monro recorded. 'He could give no account of why he had this . . . and said that he could not read or write.' There was a scrap of card with O'Malley and Stack's addresses and a letter addressed to 'Mr Philips, PO Box 36, Philadelphia'. (The contents of this letter were not revealed in any subsequent legal proceeding.)

Larkins was released from Whitehall Place the next morning, the 20th, accompanied by a posse of police. Mrs Eugenie Horan, landlady of Alfred Street, found her house bulging. Five detectives lodged in her parlour to accompany the suspect wherever he went.

Inspector Quinn meanwhile had returned to 42 Lambeth Road on the evening of the 19th, searched the dead man's room – and found a Smith & Wesson revolver plus fifteen cartridges, £21 in gold and silver and two Bank of England £5 notes. The numbers were noted. The discoveries were replaced where the inspector had found them.

Larkin's Islington lodgings were turned over on the afternoon he had crossed the river to go to Lambeth. An identical Smith & Wesson Russian-pattern revolver with fifteen cartridges was found in a portmanteau. It too was replaced.

Monro had the letter found on Larkins, alias Harry Scott, traced to a post-office box in Philadelphia. It was addressed to the same Philips that Melville had claimed had commissioned him to go to Europe as an agent for a patent lightning conductor. Monro already knew from Pinkerton's that Philips was a Mr Albert P. Burchell of 2251 North Sixth Street, who worked for the Pennsylvania and Reading Railroad. Burchell, so Monro was informed by the detective agency, was a member of the Clan-na-Gael.

On the morning of the 25th Larkins asked one of his minders, PC John Craig, to write a letter for him. 'We went out together to get some refreshment,' the policeman said in evidence, 'and then to the high street to buy paper and envelopes.'

Constable Craig's charge dictated a letter addressed to a 'Mr Burchell' asking for £14 'to get back to America' but the plea was put inside another envelope addressed to a 'Mrs Hawkins of 1939 N 2nd St, Philadelphia'.

Monro had Larkins bottled up, and a paperchase link between the suspect and Melville, bearer of General Millen's letter of introduction to the Parnellite MPs. He was sure he had found 'McTin', but the second of Cohen's American visitors had yet to be apprehended. There was still no trace of dynamite. He resolved to flush out the conspiracy in the most public way possible.

On the afternoon of the 25th the suspect Larkins was told by his police minders that he must appear as a witness in a court room the next morning. The attic room at Alfred Street was searched again in his presence and the revolver 'discovered'. Larkins said he was going to pawn it as he had no money.

Police Sergeant Walsh gave him 7s 6d from police funds and stuffed the fearsome Smith & Wesson in his blue serge uniform pocket.

---

*City and Southwark Coroner's Court, High Street,
Borough, London SE, 26 October 1887*

Mr Coroner Samuel Langham's little court was heaving. Wondering journalists sucked their pencils: why had half of Fleet Street and a bunch of New York wire-men been summoned to an inquest into an obscure consumptive? The rest of the crowd seemed to be made up of policemen. One witness appeared to be under guard.

The first witness was Elizabeth Keys, landlady of 42 Lambeth Road. Led politely by the coroner she gave her story of the death of Joseph Cohen in her upstairs room and his two mysterious 'American visitors'.

Suddenly James Monro, the assistant commissioner himself, rose to speak. The overflowing press bench woke up.

'Perhaps you will allow me, Mr Coroner, to state a few facts which will make clear my questions as to identification,' he said. 'The fact is this man was an agent of an American association called the Clan-na-Gael, whose object is to commit outrages in London and elsewhere by dynamite, Fenian fires, and assassination. The head of the association, who was over here at the time of the Jubilee, was General F. F. Millen, and his agent in London was a man who called himself Joseph Melville.'

Mr Samuel Langham was astonished. 'You are taking as facts what is not in evidence,' he said.

Monro explained that he was making this statement to 'make his subsequent questions intelligible'. He turned to the landlady. Was the man she knew as 'Brown', the dead man's visitor, in court?

'That is the man,' said Mrs Keys, pointing at the tall, well-built witness with a sandy moustache, flanked by police in the well of the court.

The American shuffled to the stand and was sworn. 'My name is Michael Hawkins [not Larkins],' he said. 'My home is in America where I am a grocer. I first got to know the deceased at the public-house near the Obelisk a month ago, and afterwards I visited him.'

Mr Monro began his arcane examination. 'What is your address in America?'

'1,939, North Second Street, Philadelphia.'

'Your wife and family live there?'

'Yes.'

'Did you ever see the deceased with a man named Melville?'

'No sir.'

'Do you know Melville?'

'Only through meeting him.'

'Did you visit the House of Commons with Melville?'

'Yes, after meeting him in a pub in The Strand – he accosted me because I looked like an American.'

'Did anybody take you round into the gallery?'

'I saw a gentleman there; but don't know his name.'

'What is his description?'

'Rather a tall man, also fair.'

'We know this fair man to be Mr Joseph Nolan, MP,' Monro told the court before turning back to Hawkins. 'I will ask you as to a mutual friend of yours and Melville's. Do you know anyone named Burchell in Philadelphia?'

'Yes.'

'Was this address found upon you?'

'Yes.'

'This is, "Mr Philips, PO Box 36, Philadelphia." Who is Mr Philips?'

'I don't know – I can't say how it got into my pocket.'

'Will you look at that newspaper. Where did you get it?'

'I cannot read.'

Monro read it – a cutting from the *Daily News* of 12 October:

' "Mr A. J. Balfour, Chief Secretary for Ireland, has accepted an invitation to address a public meeting at the Town Hall, Birmingham . . ." ' The meeting would be in eight days. The implication was clear: Balfour was an assassination target.

'How did it get into your pocket?'

'I don't know.'

In a *coup de théâtre*, Inspector Littlechild produced an enormous revolver – a Smith & Wesson – 'taken loaded from the witness yesterday – exactly the same as the weapon found in the deceased's room,' he said.

'I bought it in Chicago,' said the witness. 'I never saw any other revolver.'

There was further apparently extraneous evidence. Mrs Honour Thursting, landlady of 7 Gladstone Street, was shown a post-mortem photograph of Cohen. She testified that the man in the picture was a frequent caller at her house, where she had a lodger called 'J. Melville'. The visitor called him 'Joe'.

'Is Melville to be produced?' asked the coroner testily.

'He is in America,' said Monro. There was laughter in court.

Dr Laurent Duque gave the cause of Cohen's death as acute lung disease. There was no sign of violence, no evidence of poison. The jury's verdict was death from natural causes.

That did not concern the journalists. They rushed from the court to the telegraph office to file sensational stories on General Millen and a Jubilee plot. Morse code chattered over the transatlantic cable. DYNAMITE PLOT SPOILED, the *New York Times* proclaimed on the morning of the 27th:

> Commissioner Monro explained that Cohen was believed to be an agent of the Clan-na-Gael Society, the head of which, Gen Millen, was in London during the Jubilee celebration. His London agent is named Melville.
>
> The evidence confirmed the report sent to America during Jubilee week regarding the existence of a dynamite plot against the Queen.

The inquest had now made a publicly proclaimed link between the suspicious Americans in London, 'General Millen' and a

Parnellite MP. The policeman had made sure of it himself. 'Hawkins' had not identified the 'tall fair man' who had admitted him and Melville to the Commons. Monro had inserted his name as an aside to his questioning – 'We know this man to be Joseph Nolan, MP.'

The reluctant witness (who still had not been charged with any offence) further never mentioned the 'head of the association'. Monro had blazoned the name around the coroner's court – 'General F. F. Millen.' Somebody wanted it that way.

The next day Monro briefed astonished reporters in even greater detail on the whole grand conspiracy. DYNAMITE MYSTERY, proclaimed the *New York Herald* on the 28th:

> It was learned to-day, at Scotland Yard, that the head of the alleged dynamite gang was General Millen, whose antecedents in fenian matters as a member of the Clan-na-Gael are well known.
>
> He resided in Paris and Boulogne, but never on English soil, or he would have been arrested. Before the Jubilee festivities Scotland Yard sent a police officer to him at Boulogne, warning him that his plot was known.
>
> Then the General returned to Paris, where he remained until a few days ago, when he left for America, travelling via Brussels, Rotterdam, and Amsterdam, whence he sailed within two days after the death of Cohen, on board the steamer *Edam*, with his wife and daughters.
>
> Melville came to London as an agent of Millen . . . the police watched him closely, and found that on two occasions he called on Mr Joseph Nolan, MP, at the House of Commons. He had for his companion the man Hawkins ['McTin'], and both of them were seen in company with the dead man Cohen.

Monro's hugely revelatory press briefing mentioned Melville's trips to Paris. The assistant commissioner stated as fact that Melville had met Millen at the Hôtel du Palais, and that 'he had been seen in a cab with a man remarkably like the deceased man,

266 FENIAN FIRE

Cohen, who was absent from his lodgings about five weeks ago'.

He mentioned Miss Kennedy, gave her address in Boston, and an account of her discomfort with the New York customs. His statement named 'Mr A. P. Burchell . . . connected with other members of the secret society' – and it very deliberately disclosed Melville's New York address: 'viz – at Mr J. J. Moroney's, 925 Tenth Avenue, New York'.

The *Herald* had time to get some reactions in America. Mr Burchell of Philadelphia 'denied all knowledge of Cohen or "Melville"', while 'O'Donovan Rossa . . . and other well known dynamiters in New York had never heard of Joseph Cohen . . .'

J. J. Moroney's humble apartment was doorstepped. 'His wife' (it was the delightful Miss Kennedy) was confronted to declare her companion absent. 'She would not act the role of British spy and reveal his whereabouts,' Mrs Moroney insisted.

There was universal bafflement. 'Several people in this city well posted declare that General F. F. Millen has so repeatedly repudiated dynamite warfare that if Cohen were really connected with him, it is regarded as pretty good proof that Cohen was not a dynamiter,' said the *Herald*.

An intrepid reporter tracked down 'Mrs Hawkins' to 1939 North 2nd Street, Philadelphia, the address conveniently disclosed at the Southwark inquest. Her correct name was 'Harkins', she said. Her husband Michael had been away since April, 'working on a steamboat on Lake Erie'. The *Herald* man questioned the neighbours. 'Harkins was known in the neighbourhood as an active member of the Clan-na-Gael and has not been seen for several months past,' he discovered. There was a tearful admission on Mrs Harkins's doorstep: 'If it is he, I know what it means,' she said. 'It will be misery and destitution for me, and my children . . .'

In London, meanwhile, questioned by eager reporters that same afternoon, Joseph Nolan, MP, denied 'any knowledge of dynamiters'. He considered the inquest 'had been designed to assist the nefarious policy of the Government . . .'

There was still no sign of dynamite. But a blocked toilet in north London was about to disgorge an explosive secret.

34

---

24 Baxter Road, Islington, London N, 27 October 1887

The morning after the Cohen inquest Hannah Bright, daughter
of the landlady of a lodging house in Islington, discovered that
the water-closet in the back yard would not flush.

She called her mother, Maria Bright, who bravely plunged in
her hands and 'took out some lime and cement caked together
which she broke up with a chisel'. There was more of it stuck in
the pan – and a curious pale muddy-powder trail leading to the
back-yard wall.

Mrs Bright had a lodger, an American gentleman called
'Thomas Scott'. He was 'a quiet, respectable old person' who,
when he took the back room on the ground floor three months
before, said he was a 'traveller in the tea trade'. Called to comment
on the mysteriously blocked lavatory her lodger admitted that he
had foolishly flushed away 'some spoiled samples of tea' and
offered to pay half the cost of a plumber.

Mr George Lowe, builder, of Ball's Pond Road was summoned,
and solemnly took out 'half a pailfull of the stuff' with his plunger.
The waterlogged discoveries were deposited in the dustbin.

Aboard the SS Edam, *New York harbour, 27 October 1887*

As Maria Bright fussed over her plumbing problems, Frank Millen
and his family were preparing to step ashore from the steamer
which had borne them from Amsterdam to New York. His name
was all over the papers. In London that morning *The Times* had
boldly declared him to be 'President of the Clan-na-Gael', no
less, 'an American dynamite, fenian, fire and assassination society'.

A reporter grabbed him as he came down the gangplank. Had 'he really gone to Europe with the intention of disturbing the Queen's Jubilee by indiscriminately scattering dynamite'?

'Absurd,' said Millen; 'the British government has concocted the whole story . . . there is nothing they will not do to further their ends.

'All that story about detectives tracking me and warning me not to set foot in Great Britain and about my fleeing to Paris is a tissue of falsehoods.'

He had gone to Europe, he insisted, 'to interest the French government in a shell I have invented – which can throw either melinite or dynamite . . . and to see General Guzman Blanco relative to an emigration scheme to Venezuela'. But 'during his stay in Europe he suffered for three months from gastric catarrh and was rarely able to leave his hotel'.

John J. Moroney was buttonholed outside his 10th Avenue tenement. 'Am I Melville? Certainly not,' he answered the reporter. 'He's much shorter than me – I'll bring him to your office and you can see for yourself . . .'

21 Whitehall Place, London SW, 4 November 1887

Monro had held back some crucial intelligence from his journalists' briefing. On 4 November he drafted a long memorandum, apparently drafted for the Home Secretary but never delivered. It is in Robert Anderson's handwriting, signed by the assistant commissioner. The original survives in Anderson's 'private papers', returned to the Home Office on Winston Churchill's insistence in 1910. It would seem to be the two men's agreed account of events to date:

> SECRET. The Fenian agent F. F. Millen, whose name has lately been before the public in connection with plots of outrage in England, is a press man on the staff of the 'New York Herald', and claims the title of 'General' in virtue of military service in Mexico. He has been prominent as a Fenian for more than 20 years, and has held

office in the Clan-na-Gael ever since that organisation was established. In 1879 he visited this country on a secret mission of inspection, the result of which he reported to the convention of the order held that year in Williamstown US, and to the convention of August 1880, and reported as head of the 'Military Board'.

This man was in the UK at the close of last year and sailed for New York in January '87 to promote new schemes of outrage.

The CNG (Clan-na-Gael) leaders who had commissioned the dynamite missions of former years, were then under promise to the Parnellites at home to suspend operations until further orders; and the executive of the organisation as a body took no part in the new plot.

But as the outcome of negotiations it was arranged that two leading CNG men should meet with two of the Council of the rival organisation called the FB (Fenian Brotherhood) with a view to joint action in promoting what they described as a display of fireworks on the Queen's Jubilee . . .

These meetings took place last March; and as the result Millen started for Europe, bearing credentials for his mission and 5,000 dollars in money. He booked on the SS *Gascogne* as 'Mr Muller' and landed at Havre on 18th April. He went at once to Paris where he remained till 12th May, corresponding freely with various persons in the UK. He also put himself in communication with well known Fenians in Paris, and notably with a man named Tevis who is the principal agent of the Fenian Brotherhood in Europe.

Monro knew a great deal about Millen's activities – but he still did not seem to know (and, it seemed, neither did Anderson) that 'the man named Tevis' was the Foreign Office's principal agent in Paris.

During the whole period of Millen's stay in Europe I was kept fully informed of his plans and movements [the memorandum continued] ... and no precautions were neglected to prevent his crossing the channel unobserved.

His mission was nevertheless a cause of unceasing anxiety; and, as the date of the Jubilee approached, this anxiety was greatly intensified by discovering accidentally that before his schemes of outrage were proposed to his confederates in New York they had been communicated to the gentleman who preceded me in charge of the Secret Service Department, and that in the event of his arrest and conviction he might have made statements on the subject, of at all events a most embarrassing kind.

Indeed he might have done. That was why Chief Constable Williamson had been sent to Boulogne. The 'absolute disclosure' Monro had demanded – which the general refused to give – concerned whatever Millen had cooked up with Edward Jenkinson in midwinter Paris. But by what 'accident' had Monro stumbled on the relationship?

The veil had not been lifted by some chance discovery in White-hall. The Foreign Office guarded their files. Monro still seemed to know nothing about Mexico, the St Petersburg operation, nor of the presiding role of Charles Carrol-Tevis. Jenkinson's records were beyond reach.

So far Robert Anderson had neglected to tell his colleague how his brother Samuel had conjured Frank Millen to London to meet the commissioner of the Metropolitan Police twenty years before – although he would tell him when necessary. The identity and dealings of Thomas Beach, in contact with Millen in Paris that spring and summer on Anderson's orders, remained hidden from Monro.

The best assumption for the 'accident' was that it was a deliberate indiscretion of Anderson's. He either knew from Beach or made it his special business to discover just what the Home Office knew of his fallen rival's past manouevrings.

The memorandum ran through how Chief Constable William-son had been sent to confront Millen – 'warning him that we

were well aware of his character and prospects'. Not once, however, were Mr and Mrs Thomson mentioned. There were more
curious shifts and elisions in the statement:

> The result of [Williamson's] action was most satisfactory.
> [Millen's] agents were seen in London awaiting his
> instructions, but he feared either to cross the Channel
> himself, or to summon them to meet him in Boulogne.
> That Millen expected they would take action notwith-
> standing his absence, may be inferred from his move-
> ments on 21st June. On that day he had all his luggage
> packed and ready for flight and was evidently in a state
> of intense excitement. But the emissaries failed to act,
> and the entire scheme was rendered abortive.

That statement is curious. The only 'agents' in London that
Monro might have been alerted to before Jubilee day were Kitty
and Florence Millen. Martha Thomson, recalled from Boulogne,
had clearly been following them around leafy South Kensington.
That is what her melodramatic claim to Winston Churchill about
'getting Millen's daughters arrested on their way to the Abbey –
thus preventing a terrible disaster' meant. The Misses Millen were
not apprehended. Their continuing liberty in London would be
crucial to the transmission of their father's letters to the three
MPs. And Monro now perfectly understood that their father's
original 'mission' – to be effected apparently by the unlikely teenage regicides – had been followed by a much more businesslike
one. His statement continued:

> Millen forthwith reported by letter to the Fenian
> Brotherhood agent in Paris, and also to Richd Tilsit (the
> secret and carefully concealed alias of the Secretary to
> the CNG in New York),* attributing his failure to the
> close vigilance of the police. On June 27 he returned to
> Paris, accompanied by his wife, who had joined him on

* 'Tilsit' was the east Prussian town near which Napoleon met Tsar Alexander I
in 1807. It might be assumed to be the general's cover-name for Alexander
Sullivan.

May 24 from Dublin where he had left her on his return
to New York last January.

My information is definite that before the failure of
Millen's schemes was an accomplished fact the conspirators in America had begun to doubt his fitness for the
work entrusted to him. An emissary was accordingly dispatched to investigate what he was doing, and if necessary
to supersede him. The agent selected for this purpose
was one J. J. Moroney of 925 Tenth Ave, New York.

The first intimation I had of this man's presence in
Europe reached me in this way: there were two daughters
of Millen's here last summer on a visit at a friend's house,
and on 11th July Millen sent to their care three letters
addressed respectively to Wm O'Brien MP, Matt Harris
MP, and Joseph Nolan MP. These letters were to introduce his friend 'Joseph Melville', the name adopted by
this Moroney for the purpose of his mission.

The letters clearly indicated that the writer was known
to the men he addressed; but it is significant that tho'
written by Millen himself, and on paper bearing his
monogram, they were signed not with his own name,
but with the alias under which he is known to his co-
conspirators. The note to Harris was signed 'J. C.
Morgan', 'Morgan' being Millen's *nom de guerre* during
his secret CNG mission in 1879. O'Brien's was signed
'J. C. Mortimer'. In Nolan's case this is the more startling,
as the letter itself gave proof that the writer was known
to him to be Millen, as it acknowledged his kindness in
showing Millen's daughters the Houses of Parliament . . .

The memo continued with an account of the two visits of
Melville and Harkins to see Nolan at the Commons on 4–5
August – and the meeting, observed by PC Foley, with the man
later found dead at Lambeth Road. It covered Melville's subsequent questioning, the letter from 'Philips' in Philadelphia and
the lightning arrester ploy, the trips to Paris, the appearance of Miss
Kennedy and Melville's final departure to France on 9 September.

In Paris [Melville] visited Millen at his hotel. He also
met there in August one T. J. Dennehy of Brooklyn*
who had also just arrived from England, where, on 3rd
August, he had called on one of the Fenian leaders, asking
him on Millen's behalf to join in an outrage plot . . . [the
memorandum continued].

Melville left behind him in London the subordinate
emissaries of the plot. One of these named Harkins, I
arrested. Upon him were found a revolver, a pencil note
giving the name and postal address of the Philips mentioned by Melville; and also a newspaper cutting relating
to Mr Balfour's movements. But after full consideration
I decided not to charge him before a magistrate, but to
deal with him as I had already dealt with Melville.

Indeed. Melville had been openly warned off at the Metropole
Hotel by Inspector Littlechild before departing in leisurely fashion
with his girlfriend for Killarney. When Monro wrote his memorandum on 4 November, Michael Harkins had been released without charge. Monro seemed to want nothing less than that he
too should disappear. A trial could be most uncomfortable. His
memorandum gave the reason why:

In this I was mainly influenced by the fact already alluded
to, respecting the origin of the plot. It seemed to me un-
desirable in the extreme to prosecute the agents of a plot,
where there was even the semblance of justification for
ascertaining that in its inception the Government was privy
to it . . . I therefore took advantage of the inquest held on
the body of his confederate, 'Cohen', to put an end to the
plot altogether by publishing the details of it.†

* Thomas Dennehy – a prominent Clan-na-Gael member and Sullivan loyalist in
the split. He had defended Millen against John Devoy's accusations that he was
an 'adventurer' in New York six years before.
† He gave his son a very different reason in the Darjeeling letter:
  'Now was the time to put the public on their guard, and show them what
was going on in their midst, fomented by a treacherous MP.
  'How was this to be done? By an inquest on the dead man . . . I took care
that the representatives of the press were duly informed. I gave a little history of

Mrs Honour Thursting, Melville's landlady at 7 Gladstone Street, had, at Monro's prompting, given evidence at the inquest. After her lodger's flight in September, letters from America addressed to Mr Melville plopped through her modest letter-box. They had reached Monro – who found them enlightening. His memorandum continued:

> Two letters which came for [Melville] after his departure are of marked value as throwing light upon the conspiracy. Both were signed 'Philips'; and both were in veiled language, but their meaning is clear.
>
> In the one the writer states that the proposition and demands of 'Morgan' (Millen's *nom de guerre*) had been submitted to 'the firm' and unanimously rejected, and that Melville should proceed to carry out what he had informed 'a member of the firm', whom he had met in Paris (i.e. T. J. Dennehy), he was prepared to do without 'Morgan's' assistance and, finally, that 'Morgan' was to be immediately recalled, leaving Melville and his agents energetically to push the interests of the firm.
>
> In the second letter 'Philips' writes that the letter above cited was dictated by 'Oakley' and 'Belcher' (his principals in the plot) and that they had told him to write privately to confirm their assurance that Morgan had been sent to the right-about, and that 'the whole firm' had the fullest confidence in him (Melville) and expected to hear from him soon in a way that would prove him worthy of that confidence . . .

The same day as the memo was drafted, 4 November, the *Penny Illustrated Paper* reprised the inquest evidence with a sensational cover featuring a Faginesque Cohen, a brutish Harkins, 'Cohen's Smith and Wesson revolver' and 'Captain Melville in clover', a louche figure dining with pretty Miss Kennedy – contrasted with 'Captain Melville down on his luck', mournfully

---

the mysterious connection of the deceased with members of the dynamite party. Needless to say that the reporters were busy . . .'

breakfasting on a boiled egg. What a triumph for Scotland Yard.

When Anderson and Monro compiled their joint memor-andum, American number two – the man who had called on Cohen on the morning of his death – had yet to be found. Harkins had been discharged after the inquest – to return to Alfred Street, Islington. A posse of police was set up in the parlour to watch his every move. Where was the dynamite? Surely Michael Harkins would not be foolish enough to lead Monro to it.

35

26 Baxter Road, Islington, London N, 8 November 1887

The shabby gentility of Baxter Road was to be troubled again –
this time by something more dramatic than a blocked toilet. On
8 November Charlie Johns, the young son of Mrs Bright's next-
door neighbour, was playing in the back yard at Number 26. He
'found some white stuff by the garden wall and put it in the oven
to dry it out', the little boy was to say in evidence. He thought
'it was bird lime . . . and wanted to catch pigeons'. Fifteen minutes
later his mother's cooking range erupted in a sulphurous blue
flash. There was a 'nasty smell'. Charlie's mother, Mrs Mary
Johns, 'did not think it worth troubling the police'.

24 Baxter Road, Islington, London N,
17–18 November 1887

Mrs Maria Bright's lodger at Number 24 had retired to his room
after the water-closet incident. He stayed there for the next five
days – he was 'ill in the legs', he said, and appeared to be short
of money. He offered to sell his landlady a tin box which her
daughter Hannah had found very heavy when cleaning his room.
Now it seemed to be empty.

He had had a visitor around 10 September – a 'man with broad
shoulders', the landlady would say in evidence.

On 17 November, between 8 and 9 p.m., a mysterious second
man called asking for 'Mr Scott'. The lodger refused to see him.
The visitor insisted – he had urgent business. Mrs Bright lit a
candle and the visitor went through to the ground-floor back
room. 'He stayed about ten minutes,' the landlady would state

in evidence. 'I never saw his face . . .' she said, but 'would recognise him again if she saw him'.

The next morning a letter arrived addressed to 'Mr Thomas Scott'. It seemed to be something to do with money and he became much more cheerful. His leg ailment seemed miraculously cured. The lodger was on the move.

21 Whitehall Place, London SW, 18 November 1887

The telegram from the secretary's department at the Bank of England arrived in Monro's office early in the afternoon of the 18th. Someone had cashed £5 notes with serial numbers matching the Melville stop order. He signed his name as 'Thomas Scott'. The suspect had left but was being trailed by City of London police.

At around 5.30 p.m. a second cable came for Monro from the City police station at Old Jewry. The Threadneedle Street suspect had been observed 'buying some boots' and 'getting his whiskers shaved at a barber's in the Goswell Road'. This was the moment. Monro telegraphed back: arrest him. At around 6 p.m. the suspect was lifted and taken to King Street police station.

A steamer ticket to America was found on him, and a letter evidently about to be posted to someone called 'Joe' in New York. It said: 'I had to do away with the tea last week as two friends came to me before I got out of bed and wanted me to go to work. They have taken good care of me to make sure I did not get lost.' The suspect had evidently seen the *Penny Illustrated Paper*. 'They have got you down fine in the papers – in one of them they have you sitting in the hotel with a woman,' the letter to Joe continued.

'Joe', as far as Monro was concerned, was Joseph Melville. 'Thomas Scott' was the dead man Cohen's second American visitor.

Harkins was re-arrested that night. The two men were brought to Whitehall Place the next day and confined separately. One of them was becoming cooperative.

Harkins was brought up and placed in my room [Monro recorded]. This room communicated with that of Mr Williamson's room by means of folding doors ... 'Thomas Scott' was placed, full in gaslight, so that he could be seen clearly. The doors were suddenly opened and Harkins was asked whether he recognised Scott. He identified him as the man who had been in attendance on the deceased Cohen and whom he saw at that house.

The gaslight trick was replayed with 'Thomas Scott' as the observer. 'He had never seen the other man [Harkins] in his life.'

24 Baxter Road, Islington, 18–20 November 1887

Mrs Bright's house was turned over that evening by Sergeant Patrick McIntyre. Her lodger's back room was searched and a tin box discovered. The landlady told the story of the blocked toilet and her next-door neighbour's exploding oven. Mr Lowe, the plumber, was found: his account book revealed the date of the drama – 27 October. Islington dustmen called only sporadically in 1887. The 'stuff' was still where it had been deposited three weeks before.

McIntyre put the dustbin's contents in a box and took it to Whitehall Place that night. 'I have the tea,' he pronounced. The next day, a Saturday, Colonel Vivian Majendie, the Home Office explosives expert, arrived to pronounce it to be American-made dynamite. Flakes of paraffinned wrapping-paper proved its transatlantic origin. The 'once-heavy' tin box in the lodger's room would be found to have similar traces; so did, when examined under a microscope, cases evidently belonging to Harkins and the dead man Cohen. 'Scott' was rigorously interrogated. He confessed his real name – Thomas Callan.

Baxter Road was searched again the next day: almost thirty pounds of waterlogged kieselguhr-infused dynamite was retrieved. There were no detonators. There would be no more dissembling – no more 'warnings off' and flights to America. This time the plotters would be put on trial.

Chief Constable Williamson drafted the committal warrants that Sunday night. The next morning, 21 November, Thomas Callan and Michael Harkins were presented to a special sitting of Bow Street magistrates, charged with 'unlawfully and feloniously conspiring to cause explosions'. The evidence centred on Callan's 'tea' letter, the Balfour newspaper cutting and the discovery of a substance pronounced to be dynamite at Callan's lodging. The names 'John James Moroney' (alias Melville) and a 'General Miller or Millen' were mentioned in the indictment as part of a conspiracy to 'destroy public buildings in England by the use of dynamite'. The chief magistrate, Sir James Ingham, 'an elderly dude with a red cravat', according to a New York reporter, remained 'sunk in stupor from which he rose to ask questions of no possible relevancy'.

Callan had nothing to say. Harkins grunted: 'It don't concern me.'

The remanded prisoners were conveyed to Holloway prison with a clattering escort of mounted police with cutlasses drawn, constables armed with revolvers riding the Black Maria. The Jubilee plotters deserved maximum theatre on the streets of London.

It was a busy twenty-four hours for Britain's secret servants. Robert Anderson took personal charge of the incarceration, informing Holloway's governor: 'The name of any selected legal adviser is to be submitted before he is allowed to see the prisoners.

'Any letters written by the prisoners are to be sent to the Home Office before transmission,' he insisted.

That same Monday Major Nicholas Gosselin (the Secret Department's north of England operative) wrote gleefully to Arthur Balfour:

> There is today *evidence* which will connect the two dyna-mitards, now under remand – with Mr Joseph Nolan MP and show also that he was in correspondence with General Millen under an assumed name and for whom (Millen) a warrant will be issued.
>
> It will be proved that both men were often in the

House of Commons and that one was twice introduced by Nolan and drank with him at the Refreshment Bar in company with the man Melville (alias Moroney) for whose arrest a warrant will also be obtained – of course they, Millen and Melville, are safe from it but it will enable us to prove the connection.

At the time Nolan was introducing these two men to the House they had the dynamite at their lodgings, 28 pounds of it has been found, to say nothing of what was done away with.

All this is a secret and I only tell you as I think every crumb of encouragement is justly [word illegible] due and unless I am greatly mistaken it will seriously hurt Parnellism.

It will take a deal of talk to do away with the *fact* that the man Nolan, for whom Parnell 'took off his coat' in truth,* introduced the working agents of the Dynamit-ards into the House of Commons and was in secret corre-spondence with their chief.

Balfour was equally cheerful. He wrote to Lord Salisbury on the 25th: 'My dear Uncle Robert. I think the dynamite pro-secutions will do good. If the police authorities are not deceived, the result will show a connection between the conspirators and one member *at least* of the Parnellite party. But this must be kept dark for the present . . .'

Major Gosselin was proving very willing. On 15 December he informed Balfour:

A 'friend' of mine had a short conversation with M. Davitt a few days ago in Liverpool . . . he said enough to show that the differences between him and Parnell had reached a climax; he spoke of him in the most con-temptuous terms and made use of the harshest language

---

* Joseph Nolan had made introductions for Parnell's US tour of 1879. In a famous 1880 speech at Galway Parnell said that 'he would not have taken off his coat for the land war if he did not believe it would lead to the independence of Ireland'.

Victoria R I, Golden Jubilee portrait, June 1887.

Arthur Balfour, Lord Salisbury's 'elegant, philosophical' nephew who proved a ruthlessly pragmatic Chief Secretary for Ireland. His 'secret service' papers for the period were partially released by the Home Office in 2001 for this work; the rest still remain closed after a century and a quarter.

Top Robert Gascoyne-Cecil, third Marquis of Salisbury. His earlier dallying with Parnell in pursuit of power turned into an absolutist defence of the Union – by whatever means necessary.

Above Henry Matthews, Conservative Home Secretary 1887–91 and the first Catholic cabinet minister in two centuries. After the police failure to catch the Whitechapel killer, Queen Victoria demanded his dismissal.

Right James Monro CB, assistant commissioner to the Metropolitan Police and head of the 'Secret Department' in the year of the Jubilee. He resigned (as commissioner) in 1890 and disappeared with his entire family to build the Abode of Mercy medical mission in Bengal. Salisbury told the Queen that Monro's 'evil practices' were responsible for mutinous dissensions in the police.

The morning of 21 June 1887 as the royal procession heads for the great Jubilee service of thanksgiving in Westminster Abbey. Guardsmen line the route shoulder-to-shoulder and police cordon off the crowd. At the very last minute James Monro 'received a message' that there was a dynamite bomb in the abbey crypt. He could do nothing but 'pray for deliverance'.

Robert Anderson (KCB, 1901), veteran Fenian-finder at Dublin Castle and the Home Office, latterly assistant commissioner of the Metropolitan Police. 'If it were known what sort of man he is there would be a howl all over London,' wrote his bitter rival Edward Jenkinson on the appointment.

Alexander Sullivan, Chicago lawyer, murder suspect and ruthless head of the 'Triangle' faction of the Clan-na-Gael.

General Charles Carrol-Tevis in his Union army uniform c.1864. Appointed Adjutant-General of the Irish Republican Army in 1866, the soldier-of-fortune delivered the plans for an invasion of Canada to the British ambassador in Washington – and twenty years later was the Foreign Office's key agent in Paris.

Thomas Billis Beach, alias Henri le Caron, Robert Anderson's deep penetration agent within the Fenian Brotherhood and Clan-na-Gael for over two decades. In February 1889 he threw off his cover by giving sensational evidence in support of *The Times* newspaper at the Special (Parnell) Commission.

Front page of *The Penny Illustrated Paper*, 5 November 1887, published a week after the sensational inquest, stage-managed by James Monro, on the American 'dynamitard' Joseph Cohen found dead in south London.

Above A minute from the *Times* archive, written when the newspaper was bidding for Francis Millen to appear as a star witness at the Special Commission. It mentions 'Thomson', 'Millen', 'Paris', 'Casey' and 'Monro'. The rest of the writer's shorthand remains impenetrable.

Left Working decrypt by the defence of an intercepted cable from the *Times* agent in New York to the newspaper's solicitor in London, soon after the start of the Special Commission. It revealed that 'F. M.' would give evidence for £10,000.

Right Cable from the powerful Clan-na-Gael fixer Patrick Egan in Lincoln, Nebraska, to Michael Davitt in London, sent the day after Thomas Beach revealed on the Special Commission witness stand that there were more British-paid spies within the Clan. 'Don't mention Mexico [Millen],' Egan insisted.

Parnell presents his bill to Arthur Walter, proprietor of *The Times*, after the exposure of Richard Pigott as a forger. Cartoon from *Fun*, March 1889.

Left Sir Richard Webster, English attorney-general, prosecutor in the Old Bailey dynamite trial of Thomas Callan and Michael Harkins and leading counsel for *The Times* in the Special Commission six months later. He told parliament that he had no knowledge of any negotiations with Millen.

Below Winston S. Churchill. As Home Secretary in Herbert Asquith's (Liberal) administration of 1910, the rising politician fended off the bizarre claims of the police-man's widow Mrs Martha Thomson that she had averted 'a terrible disaster' during the Golden Jubilee of 1887 – and gave parliament a censored version of the elderly James Monro's account of the affair.

he could employ. My 'Friend' seems to think that if
Parnell opposes Davitt he will meet with a bad accident
some fine day!

I have now [illegible] in an MP who has an 'itching
palm'. But if I am to follow it up you must put funds at
my disposal. The money I get from the Home Office is
estimated for and bears no margin. Would it be worth
spending a little money sending my 'Friend' over to see
Davitt? He has invited him?

Gosselin had recruited a Nationalist MP as an informer. Mr
Balfour had a black operations fund into which the major wished
to dip. He would do so again.

On 25 November Edward Jenkinson got a message from the
War Office. He wrote to Earl Spencer: 'Another great grief has
come upon us. We got a telegraph this afternoon telling us that
our eldest son died this morning of enteric fever at Deolali.*

'We had not heard of his being ill . . . coming so soon after
Harry's death, I don't know how my wife will bear it . . .'

---

* British army base hospital in Bombay. Going 'doolally' meant you did not
come back.

36

*Court Number One, The Old Bailey, City of London,
1 February 1888*

The Jubilee plotters were brought in chains and under armed escort from Holloway to the Old Bailey. This was a high affair of state. Sir Richard Everard Webster, MP, the English attorney-general, a member of the Government, opened for the prosecution. There were two counts: one, 'conspiracy to injure persons and property by dynamite in conjunction with a man named Melville and a man named Cohen who was dead'; two, possession of 'large quantities of dynamite'.

Sir Richard reprised the committal evidence – Joseph Melville's arrival in London and cashing of drafts at the London Joint Stock Bank; the visit of Melville and Harkins to the House of Commons; the death of Cohen; the discovery of the Balfour newspaper cutting on Harkins; the arrest of Callan after the visit to the Bank of England and the finding on him of the 'tea' letter.

The attorney-general climaxed triumphantly with the discovery of 'twenty-nine pounds' of dynamite in the dustbin of 24 Baxter Street. 'It would be proved that the dynamite was of American manufacture,' he said; 'the portmanteaus were examined and found to be marked with kieselguhr, an earthy substance of which the dynamite was composed . . .'

A parade of policemen gave evidence. Maria Bright told the story of her blocked water-closet. Mr Lowe, the plumber, gave his deposition. Young Charles Johns told the tale of his mother's exploding oven. The jury spent the night in a hotel under heavy police guard. The accused were secured in the gloomy hulk of soon-to-be-demolished Newgate prison.

Expert witnesses were called the next morning. Mr George Smith Inglis, the eminent 'facsimilist', confirmed that Callan's endorsement on the banknotes and the 'tea' letter were in the same hand. Colonel Majendie revealed that the amount of dynamite used in the House of Commons crypt bomb was eight pounds; the quantity retrieved from Baxter Street was capable of doing 'very great damage', he said gravely.

The political moment had come. Joseph Nolan was called to the witness box. His encounter with the attorney-general was brittle.

'I think you are a Member of Parliament, Mr Nolan?'

'Yes.'

'And sit for North Louth, I believe?'

'Yes.'

'You were in attendance in the last session?'

'I think every day.'

'You had many applications for people to come in, had you not?'

'More than were pleasant.'

'Do you remember Mr Melville sending in a card to you?'

'I cannot say that I remember the name particularly but my attention has been called to it . . .'

'Are these entries in your writing?'

'The writing is like mine.'

'Do you recollect Harkins as a man who you have seen at the House of Commons?'

'No,' Mr Nolan replied.

Monro had been working up the investigation zealously. The timings indicated that Melville, Callan and Harkins arrived in England on or around 21 June on the SS *City of Chester*. The dead man, Cohen, had arrived some time earlier.

The passenger list was scrutinised. 'Thomas Scott' had shared a six-berth steerage cabin. Joseph Myler, the steamer's chief steward, was produced as a witness.

'Look at the prisoner, Harkins, first. Was that man a passenger on that voyage?' the prosecution directed.

'Yes.'

'What name did you know him by?'

'Scott.'

'Look at the other man, Callan – do you recognise him?'

'I cannot swear to him but I fancy I have seen him, I am not as sure as I am of the other.'

The prosecution evidence reached the moment when the police picked up Melville's part in the plot. 'On June 24, a man who we will submit was Melville cashed at the Joint Stock Bank, two bills coming from America,' said the attorney-general. 'Melville was perfectly well known to the police and his proceedings were carefully watched.'

Questioned by the judge, Inspector Littlechild stated that instructions 'were given to the House of Commons policeman as to a man named Joseph Melville . . . in the beginning of July'.

The dock brief defence was feeble. Mr Geoghegan, Callan's counsel, failed to interrogate how Melville was 'perfectly well known to the police' almost a month before he and his companion 'McTin' made the incriminating visit to the Palace of Westminster. It would have drawn out the matter of the letters of introduction from Millen – whose name had been splashed all over the committal hearings but was not mentioned once in the trial.

Yes – there was dynamite, the defending counsel admitted, and his client had indeed flushed it down the lavatory. But it was the dead man Cohen's dynamite, which his 'foolish, weak-minded' client had 'disposed of as an act of friendship'.

Mr Frith, defending Michael Harkins, was equally unconvincing: the chemical traces in the portmanteau were left by samples of his trade as a 'grocer and oil-man', he suggested. 'Who would be foolish enough to sleep with dynamite under the bed?' he asked. The jury seemed unimpressed.

Mr Justice Hawkins summed up with imperious detachment. There seemed scant doubt. At 1.25 p.m. on 3 February the jury retired. Sixteen minutes later they returned with their verdict: 'Guilty as to both prisoners.'

'Do either of you desire to say anything for yourselves?' asked the judge.

'I am innocent of the charge charged against me. I did not come here for the purpose of destroying life and property,' Thomas Callan said.

'I know the value of property too well to think of doing away with any property or any life,' said Michael Harkins '. . . as far as life is concerned I have a wife and five children now, one of which was born since I left, the eldest is a little over six years of age; and as far as life is concerned life is dear to me, the dearest thing in this world that it should bring to bear the value of other lives . . .'

Mr Justice Hawkins peered at the accused impassively. Under the Explosives Act (1883), causing explosions meant life; intent to do so meant twenty years' penal servitude with hard labour. 'The law permits me, at my discretion, to pass on you a much severer sentence than the one I am about to pronounce,' said the judge.

'If I had before me the guilty principal – for I believe there is one, perhaps there are more than one behind – who had prompted you to the commission of the crime for which you stand now to receive sentence – I should have felt my duty towards the public safety required that I should pass upon him the full extent of punishment which the law would permit me to pass . . .

'It is my painful duty to condemn you to be kept in penal servitude, each of you, for the term of fifteen years.'

The prisoners were consigned to Chatham jail. 'Fenian' prisoners did not prosper there.

An extraordinary rumour soon took hold in New York. The convicted dynamiters, who had maintained their innocence throughout, were about to confess everything. 'Callan and Harkins since they have been sentenced have offered to tell all . . . and whence the dynamite funds came from,' reported the London correspondent of the *New York Mail* two weeks after the trial.

'They promise to betray the names of certain Parnellites with whom, they say, they were instructed by their superiors to communicate. The Government will leave no stone unturned to obtain any sort of evidence which will assist them in denouncing the entire body of Parnellites as dynamiters . . .'

In his *United Irishman* newspaper Rossa commented knowingly on the report: 'We believe England's spies had a hand in
this work of Callan and Harkins and they were sold to England
as soon as they as they left America.' They were sold from the
moment they were recruited in Philadelphia.

Chatham Jail, March 1888

Perhaps it was his own high-minded quest for the truth, perhaps
it was political expediency in a bid to convict 'all Parnellites as
dynamiters' – but James Monro was indeed seeking confessions
after the Jubilee plotters' conviction. Sometime in late March
Inspector Littlechild was dispatched to Chatham. Harkins said
nothing – but Callan broke.

Monro wrote up his account in November 1891. By then
Harkins had been released, dying of terminal lung disease – and
Sir Edward Bradford was commissioner:

> There is a matter connected with police, which, before
> I leave England, I feel bound to bring to your notice
> [Monro wrote to the man who replaced him].
>
> I see that one of the 1887 dynamiters, Harkins, has
> been released. I do not know what grounds for showing
> clemency to this man existed for he was a dangerous and
> determined miscreant.
>
> But with him was convicted a man Thomas Scott, or
> Callan, who is in my opinion deserving of mercy. After
> his conviction Callan gave me most valuable information,
> which enabled me to find out how the dynamite was
> brought from America to England – how the dynamiters
> themselves came over – what were their plans – and also
> to discover the detonators which Callan had thrown away
> in Finsbury Park water . . .*

---

* The ornamental boating lake a mile north of Baxter Road was dragged and
the detonators found in 'a little purse'. Why Callan disposed of the detonators
so discreetly, yet flushed the dynamite down the water-closet, is not interrogated
in any police document.

Except myself, the only man in the police who knows
the details of Callan's actions and confession is Chief
Inspector Littlechild, and the statement of Callan must
be amongst the secret records of your office.*

Inspector John Littlechild added for the Home Secretary's
attention:

The convict made a full statement to me of the manner
in which he was engaged to come to this country and,
as far as he knew, the part that Joseph Moroney, alias
Melville (the leader on this side of the water), the released
man Harkins, and Cohen (who died just previous to his
arrest) took in the conspiracy.

His information disclosed how the dynamite was
brought ashore at Liverpool by himself and the others,
and also how he was sent to Windsor Castle provided
with a watch on a day when the state apartments were
open to the public to ascertain how long it would take
to get from the inside of the Castle to the railway station
thus showing that an explosion at the Castle was
intended . . .

There was no mention of Millen in the report. Monro stressed
that only he and Littlechild knew the true details of Callan's
actions and confession. On the eve of his departure for India he
wanted to pass on the moral burden.

* Callan's confession is not in the 1891 Littlechild file. Covering letters show
that Robert Anderson took charge of it.

37

20 Arlington Street, London W, 19 March 1888

Arthur Balfour was right when he predicted to his uncle that 'the dynamite prosecutions will do good'. Joseph Nolan's shifty denials at the Old Bailey deserved further interrogation. In early March a parliamentary select committee was appointed to examine the matter of how by now convicted American dynamiters were evidently shown round the Palace of Westminster by a prominent Parnellite. The committee would take evidence in April.

A confidential gathering was called. A scrappy letter to Arthur Balfour dated 17 March from W. H. Smith, Leader of the House of Commons, stated briskly: 'Salisbury suggests 1 p.m. on Wednesday at 20 Arlington St for the Monro meeting with Matthews and yourself.'

What passed over luncheon at the Prime Minister's London house is not directly recoverable. What follows is a reconstruction informed by subsequent events – but the gathering of the cabinet principals concerned with Ireland and the head of the Secret Department was not for example about the personal safety of ministers.*

There was in mid March 1888 a highly sensitive matter of state to consider – just what Mr Monro might tell his forthcoming parliamentary inquisitors about General F. F. Millen and a Jubilee plot. Lord Salisbury chaired. There was much harrumphing and

---

* Sir Charles Warren (who was unaware of the Arlington Street meeting) wrote to the Home Secretary soon afterwards: 'Monro as Secret Agent has no information of any special danger . . . for months now we have had no information of any definite character.' There would be a major scare in mid May over a Paris-based plot to assassinate Arthur Balfour.

throat-clearing. The Jubilee bomber so dramatically named by Monro in his public-spirited disclosures of the previous autumn was, it must be admitted, in some way a British agent. The assistant commissioner already seemed perfectly well aware of the fact – he had discovered it 'accidentally' while Millen was in Boulogne. It was the disgraced Jenkinson who had confected the scheme – to what end they might only speculate. This must stay secret.

There was, however, a continuing agenda. The dynamite found in Islington was real. Nolan had let the dynamiters into parliament; more were implicated: it was surely a public duty to expose this nest of traitorous MPs. The general might still be of singular utility in doing so. His name was not in Inspector Littlechild's précis of Callan's confession – nor had it been mentioned once at the Old Bailey trial. Just as well. As Monro had rightly noted, 'in the event of his arrest and conviction [Millen] might have made statements . . . of a most embarrassing kind'. But what if he might be caused to make statements to the discomfort of Mr Parnell? The mercenary general was greedy. There was a further inducement: was the assistant commissioner aware of the general's patriotic role in the former Fenian troubles? Mr Anderson certainly had cause to know. There was always a threat hanging over his head. Informers did not last long.

Its biddable villain must be rewritten back into the Jubilee plot. The good policeman agreed. He would splash Millen's name all over parliament. Much as he would like to do so, he would most assuredly not make any revelations concerning Mr Jenkinson.

Committee Room 15, House of Commons, 19 April 1888

The assistant commissioner faced his inquisitors impassively. Henry Matthews questioned the witness on the Jubilee plot: 'As to General Millen, was he the leading man and superior of the others?'

Monro replied obliquely: 'General Millen is a man who has been known for the last twenty years as connected with Fenian matters . . . He was connected with the Fenian rising in 1867, which was not dynamite . . .' He was wandering from the script.

'Was he in communication with those other men, Melville or Harkins or Callan last year?' Matthews asked.

'He was in communication with Melville, that is he met Melville on one occasion in Paris . . .'

Then Monro got to it: 'Millen left this country in January 1887 and went to America, and between January and April he received his instructions to come over here and commit an outrage at the time of the Jubilee.' He could not be clearer than that.

Questions and answers ran on course thereafter. The assistant commissioner laid bare the arcane business of the visits by Florence and Kitty Millen to the Palace of Westminster and the passing of their father's letter to Joseph Nolan – introducing 'Melville' as an old friend. He outlined the tracking of Melville from the Westminster pub, and his subsequent interrogation at the conveniently named Gladstone Street. 'He had bought a letter to Mr Joseph Nolan from Miles O'Brien,' Monro added ingenuously. O'Brien was New York chairman of the Irish parliamentary fund. The connection between dynamite and Parnell was given an extra nudge in *The Times*.*

Monro had new information gleaned from Callan's confession. Cohen and a mysterious 'fifth man' seen at the obelisk had arrived in England bearing a quantity of dynamite sometime in May, he revealed. Moroney, alias Melville, had travelled on the *City of Chester* with Callan and Harkins with more explosive, but 'they did not arrive here in England till the 21st of June, Jubilee Day, on account of their having missed the previous steamer, finding all the berths in it engaged . . .'

Joseph Nolan was questioned by the Home Secretary. He denied outright receiving 'any letter of introduction'. He had no

---

* A curious letter appeared in *The Times* on 23 April about the 'Jubilee dynamite gang of last summer'. It pointed out knowingly that Nolan was the interlocutor of Parnell's American tour of 1881 at the height of the land war, and that Miles O'Brien was a wealthy New York supporter of nationalist MPs. It was signed 'A Looker On'. This was probably Anderson.

'distinct recollection' of Melville and, although he had met Millen in London in 1886, had 'never heard that the General had any connection with what is known as the dynamite faction in America'.

James Monro was recalled on the 30th. This time the inquisitor was hostile: it was Joseph Biggar, MP. The former member of the supreme council of the IRB seemed to sense a loophole in the policeman's earlier reference to the 'Fenian rising of 1867'. 'What was the nature of General Millen's connection with this rising?' he asked.

'At present I do not think it would be advisable for me to say what I know about it . . .'

Indeed it would not be advisable. The youthful Robert Anderson had sent rebels to prison on Informant M's long-ago betrayals. Monro clearly knew it – so did his inquisitor.

'You are not prepared to state what his connection was?' asked Biggar.

'I do not intend to give any information regarding General Millen until it seems to me, as a police officer, expedient to do so in connection with the criminal proceedings which it is my duty to take against him . . .'

He was putting down a marker. Monro had not bent completely to the Arlington Street agenda. If the general showed up in the furtherance of some darker political purpose he would march him smartly off to Bow Street magistrates' court.

Frank Millen, meanwhile, was somewhere quite safe from any arrest warrant. A reporter from the *New York World* picked up his trail in an April interview at the Broadway office of Colonel George W. Gibbons, president of the American Annexation League, a society of ex-Civil War officers dedicated to the expulsion of European colonialism from the American continent.

The cigar-chomping colonel dramatically revealed a secret plan was being hatched in London to engineer some border dispute from British Guyana and seize gold mines in Venezuela. The colonel was raising a mercenary army of New Yorkers equipped with 'dynamite guns' to make a counter raid: '100,000 Irish' would volunteer, Colonel Gibbons proclaimed. And who was already in Caracas organising the army of national resistance? It was General Millen, of course – 'an old soldier of fortune and New York journalist . . .'

Foreign Office, London SW, May 1888

Sir Julian Pauncefote could wish for nothing more than that 'Mr XXX' might disappear for ever in some Caribbean jungle. If only Mr Monro, with his tiresome sense of a policeman's duty, had not been reading the New York papers.

His memo arrived at the Foreign Office on 18 May: 'I am informed that information concerning General Millen may be got from Venezuela. So far as outrage is concerned I do not think that Millen will give us trouble, but he may have been something in the filibustering line which it might be well to know . . .'

The eager Monro suggested scouring the jungles of Central America. HM consul in Guatemala City was wearily ordered the next day to make inquiries. An engraved portrait from the *Graphic* magazine was carefully snipped out at Scotland Yard and sent as a mug-shot. There was no sighting.

It was all a bit pointless. The Foreign Office already knew perfectly well where Millen was. The great Anglo-Venezuelan war of 1888 had been a flop. Millen had returned to his first point of departure.

Sir St John Spenser had cabled ten days earlier from Mexico City: 'The person about whom Carden reported in 1885, who may be styled "Mr XXX", arrived here a few days ago and is lodged in one of the hotels.' No one from the legation had yet made contact – what should they do? The Foreign Office sat on the intelligence for a month.

The Millen matter would not go away. Nationalist MPs were asking questions in parliament. What was this farrago of evidence before the select committee, not given in the trial of Callan and Harkins? It was a conspiracy. 'The commission was set up by Viscount Ebrington, a Liberal Unionist, in collusion with Govern-

ment members to besmirch the character of an individual member
of the House,' Timothy Healey, MP, alleged on 5 June. This was
becoming uncomfortable. It was time to act on the Mexico cable.
Lord Salisbury stirred.

Sir Julian Pauncefote sent the Home Secretary a carefully con-
structed note that evening: 'With reference to a letter which was
addressed to Mr Jenkinson on Nov 4 1885 and other correspondence in that year, I am directed by the Marquis of Salisbury to
state for the information of Mr Secretary Matthews, that HM
Minister in Mexico has reported that General Millen, the person
referred to in that correspondence, was in Mexico . . .' He
enclosed a translated newspaper report of the general's arrival.

The note was exquisitely drafted. The 'letter to Jenkinson',
sent on the eve of his tempestuous Arlington Street meeting
with Salisbury, was the dispatch from Lionel Carden giving the
recognition code for the forthcoming encounter with Millen.
That and the 'other correspondence of that year' reference was
plain. The dry memorandum folded the Home Office back into
the whole Mexican construct – the recruitment of Millen on
behalf of HM government. Henry Matthews was hugely compromised. The note implied that he, at least in the Home Office,
had had access to the Millen file all along. His interrogation of
the assistant commissioner before the select committee had been
a mummery. But how much did Monro know? Thus far that
Edward Jenkinson had been in contact with Millen in January
1887 – and again, it would seem, by letter in the Jubilee summer.
That was the embarrassment he had sought to spare HM government. So far the embarrassment had all been Mr Parnell's.

The Irish were asking uncomfortable questions in parliament.
Wearily the Home Secretary was compelled to bring the policeman in on the presiding secret. It went much higher than
Jenkinson. The man Monro had so publicly named as the head
of a dynamite plot against Queen Victoria had been recruited on
the personal sanction of the Prime Minister. What was Monro to
do – expose the whole thing? He had meanwhile need of all the
political support he could get.

Whitehall Place, London SW, June 1888

Edward Jenkinson's defenestration from Room 56 was supposed to have brought order to the counter-revolutionary apparatus. By early summer 1888 it was in uproar again. Monro's enemy this time was the overbearing commissioner, General Sir Charles Warren. The feud had begun during the pursuit of Callan and Harkins in November 1887, when Monro had complained that his department was over-worked. 'The result has been that Mr Williamson has broken down* and that I am in a fair way to break down also,' he wrote.

Monro sought help for the ailing Williamson. He suggested an old friend from Bengal, a tea-planter called Melville Mac-naghten, be appointed assistant chief constable. The Home Office agreed but Warren blocked the appointment with a mean little whispering campaign. But the most irksome burr was Monro's direct access to the Home Secretary in his parallel role as 'secret agent'. The head of the Criminal Investigation Department should devote his 'time and energy to legitimate work', Warren had insisted that spring, and 'not be burdened with the care and anxiety of duties which previously occupied the whole of the attention of an officer of undoubted experience and ability . . .'

If this was a move to rehabilitate the fallen Jenkinson, it could not have been timed better to enrage Monro.† He was burdened enough by politicians. Warren kept up the pressure: every barb in the radical press over his Kaffir-bashing public-order methods‡

* He was granted three months sick leave, suffering from 'fainting attacks'. He died in December 1889 as a result, said Monro, of his 'especially arduous labours against the Fenians'.
† There was a further blow for Monro that summer – a knighthood for the hated Jenkinson in the Queen's Birthday Honours. Sir Robert Hamilton, former under-secretary at Dublin Castle, thought it was a reward for services rendered to the Conservative government. He wrote to Earl Spencer cryptically: 'I have an uncomfortable feeling that Jenkinson is at the bottom of the "Parnellism and Crime" business of *The Times*, notwithstanding his having assured you that no connection of Parnell with crime came before him . . .'
‡ On Sunday 13 November 1887, on Warren's orders, baton-wielding police cleared Trafalgar Square of a huge anti-government demonstration, for which Irish and socialist agitators were blamed. Regular troops were engaged. Two demonstrators died. The *Pall Mall Gazette* called it 'Bloody Sunday'.

enlivened his efforts to put the assistant commissioner under his thumb. 'I must, in justice to myself, disclaim all responsibility for any unfavourable results to which the system now initiated will lead,' Monro informed Matthews on 11 June. He boiled with indignation. His 'Special Section', meanwhile, was heading for the most curious re-arrangement of its affairs.

HM Legation, Mexico City, 30 June 1888

It was Lionel Carden who remade the contact. The ambitious young diplomat must have found the encounter ironic. Frank Millen was famous; he was splashed all over the American papers as the man who had plotted to blow up Queen Victoria. Now, here he was in the legation garden offering to serve Her Majesty's government again. It was Carden's boss Sir St John Spenser who cabled the Foreign Office with the news on 30 June:

> Secret and confidential. Carden asks me to forward the following – 'With reference to my despatch Secret of the year 1885, "X" has returned to Mexico and asks me to say that he is willing to resume supplying information provided he has not to deal with the same person with whom he was dealing last summer.
>
> 'Is ready to go to London or Dublin if necessary but would prefer continent . . .'

Lord Salisbury pondered the message's utility. 'X' was ready for work 'provided he has not to deal with the same person with whom he was dealing last summer'. Last summer – June 1887 – the Jubilee plot. Sir Julian Pauncefote, head of HM Foreign Secret Service, copied the cable to Henry Matthews, who passed it to Monro.

PART NINE

The Commission

'The gentlemen that lied in Court, they knew,
and well they knew.'
Rudyard Kipling, 'Cleared'
(In Memory of a Commission)

38

Royal Courts of Justice, The Strand, London WC,
2–5 July 1888

Robert Anderson's anonymous exposés in *The Times* had produced an unlooked for result. After a heated exchange in the
paper's letters column following the 'Behind the Scenes in
America' article of 1 June 1887, an eccentric former Irish MP
called Frank Hugh O'Donnell claimed he had been personally
libelled. The case came to court on 2 July 1888, with the
ubiquitous Sir Richard Webster defending.

The attorney-general made a three-day speech, reprising the
allegations – and produced six more letters following those published in spring 1887 which pointed to even deeper complicity
by Mr Parnell in the Phoenix Park murders. The letters' authenticity was beyond doubt, Sir Richard insisted. The famous 'facsimilist' George Smith Inglis (who had studied the first batch of
letters, then been employed by the prosecution in Regina v. Harkins and Callan) again pronounced them authentic. One pur-
porting to be from Parnell to Patrick Egan, former treasurer of
the Land League, was especially damning. The judge directed
that only statements concerning the plaintiff personally were
admissible. There were none in the article. On 5 July the jury
found for *The Times* without leaving their bench.

Sir Edward Jenkinson observed the proceedings with bafflement. He had investigated the murders exhaustively and found
no link to Parnell. He wrote to Sir William Harcourt the day after
the verdict urging the opposition front-bencher go on the political
offensive. The fallen spymaster offered 'every assistance in my
power'.

Home Office, 4 July 1888

The Mexico City telegram sat menacingly on the Home Secretary's desk. Mr Henry Matthews called a grim little meeting with
the assistant commissioner. Both men were compromised. Both
men had been copied with Millen's 'the person I was dealing
with last summer' cable. Lord Salisbury seemed willing enough
to put the Jubilee bomber back on the payroll. It was James
Monro who replied to the Foreign Office on 4 July in a memo
laden with weary knowingness: 'I am to request you to inform
the Marquis of Salisbury that Mr Matthews is not disposed to
recommend compliance with Millen's proposal. This man is not
trusted in the Fenian organisation, and is not likely to be of
use . . .'

There was a flash of truncheon: 'Further it is to be borne in
mind that a warrant for his arrest is in existence and would be
executed was he to return to this country.'

The next morning, 5 July, Pauncefote cabled the Mexico legation: 'Inform X we are not disposed to accede to his proposal . . .'

The verdict for *The Times* in the O'Donnell libel case came
that afternoon. The newspaper's editor, George Earle Buckle,
sent a message to Lord Salisbury by special messenger: 'Could
you let me see you some time this evening with ref to our case
and its outcome? I could come either to the FO before dinner
or to Arlington St later . . .' They met just before midnight.
There was much the Government might do to progress matters
discreetly.

Westminster, summer 1888

The Westminster orchestra was turning up for the greatest
political opera of the age – the Special 'Parnell' Commission. It
would occupy 128 sittings; over 450 witnesses would be examined
in a trial without a jury in which sixty-three serving and two
retired members of parliament and sixty-seven 'other persons'
would be arraigned with 'conspiracy to bring about the absolute
independence of Ireland'.

Parnell drew it on himself. The Irish leader demanded the appointment of a parliamentary committee to probe the 'facsimile letters', sensationally regurgitated in the failed O'Donnell libel action. The Government countered with something much more theatrical: a 'special commission' to rake over the entire 'Irish nationalist conspiracy'. Joseph Chamberlain, the breakaway Liberal Unionist, urged the idea on his new patrons. Much of the Cabinet was reluctant but Lord Salisbury barged it through.

There was uproar in parliament. The battles over the Bill ordaining the Special Commission echoed the home rule slugging matches – but this time, some of Mr Parnell's Liberal allies kept their distance, anxious lest the mud did indeed stick. At last, on 13 August, after plentiful political arm-twisting, the Special Commission Act was passed. Three learned judges would sift through a decade's worth of evidence – boycott, mayhem, murder and outrage – in a 'huge fishing expedition'. The matter of the letters would be at its heart but, as *The Times*'s official history itself explains: 'It was essential to show the relations of the Parnellites with crime in Ireland on one hand and American promoters of dynamite outrages on the other.'

Skulking in Mexico the Jubilee bomber had taken on a sparkling new significance. There remained Monro and his inconvenient sense of a policeman's duty.

The Special Commission was politically very clever. Parnellism would be on trial – but the 'prosecution' would be conducted by a newspaper. *The Times* would even be paying for it. How much 'special information' should the Government provide? 'If we do not, it may get wasted,' Arthur Balfour explained to his uncle on 17 August; 'if we do, shall we not find ourselves in a somewhat embarrassing position?'

Lord Salisbury replied: 'There may be grounds for not stirring, if the evidence is not of a conclusive kind, or if the mode of getting it cannot be explained. If on the other hand – it has come naturally into our hands ... we shall be fulfilling an obvious and elementary duty in facilitating the proof of it before the Commission ...'

Thus it was. *The Times*'s solicitor, Mr Joseph Soames of 58

Lincoln's Inn, had been bustling round since the first stirrings of the O'Donnell libel case in summer 1887 collecting evidence. The Irish end would be pivotal. A thirty-nine-year-old former inspector of the Royal Irish Constabulary, recently appointed a resident magistrate, was briefed by the Irish attorney-general to coordinate intelligence operations at Dublin Castle. His name was William Henry Joyce. A small hand-picked team worked under him.

By late summer two tons of files were crated up ready to be shipped to the Irish Office in London. Overtures were made as to how far the secret organs of the Metropolitan Police might cooperate.

James Monro had had enough. His bruising row with Warren was the overt reason for his resignation. On 16 August he wrote to the Home Secretary: 'Grave differences of opinion on questions of police administration have arisen between Sir Charles Warren and myself ... I can no longer continue responsible for the efficiency of the Criminal Investigation Department ...'

It was not quite self-immolation. Monro knew too much to be cut loose completely. In the oddest reshuffle imaginable of the secret Whitehall chessboard, on 30 August Monro was whisked off to a room in the Home Office, keeping control of 'the secret Irish work'.

Who might replace him? Robert Anderson was appointed CID chief. He was told to keep the appointment secret, but Jenkinson still had ears in Whitehall. He wrote to Spencer on 24 September:

> It is quite true that R. Anderson has been appointed to succeed Monro as Head of the Criminal Inv Dept at Scotland Yard. What an infamously bad appointment it is! Anderson is not the 19th part of a man, and if it were known what kind of man he is, there would be a howl all over London.
>
> Gosselin writes in the greatest disgust about it all. He says 'I have lived to see a great many things in my time but the acuteness shown in finding this man (Anderson) is worthy of all admiration.'

> Matthews is too lazy or too weak, or too indifferent
> to make any stand . . .

Robert Anderson's first day in office was eventful: a woman called Polly Nichols was found murdered in a Whitechapel alleyway. Eight days later Annie Chapman was found in a back yard with her throat cut and her insides ripped open. Two dead prostitutes did not seem that remarkable. Anderson went on extended leave to the Swiss Alps, claiming 'exhaustion from overwork'. On Sunday 30 September, however, he was urgently recalled: two more women had been found dead. Anderson wrote in his memoirs: 'Letters from Whitehall decided me to spend the last week of my holiday in Paris that I might be in touch with my office. I received an urgent appeal from Mr Matthews to return – which I did.'* Why Robert Anderson should spend the first week of October 1888 in the French capital he chose not to elaborate further.

---

* A letter from Matthews to Warren in the Home Office 'ripper files' dated 5 October 1888 contains this waspish postscript: 'I shall be very glad to hear whether Mr Anderson's health has prevented him from returning to his duties . . .'

39

Mike Ledwith's Saloon, Third Avenue and 44th Street, New York, September 1888

Three thousand miles from the Royal Courts of Justice in London another quasi-judicial procedure was about to go into session. There were no bewigged barristers in this court, a Masonic lodge room above a raucous Irish-American bar on Third Avenue.

Just as the career of Charles Stewart Parnell was about to be judicially examined for specks of dynamite, so the feuding Clan-na-Gael was about to offer up its history for forensic inspection. The evidence given at this 'trial' of the record of Alexander Sullivan and his Triangle acolytes was all supposed to be deadly secret.

The Clan 'kickers' led by John Devoy and Luke Dillon had held their ground since the breakaway Brooklyn conference of February 1887. Dissenting clubs in New York and Philadelphia had defected wholesale. Aleck Sullivan had been forced to make terms. In June 1888 a 'union conference' was called in Chicago, supposedly to remake the brotherhood as one. Held at the Madison Street music hall, it was a grisly affair of bogus backslapping mixed with murderous threats.

Thomas Beach was there, scampering round the axis of Aleck Sullivan and his most important ally Patrick Egan. When John Devoy raised a suspicion that 'British spies' had penetrated their ranks, Egan stared back and growled menacingly, 'We know where the spies are.'

A fragile unity was achieved under a new nine-man committee of five Sullivanites and four antis, but Devoy pushed through his demand for a set-piece trial of the Triangle – Aleck Sullivan,

Boland and Feeley – for political and financial fraud. Among
Sullivan's loudest accusers was Dr Patrick Cronin.

The six-man trial committee – three partisans from each faction
– held its preliminary meeting in a hotel in Buffalo, New York
State, on 20 August. A young Devoy/Dillon-supporter from
Philadelphia, Michael J. Ryan, was appointed 'attorney for the
prosecution'. Cronin was one of the inquisitors. Aleck Sullivan
sat pale-lipped, anger smouldering under a lawyer's calm. It did
not last. His accusers were all 'British spies', he raged. Pistols
were drawn from bulging waistbands. Sullivan turned on Patrick
Cronin with special fury. He was his 'malignant enemy – the
brand of perjury burned into his brow'. Nothing was to be more
reviled than a former revolutionary comrade.

The proceedings were moved to the Hotel Westminster in
New York, but the press found out and started leaking sensational
reports. The trial re-adjourned to a bar-room on Third Avenue.
John Devoy was warned: 'Aleck is going to make a morgue of
the committee room in Mike Ledwith's.' He tucked a gun in his
pocket – 'a self-cocking revolver given to me by my old prison
comrade Ric Burke'.

The condemnations stacked up: Sullivan had broken the link
with the IRB, focus of the revolutionary movement's legitimacy;
he had rigged the 1886 Pittsburgh convention, packed commit-
tees and conjured favourable voting results from bogus district
conventions.

Huge sums of money supposedly spent on 'active work' had
been pocketed by Sullivan, it was alleged. The dispatchers of
dynamiters – the name of John J. Moroney (Melville) was mentioned – had handed out parsimonious amounts on the eve of
operations. The families of volunteers, dead or in English prisons,
had been abandoned by the Clan. Mrs Susan Mackey Lomasney,
the widow of the 'Little Captain' blown to pieces beneath London
Bridge, gave evidence in person, claiming she was left destitute
in Detroit. Sullivan had offered her nothing more than a $100
loan.

Luke Dillon's evidence was the most sensational. He was
famous – the man who had bombed the Houses of Parliament

on 25 January 1885, one of the very few Clan bombers to make the return journey. It was Sullivan's loyal lieutenant Moroney who had recruited him and an ex-Confederate soldier called Roger O'Neill for the mission, so Dillon revealed. On the New York dockside Moroney had provided steerage passage and $100 'to carry on work'. For further funds they were referred to 'the agent on the other side'. The agent was 'betrayed' and 'was now in prison', said Dillon.

'How many operations did you perform?' he was asked.

'Three. We always bade each other good-bye after each meeting, thinking it might be our last meeting on earth . . .'

After the Palace of Westminster attack O'Neill had 'wandered round London helped by a few Irishmen, and got back to America by working a tramp steamer . . .' Luke Dillon made it to New York the same way.

The New York press was still sniffing round. With the Special Commission about to open in London, the danger to Parnell of this explosive entrail-examining was clear. James J. O'Kelly, MP, Millen's old Havana comrade-in-journalism, was dispatched to New York to quieten things down. The gravest fear was that John Devoy would pursue his allegation that Patrick Egan had turned over $100,000 in Land League money to the Clan during the dynamite campaign. The saloon-bar trial adjourned on 16 September to allow the warring factions to campaign for the Republican presidential candidate Benjamin Harrison. It would reconvene in January.

Royal Courts of Justice, September 1888

The Special Commissioners held their preliminary meeting at the Law Courts the next day, 17 September. The three judges made a ruling that would transform the 'trial' from a libel case into a political grand inquisition. Instead of 'defending' itself by proving the alleged libels against a plaintiff were true, *The Times* newspaper was instructed to proceed as if Parnell and his entire party were indicted on all the allegations in the articles.

The newspaper would effectively act as the prosecutor. Witnesses must be found, informers induced to testify. The letters, sensational as they might be, would be a sidebar. *The Times* was given powers to subpoena, complete with relevant police records, members of the Royal Irish Constabulary. It remained to be seen what assistance Whitehall might provide on higher matters.

The Times's counsel had to work hard to structure the sprawling allegations into charges that could be substantiated. They emerged under nine heads, embracing three main issues. It was alleged first that the 'respondents' – sixty-three serving and two retired members of the Irish Party – were members of a conspiracy to bring about the absolute independence of Ireland; that they had promoted by intimidation an agrarian campaign of rent strikes to bring down the landlord system; and thirdly that in pursuit of these objectives they had either committed or condoned crimes themselves and associated with notorious advocates of crime and dynamite.

Michael Davitt (who was not then an MP) was charged separately with being the broker of the alliance between the parliamentary party and American extremists – the 'new departure' of 1879. Underpinning this charge was the early history of the Land League and its clandestine funding by the Clan-na-Gael. The Dublin meeting of Davitt and Millen was pivotal.

The Government had its own problems. The attorney-general, Old Bailey hammer of the Jubilee bombers, victor in the O'Donnell libel case, clearly thought that leading in the Special Commission might be a prosecution too far.

'My position as counsel for *The Times* in defending an action brought by a private individual is altogether different from my appearing in support of charges against the Parnellite party,' Sir Richard Webster wrote to Balfour. 'It will be said that the Govt have been conducting the prosecution and no amount of argument will satisfy the public of the contrary,' Lord Salisbury insisted. To 'run away from the case', as he put it, would look as if the chief prosecutor did not believe the evidence.

There was indeed a problem. Pigott was the black hole at the heart of *The Times*'s case. The prosecution knew it; so did ministers.

40

Vienna, Austria-Hungary, 18 October 1888

The Special Commission's formal opening was just a few weeks away. Sir Edward Jenkinson embarked meanwhile on a continental journey – on whose account (probably Earl Spencer's) and to what precise itinerary remains enigmatic. But as the lawyers in London laboured over their briefs, the newly made knight can be definitely placed in Paris and Vienna, from where he wrote a very conspiratorial letter to his old patron on 18 October:

> P. S. Cassidy, who as you know was Rossa's secretary and head of the extreme party in New York, has just written a long letter to an Irish friend of his.
>
> Parnell will never get any more money from America' [Cassidy had told his mysterious 'friend'] . . . and points out in detail what I have always said should have been Parnell's attitude in regard to the extreme party. Instead of denying all knowledge with the dynamiters, Parnell, says Cassidy, should have boldly showed his connection with them, showing their strength and at the same time, saying he disapproved of their methods, but was only biding his time to get the upper hand of them and to use constitutional agitation.

How Sir Edward was still reading Mr Cassidy's transatlantic communications was curious enough. His prescription for Mr Parnell – to have boldly declared his connection with dynamiters – was even stranger.

'This Cassidy is the man who came over . . . to Ireland and

had a dinner given to him at an hotel in Dublin at which two MPs with Parnell's knowledge were present,' he reminded Earl Spencer. 'Before he left, he promised to use all his influence to keep the extreme party in America quiet and to prevent outrages. From that time there have not been any dynamite outrages in England . . .' James Monro had informed the Home Secretary in June 1887 that Millen was Cassidy's accredited agent. Jenkinson depicted Cassidy as keeper of the Parnellite peace.

He had more news:

> M. Davitt has been in Paris working for Parnell and has been trying to collect evidence for him. He has run down Pigott (the rascal who has been working for *The Times*, as I know, against Parnell) and has subpoenaed him for the trial. Pigott is in a great fright and has offered (as I anticipated) to go over to Parnell and make certain confessions . . . rather than go into the witness box. But on Davitt's advice, Parnell won't have this.
>
> The chief thing we can say is that Pigott went to [Eugene] Davis and offered him £100 if he would go into the witness box and swear that Parnell had a hand in the PP murders. I saw Davis's letter about it, highly indignant and abusing Pigott . . .
>
> Davitt is working hard for Parnell and he has got men of all shades of opinion working with him. I shall know more on my way back through Paris next week . . .

Paris, 19–20 October 1888

The traveller would indeed know more. On the eve of the Special Commission's opening Sir Edward Jenkinson met Michael Davitt in Paris.

The old adversaries had much to discuss. Davitt had indeed run down Pigott – if not literally: the 'rascal' had departed Paris for Dublin on the 4th, the day Robert Anderson also left the French capital. Davitt had a neurotic fear of alcohol, but he had

braved the absinthe fumes in Reynolds' Bar long enough with
Joseph Casey to get at least some of the story of the black bag
and the handover of its contents at the Hôtel des Deux Mondes
to the *Times* agent.

Davitt had also interviewed General Carrol-Tevis. They had
a gentlemanly conversation about journalism. The general's
employment by the *New York Times* had ended. How about a
job with the Parnell-supporting *Freeman's Journal*, he enquired.
'I am a welcome guest where the majority of journalists are at
least only tolerated if admitted at all,' Tevis declared.*

The Foreign Office agent had been astonishingly forthcoming.
It was from Tevis that Davitt learned of the Cassidy-Hayes-Katkov
manoeuvres of 1886. It was from Tevis that he learned of Millen's
diplomacy on behalf of the Fenian Council in spring 1887. (He
scribbled in his notebook: 'Interview with Z. Read me letter from
SC in which Parnell was denounced and ridiculed . . . and Gentle
T talked of as a kind of grand pacificator.')

It was from Tevis that he learned of Duleep Singh's dispatch
to Moscow and the Casey passport switch. It was from Tevis that
he learned of Richard Pigott's meetings with Frank Millen at the
Hôtel St Petersbourg the previous summer.

It was from Tevis that he learned of Millen's sojourn in
Boulogne and his 'pretence of preparing things in England'.

Davitt also knew that Jenkinson and Earl Spencer were being
blackmailed. Matthew O'Brien – who had been the intermediary
in the days of Red Jim McDermott's entrapment plots – claimed
to have 'two letters' that would destroy the fallen spymaster and
his patron with him. (Jenkinson's alarmed replies to the threats
are in Davitt's papers.)

The two old adversaries made a deal. In the forthcoming grand
inquisition Davitt would not expose to official glare the wilder

* There was an interesting aside: the general was anxious to introduce Davitt to
a young woman, Irish-born daughter of the British military attaché in
St Petersburg. She was the famously beautiful and burningly nationalist Miss
Maud Gonne, later the inspiration of W. B. Yeats. She wanted to meet Davitt to
serve 'our dear country'. 'What is this little game?' he scribbled on her letter.
'Probably a *Times* plot.'

operations run out of Dublin Castle and Room 56. In return Sir
Edward Jenkinson gave Davitt the extraordinary truth about Her
Majesty's government and the Mexican general. Davitt needed
to know: his meeting under the cover-name 'Mr Black' with 'Mr
Robinson' in Dublin in 1879 when Millen was making his military
tour of inspection would be at the centre of the prosecution case
against him.

Davitt noted in his little black book: 'Millen in pay Hoare
[British Consul in New York]. Came over 1887. Monro applied
for warrant for arrest Millen fortnight after he had gone. Applied
for warrant . . . knowing he was away . . .'

There was something else in his notes – a one-line scribble:
'Tevis, [Patrick] Casey all in [British] service.'

Maybe Jenkinson told him. Maybe Davitt found out for himself
– but as Parnell's intelligence chief dispassionately interviewed
the 'representative of the Fenian Brotherhood in Paris' he realised
that every move made in the French capital since the fall of home
rule was a conjuring trick. The deadly dynamiter Patrick Casey
was in British pay. The affable Tevis, former adjutant-general of
the Irish Republican Army, was the conduit to Whitehall. Why
Tevis himself chose to reveal so much remains a mystery. Perhaps
Davitt knew enough of his long ago – and more recent – betrayals
to apply some discreet pressure.

Davitt had already learned enough about Richard Pigott to
stop the tribunal even before it began. He had enough information on the Jubilee plot to put the Government on trial. He
bundled up his papers and prepared to return to London for the
Special Commission's imminent opening. How could they lose?
The defence had staged another intelligence coup. An Irish sympathiser at the Western Union telegraph office on 38th Street
noticed incoming cipher cables from an address in London –
'Assert'. The code was impenetrable but the telegraphic address
was spelled out – Soames Edwards at Lincoln's Inn, *The Times*'s
solicitors. The messages were routed via New York to someone
code-named 'Mohawk' in Colorado. The messages were copied
and discreetly relayed back across the Atlantic to the defence.

Lewis & Lewis, Solicitors, 10–11 Ely Place, Holborn,
London WC, 21 October 1888

Sir Edward Jenkinson arrived in London on the night of the 20th
and went next morning to the offices of Parnell's solicitor. He
confided to Spencer:

> I had a long talk with George Lewis today. They have
> got Pigott quite in a hole. He will be put in the witness
> box and declare the letters to be forgeries. This will smash
> up the *Times* case about the letters v Parnell which is the
> kernel of the whole business . . .
>
> No doubt *The Times* has been awfully humbugged . . .
> and the Govt has made a great mistake in giving it so
> much support . . .
>
> I take a fitful pleasure in looking on because I have
> such an intimate knowledge of the whole business . . .
> and could have prevented them falling into a trap if they
> had asked my opinion.

For once the motives of this supremely convoluted man seemed
simple. Jenkinson's defection, if that is what it was, was a matter
of a secret policeman's wounded pride.

Clinging to Pigott, *The Times* was sleep-walking towards disaster. It was becoming clear to certain figures in London that the
newspaper needed a magic bullet to destroy their enemy. Robert
Anderson held one – the informant in America whom Jenkinson,
try as he might, had never been able to flush out. Thomas Beach
wanted to give evidence in person. He had written to his controller from Chicago on 18 September:

> The feeling here is that the commission will result in
> a great victory for the Irish party . . . why they are so
> confident I cannot see.
>
> Parnell's conversations with me and others repres-
> enting the Rev Org on this side commit him to a perfect
> knowledge of and a union between it and the League. I

wish it were possible to testify. I am perfectly willing if
it would result in good . . .

The Times meanwhile had been pursuing a surprise witness of
its own, whose discreet overtures the Foreign Office had put on
file two years before. On 15 October 1888 a man named J. T.
Kirby, a private detective from Montreal, arrived at remote ranch
house in Pueblo, Colorado. He had an offer for the wool-rancher,
Patrick Sheridan, the 'notorious Invincible' according to the prosecution indictment – the same man who had approached the
British ambassador in Washington in March 1886 under the cover
name 'Henry'. The Canadian detective had an offer: testify against
Parnell and the paper would 'buy' his ranch for no less than
£20,000.

Coded messages flew back and forth between 'Mohawk' and
'Assert'. The patriotic cable-clerk at the Western Union office
relayed them to the Parnellite camp in London. They would take
a week to decipher.

Probate Court Number One, Royal Courts of Justice, 22 October 1888

The Special Commission opened at three minutes past eleven
precisely. The chamber was packed – entry was by ticket only,
and it was heaving with press and spectators. The chief 'respondents', Mr Parnell and Mr Davitt, sat at the front, half solemn,
half mocking like clever schoolboys up before the beak. They
knew something. A curtain was raised and the three learned judges
trooped to the bench. Sir Richard Webster and Sir Henry James
would lead for *The Times*; the distinguished barrister and Liberal
MP Sir Charles Russell and the rising young lawyer Herbert
Asquith, MP, for the defence.

Everyone expected an immediate set-to over the letters. The
prosecution opened instead with a rag-bag of obscure witnesses
from the days of the land war – bucolic policemen and intimidated
peasantry in picturesque garb, 'evidently bent', according to one
observer, 'on playing the simple game of wearing down the other

side'. It was a phoney war. Both sides well knew that Pigott was
the rotten plank in the causeway. The question was at what point
it would be reached.

It nearly collapsed in the first week. Henry Labouchere, the
flamboyant radical MP, proprietor and editor of the magazine
Truth, an ardent Parnell supporter, had hired a private detective
– a 'Mr John Sinclair'. Sinclair was recommended by Patrick Egan,
for whom he was already working as a transatlantic courier.
Labouchere sent him in mid October to a shabby seaside terrace,
11 Sandycove Avenue, in Kingstown, Dublin. His mission was
to 'induce' Richard Pigott to come to London. The threat was
simple. In his negotiations with Houston Pigott had made his
conspiratorial visit to Eugene Davis in Lausanne the key to the
discovery of the 'black bag'. On his energetic mission to Paris
Davitt had managed to turn Davis for the defence and Pigott
knew it. Davis's promised appearance before the commission
would expose everything.

On the night of 25 October Pigott went to Labouchere's
house at Grosvenor Gardens near Buckingham Palace. Waiting
in the library was Charles Stewart Parnell. Pigott confessed that
the letters were forged.

The Irish leader was jubilant; Davitt was appalled. He knew
just who 'Sinclair' was – it was Matthew O'Brien, the man who
had been involved in Jenkinson's earlier entrapment plots. He
foresaw a disastrous outcome: that *The Times* would pay Pigott
£5,000 to vanish, and when the time came to produce Pigott in
court the prosecution could report that Parnell had secretly met
him and had induced him by blackmail threats or money not to
testify. The rotten plank would be skipped over.

Joseph Soames, *The Times*'s solicitor, was to give his version
in later testimony to the commission:

> The matter came about in this way. A man wrote to me
> . . . and offered to give me information, I knew
> the handwriting. I knew it was from a man named
> O'Brien. The whole thing was an attempted plant on
> me. I had this man watched and traced that he was sent

over at the instance of Mr Labouchere to see Pigott in Dublin.

The man took the name of 'Sinclair'. I had him followed, and I traced him to Mr Labouchere's, then to Mr Pigott and then I traced Mr Pigott, Mr George Lewis and Mr Parnell together in the house of Mr Labouchere.

O'Brien admitted to me under the name of 'Roberts' in America – it was a man named Roberts who imposed the letters on Mr Moser. Mr O'Brien was at one time a solicitor in Dublin . . .

Matthew O'Brien (alias Sinclair, alias Roberts) would work for anybody. *The Times* had also employed him during ex-Inspector Maurice Moser's farcical 'Sheridan letter-finding' mission to New York in summer 1887. While acting as the defence's threatening emissary to Pigott in Dublin, he was, so later testimony to the commission showed, telling *The Times* precisely what he was up to.

O'Brien was also meanwhile being leant on by Major Gosselin, who was relaying information to Arthur Balfour.*

Thomas Beach in Chicago, meanwhile, was reading press reports of the commission's proceedings. He was baffled as to why the prosecution seemed so limp – 'a rehash of what we have heard for the past five years', he told Robert Anderson in a letter dated 30 October. There was some urgent new intelligence. He had met Patrick Egan – who seemed to know all about Pigott and the forgeries. 'If the case is confined to the letters we have evidence which completely explodes the *Times* case,' Egan had confided. His greatest fear was 'evidence of informers', the spy reported. Robert Anderson took note. He had an informer who might demolish Parnell and his party before the letters need be considered at all – Thomas Beach himself.

*　　　*　　　*

---

* A letter from Gosselin to Balfour's private secretary of 15 March 1889 states: 'All I can hear up to this is that the Brixton man is in very low water indeed and has been in touch with the *Times* people. I don't think it would be judicious to touch him until I hear further at least.' O'Brien's address was 70 Somerton Road, Brixton SW.

The tedium of the commission's opening rounds was suddenly broken the next day, 31 October, by the appearance of the *Times* witness Captain William O'Shea, Joseph Chamberlain's political henchman and cuckolded husband of Parnell's mistress. Much of his deposition concerned the Kilmainham negotiations of 1882 in which he had acted as a go-between in securing the armistice in the land war. The attorney-general, Sir Richard Webster, made particular play of Parnell's desire at the time 'to see Sheridan . . . an organiser in the West . . . to use him for the purpose of putting down outrages'.

The witness was shown the 'letters' and questioned on the signatures. 'I believe them to be Mr Parnell's,' O'Shea replied firmly.

Sir Charles Russell rose to cross-examine. The surprise witness had to be handled with the utmost care. What might he say of Mr Parnell's relationship with his wife?

Davitt had briefed Russell with his Paris-derived intelligence on the captain's collusion in the production of the Black Pamphlet – the propaganda sheet cooked up in Soho in the last months of Salisbury's caretaker administration – indicting Parnell and depicting Patrick Casey and General Charles Carrol-Tevis as ferocious revolutionaries. After his rejection by the Clare home rule constituency association, O'Shea's search for ultra-nationalist credentials had led him into some strange company.

Had he employed a man named Mulqueeny? asked Sir Charles, 'a member of the old Nationalist Party', to go to France and obtain the signature of someone called Patrick Casey, a 'professed dynamitard', on a testimonial protesting against his exclusion from politics?

'I do not remember – it is possible,' O'Shea answered.

Did he know a notorious public house in Wardour Street? 'I might have been there once.'

'You do personally know Richard Pigott?'

'I have never seen him.'

'Have you said you will be revenged on Mr Parnell?'

'No . . . I never have been revenged,' O'Shea replied.

'Have you said that you have a shell charged with dynamite

to blow him up?' asked Sir Charles (Katherine O'Shea had given the defence her husband's 'the blackguard's reputation is about to be sent to smithereens' letter of 2 November 1885).

'I should say not – what kind of shell?'

The questioning deepened. 'Did you hear that in the winter of 1885–6 there were some American Fenians in London who were hostile to Mr Parnell and who held documents supposed to compromise him?' asked Sir Charles. The answer was yes.

'Do you believe these men were opposed to his policy?'

'Of course, if his policy was not dynamite and they came over with dynamite, they were opposed to his policy.'

'You believe he [Parnell] was opposed to dynamite?'

'Most certainly.'

The news of the Americans' presence in London had come from Mulqueeny, O'Shea admitted. They had met at the Bedford Hotel in Covent Garden. One of the visitors had threatened him with a gun. 'What was his name?' Russell asked.

'I think he mentioned a General Carrol-Thalis [sic], or some such name,' said the witness. The second man was a civil engineer 'established in London' named 'Hayes'.*

'Do you recollect the name of Cassidy?' asked Sir Charles.

'No,' O'Shea replied.

The exchange ended. 'Carrol-Thalis' (Tevis) and Patrick Sarsfield Cassidy were never mentioned again in Probate Court Number One. It seemed completely opaque to anyone outside a very secret knot. The defence had put down a marker. They knew all about the Hayes-Cassidy-Tevis dealings of 1885–6 which inspired the 'mission to Katkov' in Moscow and was the germ of the Jubilee plot.

But as menacing for the prosecution, the defence had flushed

---

* John P. Hayes, the Philadelphia informer who had provided Jenkinson with warning of the Thames bridges bombs and plotted in Paris with the Casey brothers, Eugene Davis and Captain Stephens in the summer of 1884. Hayes was induced with the offer of money to return to Paris in late October 1888. Davitt confronted him with a revolver and extracted the information used in the cross-examination of Captain O'Shea.

out Tevis himself – O'Shea had met him in London – the result was 'a shell primed with dynamite' aimed at Parnell.

Tevis was the instrument of HM Foreign Office. Davitt knew it. So did Lord Salisbury. Should the defence choose, they could expose Whitehall's collusion with O'Shea at will. Far better, from the Government's point of view, that the cuckolded captain should forbear from his desired 'revenge' – for now at least. There was a meeting of the defence that night – but it was not the captain's testimony that seemed to concern them most. The *Times* agent's cipher cables from Colorado had been broken. Patrick Sheridan was prepared to give the 'whole history of Land League that will convict', according to one decrypted 'Mohawk' cable. Matthew O'Brien was at the meeting. A scrappy note in the Davitt papers gives his account of what happened:

> 31 October. Meeting at Labouchere's House with Parnell. Long conversation about Sheridan. P said he is to be prevented [from coming to London] at all cost and risk. But *The Times* has offered him a lot of money. I don't mean that, said P, I would not give him any money. Tell Egan and he will understand. I told Labouchere surely he means Sheridan should be removed if necessary. Mr Labouchere replied: Yes.

The note was addressed to *The Times*'s solicitor – and was very much a version of events he wanted to hear. But Mr Parnell, according to the duplicitous private detective, seemed prepared to play as rough as anybody. Patrick Egan would understand.

Whitehall Place, London SW, November 1888

The Special Commission continued with a pettifogging parade of very unsensational evidence. The Metropolitan Police in contrast was about to enact its own high drama. Sir Charles Warren was being roasted in the press for the failure to catch the Whitechapel killer. Queen Victoria sent her Prime Minister a stream of telegrams with her own prescriptions for re-addressing the failures of the Home Office and the Criminal Investigation Department. Henry Matthews, she said bluntly, was not up to the job.

Salisbury contemplated his dismissal. Warren meanwhile published an extraordinary statement of his own in a magazine article implying that in internal matters of police administration and discipline he should not be under the orders of the Home Secretary. It was the general who lost the Whitehall war: on 10 November he offered his resignation and returned with relief to the War Office.

Two weeks later Matthews submitted the Cabinet's choice of successor for the Queen's approval: 'Your Majesty is doubtless aware that Mr Monro was lately Assistant Commissioner in charge of the Criminal Investigation Department and resigned that office in consequence of differences of opinion that had risen between him and Sir Charles Warren . . .'

'Mr Monro is lame, and rides with difficulty now,' the Home Secretary added. 'Mr Matthews hopes that he would be able to accompany your Majesty's carriage on State occasions . . . in the usual manner, on horseback, but it is scarcely possible to say confidently, without a trial.'

Lame or not James Monro was brought out of his secret limbo at the Home Office to take the top job. Robert Anderson was his deputy. The 'close friends' were running the whole show.

Gilsey House Hotel, Broadway and 38th Street, New York, 21 November 1888

James and Martha Thomson could not believe their luck. Here they were in Manhattan, staying at a fashionable hotel on a mission to save the British empire from imminent dissolution. They had oceans of dollars. They were here to make a deal with an old acquaintance from Boulogne-sur-Mer, someone they would refer to in their London-bound cables as 'FM'. Their own curious code-name was 'Ladybird'.

Someone in Whitehall had parcelled up Frank Millen as a witness for *The Times*. Someone in Whitehall had propelled the retired Metropolitan Police detective and his wife towards New York in the service of the newspaper's solicitor.

In *The Times*'s Wapping archives is a box of scrappy undated notes in that most difficult cipher, the personal shorthand of a journalist (it appears to be the *Times* leader-writer John Woulfe Flanagan's). Many of the words are illegible.

Note one reads: 'Eugene Davis xxx £20,000 Egan xxx Invincibles, Davis xxx, Soames offer xxx Anderson and Monro.'

Note two reads: 'Thomson, Supt. Bow St. xxx Millen, xxx promised xxx In Paris, Thomson xxx Millen, Monro, Nat. League offices xxx Casey, Monro, xxx O'Brien xxx £2000 Casey xxx Pigott.'

Note three reads: 'General Millen 437 West 57th Street New York. BCNY Hoare xxx Kirby.'

Note four reads *en clair*: 'It is stated that F. F. Millen was in New York on Monday June 6 or Monday May 30 1887. Does this agree with what is known of his movements? This is of considerable importance.'

It was indeed important. Frank Millen was supposed to be tucked up at the Hôtel Poilly on those dates, plotting the destruction with dynamite of Queen Victoria. Very secret information, however garbled, was reaching Printing House Square. Who better to clarify matters than the Mexican general's seaside companions. In November 1888 James and Martha Thomson went on Printing House Square's clandestine payroll and were smartly sent across the Atlantic.

The first one-line cable, announcing Ladybird's arrival in New York, was sent to 'Assert – London' (Joseph Soames's telegraphic address) on 21 November. The second was sent three weeks later. This time it was in code:

> sgde hmzk cdbh rhnm neel hrsq zsgd hrmn vqdz cxsn
> bnld nudq zmcf hudd uhcd mbdn msgq ddcz xrmn shbd
> tonm ozxl dmsn eehu dsgn trzm cont mcrc . . .

Scribbled on the original is a note: 'this is the old Z for A cipher.'*
A single-letter forward transposition gives:

> The final decision of FM is that he is now ready to come over and give evidence, on three days' notice, upon payment of five thousand pounds down, and the remaining five thousand to be paid him after his evidence and cross-examination, and he is no longer required. I think him of the utmost importance.

A sequence of telegrams followed:

> 17th December, '88. New York. To Assert, London.
> Reply cable twelfth urgently needed. Brown Bros. have no advice yet of remittance – five hundred.

> 20th December, '88. London. To Thomson, New York.
> Am waiting final instructions of counsel. Will wire the moment I get them. – Assert.

> 24th December, '88. New York. To Assert, London.
> With General, daily, and thus gather: Henry can prove

---

* The original transcripts are in the papers of Timothy Harrington, MP, held in the National Library of Ireland. The cables were copied to the Parnell camp in London by a source at the Western Union telegraph office in New York.

sixth May case.* So can he, and far more, both before
and after, if you close with him at once. Will come over
with me in 'Servia', Saturday. Reply immediately. Refuses
to [unrecoverable] time and you risk losing your best
witness.

28th December, '88. Eastbourne – To Thomson, New
York.

Counsel thinks Henry the most important witness. He
says we must know what he can prove, and if he has
papers, will he give you a written statement, not to be
used unless we agree – Assert.

Chicago and London, Christmas 1888

The Special Commission had gone into a five-week Christmas
recess. In Chicago meanwhile the Clan's trial committee was
about to reconvene. Early in January 1889, with the Republican
Benjamin Harrison safely installed in the White House, the tribunal met again in Chicago to take stage-managed depositions
for the defence. John Moroney and Thomas Dennehy – Frank
Millen's visitors in Paris in August 1887 – spoke glowingly of
Alexander Sullivan's revolutionary zeal and financial probity. An
affidavit was read from Henri Le Caron – the Triangle chief was
a 'gentleman of the highest integrity', said the Illinois Clansman.
Thomas Beach was absent. He had set off for Europe summoned
to the bedside of his dying father and for another reason.

The tribunal pronounced its verdict. It was a triumph for Sullivan: he was cleared on all charges – his 'patriotism and integrity'
endorsed absolutely. Two members dissented, both physicians:
Patrick Cronin and Peter McCahey. All records were to be
destroyed, they were ordered. Cronin refused. He returned warily
with his sheaves of longhand notes to his shabby surgery on South
Clark Street, Chicago.

Thomas Beach arrived in England just before the verdict.

* 'Henry – le Caron' is scribbled on the original decrypt. 'Sixth of May' refers
to the Phoenix Park murders.

Robert Anderson would later claim that he himself was hugely reluctant to advance the spy towards the witness box. Correspondence in the Anderson papers speaks for itself. Beach wrote to his controller from Colchester on new year's eve 1888: 'I have thought over the question and have come to this determination viz that if I can accomplish great good I am willing to accept the risk which may follow and testify . . .'

He offered to prove how Parnell and Davitt's American tours had been controlled by the Clan. He would testify to his own meeting with Parnell and Egan in the House of Commons in 1881. He would demonstrate how 'the dual positions occupied by the leaders furnish proof of the knowledge of the conspiracy to use armed force . . .' He would prove the bombing truce was only put on hold against a time-limited promise that home rule would be delivered by constitutional means.

'In reference to the amount which I should receive I would quote either a lump sum of ten thousand pounds or an annuity for life of 400 pounds per year.

'I shall be in London Thursday and Friday evening. I leave my whole interests and dispositions to you.'

It was a huge sum. John Cameron MacDonald, *The Times*'s manager, thought it more than worth it. 'I will come to you early tomorrow and meanwhile I telegraph to Houston whose advice and knowledge may be useful,' he messaged Anderson on 5 January 1889.

'The American case is to be taken after the letters which the Attorney General expects to take next week. If my proposal can be carried out it is to the last degree desirable.'

Joseph Soames drew up the contract. It was sent to Anderson on the 10th with a note from MacDonald:

> Disclosures are now pressing on us in such a way that if your man is not available as quickly as steam can carry him the case will have been virtually concluded and that section of it embraced in your articles no longer needful to be gone into . . .
>
> Therefore I hope to hear tomorrow that you have

despatched the requisite summons by cable. I consider
that you must be left to your own discretion as to the
moment for making the disclosure . . .

Anderson might produce his star witness 'at his discretion'.
The attorney-general intended producing the letters before hearing 'the American case'. That would be a mistake – it must be
the other way round. Beach was urgently summoned from Essex
to 39 Linden Gardens, where the assistant commissioner had
already 'culled' the most interesting extracts from his cache of
Clan circulars. They were bundled up and taken by cab to an
address in fashionable Cork Street, the comfortable rooms of
Edward Houston. Beach bore with him a single-line letter of
introduction initialled 'RA'.

For ten days the spy and the youthful propagandist waded
through the pile of papers. There were plenty of references to
the swashbuckling career of a certain General Millen. The documents were carefully screened in case the defence were permitted
to examine them and a page of one letter containing certain
sensitive names was deleted. The prosecution was briefed in detail
on what the surprise witness might reveal. By the first week of
February 1889 Thomas Beach was ready to go into the witness
box.

42

The Special Commission entered its forty-fourth day. That morning the press bench was livelier than of late – it was rumoured
that at last the letters would be produced. At 10.30 the judges
entered. Sir Richard Webster solemnly announced – to everyone's
astonishment – that he was now going to take the 'American part
of the case'. A witness clambered into the box, a spare-framed
man aged around fifty, with the pointy, waxed moustache then
so fashionable among military men – 'a little ferret-eyed, sharp-
visaged person', said the *Daily Chronicle*. American reporters
noted his lapel pin: the badge of a veteran of the Grand Army of
the Republic.

'What is your name?' asked Sir Richard.

'My baptismal name is Thomas Billis Beach.'

'Under what name have you been known for a number of
years?'

'Henri Le Caron.'

The defence was stunned. 'He was the only important witness
we had not been warned about by our agents in America,'
recorded Davitt in his memoirs. 'I had learned that a "Colonel"
or "General" had left New York for London – and Mr Labouchere said that a Chicago apothecary was to give evidence for *The
Times*. Neither description fitted the real person.'

The witness delivered his testimony with crisp precision. He
covered the Fenian 'invasions' of Canada and his contribution to
their confounding; his proposal as a Clan member by Alexander
Sullivan; the rituals and codes of the United Brotherhood and its

commitment to armed force. He dwelt at length on Devoy and Millen's mission to Ireland in 1879 and James O'Kelly's gun-running efforts. He described Parnell's 1880 Chicago visit, flanked by armed Clansmen. The attorney-general steered the prosecution witness all the while towards the whispered meeting with Parnell in the corridor leading to the House of Commons library. The 'I have long ceased to believe that anything but force of arms will ever bring about the redemption of Ireland' line fell like a thunderbolt.

The evidence piled up the next day and the next – interminable readings from Clan-na-Gael circulars enmiring Irish nationalism in dynamite. The witness, under Webster's well-briefed lead, moved through Millen's Belize invasion plan, the 'submarine tor-pedo-boat', the instigation of the bombing policy in 1881 and the Lomasney and Gallagher bombing missions. He reported Alexander Sullivan's judgement on Gallagher's failure: 'The doctor disobeyed instructions and gave himself away . . . he got in with some of Rossa's men who told Jim McDermott who informed the Government.'

On a defence interjection, the witness brought up the case of Patrick Cronin – expelled for 'treason, lying and violation of his oath . . . he had been a determined opponent of the Sullivan regime,' said Beach.

Sir Richard led the witness determinedly towards the crucial Chicago 'Delusion' conference of August 1886 and the presence of Michael Davitt and the three Nationalist MPs. It all seemed damning.

'Did you visit England in April 1887?' asked Sir Richard.

'Yes.'

'You returned to the United States in October 1887?'

'Yes.'

Apart from extracting a sly little reference to the witness's meeting with Dr Joseph Fox, MP, at Gatti's restaurant in London, the attorney-general chose not to probe any further the activities of Thomas Beach in the summer of the Jubilee.

The commission had caught light. The newspapers reported 'extraordinary revelations' and 'startling evidence'. The public gallery filled with fashionable figures gasping and tutting at Beach's disclosures. Parnell stayed away. Davitt scribbled notes.

Late on the afternoon of the 7th Sir Charles Russell rose to conduct the cross-examination. He addressed the witness studiedly as 'Mr Beach'.

What was his role? 'I looked on myself as a military spy in the service of my country,' Beach replied.

'After 1868 through whom did you communicate?'

'Directly to the Home Government,' said the witness.

'And from that time up to the present you have been in such communication?'

'Yes, sir; until February 1 this year. By coming here I have stopped my usefulness to the cause.'

'Were your communications direct to the Home Office or were they sent through any intermediate source?'

'They were sent at different times to different officials of the British government,' said the witness. He had seen a 'bundle of my correspondence the other day'. He made a gesture indicating the pile of paper's height.

Sir Charles saw an opportunity. Where had he seen them? The witness refused to answer. The commission president directed him to do so. Beach admitted he had been given the papers by Mr Robert Anderson and inspected them at Number 3 Cork Street, Edward Houston's address.

'Is Anderson employed at Scotland Yard?' asked Sir Charles.

'I know that he has been connected with the Home Office for a great many years . . .'

Defence spirits soared. They had found a chink. Beach, alias Le Caron, was a spy – but what was a high government official doing handing over a very secret agent to *The Times* newspaper?

Russell banged away at the Anderson connection. He had been examining the papers closely himself. One document had been clipped. Beach admitted under questioning that the initials 'RA' had been removed. 'Look at this document. You see one page is cut off?' he asked.

'Evidently.'

'Did you take that off at Cork Street?'

'I did.'

'Just make a note to bring it with you tomorrow . . .'

The witness replied sharply: 'Do you want me to risk the lives of men in America . . . ?'

'Do not ask me questions, sir,' growled Russell; 'the judges will see the names and I shall not read them without their approval.'

American reporters rushed to wire their news desks sensational stories about the existence of more British spies in the ranks of the United Brotherhood.

Camp 20, Clan-na-Gael, Chicago, 8 February 1889

There was uproar in the Clan. That Major Henri Le Caron of Braidwood, Illinois, had been relaying secrets to London for almost two decades was bad enough. There were more enemies within. Newspapers pounced on the testimony about the cut-off page that would 'risk the lives of men in America'. One of them was already at grave risk. The *Chicago Tribune* reported: 'Dr P. H. Cronin, one of the moderate men in the Clan-na-Gael who wanted the organisation to support Parnell, was referred to yesterday in a way he must despise – Le Caron says he was on the committee which tried Cronin for treason to Ireland . . .'

Sullivan's enemies, however, could draw their own comfort. Beach the British agent was the Triangle chief's must trusted acolyte. Patrick Cronin, skulking in Chicago with his notes of the saloon-bar 'trial', was now loudly relaying the accusations to anyone who would listen. Aleck Sullivan had an answer. Le Caron had suckered him, yes – but Cronin was the real and most dangerous spy. 'An atmosphere of terror and distrust was created by Sullivan . . . the last component of which was absurd but widely believed,' recorded John Devoy. 'The story was that while Sir Charles Russell, by permission of the Parnell Commission, was examining a letter to Le Caron from a confederate in America, Asquith looked over his shoulder and saw the name "Cronin". He told Davitt and Davitt told Sullivan.'

On the night of 8 February there was a stormy meeting in

Chicago of Camp 20 of the Clan-na-Gael – where rumours were
reported that the secret trial committee's minutes had been produced and read at another camp, the Columbia Club – of which
Patrick Cronin was a prominent member. Camp 20's 'senior guar-
dian', a Sullivan partisan named John F. Beggs, deputed three
men to root out the sedition: Daniel Coughlin, a detective in the
Chicago police department, Martin Burke and Patrick O'Sullivan,
an 'ice-man' with a works near Lake Michigan, would form the
removal committee.

Royal Courts of Justice, 14–15 February 1889

Beach had held his ground even under Russell's pounding. The
'American part of the case' seemed damning. It was time to take
the letters. Joseph Soames was called by the prosecution to pronounce on their provenance. The body of the principal letters
had been written by Henry Campbell, Parnell's secretary, and
signed by Parnell himself, he explained. Specimens of handwriting
were produced for comparison.

Edward Houston was called. The young journalist explained
sanguinely that he had been at pains not to enquire too deeply
into the original source of the letters. Parnell gazed at him
throughout, according to an observer, 'with intense amusement'.
On 14 February Russell rose to cross-examine. Soames was
recalled.

'Have you been directed by Mr MacDonald to pay any sums
to anyone else except Mr Houston?'

'No.'

'Not to Moser?'

'Yes – but I did it myself.'

'What is Moser?'

'A detective.'

'What did you pay him?'

'I cannot tell you.'

'When?'

'August 1887.'

'Was anyone else employed?'

'Yes.'

'Who?'

'Mr Kirby.'

'Was there anyone else you employed?'

'I sent one other agent to America.'

'When?'

'Last autumn.'

'How much was he paid?'

'I think £300.'

'What was his name?'

'Thomson.'

The defence were poking into some very sensitive territory, *The Times*'s intelligence operations in America. Ex-Inspector Maurice Moser was the veteran of Monro's hunt for Jenkinson's agents in Paris and for Invincibles in Manhattan.

'Mr Kirby' was the Canadian detective who had been negotiating with Patrick Sheridan in Colorado the previous autumn. The defence had been reading his New York-routed cables to *The Times*'s solicitor throughout.

Sir Charles resumed the cross-examination the next day. He returned to the matter of Kirby. 'What was his authority?' he asked.

'It was to go and visit Sheridan and get from him a letter written by Mr Parnell which was identical in terms with the letter of 15 May 1882,' said Mr Soames.* The solicitor's testimony appeared in wire-relayed press reports the next day. Anyone reading the newspapers in New York or Chicago now knew *The Times* was bidding for a second Le Caron to cross the Atlantic. This time his name had been openly declared before he even got on the ship. It was Patrick J. Sheridan, wool-rancher of Colorado and Fenian firebrand.

The defence knew from the cable decrypts that there was a third informer on the hook – 'FM' in New York. A *Times* agent was also at his side. But for now Sir Charles Russell chose not to

---

* The letter, sensationally published in *The Times* on 18 April 1887, in which Parnell seemed to condone the Phoenix Park murders.

probe, in public at least, just what the mysterious 'Thomson' might be up to.

Pigott would be the next prosecution witness (Webster had issued his own subpoena after Pigott expressed extreme reluctance to go into the box). The defence had got there at last. When it came to his cross-examination, Pigott's forgeries could be picked to pieces at will.

Royal Courts of Justice, 20 February 1889

Richard Pigott took the stand on the afternoon of the 20th, blinking under the none too rigorous interrogation of the attorney-general. The witness, 'white-bearded, bald-headed, bland, smiling . . . having the appearance of a cheapened Father Christmas', according to one observer, was questioned on the letters' origins. He reprised the story of the black bag – and the encounter with 'Maurice Murphy' and 'Thomas Brown' at the Hôtel des Deux Mondes. He had made 'five or six trips to Paris in 1887 in the hope of seeing someone who would give me further information', Pigott revealed (certainly not that he had met Frank Millen that summer). It all seemed plausible enough.

Then, just as Davitt had predicted, Pigott told the story of the approach made in Kingstown by 'Mr John Sinclair of 17 Henrietta Street' and the inducement to go to London – followed by the encounter on 24 October 1888 with Parnell in the ground-floor library at Henry Labouchere's house. The MP had drawn him aside in the entrance hall, the witness claimed, and offered him £1,000 if he would declare the letters to be forgeries.

Sir Charles Russell rose to cross-examine the next day. He was well briefed. Had the witness offered, three days before the first facsimile letter appeared in *The Times*, to Archbishop Henry Walsh of Dublin 'the means to defeat an impending attack on the Irish party'?* It was possible, Pigott stammered – but it was not the

---

* Pigott had approached the home rule-supporting archbishop in an apparent attempt to secure either a counter-offer or the absolution of the confessional. When the commission got down to business, Dr Walsh tipped off the nationalist camp that Pigott had apparently been prepared to admit being the forger before

matter of the letters he was referring to, it was some other impending attack.

Had he written a pamphlet attacking the Land League for
Lady Florence Dixie in September 1882? He might have done –
but it was never published.

The question of the Black Pamphlet was raised. Had Pigott
supplied the information?

'Nothing whatever,' Pigott insisted – that was written by a
'Captain Steward, a Captain somebody . . .'

The witness was casually invited to write down certain words
and phrases under Russell's dictation. In a famous piece of
court-room theatrics, Russell demonstrated the same verbal tics
were repeated in the letters. 'Hesitency' damned him. Pigott
blustered, he denied, he still would not admit to forgery. On
Friday 22 February the court was adjourned until the following
Tuesday.

At midday on the 26th the witness was summoned again. There
was no response. A short adjournment was called: Soames's clerk
explained that a search had been made at his hotel in Fleet Street,
Anderton's. The witness 'seemed to have disappeared'. The commissioners, on Russell's urging, applied for an arrest warrant. It
went to Robert Anderson.

The Home Secretary scribbled a note to the assistant commissioner that night: 'It is suggested that there is some delay in
dealing with the warrant against R. Pigott. I trust there is no
truth in this. I should be glad if you would come over to the
Irish Secretary's room here and speak to me . . .'

Pigott had already flown. On the morning of Saturday the
23rd he had returned to Henry Labouchere's house. He wanted
to make a statement. The eminent journalist George Augustus
Sala was summoned as a witness. Pigott dictated and the MP
scribbled furiously. Each page was countersigned. He confessed
to forging everything. The document was sent to George Lewis's

---

the letters had even been published. The learned cleric meanwhile, a keen amateur
code-breaker, was deciphering the intercepted cables from 'Ladybird' in New
York.

offices at Ely Place but Parnell loftily refused to touch it. It was
returned by hand to Anderton's Hotel.

Then Pigott had had second thoughts. On Sunday night he
and a Dublin solicitor named W. J. Shannon, a Soames employee,
drafted a second statement. The Grosvenor Gardens confession
had been made out of fear and under renewed cash inducement,
he said. He had not forged all the letters: some genuine originals
had been obtained from a man in Paris named Patrick Casey; the
remainder he and Casey had forged together. The statement was
sworn as an affidavit on Monday morning. Then he posted two
small Bank of England notes to his housekeeper, Anne Byrne, in
Kingstown.

At around 4 p.m. on Monday the 25th Pigott left Anderton's
Hotel, where two plain-clothes RIC men were supposedly
guarding him against 'being mobbed'. Constable Gallagher testified he had observed two men in the smoking room who appeared
to be 'shadowing' the witness. Pigott scurried up The Strand
towards Charing Cross Station and took the evening boat-train
to Paris.

The Shannon affidavit was read to the commission by the
attorney-general on the afternoon of the 26th, the day of
Pigott's non-appearance in court. It was still not a full confession.
Maybe it was a last-ditch bid for money: the fugitive Pigott had
nothing left to lose; but transiting Paris he had meanwhile posted
the Labouchere document, the one Parnell had so diffidently
refused to handle, to *The Times*'s solicitors.* Joseph Soames
brought it into court unopened the next day. The commission
president theatrically extracted the enclosure from its crisp envelope. The secretary read it gravely: 'I grieve to have to confess
that I myself fabricated them using genuine letters of Messrs

---

* Pigott stayed in Paris only a few hours before catching the train to Madrid.
Davitt rushed across the Channel but missed him. He interviewed the Caseys and
certain Parisian booksellers, who revealed that Pigott took only the 'most scandalous books' but never paid for them. Davitt's notebooks reveal he claimed to
represent a club of Tory connoisseurs of the erotic and suggested the pornogra-
phers send their bills to members of the Irish Loyal and Patriotic Union for
settlement.

Parnell and Egan simply placed against the window ... I then wrote to Houston telling him to come to Paris for the documents ... placed them in a black bag with some accounts and old newspapers ...'

The conspiratorial meeting with Eugene Davis in Lausanne had been nothing more than 'mere gossip', he confessed. The batch of letters produced during the O'Donnell v. Walter libel case he had also forged. The meeting with Clan chiefs in America to 'obtain permission' for the black bag to be handed over was fantasy, he admitted.

The attorney-general blanched. He hurriedly consulted his clients. 'My Lords ... those whom I represent request me to express their sincere regret that these letters were ever published ...'

That day, 27 February 1889, seemed to be Ireland's apotheosis in The Strand. But it was not over yet.

Hotel los Embajadores, Madrid, 28 February 1889

The story of Pigott's self-immolation has often been told – the flight from Paris to Madrid, and his furtive stay at the Hotel los Embajadores under the name 'Roland Ponsonby'. On Thursday the 28th he wired care of Joseph Soames's chambers in London for money. Chief Inspector John Littlechild was summoned; he ordered a dummy reply sent 'with the object of detaining Pigott in Madrid until he could be arrested'. Robert Anderson moved ponderously into action.

The British minister in Madrid was cabled to apply to the Spanish police for the fugitive's arrest on an extradition warrant. On Friday afternoon an inspector called. Pigott asked if he could get his hat, went into an adjoining room, opened his bag, took out a revolver, put it in his mouth and blew off the back of his skull.

Michael Davitt rushed to Dublin to search Pigott's house. Anne Byrne, the housekeeper, was left forlornly in charge of his sons, Jack and Dick. She explained that a 'Mr Sinclair' had already called the previous evening and taken bundles of correspondence. Her employer, 'the kindest of men', had already written to her authorising 'Mr Sinclair' to do so. She was to burn the rest. Some letters survived.

There was panic at Printing House Square. A note by Arthur Walter, principal proprietor of *The Times*, reads: 'I have just heard about Pigott. If possible steps should be taken *at once* to see that his papers, if any, are not secured by the other side. A bribe will probably prevail with the Spanish police and Labouchere and Co will not hesitate to offer it.'

Thus it was. Inspector Patrick Quinn and Sergeant Lowe arrived in the Spanish capital on 5 March. The deceased's effects were released by the investigating magistrate and borne safely back to Robert Anderson in London.

Gloom descended on the Government. Arthur Balfour wrote: '*The Times* has been stupid beyond all that history tells us of stupidity.' Salisbury stayed calm enough. He told the Queen: 'Pigott was a thorough rogue – whose testimony ought not to be taken seriously.' George Buckle, editor of *The Times*, offered his resignation. Mr Walter would not accept it. There was still hope. 'FM' might still be conjured across the Atlantic to the rescue. And there was always 'Henry'. On 13 March the case for the prosecution stuttered limply to its conclusion. The case for the defence would open on 2 April.

There were bruising exchanges in the Commons. With Pigott destroyed, Le Caron's damage might be rolled back. Sir William Harcourt, the opposition front-bencher, laid into the Home Secretary: Who had given authority for Mr Anderson to hand over the papers? 'That was not with my cognisance,' said Henry Matthews, 'but . . . he acted in accordance with what was due to the Special Commission.'

Special indignation was expressed at Le Caron's 'Do you want me to risk the lives of men in America?' outburst under cross-examination. Why was Houston put in possession of information that would expose the lives of men in America to the fate of informers – assassination? asked Mr T. P. O'Connor. Matthews made no coherent reply.

Robert Anderson was the juiciest target. 'The Assistant Commissioner of the Metropolitan police has betrayed the secrets of his department,' Sir William Harcourt thundered '. . . he has allowed himself to be made a tout for *The Times* . . .'

The enraged civil servant's response was published in *The Times* on 21 March. 'A complete explanation of my conduct would involve such an appeal to documents and details as would amount to a disclosure of the secret service arrangements of that period,' he said conspiratorially. 'To me that would be intensely gratifying . . . it would moreover supply a missing chapter of uncommon interest in the political history of recent years.' It certainly would.

Le Caron had pressed the matter on him, so Mr Anderson insisted – and he had pleaded

> to be put in touch with *The Times* . . . This I point blank refused to do, I told him I had no contact with *The Times* relative to the conduct of the case before the Commission. I would bear his request in mind if I should be applied to. This was in December. Next month Mr MacDonald appealed to me to find a witness to prove what he called the 'American part of the case'.

The Times was on the ropes in The Strand. The Government was being punched round the ring in parliament. The time had come for some extra-curricular help.

Irish Office, Great Queen Street, London SW, winter 1888–9

Just as Mrs Martha Thomson espied a little money-making opportunity during the Anderson memoirs rumpus, so in spring 1910 another former spear-carrier in the long-ago political drama in The Strand felt moved to break his silence. He was William Henry Joyce, the Irish resident magistrate deputed in May 1888 to collate crime papers at Dublin Castle in support of *The Times*–O'Donnell libel case. His secret activities were to expand dramatically during the Special Commission.

Almost a quarter of a century later the embittered ex-official, dismissed in 1901 for 'excessive ingestion of alcohol', pounced

with outrage on the outcome of the Anderson debate. The Liberal
government had acquitted its Conservative predecessor. Asquith
and Balfour were colluding: there was no funny business during
the Parnell Commission, they claimed; 'bunkum', said Joyce. He
composed a long memorandum. A copy is in the *Times* archive
in Wapping. It rambles and bleats but is studded with revelatory
nuggets on what he called 'events occult and otherwise'.

He was in a position to know. In October 1888 Joyce was
seconded to the Irish Office in London to turn police reports
into witness subpoenas for *The Times*. He toiled in a special room
at Great Queen Street – Arthur Balfour deliberately stayed aloof.
For the next three months Joyce, on his account, worked through
Major Nicholas Gosselin, 'who had cognizance of many strange
things going on behind the scenes and was in constant communication with Mr Soames *and others*'.

The Times's quest for 'Henry' crossed his desk. Joyce had prepared a dossier on Patrick Sheridan's activities in the land war
when at Dublin Castle. He was summoned to a meeting at 58
Lincoln's Inn, where Joseph Soames introduced him to the
Canadian detective Kirby. Joyce found him 'garrulous' and
'knowing nothing about Ireland'. After some argument the
Sheridan dossier was handed over, and Kirby dispatched on his
mission to the Rocky Mountains.

Joyce's most significant encounter in the autumn of 1888,
however, was with Robert Anderson. The assistant commissioner
clearly did not want this Irish prodnose prying into his own larder
of secrets. He could produce no information on the dynamite
campaign because, so Joyce was told, 'Sir Edward Jenkinson,
when giving up his secret service work, had deliberately destroyed
all the confidential records.' James Monro concurred: nothing
much survived of the scandalous goings-on in Room 56. Joyce's
opinion of the set-up was coruscating: 'The whole system as
revealed to me turned out, if not a huge *fraud*, most certainly a
gigantic farce.'

Things became less farcical after the flight of Pigott. Balfour
urgently asked the Home Secretary on 24 March 1889: 'I should
be greatly obliged if you would ask Mr Anderson to communicate

freely with Mr Joyce RM as to all matters in the Home Office which have any bearing on the Special Commission . . .'

Great precautions were taken. The next day the documents were transported from the Home Office to the home of John Satterfield Sandars, Henry Matthews's private secretary – where they would be safe, so Joyce was told, from 'sympathisers with opposite political parties who might be observant'.

> They were very bulky, numbering about 100 important files from various American consuls with statements from informers . . . the material portions of these documents were copied at the Irish Office and handed over to Mr Soames [noted Joyce]. Shortly after this it was arranged by Mr Balfour that I should visit the Foreign Office with a similar object. The matter was settled by Mr Villiers* who had custody of the Irish papers . . .

But something was missing. Where were the reports from the most sensitive intelligence station of all – HM consulate in New York? 'I became aware of the existence of a system whereby the British consul at New York (Mr Hoare) supplied information direct to the Special Branch at the Home Office,' continued Joyce. 'This was inaugurated by Sir E. G. Jenkinson and when he retired was continued by Mr James Monro.' The New York reports 'were kept in Mr Monro's custody . . .'

> I reported this to Mr Balfour who then had a cable message dispatched through the FO requiring Mr Hoare's attendance in London.
> The main object in getting him to London was to secure his co-operation in having one of his agents in New York brought over to give evidence for *The Times*, however Mr Hoare refused to move in this direction . . .

* Francis Hyde Villiers – Sir Julian Pauncefote's private secretary.

HM Consulate, 24 State Street, New York, 1–2 April 1889

Indeed, William Hoare did not seem minded yet to become the
Foreign Office's tout for *The Times*. Mr Anderson sitting comfortably in Whitehall might have delivered Beach up to the prosecution, but life for a British intelligence officer in Manhattan
was more dangerous. Besides, what might the consul's own special
asset choose to reveal?

The Parnell camp in London, preparing feverishly for the opening of their defence, were still reading Assert's transatlantic cables.
A sequence of decrypts made it clear that Millen was still on the
hook but, just as Joyce reported, Mr Hoare was proving reluctant
to hand him over.

Assert cabled on 1 April: 'Hoare, British Consul has authority
to give you names of some informants like Major Le Caron. See
him. Get all particulars and induce one or two men to come over.
Assistance will be sent to you for Millen.'

The Times's agent messaged back from New York that afternoon: 'Hoare very civil. Cannot assist us in any way.' That would
have to change.

There was an intense round of meetings in Whitehall. Monro
was clearly up to his ears in it. In his rambling revelations of 1910
Joyce indicated that it was Balfour who progressed the move to
ensure the reluctant consul's cooperation – but it went higher
than that. The recall order was sent on 4 April by Sir Philip Currie,
deputy permanent under-secretary at the Foreign Office, with the
special instruction scribbled on the message form: 'Give some
reason for your journey unconnected with Irish business such as
private affairs or consular business.' The consul replied: 'Will leave
on 13th or sooner if required. Necessary to make arrangements
before departure . . .'

On the message form there is a sequence of notes:

'Sent to Monro, morning 5 April.'

'6 April. Mr Hoare was told by tel of 4 April to give some
reason unconnected with Irish business for his departure.'

'Will the 13th be early enough? – he had better be told by
tel.'

'Yes: that will do: provide some excuse for [illegible] US journey – S.'

The last line is in Lord Salisbury's handwriting.

The Prime Minister had put his imprint on the matter. Things should henceforth progress much more smoothly. Two days later, on 8 April, *The Times*'s solicitor cabled his agent in New York: 'Difficulties will be removed and assistance in other quarter. Remain for the present.'

Montevista, Colorado, 4–5 April 1889

There was still the matter of 'Henry'. Joseph Soames had revealed under cross-examination that Patrick Sheridan had been offered enormous sums to give evidence for the prosecution. It was not a shrewd move. Whatever message may have been sent by Parnell to Patrick Egan the previous autumn concerning Sheridan's 'removal', it was *The Times*'s solicitor's outburst that had condemned him. On 5 April *The Times*'s agent cabled from Colorado:

> Sheridan met me yesterday; your evidence saying he offered to go to London and give evidence for twenty thousand pounds caused Clan-na-Gael to sentence him to death.
>
> Two parties of the Clan were ordered to carry out sentence of the executive. His life is sought; hence he threatens that he will now go to London and prove *The Times*' justification.

'Henry's' promised evidence still looked devastating – 'it would lead Parnell either into the dock or to fly the country'. That is, if he lived long enough to give it. 'He showed me documents connecting Parnell and Dillon with himself as of the [Invincible] Executive existing at time of Parnell's arrest, 'eighty-one,' Kirby cabled. The message was intercepted and decrypted by the defence.

At least no one had been foolish enough to mention Millen in open court as a potential prosecution witness. The obstructive New York consul had been recalled. He would leave on the 13th.

'Difficulties will be removed,' Soames had messaged his New York agent. The Foreign Office was being very accommodating in the matter of the general. There seemed nothing to stop him, as James Thomson had proposed, jumping on the SS *Servia*, the fastest ship on the Atlantic, and steaming to the thunderer's rescue.

But what might the surprise witness reveal for his promised £10,000 on the witness stand of the Special Commission? That Charles Stewart Parnell was a 'thorough-going Revolutionist'?

Or might General Millen – Dynamitard – have declared that in the year of the Jubilee he was an agent of the British Prime Minister? Either way he would have stopped the show.

Royal Courts of Justice, 11 April 1889

Sir Charles Russell's opening speech for the defence was in its sixth day of towering oratory – rubbing *The Times*'s nose in its self-made Pigott debacle. However, the little lunchtime gathering of the prosecution principals on 11 April was not totally downcast. In the Venetian-gothic gloom of the Royal Courts of Justice Arthur Fraser Walter, Joseph Soames, Sir Henry James and Sir Richard Webster, the attorney-general, considered the prospects of redemption from America:

> Question. Whether we should try to get Sheridan and Millen or either of them? Attorney-General in favour [Arthur Walter minuted that afternoon]. Because he was convinced they could prove certain charges if not against Parnell at all events then against some of the incriminated . . .
>
> I said that in my opinion our case was so bad, our performance had fallen so far short of our promises, that I doubted if any single witness, uncorroborated, could do much to remedy it. Further, that if Sheridan really were in a position to prove what was expected of him . . . I doubted if anything would induce him to give evidence, in face of the almost certain risk he would run of vengeance and death . . .

Later on the evening of the 11th (London time) the Reuter's cable arrived at Printing House Square with the news of a death in New York. *The Times* ran the briefest of notices the next morning: 'General Francis Millen, a member of the Irish Nationalist Party, is dead.' Arthur Walter recorded that night: 'Considering the gravity and the pointedness of our charges against Parnell himself, we shall not escape condemnation unless we bring home to him personally, direct complicity in crime . . .

'Gen Millen is dead so we can hope for nothing from him . . .'

Woodlawn Cemetery, The Bronx, New York City, 12 April 1889

Old rebels, garrulous pressmen and distinguished diplomats shuffled into the Millen parlour on West 57th Street to pay their last respects – 'filing past the coffin, taking a last look at the manly face so rigid in death', the *New York Herald* reported. Fenian legends were on parade: Thomas Clarke Luby, co-founder of the Irish Revolutionary Brotherhood, sentenced to twenty years in 1865; and Dr Dennis Mulcahy, whose girl Frank Millen had snatched and brought to America while her rebel-betrothed was in Mountjoy jail. Long ago in Mr Edward Archibald's shuttered consulate library he had betrayed them all.

The former American ambassador to Mexico, 'members of the Cuban Society' and a delegation from the New York Press Club boarded the coaches to follow the cortège to Woodlawn Cemetery in the Bronx.

The *Herald* reported:

> Across the foot of the black casket were crossed the swords that he had carried in various campaigns under President Barrios in Guatemala, and Generals Coman-fort, Juarez, and Corona in Mexico.
>
> On the breast of the corpse rested a sprig of shamrock sent some time ago from the birthplace of the deceased in Tyrone, Ireland.
>
> It was a soldier's funeral – simple, but impressive; kind

words spoken around the casket by stern-faced men who
had known of his deeds in many climes. Here and there,
the echo of an anecdote telling of his courage and patriotism, mingling with the half smothered sobs of the ladies
of the family . . .

44

Probate Court Number One, Royal Courts of Justice,
1 May 1889

The drama of Special Commission reached another turning
moment. The first witness for the defence was Parnell himself.
He took the stand on 1 May for Sir Charles Russell to guide him
graciously through a set-piece exposition of Ireland's ills and
home rule's boons. The witness displayed remarkable innocence
of the American connection.

'Were you aware until the publication of these libels that the
Clan-na-Gael organisation was what has been called a murder
club?' asked Russell.

'No, I never supposed such a thing for moment,' Parnell
replied.

'Did you know that Alexander Sullivan was a member of the
Clan-na-Gael?'

'Never. I had met him . . . he seemed very anxious to secure
the success of my movement in America.'

'Had you at any time any information that Mr Sullivan was
engaged in dynamite or assassination?'

'Not the slightest . . .'

The attorney-general, Sir Richard Webster, cross-examined.

'Until Le Caron's evidence you had no knowledge that Sullivan
was connected with the Clan-na-Gael?' he asked.

'Not the slightest,' Parnell replied. He was lying.

The attorney-general raised the admission of Melville and
Harkins to the Palace of Westminster by Joseph Nolan, MP. 'Was
Mr Nolan a member of the physical force party?' he asked.

'I have no reason to believe that any members of my party

have been members of the physical force party,' Parnell replied.

The attorney-general let that go. That was all there was of the Jubilee plot at the Special Commission – apart from a curious further aside.

'Mr Jenkinson was connected with the Home Office?' said the attorney-general enquiringly.

'He may have been,' Parnell answered.

'Did you know him?'

'No.'

But his intelligence chief did.

North Clark Street, Chicago, 4 May 1889

As Parnell answered his interrogator, the three-man Cronin removal committee was about to go into action in Chicago. The planning had already taken months. Martin Burke rented an apartment on Clark Street opposite the doctor's down-at-heel surgery. Two attempts to lure him to his death by bogus medical calls had misfired. On 20 March a remote house was taken – the Carlson Cottage in Lakeview, Lake Michigan, close to Patrick O'Sullivan's ice-works. Cronin accepted a contract to tend the medical needs of the workers.

On Saturday 4 May the Chicago police sergeant Dan Coughlin rented a horse and buggy at a livery stable on North Clark Street. He went to Patrick Cronin's apartment and was admitted by the landlady, a Mrs Conklin. An ice-man had been injured – out on the lake, the visitor claimed. The doctor bundled up his medical instruments and headed in Coughlin's buggy for the cottage.

As he entered he was immediately struck from behind with an ice-hatchet by Burke. Seven more blows killed him.

The body was stripped and put in a trunk. A Catholic medallion around the neck was left untouched. The body was tipped into a storm drain.

Irish Office, Great Queen Street, London SW, 5 May 1889

Parnell was getting away with it. The prosecution had set up some traps, but still the Irish leader skated lightly over all knowledge of dynamite plots. *The Times*'s needs remained pressing. The separate case against Michael Davitt was about to open. After Parnell's insouciant denials, revelations from within the Clan were at an even greater premium.

William Hoare had duly arrived from New York after the recall order – but was still proving 'difficult to manage'. His reluctance to play politics remained unbending.

Arthur Balfour called a conference at the Irish Office on 5 May to discuss the Hoare business. William Joyce recorded it in his memorandum.

Present were Joyce, Sir West Ridgeway, the permanent under-secretary at Dublin Castle, and Peter O'Brien, attorney-general for Ireland. The youthful John Sandars, William Matthews's private secretary, represented the Home Office.

James Monro was the custodian of the consul's past dispatches, Mr Sandars revealed, but was 'reluctant to part with the papers due to the notoriety of the Le Caron incident', according to Joyce. The policeman's reluctance was evidently quickly over-turned.

Sandars wrote to Joyce that night: 'I think I may say my mission has fairly prospered. Monro is most anxious to allow every use to be made of the material portions of the reports and will be glad to see you tomorrow and settle [the] basis of working arrangement.' On Joyce's account the secret consular papers had already been moved to Monro's private house at 35 Eaton Square 'to avoid observation by Liberal sympathisers at the Home Office'.

Chicago, May 1889

News of Patrick Cronin's disappearance was published on 6 May. His allies proclaimed it was murder and set out to track down his killers. Alexander Sullivan in return stoked the spy-frenzy. A girl claimed she had seen the doctor heading by streetcar for the railroad station. For two weeks mysterious telegrams were published in the Chicago papers plotting Cronin's movements by train across Canada from Montreal to Halifax – evidently heading for the transatlantic steamer to bear him to the witness box in Probate Court Number One.

Patrick Cronin had been mentioned as an aside in Thomas Beach's testimony as a bitter enemy of Sullivan. *The Times* had indeed made an effort to get the vanished doctor to testify. According to William Joyce, Balfour asked him to enquire of Thomas Beach, now under police guard with his wife in a London safe house, what might induce the doctor, his old Illinois Clan-comrade, to testify. Beach replied: 'For years past I have known him to be a professional scoundrel and a liar of the Millen type and I would not take his word or trust him one inch . . .' But it was all too late anyway.

On 21 May a Chicago sewer on 59th Street was reported blocked. 'Dog in here!' shouted one of the repair gang as the manhole was opened. A man's body floated feet first to the surface. Storm water had washed it for miles under the city streets. A Clan-na-Gael committee arrived at the city morgue to declare that the mutilated body was not Dr Cronin's. According to a priest: 'Everyone knows the traitor is in London about to take the stand at the Special Commission.'

Millen was dead. So was Cronin. Le Caron was in hiding under armed guard. 'Henry' was in fear of his life, the Sheridan ranch prowled by hired guns armed with Winchester rifles. Cables continued to fly between *The Times*'s solicitors and their agent in Colorado. On 20 June he messaged: 'Satisfied he will go, as determined to revenge those who ordered his death. Believe he possesses full testimony and has documents here, but won't divulge same till on ship . . .'

Patrick Sheridan knew how to save himself. He continued the tortuous telegraphic negotiations, while from 3 June 1889 onwards relaying full details by cable to Davitt. He in turn indicated to the Clan (via Patrick Egan) that Sheridan was now cooperating with the defence. The threats might continue but the devious wool-rancher was not to be touched. 'Assert's' cables revealing the huge sum *The Times* was prepared to pay to an alleged terrorist were published later in Dublin and New York newspapers – to the great embarrassment of Printing House Square.

The Special Commission had become a poker game played in a hall of mirrors – the players knew what their opponents were holding. The exchanges were knowing, counsel on each side proceeding to a point of a revelation, then retreating. Michael Davitt knew enough to bring down the government.* There were those advising the prosecution who knew it too.

Taking the witness stand on 3 July Davitt was questioned by Webster about the meeting with Millen, described as 'head of the Clan-na-Gael military council', in Dublin in 1879. It was at the core of the prosecution case against him. The witness refused to answer – he was 'bound by an oath of secrecy'. The attorney-general let that seemingly damning admission pass. He turned smartly instead to the 'new departure' telegram intended for Parnell – the founding link forged a decade before between the constitutionalist movement and American terror. It had been signed by General Millen.

'Was [Millen] a member of the Clan-na-Gael?' asked Sir Richard.

'I cannot answer,' the witness replied, 'it might hurt him.'

'Do you believe he was?'

'He is dead now,' said Davitt.

'Well then – he cannot be hurt by your answer.'

'It might hurt his relatives. It might give them pain . . .'

How much more painful surely for Frank Millen's wife and daughters to know what Davitt had learned from Sir Edward Jenkinson in Paris nine months before: that the Mexican general was a British-paid spy.

James Monro wrote the next day to Sandars about Webster's

---

* Davitt kept to his bargain not to incriminate Jenkinson. Later in the commission's proceedings Henry Labouchere urged Davitt to track down and subpoena Red Jim McDermott and expose his bogus bomb plots. Davitt referred to his activities only as an interrogatory aside and accused the Dublin Metropolitan Police – not Jenkinson.

curiously lenient interrogation of Davitt. 'For the V in his name substitute M and you have my feelings. It is too disgusting. I feel crushed again.' He had co-operated to his utmost. The policeman had bent and bent again to political pressure. The prosecution was muffing it. Monro did not know what Webster clearly suspected – that the defence knew all about Millen.

Sir Charles Russell delighted in dropping little hints. A week later Joseph Soames was recalled for the defence. There was a playful reference to the matter of 'Ladybird' and the late general.

'Who is Mr Thomson?' asked Russell.

'He is nothing at all,' said *The Times*'s solicitor; 'he is an independent person.'

'A private detective, I suppose?'

'Not exactly. He would be rather offended to be called that.'

'Is there any witness you described as "M"?'

Soames replied: 'No, I have not the slightest recollection of any such person . . .'

Cook County Coroner's Court, Chicago, June 1889

The Cronin murder investigation in Chicago had meanwhile become a Special Commission by proxy. At the inquest in June 1889 the feuding Clan was compelled to pry open its tabernacle of secrets. On the 11th the coroner's jury announced their verdict: it was a murder conspiracy. Five men were named, including Alexander Sullivan, the only one not yet in custody. He was arrested that night at home in his pyjamas and taken to Cook County jail loudly protesting his innocence. The next day John J. Moroney, 'a known associate of Sullivan', was arrested in New York at the request of the Chicago police. The *New York Times* went to town on the story.

Moroney, a native of Galway, had 'never been known since he came to this country to do a stroke of work', said the rumbustious report. He was, according to prominent Irishmen in Philadelphia, 'a dangerous agitator interested in personal revenue only' who had fled the city when 'it got too hot'. The newspaper's readers were reminded of the events of summer 1887 when:

at the Queen's Jubilee, Moroney went to England with
a party of men of similar characteristics, bearing with him
it is said $75,000 for the purpose of carrying terror into
the hearts of the English people.

Somehow Moroney forgot to blow up anything . . .
flitting like a honey-bird from city to city on the Continent enjoying himself as thoroughly as his money would
permit . . . by a queer coincidence two of his companions
were arrested.

The story continued with the return of 'Melville' in October
1887 alongside the lace-smuggling Miss Kennedy, who was 'now
believed to be his present wife'. Mrs Moroney, an 'attractive
brunette', was retraced to the four-room tenement on Tenth
Street but, just as she had done after James Monro's revelations
at the Southwark inquest, refused to say anything about her
husband's wanderings.

Michael Ryan, however, who had acted as 'attorney for the
prosecution' in the trial of the Triangle at Mike Ledwith's Saloon,
had a great deal to say: 'There is no doubt that money was spent
in sending John Moroney plus a female companion and Thomas
Dennehy of Brooklyn to England,' he told the *Philadelphia
Inquirer*, 'a mission that gave those patriots excursion trips to
the Lakes of Killarney – and in securing sentences of imprisonment
of fifteen years each to Michael Harkins, a poor dupe, a tool of
others – and Philip Callan, from whom I personally saw a letter,
written a day before his capture, saying he was starving.'

It was all a Triangle racket. Rattle the cash-box for 'active
work', send useful idiots to blunder around with dynamite. Then
betray them. Jubilee Plot part two – the dispatch of Cohen, Callan
and Harkins – was a scam. Moroney had cooked it up for the
money, Sullivan to save his skin by blowing up his political
enemies.

The Cronin murder trial began in late October before a
Chicago grand jury. The cases against Moroney and Sullivan were
dropped for lack of evidence. The prosecution nevertheless tore
into the Triangle's record as a 'junta whose sole object was to

steal the organisation's funds'. On 16 December Martin Burke, Daniel Coughlin and Patrick O'Sullivan were sentenced to life imprisonment.

London, winter 1889–90

The Secret Department had a new task. On Christmas Eve 1889 Captain William O'Shea filed for divorce on the grounds of adultery.* Mr C. S. Parnell was cited as the co-respondent. Reports from Inspector John Littlechild in Anderson's private papers reveal that from mid November onwards he was watching the house – 'St John's Lodge, Tressillian Road, Lewisham (or Brockley)' – where Parnell and Katherine O'Shea were trysting. Nicholas Gosselin was also on the case. He reported very secretly to Balfour in early January 1890: 'As the O'Shea suit may have a great influence on future events I hope it not out of place if I let you have some facts connected.' The major reported gleefully how the O'Sheas' son Gerard had found his mother's bedroom strewn with Parnell's clothes and personally labelled medicine bottles. 'On this the lad attacked her . . . she retaliated and made admissions which he told his father [who was] there and then consented to the [divorce] suit.'

There was a sinister note. O'Shea 'was in a great state of terror', said Gosselin, but if he was too frightened to proceed there was 'abundant evidence' of the affair otherwise. Parnell might yet be brought to the sticking point.

The Special Commission had expired the month before under the weight of its own epic oratory. Davitt, defending himself, spoke for five days. Sir Henry James closed for the prosecution in a speech lasting a day longer. 'Henry' was still negotiating with

---

* Katharine's wealthy aunt had died in April 1889, leaving her fortune almost exclusively to her niece. Her relatives contested the will, which also froze the captain out of his marriage settlement. In the eventual divorce hearing Katharine alleged her husband had connived in and condoned the affair from the beginning for material advantage. The captain insisted he did not suspect his wife's adultery until 1887.

The Times almost to the very end, claiming to be 'hoodwinking' the newspaper all along. In late November the commissioners at last retired to draft their juryless conclusions. They were published on 13 February 1890 under the nine headings of the original charges: 'We find that the respondent members of Parliament collectively were not members of a conspiracy to achieve the absolute independence of Ireland,' read point one – but the judges found that seven of the accused had indeed conspired to promote an agrarian agitation.

'We entirely acquit Mr Parnell and the other respondents on the charge of insincerity in their denunciation of the Phoenix Park murders,' read paragraph three. On charge nine (associating with named advocates of crime, of whom Frank Millen was one) the judges concluded: 'It has been proved that the respondents invited and obtained the assistance and co-operation of the physical force party in America, including the Clan-na-Gael . . .' That charge stuck.

As for the further allegation against Michael Davitt – that he was the broker of the alliance between 'the party of violence in America and the Parnellite Party in Ireland' – the judges found that he was 'mainly instrumental'.

Both sides claimed victory. Lord Salisbury appeared supremely aloof. *The Times* paid Parnell £5,000 in an out-of-court settlement in an action brought for libel in Edinburgh. The parliamentary debates on the report's adoption were bruising. On 4 March Timothy Harrington rose to speak: 'I'll prove a foul conspiracy,' he said, 'by statements which will show that while we were accused of associating with dynamitards and murderers, our accusers were in constant association with dynamitards.'

He read out the cable intercept of 13 December 1888 from Thomson to 'Assert': ' "The final decision of FM is that he is now ready to come over and give evidence, on three days' notice, upon payment of five thousand pounds down, and the remaining five thousand to be paid him after his evidence and cross-examination . . ."

'But when the House is informed who FM is I think they will be even more surprised.

'That name was General Frank Millen ... Well, Sir, did that telegram or that cipher come under the notice of the Attorney General?'

'Not one of them,' Sir Richard Webster replied. He was lying his head off.

_____

Trinity College, Dublin

In the judicial drama of the Special Commission, with all its twists
and revelations, there remained a presiding question. Why did
Michael Davitt, briefed in Paris on the eve of the tribunal's opening by Sir Edward Jenkinson, choose not to bring the whole
house down by exposing General F. F. Millen's relationship with
the British government? His name had been splashed by James
Monro all over the press and parliament as the head of the 'Jubilee
dynamite gang'. Two of his 'dupes' were serving long terms in
prison.

When the prosecution knives at last came out in Probate Court
Number One with the devastating disclosures of Thomas Beach,
Parnell's intelligence chief knew from the cable decrypts all about
The Times's continuing bargaining with 'FM' in New York. Huge
sums were on offer to the man who had evidently plotted to
blow up Queen Victoria. The Government was colluding in the
newspaper's negotiations. Their target was an agent of HM
Foreign Office. The scandal would have been enormous.

Davitt's papers held at Trinity College, Dublin, contained an
answer. It was a one-line cable from Patrick Egan sent from
Lincoln, Nebraska, dated 9 February 1889, the day after Beach
made his sensational 'more spies in America' outburst on the
witness stand. It read: 'Don't mention Mexico. Will cable again.'
Mexico was Millen.

The very respectable Patrick Egan (he was about to be
appointed US minister to Chile) was former president of the Irish
National League of America, the 'open movement' whose funds
had underwritten the home rule campaign. He was also Alexander

Sullivan's chief political ally in the Clan-na-Gael and Davitt's continuing interlocutor with the hard-men in Chicago. Egan was
relaying orders from Sullivan. Beach had sponsored Alexander
Sullivan as a Clan member in the first place. His enemies were
jubilant at his exposure. Now Millen was a spy – he was a traitor
too far.

Egan messaged again cryptically on 13 March: 'While this
Mexican question is pending, I am like the Cork fisherwoman
who was in a state of grace and couldn't tell her old enemy what
she thought about her, but perhaps I won't be always so!' Patrick
Egan thought himself without sin at that moment – but it seems
he was prepared to fall from grace in the future. Whatever he
meant, it did not sound healthy for Frank Millen. Less than a
month later the general was dead – apparently from natural causes.
Far better for the sundered Clan, sunk in its own murderous
corruption, that his duplicity should now stay buried with him.

There were plenty of non-revolutionaries with an interest in
discomforting Lord Salisbury's government who knew about
Millen. Sir William Harcourt, the former Liberal Home Secretary,
hammer of the Tories in the Special Commission debate, was
aware of the Mexico contact. Earl Granville the former Liberal
Foreign Secretary knew of it; Earl Spencer certainly did. So, probably, after Jenkinson's clandestine 'back Parnell or expect disaster'
overtures of December 1885, did William Gladstone.

But apart from the Nationalist MP Timothy Harrington's accusations in the Commons Special Commission debate of March
1890, the Jubilee plot was never raised again in the press or
in parliament until Sir Robert Anderson's *Blackwood's Magazine*
outbursts of twenty years later. A seamless Civil Service took over.
British governments did not manufacture dynamite plots. No
respectable politician was going to fling such wild accusations –
where was the proof? One would have to dig very deep to find
the cable traffic of HM legation at Mexico City in the summer/
autumn of 1885 when Millen was recruited. But the message of
three years later when Millen made the renewed offer of his services from the same very discreet letter-box was the real smoking
gun. That short cable from Sir St John Spenser to Lord Salisbury

of 30 June 1888 read: 'Agent X is willing to resume supplying information provided he has not to deal with the same person with whom he was dealing last summer.'

Agent X was Millen. Last summer was the Jubilee. Who – to the apparent unspoken recognition of HM Foreign Office – was the person the general was dealing with? There are several candidates.

Sir Edward Jenkinson is one. He was of course known to the FO: they had passed him the Mexico contact in the first place.

James Monro discovered 'accidentally' while the general was at Boulogne in June 1887 that 'Millen's schemes of outrage' had been communicated to his predecessor before they had even been brokered in New York. Perhaps the very discovery, probably through an intercepted letter, that the two men were somehow in contact* persuaded the policeman that it must be so. His colleague Robert Anderson would have eagerly nudged him in pursuit of their loathed former rival.

That dates the Jenkinson–Millen dealings to the previous January – when the dismissed spymaster made his last mysterious trip to France. He was not the Whitehall-connected figure that Millen was 'dealing with last summer'. But they had indeed met in Paris. The general had returned to New York thereafter to make his overtures to the Fenian Council. If Jenkinson had inspired him, what was his motive? His every move since their first meeting in November 1885 had aimed to keep the dynamite war on hold. Home rule was the only answer, so he had told Lord Salisbury, and got no thanks for it.

There was, however, a very curious admission made in the Vienna letter of October 1888 to Earl Spencer. Jenkinson quoted the views of Patrick Cassidy, one of the evident sponsors of the Jubilee plot:

---

* That Jenkinson and the general continued some sort of relationship is hinted at by a letter of January 1889 to Earl Spencer announcing that Sir Edward was setting off, at the invitation of an American syndicate offering an abundant salary, to manage a colossal ranch and mining enterprise in Baja California, Mexico. The coincidence seems too great. The elusive Colonel Farrer, to whom Millen wrote from Boulogne, died in an 'accidental' fire at his London lodgings in October 1893.

He says Parnell will never get any more money from
America and points out *what I have always said* should
have been Parnell's attitude in regard to the extreme
party.

Instead of denying all knowledge of the dynamiters,
Parnell should have boldly showed his connection with
them, showing their strength and at the same time, saying
he disapproved of their methods . . .

Jenkinson was at one with the head of the Fenian Council.
The bigger the terror threat the better – kept on hold only because
Parnell ordered it so. The master of the bogus bomb-plot had
rattled enough dynamite to push Gladstone towards home rule.
In the winter of 1886–7 the Conservative government seemed
far less fearful. If the Irish leader would not be a revolutionist,
the spymaster would make him one. What was needed was the
biggest scare imaginable.

It was as messianic as it was dangerous, but Monro was right
– the 'schemes of outrage' began with Jenkinson. The dismissed
spymaster had primed the bomb for his own bizarre ends. Then
he had walked away. Millen meanwhile, enmeshed in his own
Byzantine dealings with both Sullivan and the Fenian Council,
had no choice but to proceed. He was being paid for it several
times over after all.

What the humiliated Jenkinson did not seem to be doing in
the spring and summer of 1887, grubbing round Lord Salisbury
for a 'colonial governorship' and mourning the death of his son,
was continuing to mastermind some wild plot from the wings.
But somebody connected to Whitehall was.

Four months after Jenkinson's dismissal information reached
Monro that explosives were on their way to Europe consigned
to one 'Muller or Miller at Paris'. The warning came from
Thomas Beach in Chicago. Robert Anderson's agent in the Clan
was relaying intelligence from April 1887 – on the Triangle
component at least – of Millen's mission. As he was penning his
anonymous dynamite exposés for *The Times*, Anderson fed the
information of the great transatlantic threat to his good friend

and colleague Monro. It all fitted the 'anti-Fenian conspiracy'. The description was his own. Then Beach went to France to track down the general. Robert Anderson sent him.

Was Beach the general's mysterious contact? Almost certainly not – his identity was unknown to the Foreign Office or anyone else in Whitehall. Monro called him 'the man in America whose name I never knew'.

Another potential candidate is Inspector James J. Thomson. Just who sent the Thomsons to Boulogne to baby-sit the general remains contradictory, but the Met commissioner and the permanent under-secretary at the Home Office both concluded in 1910 that it was Anderson. The secret civil servant had his own interest in Millen's progress. He knew enough about 'Informant M's' past betrayals of the Irish revolution to bend him to whatever purpose he chose. What that was would become clear once the Jubilee had passed – but not quite yet.

Beach – the Thomsons – were walk-ons in the drama. A much bigger player was receiving directions from the centre all along. It was General Charles Carrol-Tevis. He had been running the Paris end since his reactivation as a Foreign Office spy in 1885. His black propaganda activities thereafter were remarkable. He had came to London to collude with Captain O'Shea. He had brokered the Fenian Council–Katkov overtures in the year of home rule's fall – while mysterious Russian emissaries were in London asking for Parnell's ring to bear back to St Petersburg as a token of commitment. He depicted Frank Millen – 'one of our dearest friends' – as the man who would establish an American military colony in Afghanistan in pursuit of the Russian conquest of India. He had picked up the general's trail again when Millen departed New York.

If Michael Davitt is to be believed (there is no archival evidence in the consulate's secret dispatch book), Tevis knew Millen was on the move because Vice-consul Hoare was briefing London direct. That would cover the period between Jenkinson's eviction from Room 56 and Millen's re-arrival in Paris. The fallen spymaster might have set it up but the Jubilee plot was now a Foreign Office affair.

In the spring and summer of 1887 Tevis energetically progressed the dispatch of the hapless Maharajah Duleep Singh to Russia posing as Patrick Casey. The loud noises drummed up in New York and London of a dynamite conspiracy against Queen Victoria ensured that operation succeeded brilliantly.

When Frank Millen arrived back in Paris in April 1887 he went straight into Tevis's counsels. Then he moved to Boulogne. When Chief Constable Williamson arrived in the Channel port on Monro's orders to 'frighten' the general away, Millen immediately contacted Tevis. Monro instructed the Foreign Office to inform the French government that a dynamite plot was being directed from their soil. But instead of fleeing to America, as Monro expected, Millen and his wife went instead to Paris. Tevis fixed it. Jubilee day passed. There was no explosion. As far as Millen was concerned there was never going to be.

Then came Jubilee plot part two. In Chicago, Alexander Sullivan still needed his outrage. His motive was to destroy Parnell politically and thus his own enemies in the breakaway Clan-na-Gael. John Moroney was dispatched in a hurry to find out just what Millen was up to. Thomas Callan and Michael Harkins were recruited in Philadelphia. The Civil War veterans were hardly young hot-heads – they were guileless patriots, expendable stooges. They all sailed aboard the SS *City of Chester* to arrive in Liverpool on Jubilee day. The dynamite in their steamer trunks was real.

Fatefully and dangerously, Robert Anderson meanwhile proceeded with his own agenda. Jenkinson might have inspired the plot to frighten his own government into appeasing Parnell. Anderson turned it round to destroy him – using Thomas Beach as his go-between.* In Paris, Millen colluded with Beach and Pigott in the entrapment operation against the three Nationalist

---

* 'No man is fit to be head of the Criminal Investigation Department if he is not clever enough to make mistakes without being caught,' Anderson wrote in his 1910 memoir, 'and I can boast that I never received a word of censure for a single one of my errors and – in this instance – it was a matter that caused me much distress and some searching of heart for it related to the safety of the Queen.' It sounded like a confession.

MPs. The letters introducing 'Joseph Melville' reached Monro's desk via Inspector Thomson – four days before they were placed by Kitty Millen in the hands of their intended targets at the House of Commons. 'Joseph Melville' was John Moroney.

Moroney duly made the set-piece visit to the House of Commons, where Monro's men were waiting. Inspector Patrick Quinn confronted him at Gladstone Street. Then he too suddenly disappeared to France.

In the autumn of 1887 the good policeman was still blinking through the fog. He really believed he was in pursuit of 'treacherous MPs'. The sensationally reported Southwark inquest in October 1887 served his purpose by bringing the conspiracy into the open. The inquest at last linked the now publicly named 'Millen' and an aborted dynamite conspiracy with the Irish Party. Monro at this stage wanted nothing more than that any remaining conspirators should disappear to America. But then he found Thomas Callan – and the trail that led him to the dynamite in Mrs Maria Bright's blocked Islington water-closet. That was real enough, as it seems were the detonators in the Finsbury Park lake. A trial was inevitable.

The question was how to reap the maximum political advantage. As Arthur Balfour wrote his uncle: 'I think the dynamite prosecutions will do good . . . the result will show a connection between the conspirators and one member *at least* of the Parnellite party. But this must be kept dark for the present . . .'

The committal proceedings named Millen. The Old Bailey trial of Callan and Harkins did not mention him once. The Special Commission was stirring in the wings. The biddable general had to be rewritten back into the Jubilee plot. Without him there was no connection to Parnell himself. He had 'met' the Irish leader – he was a 'thorough-going Revolutionist', so Pigott's forged letter in Robert Anderson's private papers claimed. He could be sprung as and when Anderson chose. The question is how much did ministers know of what the civil servant was up to? They seemed to know everything.

The Arlington Street meeting on 19 March 1888 was the moment Monro bent to the higher agenda. At the parliamentary select committee that followed he and the Home Secretary went through a grim little script naming Millen as the head of the Jubilee dynamite gang.

Then Millen came on line again with the 'willing to resume work' cable to the Foreign Office. It was passed via the Home Secretary to Monro.

At last the dutiful policeman made a stand and 'refused to do what he considered to be wrong'. If the general showed up he would arrest him on sight. Then Monro resigned as head of the CID (he stayed on as head of the Secret Department) and was replaced by Robert Anderson.

The temptation was Faustian. Five months later, with the Whitechapel murderer's crimson reign at its height, Monro was offered the commissionership. There was a discreet understanding: Anderson would remain in post as his deputy – they must pull together. In the late autumn of 1888, as the looming disaster of the Pigott forgeries became obvious to the Government, Millen and the ever-loyal James and Martha Thomson were handed to *The Times* newspaper. It was Anderson's doing but Monro colluded.

Seeking to spirit the general from New York to testify was politically risky but great risks were already being taken. Thomas Beach alias Henri Le Caron was propelled by Anderson to the witness stand of the Special Commission. His evidence was damning. Then came Pigott's confession, flight and suicide – and it was *The Times* which was under siege. 'FM', still haggling over money in New York, looked like the relief column on the horizon but Consul Hoare was obstructive. Lord Salisbury himself ordered his recall to London on 'private business'. As the consul packed his steamer trunk, Frank Millen was found dead.

A Chicago journalist called John McEnnis, investigating the Cronin murder in 1889, wrote of the Jubilee plot: 'All the original information had come, it is now known, from Le Caron [Thomas Beach] in Chicago. It had absolutely no foundation in fact whatsoever, but the dove-cote at Scotland Yard was fluttered, and detectives absolutely worked over the whole of America and France to find a foundation for their blood-curdling romances.'

The writer was a Sullivan partisan in the Cronin feud and had his own agenda. But he was right in this sense – it was a 'blood-curdling' scare cooked up by a counter-intelligence operation which had gone to war on itself.

What the sceptical Chicago journalist could not know is how high the political conspiracy reached. It went to Lord Salisbury. His fingerprints were on the Mexico cables; he read the Tevis material; the Duleep Singh-Casey-Katkov operation was his and Sir Julian Pauncefote's own exquisite project. Every court-room reference to Millen was to someone whose recruitment as a British agent he had personally sanctioned.

He chaired the Arlington Street meeting which prompted Henry Matthews and James Monro to go through their charade in the Commons. He was blithely aware of the Agent X cable. His minutes were scribbled on the order recalling William Hoare when the New York consul proved reluctant to turn Millen over to *The Times*.

His motive was the destruction of home rule Liberalism. Defence of the Union was the justification. The secret apparatus of the state was used to that end. Those who colluded were rewarded; those who demurred were banished.

The Prime Minister, it might be said, had hazarded the life of his sovereign. When Lord Salisbury had first flirted with Parnell in pursuit of power, Sir William Harcourt accused the Conservatives of 'tampering with treason and dynamite'.

In pursuit of the Irish enemy, the highest Tory of all might do just that.

EPILOGUE

On 12 June 1890 James Monro resigned for the second time. Henry Matthews begged him to keep it secret, but the policeman refused. There was an emergency statement to the Commons. The reason was a row over police pensions and his desire to appoint a new assistant commissioner, like him a professional policeman. This was 'contrary to the wishes of the Home Secretary, who, it is understood, desired to transfer an official of the Home Office, as in the case of Mr Anderson,' reported *The Times*.

The Queen wrote in alarm to Lord Salisbury. Why had the commissioner resigned? Why had she not been informed before Parliament? The Prime Minister's reworking of recent history was remarkable. 'Mr Monro . . . posed not as your Majesty's servant . . . but as if he had been captain of a band of allied troops taken into your service,' he replied . . . 'It was owing to this contrivance that first Mr Jenkinson, afterwards Sir Charles Warren, were induced to resign.'

There were seditious meetings at Bow Street police station. Forty men were sacked. After a week in which London's police seemed on the brink of mutiny, Sir Edward Bradford, the business-like secretary of the India Office's Secret and Political Department was appointed commissioner. The destruction of Monro however was complete. The trouble was all due to his 'evil practises' Salisbury told the Queen.

He left one enduring memorial. It was Monro who in his last months of office commissioned the Met's new headquarters on the Thames. He insisted it should be called New Scotland Yard.

James Monro, CB, prepared to set off with his entire family for Bengal to build the Abode of Mercy.

Robert Anderson remained head of the Criminal Investigation Department. He was knighted in 1901. Major Nicholas Gosselin took over the Secret Department on a salary boosted by £800 per year paid from an annuity sanctioned by Lord Salisbury from Home and Irish Office funds 'against the abolition of SS money by a rival Government'. The reason for the beneficial deal is given in Salisbury's correspondence as 'services rendered'.

Gosselin went to New York and sacked William Hoare. The consul who, at the end, had been so reluctant to cooperate in bundling up Frank Millen as a witness for *The Times* was reposted first to 'Brest, Finisterre', according to his record of service (an arch civil servant's joke perhaps), and thence to represent Her Majesty's government at Honolulu in the Sandwich Islands. Sir Julian Pauncefote became ambassador to Washington.

Sir Edward Jenkinson's Mexican venture did not prosper. The colossal land-grab scheme on the desert isthmus of Baja California turned out to be a front for a bunch of retired US army generals aiming to declare an independent 'Republic of Lower California'. Lord Salisbury was messaged by the ambassador in Mexico City: 'The only circumstance in this affair which caused me any uneasiness was a series of telegrams which arrived accusing the English Land and Colonisation Company of which Sir Edward Jenkinson is the chairman of being mixed up in this proposed piratical expedition.'

It appeared, however, 'that little had been done beyond giving pompous titles to those who were to lead the invasion'. That was very Millen-like. Sir Edward thereafter retired to Wales and kept his mouth shut, still fending off blackmail threats from Red Jim McDermott and Matthew O'Brien.

Florence Millen found a post with the US census office in Washington. Kitty Millen married Thomas Clarke Luby's son Jack, but seems to have decamped thereafter as governess to a 'wealthy family in Havana, Cuba'.

Frank Millen's rest in Woodlawn cemetery was not peaceful. A strange letter of November 1889 from Luby describes his and the family's shock on discovering 'The disinterment of my poor friend Millen and his re-interment with Masonic ritual in a better plot'. By who and why is not elaborated.

Thomas Beach lived with his wife under police guard, shuttling round safe houses under the alias 'Dr Howard'. He published his (Anderson-censored) memoirs in 1892 – *Twenty Five Years in the Secret Service, the Recollections of a Spy*. It was a best-seller. He described the Jubilee plot as 'an undertaking shrouded in mystery'. Beach added a mysterious line of his own. Arguing, not unnaturally, that a parsimonious government should provide more Secret Service money to pay informers, he wrote:

> There is no use thinking that mere tools like Callan and Harkins – the men now in prison in connection with the Jubilee Explosion Plot – would be of any service. These men know nothing.
>
> It is the Millens and Moroneys of the conspiracy who should be in government pay – and they have no mean price . . . Imagine offering these men a retainer of £20 per month . . . The idea is ridiculous.

The spy was sending a last conspiratorial wink to Whitehall.

Thomas Beach, alias Henri Le Caron, died two years later of bowel disease in a house in Tregunter Road, Fulham. Inspector Littlechild formally identified the body. He was buried in Norwood cemetery, south London – although there were plenty of sightings from around the world of a heavily disguised ferret-faced man well into the 1900s.

Parnell did not contest the O'Shea divorce suit, which was heard in November 1890. He was an adulterer. Gladstone abandoned him; so did the Catholic bishops. Salisbury made rude jokes in parliament. The Irish Party split and took years to regain its political cohesion. Parnell married Mrs Katharine O'Shea in June 1891.

Major Gosselin stayed on the case to the end. He reported secretly to Balfour on 8 September: 'There is not enough vitality in Irish disaffection to get up a plot capable of breaking the pipe of the oldest charwoman who cleans the smallest police hut in this island . . .

'I have had some information about Parnell for some time which I hesitated to send . . . it is that he is looking about to make an honourable compromise with the other side . . .'

There was no compromise. Parnell died a month later aged forty-five.

Dr Thomas Gallagher was released insane from Portland prison on 29 August 1896. John Daly was released the same day after a vocal amnesty campaign claiming that the bomb evidence against him was planted. He became mayor of Limerick. Jeremiah O'Donovan Rossa died in New York and was given a Republican hero's funeral in Dublin in 1915 when a new generation of Irish revolutionaries were negotiating with England's enemies. Pigott's orphaned sons, Jack and Dick, were 'sent away to sea' under a new surname. Joseph Soames donated £10 to their welfare.

The Times paid the ruinous costs of the Special Commission.* For years afterwards George Buckle went on corresponding with Anderson and Balfour, seeking proof that the Pigott letters were genuine. In 1907 the newspaper was swallowed by Lord Northcliffe.

William Gladstone became Prime Minister for the fourth time in August 1892. A second attempt at a home rule bill was made in 1893 – it scraped through the Commons only to be crushed in the Lords. Lord Salisbury was returned to power by a Conservative/Liberal Unionist landslide two years later.

Queen Victoria celebrated a dynamite-free Diamond Jubilee. She died in her bed at Windsor Castle cradled by her grandson, the German Kaiser, on 22 January 1901.

The 'Jubilee bombers' did not serve full sentences. Michael Harkins was released from Chatham jail in October 1891 suffering from a tubercular aneurysm. He died in Philadelphia a year later.

Thomas Callan stayed in jail. The Massachusetts Veterans Post of the Grand Army of the Republic petitioned HM government for 'An act of clemency, duly appreciated by the Irishmen in this country, if the Imperial government would commute the imprisonment of our American fellow citizen and soldier.' Just before his departure for India, Monro had written privately to Sir

---

* The legal fees amounted to almost £250,000 – the equivalent of at least £12 million today.

Edward Bradford that it should be so. Callan was instead transferred from Chatham to Portland prison.

He wrote to a friend in Philadelphia:

> We had a ride in a brougham from the prison to the
> station and it took us about seven hours for it to get to
> Portland. Then we had another ride in the black maria
> from the station to the prison. It was quite a picnic for
> us after being shut up for four years where you couldn't
> see nothing but bleak walls and thick fogs.
>
> I suppose you are making great preparations for the
> presidential election. I imagine myself marching up the
> street as big as life with a torch on my shoulder but I
> think it will be a long while before that will be.

The prisoner quoted a sentimental poem. 'Oh where is my door
post by the wild wood sisters and sure did ye weep for its fall . . .
Where is the mother that looks on my childhood and where is
the bosom friend dearer than all . . .'

With ten years of his sentence still to run, Thomas Callan was
quietly released from Portland prison on 23 January 1893.*

* Callan arrived in New York soon afterwards on a German steamer 'emaciated,
gray and weak', according to his hometown newspaper, the *Lowell Daily Courier*,
which quoted a conspiratorial London dispatch in the *New York World* of 29 January
1893, evidently derived from a nationalist MP: 'One of the last official acts of Mr
Matthews, the late Tory home secretary [Salisbury's government had fallen] . . . was
to order that dynamiter Callan be set free. The case was then reviewed by his successor, Mr Asquith . . . Mr Matthews . . . knew that when the Liberals came into
power they would be forced to look into the sentences of the dynamiters, and he
wanted to prevent an investigation . . . Cohen, who was a police agent from the first
and the prime mover in the [Jubilee] plot, died in London before Callan and Harkins
had made use of the dynamite which had been supplied . . . and it is said Dr (Robert)
Anderson, head of the criminal investigation department, fearing that the whole
plan would fizzle out and that the political effect it was hoped to obtain would be
lost, had Callan and Harkins arrested.'

'With Harkins dead,' the report continued, 'Matthews hoped to close the
incident by releasing Callan and preventing inquiry into the origin of the Great
Jubilee Plot. When Callan's release was announced, the Unionist newspapers
fiercely attacked Mr Asquith, but they suddenly dropped the subject . . . If he is
attacked, Mr Asquith can show that the Jubilee Plot was planned by English
police agents in America . . .'

Thomas Callan spared the authorities any further discomfort. He was killed
'falling from a garbage cart' in Lowell on 26 May 1894.

DRAMATIS PERSONAE

Rebels

CALLAN, THOMAS (alias THOMAS SCOTT)
Philadelphia Clan-na-Gael member. Civil War veteran. Arrived in Liverpool 21 June 1887; arrested in November. Described at his Old Bailey trial as a 'sock-darner'. Sentenced to fifteen years for possession of explosives. Released after US amnesty campaign in 1893.

CASSIDY, PATRICK SARSFIELD
Sligo-born poet and journalist – business editor of the *New York Sunday Mercury*. Clan-na-Gael member who defected to Rossa. Toppled Rossa in November 1886 as head of Fenian Council, accused by his rival thereafter of being a British spy.

COHEN, JOSEPH (alias MR BROWN)
American found dead of consumption in London in October 1887. No personal details were revealed at his inquest or thereafter. Named by James Monro as a member of the 'Jubilee dynamite gang' and courier for money and explosives.

CRONIN, DR PATRICK
Chicago Clansman. Accused Alexander Sullivan of fraud; member of the 'trial' committee in 1888. Murdered in May 1889.

DAVITT, MICHAEL (1846–1906)
Nationalist visionary. Brought as a child from Mayo to Lancashire, where he lost an arm in a mill machinery accident. IRB member sentenced in 1870 to fifteen years for gun-running. Released from Dartmoor in 1877. Went to America to broker

'new departure'. Inspirer of Land League. Imprisoned in Portland prison (1881–2).

Politically estranged from Parnell post 1884, he nevertheless
acted as intelligence chief during Special Commission at which
he himself was arraigned separately. Editor *Labour World*, 1890.
Elected anti-Parnellite MP for North Meath 1892. (Alias: Mr
Black.)

DEVOY, JOHN (1842–1928)

Revolutionary and journalist. Born in Kildare, joined IRB in
1861. Served French Foreign Legion in Algeria. Appointed by
James Stephens organiser in the British army, Dublin (1865–6).
Sentenced for treason-felony, amnestied in 1871, exiled
to New York. Joined Clan-na-Gael and became one of its most
important figures. Inspired *Catalpa* mission to Australia.
Brokered 'new departure' with Michael Davitt in 1879 and
walked tortuous line between the violent and moral persuasion
route to Irish independence thereafter. Became Alexander
Sullivan's most bitter enemy. Formed breakaway Clan with Luke
Dillon in early 1887.

DILLON, LUKE (1848–1930)

Yorkshire-born Clansman brought to US as a child. Bombed
the House of Commons in 1885. Joined Devoy in split from
Triangle. Reported Millen–Cassidy overtures of 1887 to Devoy.
Accused Sullivan and Moroney of fraud and murder. Bombed
Welland Canal, Canada, during the Boer War. Released from
prison in 1914.

EGAN, PATRICK (1841–1919)

Longford-born member of IRB supreme council (1877). Successful Dublin businessman. Land League treasurer – transferred
funds to Paris in 1882 and made secret subventions to Alexander
Sullivan. Went to America; became president of National League
of America and a key Sullivan ally in the Clan. Remained a
contact of Davitt's throughout and played a major part in exposing Pigott as a forger.

HARKINS, MICHAEL (alias HARRY SCOTT)
Philadelphia Clan-na-Gael member. Recruited by Joseph
Moroney for Jubilee mission. Sentenced to fifteen years for possession of explosives. Released from Chatham jail terminally ill
in 1891.

LOMASNEY, WILLIAM MACKEY (1841–84)
Born in Cincinnati – made arms raids in Ireland. Arrested in
1867, amnestied in 1871. Became a Detroit bookseller and
'fanatic of the deepest die'. Met Parnell in France in 1881 and
sent admiring reports. Led Clan dynamite offensive in London
(1883–4) and blew himself up under London Bridge.

O'MAHONY, JOHN (1816–77)
Gaelic scholar, founder and 'head centre' of Fenian Brotherhood
in New York, toppled by his 'senate' wing rivals when 1865–6
rising in Ireland failed and stranded hundreds of Irish-American
veteran soldiers. Appointed Millen head of 'expeditionary
bureau' in New York with plan to send force to the rescue. Died
in poverty and given hero's funeral in Dublin.

MORONEY, JOSEPH
Sullivanite Clan-member from Philadelphia. Dispatcher of dynamiters, later accused of stealing operational money. Arrived in
Liverpool on Jubilee day 1887 – turned up at the House of
Commons six weeks later as 'Joseph Melville'. Shadowed by
police around London and Paris – retired to America. Accused
of complicity in 1889 Cronin murder.

ROSSA, JEREMIAH O'DONOVAN (1843–1915)
Cork-born journalist-revolutionary. Arrested in Dublin in 1865
and suffered brutalising imprisonment. Exiled to America in
1870. Militant of militants he was expelled from Clan for intransigence. Sent first 'skirmishers' to launch gunpowder attacks on
Britain in 1881 – funded by his inflammatory paper the *United
Irishman*. Revived Fenian Brotherhood in 1886 to be expelled
again. Given hero's funeral in Dublin in 1915.

STEPHENS, JAMES (1824–1901)
Veteran rebel, founder of the Irish Revolutionary Brotherhood
(1858). Recruited followers in the warring Union and Confederate armies promising an armed rising in Ireland. Arrested in
Dublin in 1865 to be supplanted (briefly) by Millen. Escaped
from prison back to America and summoned Millen from Mexico
to make a plan for a renewed rising. Toppled by hardliners after
the autocratic 'Captain' ordered the fight to be postponed yet
again and was repudiated by the IRB thereafter. Spent long exile
in Paris. Died in Dublin.

SULLIVAN, ALEXANDER (1847–1913)
Chicago lawyer and politician, born in Maine of Cork emigrants
(according to Devoy in Canada, son of a British soldier). Rose
through Republican Party machine. Tried and acquitted of one
murder and another gunshot wounding. Joined Clan-na-Gael
c. 1877 – elected president in 1881. Elected president American Land League 1883 (soon afterwards the National League),
the primary US fundraiser for Parnell's party in parliament.
Embarked in secret on dynamite attacks (1883–5). Retrenched
power in Clan in 1884 with a three-man executive, the Triangle,
and dissolved link with the IRB in Europe. Accused of fraud by
Clan schismatics, arraigned in a 'trial' in 1888–9 but acquitted.
Indicted by Chicago coroner's jury of complicity in murder of
Patrick Cronin.

Spies

BEACH, THOMAS BILLIS (1841–94)
Essex-born, ran off to France then America aged twenty to fight
for Union in Civil War. Afterwards joined Fenian Brotherhood
as 'Henri Le Caron' (also known as 'Informant B', 'Thomas',
Dr Howard'). Recruited as informer soon afterwards when in
England. Betrayed Canada invasion of 1870. Joined Clan-na-
Gael and posed as Sullivan ultra-loyalist. Robert Anderson was
his Whitehall control throughout. Self-unmasked when he gave
evidence to the Special Commission in 1889. Lived in hiding
thereafter. Died in London; buried in Norwood Cemetery.

CASEY, PATRICK
Kilkenny-born cousin of James Stephens. In Paris exile since 1870 with brother Joseph. Worked as printer. Invented dynamite plots (1884–5) on tide of 'absinthe and cognac'. Colluded with Captain Stephens in Daly rescue plan and provided Pigott with the 'black bag'. In March 1887 swapped identity with Maharajah Duleep Singh, who went to Moscow on his passport. Named by 'Scotland Yard source' as prime plotter versus Queen on Jubilee eve. Later offered to appear for the defence at the Special Commission and reveal all. Offered large sum by *The Times* in parallel. 'In [British] service', according to Davitt.

CARROL-TEVIS, GENERAL CHARLES (1831–1900)
American soldier-of-fortune and British Foreign Office spy. Philadelphia-born, West Point class of 1849. Served Turkish Sultan in the Crimean War, US cavalry Civil War. Adjutant-general Irish Republican Army (senate wing) in 1866–7, when he sent Canadian invasion order of battle to HM minister at Washington. Based in Paris thereafter – fought for Pope Pius IX (1868), in Franco-Prussian war, for Turks in 1877, and Egyptian Khedive. Re-animated as Foreign Office spy in 1885. Appointed Fenian Brotherhood's representative in Europe by P. S. Cassidy. Colluded in abortive Irish-Russian alliance plot (1886), which came live in March 1887 when Maharajah Duleep Singh was sent to Moscow as 'Patrick Casey'.

HAYES, JOHN P.
Philadelphia informer – reporting ultimately to Jenkinson. Gave warning of the House of Commons attack. Colluded with Casey, Captain Stephens and Red Jim McDermott in bogus Paris dynamite plots of 1885 and anti-home rule propaganda campaign in London the following year. Set up mission to Moscow with P. S. Cassidy and Tevis in Paris in 1886, but did not go through with it. Paid by *The Times* to find witnesses in winter 1888–9.

McDERMOTT, JAMES ('RED JIM')
Long-time informer within O'Mahony wing, Fenian Brotherhood. On Jenkinson's *agent provocateur* payroll from 1882 onwards, operating in New York, Dublin, Cork, Paris and London. Set up for phoney trial by Jenkinson. (Alias: Peter Quigley.)

MILLEN, BRIGADIER-GENERAL OF ARTILLERY FRANCIS FREDERICK (1831–89)

Tyrone-born soldier-of-fortune. Served British army (allegedly) in Crimean War. Fought for Guatemala 1863 – then for 'liberal' forces of Benito Juárez in Mexico versus Church party and Emperor Maximilian (1864–7) – rose to general. Joined Fenian Brotherhood in Mexico – sent by John O'Mahony on military reconnaissance to Ireland. Elected (Provisional) Chief Organiser Irish Republic in Dublin during failed coup attempt of 1865. Offered services as informer to HM consul in New York in 1866. Joined Clan-na-Gael, became chairman of military council. Devised plans for war versus British empire in alliance with Afghans, Zulus, Boers etc. and US invasion of Ireland in 1877–9 – plans reached Whitehall via Spanish consul in New York. In 1879 made secret tour of inspection in Ireland, where he met Michael Davitt. Correspondent for the *New York Herald* in Cuba, Panama etc. meanwhile. Remained loyal to Alexander Sullivan during the Clan-na-Gael split. In 1885 was chief of staff to General Barrios, Guatemalan dictator; also made overture to HM Foreign Office to act as informer from Mexico City. Commissioned by Alexander Sullivan to form an alliance with Paris Fenian exiles in January 1887. In Boulogne/Paris in summer 1887. Named by James Monro before Commons select committee as head of Jubilee plot. Made offer to resume work in summer 1888. Negotiated with *The Times* via Inspector James Thomson in winter 1888–9 to testify at Special Commission. Died in New York in April 1889 and given a patriot's funeral. (Aliases: Informant M, Frank Martin, James Thompson, Mr G. G. Robinson, Mr Morgan, Mr Mortimer, Agent X, Agent XXX, Mr Muller or Miller, the Gentle Torpedo, FM, Jenks, Jinks.)

O'BRIEN, MATTHEW

Failed Dublin lawyer who acted as Jenkinson agent in New York (1883–4). Colluded with Red Jim McDermott on entrapment operations. Duped Inspector Moser in the *Times* hunt for 'Henry' in New York in 1887. Set up private investigation agency in London. Later employed by Patrick Egan during Special Commission and by Henry Labouchere MP, editor of *Truth* magazine in Parnell's camp. Working as a double for *The Times* and Major Gosselin meanwhile. Blackmailed Edward Jenkinson and Earl Spencer. (Aliases: John Sinclair, Mr Roberts, Mr Wilson.)

PIGOTT, RICHARD (*c.* 1831–89)
Dublin journalist. Sold his nationalist paper the *Irishman* to
Parnell and Patrick Egan in 1881. Made money afterwards as
anti-Land League propagandist and 'dynamite-revalationist'.
Duped Irish Loyal and Patriotic Union and *The Times* into buy-
ing 'Parnell' letters. Consorted with Millen in Paris 1887. Com-
mitted suicide in Madrid after being exposed as a forger at the
Special Commission of 1889.

SHERIDAN, PATRICK
Land League organiser linked to Phoenix Park murders.
Addressee of one of the Pigott 'Parnell' letters. Fled to America
and made provocative dynamite speeches. Approached British
ambassador under cover-name 'Henry'. *The Times* offered him
£20,000 for his testimony.

STEPHENS, CAPTAIN DARNLEY STEWART
Dublin-born ex-colonial policeman. Recruited by Jenkinson as
agent, sacked for drunkenness in 1885 after misfired entrap-
ment plots. Worked thereafter as propagandist and agent for
Conservative-Unionist interests and *The Times*. Exposed by
Davitt in New York and had to flee for his life.

Home Office/Police

ANDERSON, SIR ROBERT (1841–1918; KCB 1901)
Dublin-born lawyer and civil servant. In 1866 he fielded the first
Millen informer reports at Dublin Castle with his brother
Samuel. Joined Secret Service in London in 1867–8. At Home
Office thereafter – running Thomas Beach first in Fenian
Brotherhood, then in Clan-na-Gael. Debriefed Beach in 1881
after Parnell meeting at the House of Commons. Sacked by
Jenkinson in 1884, re-employed by Monro in 1887 as 'assistant'.
Ran Beach on entrapment operations versus Nationalist MPs
1887 while anonymously providing *The Times* with 'Behind the
Scenes in America' exposés. Appointed assistant commissioner in
charge of CID when Monro resigned in summer 1888. Proposed
Beach as witness to *The Times*. Retired in 1901. Connection
with Beach was revealed in 1889 at Special Commission – and
with *The Times* in his own memoirs of 1910, when he insisted

he had acted with Monro's approval on 'anti-Fenian conspiracy'. Wrote many books of millenarist Christian theology which still enjoy lively following on US Internet sites.

GOSSELIN, MAJOR NICHOLAS, RM (KCB 1901)
Former Royal Irish Fusilier. Appointed Jenkinson's de facto deputy in 1884, responsible principally for north of England intelligence. Eager undercover operator who acted as a freelance for Arthur Balfour. Head of Secret Department 1888–1901, when paid special annuity established by Lord Salisbury. Known as 'the Gosling', 'Malcolm'.

HARCOURT, SIR WILLIAM VERNON (1827–1904)
Liberal Home Secretary 1880–85. Faced Rossa and Clan-na-Gael dynamite campaigns. Pleaded with Spencer for Jenkinson to operate from London. Parliamentary hammer of Conservatives during Special Commission debates. Called Robert Anderson 'tout for *The Times*'. Liberal leader 1896–8.

JENKINSON, EDWARD GEORGE (1835–1919; KCB 1888)
Harrow-educated Indian civil servant. Private secretary to Earl Spencer; appointed assistant under-secretary for police and crime at Dublin Castle after Phoenix Park murders – unofficially dubbed 'spymaster-general'. Acted secretly in same capacity at Home Office in London. Built network of agents answerable to him personally, causing huge rows with Metropolitan Police. Monro accused him (rightly) of extra-legal activities. Ran Millen file in winter 1885–6. Became Parnell partisan who tried to swing Lord Salisbury to home rule. Sacked in December 1886. Secretly fed Michael Davitt information at opening of Special Commission. Used alias 'George Jones'.

JOYCE, WILLIAM HENRY
Dublin Castle civil servant seconded to London during Special Commission to collate evidence in favour of *The Times*. Ran 'Henry' file. Sacked for drunkenness in 1903. In 1910 he claimed massive collusion between Home/Irish Office and *The Times* – and that Consul Hoare was recalled on government orders when reluctant to hand over an unknown potential witness in New York – Millen.

LITTLECHILD, CHIEF INSPECTOR JOHN

Scots-born policeman, member of original Special (Irish) Branch. Appointed head of Section D in 1887, answering to Monro. Tracked Joseph Moroney round London and confronted him at the Metropole Hotel. Obtained Thomas Callan's confession in Chatham jail in 1888.

MCINTYRE, DETECTIVE SERGEANT PATRICK

Irish-born Special (Irish) Branch man. Sacked from police by Anderson in 1889. Employed by *Times* interests in attempt to prove Pigott letters genuine. Published sensational reminiscences in *Reynolds's Newspaper* (1895), claming that most dynamite plots of 1883–5 were *agent provocateur* stunts.

MATTHEWS, HENRY (1826–1913)

Conservative Home Secretary 1886–90, Catholic criminal lawyer, Paris-educated. Won Irish seat of Dungarvan in 1868. Protégé of Lord Randolph Churchill. Sacked Jenkinson. Pilloried for police failure to catch Whitechapel killer 1888. 'Weak and lazy', according to Jenkinson. Later denied all knowledge of Anderson's propaganda activities.

MELVILLE, INSPECTOR WILLIAM (1852–1918)

Kerry-born Met policeman. S(I)B port-watcher in France 1883–4. Detached by Monro to watch Millen in France. Later head of the Special Branch and the War Office Intelligence Department under the title 'M'.

MONRO, JAMES, CB (1838–1920)

Edinburgh-born policeman. Inspector-general of police, Bengal – appointed assistant commissioner Metropolitan Police in 1884 as head of CID. Appointed head of 'Secret Department' in parallel in January 1887. Resigned as CID chief in 1888 after rows with Commissioner Sir Charles Warren but stayed head of Secret Department. Appointed commissioner at the end of 1888; resigned in 1890. Founded Abode of Mercy medical mission, Ranaghat, Bengal (1891–3). Retired in 1905. Published one book of millenarist theology, *Preparing for the Second Coming.*

MOSER, INSPECTOR MAURICE
> Scotland Yard detective who pursued Jenkinson's agents in Paris. Employed by *The Times* in 1887 in New York hunt for 'Henry'.

THOMSON, INSPECTOR JAMES
> Levant-born policeman employed on anti-Fenian operations from 1867. Worked with Robert Anderson in short-lived Secret Service of 1867–8. Retired from Met in spring 1887 to be 'employed by Anderson on some inquiry'. Went to Boulogne with his wife Martha to meet Millen. Both employed by *The Times* in 1888–9 to negotiate with Millen in New York.

WILLIAMSON, CHIEF CONSTABLE ADOLPHUS FREDERICK ('DOLLY') (1834–89)
> Veteran Scotland Yard detective – worked with Thomson after Clerkenwell explosion; first head of Detective Department and chief superintendent CID. Head of Special (Irish) Branch 1883. Monro's deputy in 1887. Sent to Boulogne to 'frighten' Millen. Died of 'overwork'.

Foreign Office

ARCHIBALD, EDWARD (KCB 1882)
> HM consul-general at New York City 1862–82. Relayed Millen contacts of 1865–7 to London and Dublin Castle.

HOARE, WILLIAM ROBERT
> Acting consul-general New York (1882–9); Millen's contact in the city, according to Davitt. Proved obstructive during the *Times* negotiations with Millen and was recalled to London. Posted thereafter to Hawaii.

PAUNCEFOTE, SIR JULIAN (1828–1902)
> Permanent under-secretary in the Foreign Office from 1882; ambassador to US in 1893. Operational head of HM Foreign Secret Service.

ACKNOWLEDGEMENTS

I am grateful to all who have helped me along the foggy and some-times lonely path in pursuit of the Jubilee plot. I thank the librarians, keepers, staff and IT systems managers of the British Library at St Pancras and Colindale, the Oriental and India Office Collection, BL, the Public Record Office, the Bodleian Library, the University of Birmingham Library (CMS collection), the Salisbury Archives Hat-field House, the Times Newspapers Ltd archives at Wapping, Trinity College, University of Dublin, the Royal Archives, Windsor Castle, the National Library of Ireland and the National Archives of Ireland. I am grateful to David Gale of the Home Office and Val Traylen of the PRO for assistance in the partial public release of the Secret Service papers of Arthur Balfour, Andrew Brown of the Metropolitan Police Service records management service, Eamon Dyas of *The Times* and Ray Seal of the MPS Museum – its remarkable contents now stored in an industrial docklands warehouse – and wish him well with his plan to bring it to the now-shuttered police station at Bow Street, Covent Garden, where many key episodes of this story were enacted.

I am grateful to Susan Donnell of London and New York and to Zoe Lappin of Denver, Colorado for sharing family information on participants in this story, alerted by its first publication. Thanks too to Owen McGee of UCD for further information on IRB figures of the era.

I cannot praise my editor Sophie Nelson enough for bringing towards coherence a narrative embracing a revolutionary organisation that splits like an amoeba, a Whitehall secret service that is not meant to exist, administrations that last six months, and principal characters who change their aliases as readily as they might don a false beard. Thanks to Vivienne Schuster of Curtis Brown and Richard Johnson for making it happen, to Kirsty Hickey and Trevor and Sandra Price of Sodbury House, Clacton, and to my wife Clare and children Katy, Maria and Joe for putting up with a house transformed by files and documents into Probate Court Number One, The Strand, 1889.

PUBLISHED SOURCES

Contemporary Pamphlets

Anderson, Robert, *Behind the Scenes in America* (*Times* reprint, London, 1887)

Anon. *Incipient Irish Revolution* (London, 1888)

Anon., *The Repeal of the Union Conspiracy – Mr Parnell MP and the IRB* (the Black Pamphlet) (London, 1886)

Dixie, Lady Florence, *Ireland and Her Shadow* (Dublin, 1883)

ILPU, *Parnellism Unmasked* (London, 1885)

'Veritas', *Lady Florence Dixie Vindicated* (London, 1883)

Newspapers and Magazines

GREAT BRITAIN AND IRELAND

The Times, *The Echo*, *The Globe*, *The Daily News*, *The Morning Post*, *The Morning Advertiser*, *The Standard*, *The Star*, *The Pall Mall Gazette*, *The Aberdeen Free Press*, *Reynolds's Newspaper*, *Penny Illustrated News*, *Blackwood's Magazine*, *Murray's Magazine*, *The Quarterly Review*, *The Graphic*, *The Labour World*, *Mercy and Truth*, *The Gleaner* (Church Missionary Society), *Akbari* (Journal of the Indian Temperance Association), *The Freeman's Journal*, *The Freeman's Weekly* (Dublin), *United Ireland* (Paris and Dublin)

UNITED STATES

The New York Times, *The New York Herald*, *The New York Mail*, *The New York World*, *The New York Sunday Mercury*, *The Chicago Tribune*, *The Irish World and Industrial Liberator*, *The Irish Nation*, *The United Irishman*, *The Gaelic American*

Memoirs, Biography, Collected Correspondence

Anderson, Sir Robert, *Sidelights on the Home Rule Movement* (London, 1906)

Anderson, Sir Robert, *The Lighter Side of My Official Life* (London, 1910)

Beach, Thomas (Henri Le Caron), *Twenty-five Years in the Secret Service: The Recollections of a Spy* (London, 1894)

Bew, Paul, *C. S. Parnell* (Dublin, 1980)

Blake, Robert, *Disraeli* (London, 1966)

Boyce, D. George, and Alan O'Day (eds.), *Parnell in Perspective* (London, 1991)

Buckle, George Earle, *The Letters of Queen Victoria* (third series, vol. i. 1886–1890; London, 1930)

Churchill, Randolph, and Martin Gilbert, *Winston S. Churchill*, vol. ii (London, 1966)

Cyon, Elie de, *Mémoires et Souvenirs 1886–1894* (Paris, 1895)

Davitt, Michael, *The Fall of Feudalism in Ireland* (New York, 1904)

Denieffe, Joseph, *A Personal Narrative of the Irish Revolutionary Brotherhood* (New York, 1906)

Devoy, John, *Recollections of an Irish Rebel* (New York, 1929)

Gardiner, A. G., Sir William Harcourt, 2 vols (London, 1923)

Gathorne Hardy, A. E., *Gathorne-Hardy 1st Earl of Cranbrook: A Memoir* (London, 1910)

Golway, Terry, *Irish Rebel – John Devoy and America's Fight for Irish Freedom* (New York, 1998)

Gordon, Peter, *The Red Earl, the papers of the 5th Earl Spencer*, vol. ii (Northampton, 1986)

Hardinge, Sir Arthur, *Carnarvon, 4th Earl*, vol. iii (Oxford, 1925)

Hibbert, Christopher, *Victoria: A Personal History* (London, 2000)

Littlechild, J. C., *The Reminiscences of Chief Inspector Littlechild* (London, 1894)

Lyons, F. S. L., *Parnell* (London, 1977)

Marlow, Joyce, *Katharine O'Shea* (London, 1975)

McIntyre, Sergeant Patrick, *Scotland Yard: Its Mysteries and Its Methods* (serialised in *Reynolds's Newspaper* Feb.–Jul. 1895)

O'Connor, T. P., *Memoirs of an Old Parliamentarian*, 2 vols (London, 1928)

O'Leary, John Marcus Bourke (Tralee, 1967)

O'Brien, Conor Cruise, *Parnell and His Party* (Oxford, 1957)

O'Brien, R. Barry, *Parnell*, 2 vols (London, 1899)

O'Brien, William, and Desmond Ryan (ed.), *Devoy's Post Bag*, 2 vols (Dublin, 1948–52)

O'Brien, William, *Evening Memories* (London, 1928)

O'Brien, William, *The Parnell of Real Life* (London, 1926)

Ó'Broin, Leon, *The Prime Informer: A Suppressed Scandal* (London, 1971)

O'Connor, T. P., *A Memory* (London, 1892)

O'Shea, Katherine, *Charles Stewart Parnell: His Love Story and Political Life*, vol. ii (London, 1914)

Robbins, Sir Alfred, *Parnell: The Last Five Years* (London, 1926)

Robert Rhodes James, *Lord Randolph Churchill* (London, 1959)

Roberts, Andrew, *Salisbury: Victorian Titan* (London, 1999)

Ryan, Desmond, *James Stephens, The Fenian Chief* (Dublin, 1967)

Thorold, L., *Henry A. Labouchere* (London, 1913)

Williams, Watkin, *Life of General Sir Charles Warren* (Oxford, 1941)

Young, Kenneth, *Arthur James Balfour* (London, 1963)

Special Studies

Curtis, L. P., *Coercion and Conciliation in Ireland 1880–1892, a study in Conservative Unionism* (Princeton, 1963)

D'Arcy, William, *The Fenian Movement in the United States* (Washington DC, 1947)

Ennis, James T., *The Clan-na-Gael and the Murder of Dr Cronin* (Chicago, 1889)

Fido, Martin, and Keith Skinner, *The Official Encyclopaedia of Scotland Yard* (London, 1996)

Funchion, Michael, *Chicago's Irish Nationalists* (New York, 1976)

Ó'Broin, Leon, *Fenian Fever* (Dublin, 1975)

O'Callaghan, Margaret, *British High Politics and Nationalist Ireland* (Cork, 1994)

Porter, Bernard, *The Origins of the Vigilant State* (London, 1988)

Short, K. R. M., *The Dynamite War – Irish American Bombers in Victorian London* (Dublin, 1976)

Williams, T. Desmond (ed.), *Secret Societies in Ireland* (Dublin, 1973)

NOTES

Abbreviations

AJB	Arthur J. Balfour Papers
AJB-SS	Secret Service papers of Arthur Balfour
AP	Althorp Papers
And	Anderson Papers
BL	British Library
Carn-P	Carnarvon Papers (PRO)
Carn-B	Carnarvon Papers (BL)
CMS	Church Missionary Society
CSO	Chief Secretary's Office
Dev	Devoy Papers
Dav	Davitt Papers
DPB	*Devoy's Post Bag*, edited by William O'Brien and Desmond Ryan, 2 vols (Dublin, 1948–52)
DS-Secret	Duleep Singh Secret Correspondence OIOC
Har	T. Harrington papers
Joyce	W. H. Joyce memorandum NLI
JSS	J. S. Sandars Papers
M-MPS	Monro (Darjeeling memorandum) in the Metropolitan Police Service Museum
MEPO	PRO Metropolitan Police
NAI	National Archives of Ireland
NAI FP	Fenian Papers
NLI	National Library of Ireland
OIOC	Oriental and India Office Collection
PRO	Public Record Office
PROCAT	Public Record Office on-line catalogue
RA	Royal Archives, Windsor
RAC	R. A. Cross Papers
Sals	Salisbury Papers (Hatfield House)
SC	Special Commission Act 1888, Report of the Proceedings reprinted from The Times 4 vols. (London, 1890)
TCD	Trinity College, Dublin
TNL	Times Newspapers Ltd
WEG	W. E. Gladstone Papers
WVH	W. V. Harcourt Papers

A Note on Sources

xxii 'certain Irish revolutionary' Hansard 21 Apr. 1910

xxii 'From its inception' PRO PROCAT MEPO 38

xxii 'No records in the series' Statement to the author by Mr Andrew Brown, Assistant Department Records Officer, Metropolitan Police Service, Aug. 2001

xxii 'All pre-1914 material' Bernard Porter, *Historiography of the Early Special Branch Journal of Intelligence and National Security*, vol. i (London, 1984), p. 382

PART ONE: The Missionary

1

4 'to ask the time' 'Veritas', *Lady Florence Dixie Vindicated* (London, 1883)

5 'the arbitrary force of England'
   Nation, 11 Nov. 1876, quoted in
   (ed.) D. George Boyce and Alan
   O'Day, *Parnell in Perspective*
   (London, 1991), p. 160

6 'You can no more shut' *The
   Times*, 12 Oct. 1887

7 'In former Irish rebellions'
   Harcourt to Hartington, 24
   Dec. 1885 in A. G. Gardiner,
   Harcourt, vol. i (London, 1927),
   p. 553

7 'The highest interests' *Quarterly
   Review*, Oct. 1883, quoted in
   Andrew Roberts, *Salisbury:
   Victorian Titan* (London, 1999),
   p. 275

8 'The gospel of freedom' Lady
   Florence Dixie, *Ireland and Her
   Shadow* (Dublin, 1883)

9 'They all say here' Jenkinson to
   Spencer, 22 Mar. 1883 AP KS
   246

9 'It was all very mysterious' Det.
   Sgt Patrick McIntyre, *Scotland
   Yard – Its Mysteries and Its
   Methods*, *Reynolds's Newspaper*,
   3 Feb. 1896

9 'God knows I would' Dixie to
   Ponsonby, 29 Mar. 1883 RA
   Vic/Z210/24

10 'she did not wish to have' Yvonne
   Demskoff, 'Assassination Attempts
   on Queen Victoria' 2001
   www.users.uniserve.com/
   ~canyon/attempts

11 'It is worth being shot at' ibid.

11 'It is stated in "The Observer"'
   Ponsonby to Granville, 3 Apr.
   1881 FO 5/1776

2

13 'General Millen – Dynamitard'
   SC, i, p. 4

14 'General Francis' *New York
   Herald*, 11 Apr. 1889

15 'When 19 years old' *New York
   Times*, 11 Apr. 1889

16 'a series of pyrotechnical displays'
   The Times, 1 June 1887

16 'The more this Irish conspiracy'
   ibid.

3

18 'And Jesus sent them' James
   Monro, 'A Medical Mission to
   Rural Bengal' *Mercy and Truth*
   (Journal of the Church
   Missionary Society, 1897),
   pp. 55–9 and letters in the CMS
   archives

19 'From early morning the crowd'
   ibid.

19 'The time will surely' ibid.

19 'The Secret Agent of State' PRO
   HO 144/208/148000M, HO
   144/189/A46281

19 'the enmity of certain aristocrats'
   M-MPS

20 'because he had' M-MPS

21 'Stimulate the police' quoted in
   Beggs and Skinner, *Jack the
   Ripper* (London, 1991), p. 311

21 'I know that, when he died' I. C.
   Monro to Scott, 26 Dec. 1951
   PRO MEPO 2/1041

21 'The times needed' *The Times*,
   30 Jan. 1920

22 'It appears that we have' Scott to
   Monro, 20 Dec. 1951 PRO
   MEPO 2/2041

22 'noiseless shoes' *Cassell's
   Magazine*, Feb. 1890

25 FN *The Star*, 19, 28 Nov. 1888

4

26 'My dear Charlie,' M-MPS

27 'We understand that Mr Monro'
   The Times, 16 June 1890 in PRO
   HO 144/307

27 'wished his children' M-MPS

28 'suggestions involving illegal'
   Monro to Home Secretary, 28
   May 1886 HO 144/721

28 'I remember as though' Sir

Robert Anderson, 'The Lighter
Side of My Official Life',
Blackwood's Magazine, Feb.
1910
29 'This was the Jubilee year'
M-MPS

5

32 'There was a hellish plot'
Anderson, *Blackwoods'*, Feb. 1910
32 'He ["Jenks"] brought his wife'
ibid.
32 FN 'Jinks' Anderson, *Lighter Side*
(London, 1910)
33 'The article written' Mrs M.
Thomson to W. S. Churchill, 2
Feb. 1910 PRO HO/144/926
A49962/5a
33 'a secret intelligence system' ibid.
33 FN 'Home Office records' see
minute from Henry to Troup, 28
Mar. 1910 PRO HO/144/926/
A49962/5b
34 'Later, as my husband' Thomson
to Churchill PRO HO/144/926
A49962/5a

6

35 'To the present hour' *Blackwood's*,
Apr. 1910
36 'More than a month' Thomson to
Churchill, 28 Mar. 1910 PRO
HO/144/926/A49962
36 'Mr Thomson retired' ibid.
37 'Amazing Confession' *Daily
News*, 7 Apr. 1910
37 'I disclaim any connection'
Morning Post, 8 Apr. 1910
38 'The alleged statement' PRO
HO/144/926/A49962/35
39 'Mr Monro is desirous' D.
Littlejohn to E. Wason MP, 9
Apr. 1910 PRO HO/144/926/
A49962
39 'Mr Anderson' Troup to Asquith,
8 Apr. 1910 PRO HO/144/
926/A49962/7

7

42 'extreme gravity' Hansard, 11
Apr. 1910
42 'If Sir Robert Anderson' ibid.
43 'If only the Government' *The
Times*, letters, 12 Apr. 1910
43 'I have communicated with'
Hansard, 13 Apr. 1910
43 'Mr Monro did not' Monro to
Troup, 13 Apr. 1910 PRO HO/
144/926/A49962/36
43 'Why is it that Sir Robert'
Hansard, 14 Apr. 1910
43 'Has the Right Hon Gentleman
seen' ibid.
43 'Had the Home Secretary' ibid.
44 'In 1887 I was' Monro to Troup,
13 Apr. 1910 PRO HO/144/
926/A49962/36
46 'I think that in reply' PRO HO/
144/926/A49962/43
46 'Please point out to S of S' ibid.
46 'The heading should be' ibid.
46 'I take it that' Hansard, 21 Apr.
1910
47 'gross boastfulness' ibid.
47 FN 'If you wish to stop' PRO
HO/144/926/A49962/56
47 FN 'To me it is an echo' *The
Times*, 30 Apr. 1910
48 'Sir Robert has behaved' WSC to
King Edward VII, 22 Apr. 1910
in Randolph Churchill and Martin
Gilbert, *Winston S. Churchill*
(London, 1966), vol. ii,
pp. 1010–11
49 'It is a public scandal' PRO HO/
144/926/A49962/5b
49 'no reference in our archives'
PRO HO/144/926/A49962

PART TWO: The General

8

54 'Friends of Ireland Club' 'An
Account of Fenianism by one of
the Head Centres for Ireland
1865–1866' (F. F. Millen) in

S. L. Anderson papers NLI Ms 5964

54 'like a ruffian' ibid.

55 'She had been talking that day of America' Queen Victoria's Journal, 12 Feb. 1865 RA

55 'My General's pay' Millen, op. cit. NLI Ms 5964

56 'Next year is the year' John Devoy, *Recollections of an Irish Rebel* (New York, 1929), p. 55

56 'We'll get all the arms' ibid., p. 55

56 'after fourteen years' Millen, op. cit. NLI Ms 5964

56 'Ireland would be as loyal' ibid.

57 'would like to see the view' ibid.

57 'When I complained' *New York Times*, 6 Dec. 1866

58 'Between June and September' Millen, op. cit. NLI Ms 5964

59 'felt hats' W. D'Arcy, *The Fenian Movement in the United States 1858–86* (Washington DC, 1947) p. 72

60 'We found Millen at tea' Devoy, op. cit., p. 75

60 'they had no confidence' ibid., p. 73

60 'It was too dangerous' Millen, op. cit. NLI Ms 5964

61 'Seeing the thing was run' *New York Times*, 6 Dec. 1866

61 'General Mellon' Archibald to Larcom, 22 Dec. 1865 NAI CSO A.123

9

62 'I have just got your note' O'Mahony Papers NLI pos. 740

63 'O'Mahony could not even afford' Millen, op. cit. NLI Ms 5964

64 'a complete circle round the city' Supt Ryan to HO, 18 Feb. 1866 PRO HO 45/7799/74

65 'shoot her father dead' Edith Archibald, Life and Letters of E

M Archibald (Toronto, 1924) p. 166

65 'proceed to England' 10 Mar. 1866 FO 5/1336

65 'Frank Martin' 13 Mar. 1866 NAI FP A.139

66 'The city is alive' Archibald to FO, 17 Mar. 1866 FO 5/1336

66 'active service muster' ibid.

66 'He is a native of the County Tyrone' Archibald to FO, 20 Mar. 1866
PRO FO 5/1336; also NAI FP A.125

66 'He has today furnished me' ibid.

67 'Herne in Dungarvan' NAI FP A.125; also PRO FO 5/1336

67 'The greatest precautions' Wodehouse to Larcom, 28 Apr. 1866 NAI FP A.139

68 'I have a son' John Beach to FO, 28 Mar. 1866 HO PRO 5/1366

69 'I arrived here' 'James Thompson' (Millen) to Archibald, 9 May 1866 PRO FO 5/1338

70 'the unlawful expedition' PRO FO 5/1340

71 'deemed so secret' Sir Robert Anderson, *Sidelights on the Home Rule Movement* (London, 1906), p. 37

71 'Informant M' NAI Police Reports Box 4

71 'The first blow' Pierrepont Edwards to FO, 6 Nov. 1866 PRO FO 5/1340

72 'I have the honour to report' ibid., 27 Nov. 1866

72 'Edward Duffy' ibid., 28 Nov. 1866

73 'Stephens declared for battle' *New York Times*, 6 Dec. 1866

73 'would interfere with' 7 Dec. 1866 PRO FO 5/1340

73 'The number of serviceable' 'Smith' (Tevis) to Bruce, 7 Jan. 1867 ibid.

74 'Would the British Government'
   21 June 1867 ibid.
74 'he incurs considerable' S. L.
   Anderson to Naas (Earl Mayo),
   19 July 1867 NAI Fenian Police
   Papers 3/629/1742
74 'I have arranged' Mayo papers
   NLI Ms 1146

10
75 'without the knowledge'
   Thomson typewritten memoirs in
   PRO HO/144/926/A49962
76 'By God, Burke' Court Report,
   The Times, 25 Nov. 1867
77 'The mob were quiet and orderly'
   The Times, 24 Nov. 1867
78 'overworked' Thomson
   memorandum, 18 Dec. 1867
   PRO MEPO 3/1788
78 'man with a brown overcoat' *The
   Times*, 18 Dec. 1867
79 'so many doll's houses'
   *Reminiscences of Chief Inspector
   Littlechild* (London, 1894), p. 11
81 'With a force of 8,000 men'
   Hardy to Disraeli, A. E. Gathorne
   Hardy, 1st Earl of Cranbrook, *A
   Memoir* (London, 1910), p. 221
81 'set up in an anonymous'
   Anderson, *Sidelights on Home
   Rule*, p. 37
81 'If Mayne will not have' Gathorne
   Hardy, op. cit., p. 224
82 'Little better than' ibid., p 249
82 'In a few days I received' Beach
   (Le Caron), *Twenty-five Years in
   the Secret Service* (London, 1894),
   p. 37
82 'Informant B' NAI Police Reports
   Box 4

PART THREE: The Clan
11
86 'You may look upon', 19 Jan.
   1872 DPB, i, p. 9
87 'You would marvel at' quoted in

Desmond Ryan, *James Stephens,
The Fenian Chief* (Dublin, 1967),
p. 274
88 'Those of Irish birth' Le Caron,
   op. cit., p. 117
88 'grotesque' *Gaelic American*, 29
   Nov. 1924
89 'There are Americans in
   England' 17 Feb. 1868 PRO FO
   5/1343
89 FN 'His remarks proved' Devoy,
   Recollections, p. 250
90 'unkind reply' R. Smith to FO,
   9 July 1868 PRO FO 5/1344
90 'Plots for such purposes'
   Thornton to Granville, 10 July
   1869 PRO FO 5/1346
91 'cold, quiet voice' Devoy, op cit.,
   p. 189
91 'be treated with every' John
   Denvir, *Life Story of an Old Rebel*
   (Dublin, 1910) p. 72
92 'It seems humiliating' *Perth
   Inquirer*, quoted in *The Times*,
   'The Escaped Fenians', 4 Aug.
   1876

12
95 'Fancy autonomy' quoted in
   Robert Blake, *Disraeli* (London,
   1966), p. 579
96 'friends returning to relatives'
   Carroll to Devoy, 19 Oct. 1876
   DPB, i, p. 207
96 'salt-water enterprise' Carroll to
   Devoy, 1 Feb. 1877 DPB, i,
   p. 230
96 'That war between England'
   Devoy, op. cit., p. 400
97 'most isolated and defenceless'
   Callaghan to Carnarvon, 18 May
   1877 PRO FO 5/1559
97 'cool – extremely so' O'Kelly to
   Devoy, 5 Aug. 1877 DPB, i,
   p. 268
97 'I think it would be well' O'Kelly
   to Devoy, 30 Oct. 1877 DPB, i,
   p. 276

97 'I have lately read' Millen to Carroll, 20 Nov. 1877 DPB, i, pp. 282–3

98 'Brothers. Not Since the time' 23 Dec. 1877 DPB, i, pp. 288–92

99 'General F. F. Millen, believed' Crump to Thornton, 5 Apr. 1878 PRO FO 5/1706

99 'A rising of the Fenians' Crump to FO, 16 May 1878 FO 5/1707

100 'If he was in favour' Carroll to Devoy, 24 July 1906 DPB, i, p. 298

13

102 'Nationalists here' Michael Davitt, *The Fall of Feudalism in Ireland* (New York, 1904), p. 125

102 'well-known revolutionist' Davitt to Special Commission, 3 July 1889 SC iii, p.592

102 'I fear your proposal' Davitt to Devoy, 13 Feb. 1879 DPB, i, p. 391

102 'I feel certain' Millen to Carroll, 10 Sep. 1878 DPB, i, p. 352

103 'I say that one million' O'Kelly to Davitt, 10 Mar. 1879 DPB, i, p. 409

104 'It is proper to state here' Carroll to Devoy, 11 Mar. 1879 DPB, i, p. 413

104 'an agricultural instructor' DPB, i, p. 430

104 'noted for its arms factories' 'Morgan' to the FC of the VC, 8 Aug. 1879 FO 5/1745

105 'talk was at an end' Carroll to O'Leary, 23 Apr. 1879 DPB, i, p. 431

105 'The men were very earnest' FO 5/1745

105 'A system of time torpedoes' 12 Apr. 1879 FO 5/1707

105 'It is signed by' Archibald to FO, 17 Oct. 1879 F0 5/1707

106 'as wrong as possible' Carroll to Devoy, 17 June 1879 DPB, i, p. 447

106 'Gentle Torpedo' Davitt, 6 Feb. 1880 DPB, i, p. 483

14

109 'the land of Ireland' Davitt op. cit. p. 160

110 'a political adventurer' Carroll DPB, i, pp. 523–5

111 'queerest Irish paper' Devoy, *Recollections*, p. 329

111 'soaped the stairs at Windsor' *Labour World*, 11 Oct. 1890

111 'workman's son' *The Times*, 18 Jan. 1881

111 'extended system of terror' Queen's Speech, 7 Jan. 1881

111 'For every Irishman' Devoy speech, 18 Jan. 1881 DPB, i, p. 42

112 'to devote himself exclusively' Bernard Porter, *The Origins of the Vigilant State* (London, 1988), p. 41

112 'a fanatic of the deepest dye' Devoy, op. cit., p. 212

112 'the manufacture and preparation' Lomasney to Devoy, 24 Dec. 1880 DPB, ii, p. 27

113 'to scare and scatter an empire' Lomasney, Mar. 1881 DPB, ii, p. 54

113 'I feel he is greatly' Lomasney, 18 Feb. 1881 DPB, ii, p. 40

113 'The lives of your Queen', anon. to Thornton, 25 Jan. 1882 FO 5/1776

113 'Knights of Hassan' C. C. Montague to Thornton, 23 Mar. 1881 FO 5/1777

113 'Dynamite will be deposited' Thornton to Granville 11 Apr. 1881 PRO FO 5/1777

NOTES 393

114 'I am informed that explosives' Clipperton to FO, 24 Mar. 1881 PRO FO 5/1777
114 'Another scheme is' ibid.
114 'I hear from different secret' ibid.
115 'one of our friends' Le Caron, op. cit., p. 171
115 'You furnish the sinews' Beach op. cit, pp. 172–87
115 FN 'that conversation' DPB vol. ii, pp. 85–6
116 'sharp-toothed, thin-lipped' William O'Brien, *Evening Memories* (London, 1928), p. 142
116 'forty lawyers, two judges' Beach, op. cit, p. 203
117 'We mean war' SC, 9 Feb. 1889
117 'they were prepared to use' ibid.
118 'invested in US bonds' Beach to Anderson, Jan. 1882 PRO HO 144/72

15
122 'of polished wood' 28 June 1882 PRO FO 5/1818
122 'a fishing and shooting' 20 June 1882 PRO FO 5/1818 (this cable is minuted 'not to go to the Queen')
122 'masculine-looking woman' Naples consul to FO, 15 July 1882 PRO FO/5/1819
122 '*mitrailleuse*' NY consul to FO, 25 July 1882 PRO FO/5/1819
123 'mutiny magistrate' Hansard, 3 Aug. 1882
123 'mules destined for Egypt' NAI A739/740
124 'like a gascock' ibid.
124 'Several at the table' Harcourt to Spencer 10 Mar. 1883 Gardiner, Harcourt i, p. 479
124 'Irish Bureau' see McIntyre, *Reynolds's Newspaper*, 2 Oct. 1895 for a sketch of the department's early days.

Catholics with Irish roots were preferred candidates.
125 'Head of Political Crime' Jenkinson memo, 22 Mar. 1883 WVH 103
125 'There seem to be great' Jenkinson to Spencer, 22 Mar. 1883 AP KS 246

16
126 'Egan expressed strong' *Gaelic American*, 17 Nov. 1923
127 'he might have been an actor' McIntyre, *Reynolds's Newspaper*, 24 Feb. 1895
127 'Jenks has done splendidly' Harcourt to Spencer, WVH 72
127 'unlawfully compassing' trial reports, *The Times*, 11–16 June 1883
128 'from the old man' ibid.
129 'Where is he living now' Jenkinson to Anderson, 21 Dec. 1882 PRO HO 144/1538

17
130 'James McDermott, NY' the original is in Dav TCD Ms 9441
130 'he was on a visit' *Labour World*, 4 Oct. 1890
130 'ex-member of the secret service' ibid.
131 'romantic marriage' ibid.
131 'Peter Quigley' Dav TCD Ms 9441
131 FN 'I have had a cypher' Jenkinson to Doyle, 27 Dec. 1882 AP KS 246
133 'very amused' Jenkinson to Harcourt, 31 May 1883 WVH 103
134 'This is the body' *New York Herald*, 22–23 July 1883 in PRO FO 5/1862
134 'Jim McDermott was safe' Jenkinson to Spencer, 19 Aug. 1883 AP KS 247

135 'I have had James McDermott
    arrested' 7 Aug. 1883, ibid.
135 'Mr Nicholson' *Labour World*,
    25 Oct. 1890

18

136 'an adventurer' DPB, ii, p. 131
136 'I have never seen' O'Leary to
    Devoy DPB, ii, p. 132
137 'one of the many expedients'
    St John to FO, 3 July 1883
    PRO FO 252/193
137 'General Millen's antecedents' 6
    Sep. 1883 FO 252/192
137 'The head of the Irish
    assassination' Carden to FO, 6
    Apr. 1883 PRO FO 5/1861
137 'lack of courage' Beach, op. cit.,
    p. 217
138 'The [Clan] leaders now'
    Jenkinson to Spencer, 18 June
    1883 AP KS 247
138 For the underground railway
    attacks see PRO HO 45/9638
138 'I gave Harcourt warning'
    Jenkinson to Spencer, 31 Oct.
    1883 AP KS 247
138 'It is impossible to get legal' ibid.
139 'D. O'Brien, the Famous Irish
    Story Teller' police report, 24
    Dec. 1883 in WVH 102
139 'very dry' ibid.
139 'there is something big afoot' 17
    Oct. 1883 AP KS 247
139 'blossom into the most'
    McIntyre, *Reynold's Newspaper*,
    17 Mar. 1895
140 'unusual quartz buttons' trial of
    Burton and Cunningham, *The
    Times*, 11–18 July 1883
140 'We have several plans'
    Clipperton to FO, 3 Mar. 1884
    PRO FO 5/
140 FN Dupont *see* Clipperton to
    Sackville-West, 4 Mar. 1884
    PRO FO 5/1928
141 'men sent over' ibid.
141 'explode a little dynamite' ibid.

141 'We must bury this' Harcourt to
    Spencer, 8 Mar. 1884 AP KS 150
142 'the English people' Clipperton
    to FO, 14 Mar. 1884 PRO FO
    5/1928

19

144 'Gentlemen, I am no assassin'
    DPB, ii, p. 242
144 FN 'They had the most perfect'
    Clipperton to FO, 12 Oct. 1883
    PRO FO 5/1862
144 'Daly is still' Jenkinson to
    Spencer, 3 Apr. 1884 AP KS
    247
144 'These things are three hand
    bombs' Jenkinson to Spencer,
    12 Apr. 1884 AP KS 247
145 'The bomb only had' Lewis
    Harcourt diary, 27 Apr. 1884
    WVH 44
145 'a little game going' Jenkinson
    to Spencer, 3 Apr. 1884 AP KS
    247
146 'Hand in hand' Jenkinson to
    Spencer, 18 Apr. 1884 AP KS
    247
146 'It was all due to' 12 Apr. 1884
    AP KS 247
146 'relieved of all duties', Porter op.
    cit. p. 46
147 'You cannot imagine' Jenkinson
    to Spencer, 31 May 1884 AP KS
    247
147 'to deal with secret societies'
    Harcourt to Queen, 25 June
    1884 WVH 692
148 'little energy or originality'
    Jenkinson to Spencer, 15
    Dec. 1884 AP KS 250

PART FIVE: Spymaster-General

20

151 'wig and false beard' Carnarvon
    to Salisbury 7 Jan. 1886 Carn-P
    PRO 30/6/53. 'His work is

very difficult and dangerous, the
Lord Lieutenant told the Prime
Minsister, ' he is obliged to take
his life in his hands, to give
meetings and wear disguises and
go very quietly without anyone
knowing it.'

151 'extreme revolutionary views'
Davitt, op. cit., p. 438; also
United Ireland, 2 July 1884

151 'conspirator after conspirator'
ibid.

152 'Jenkinson is dangerous'
Hamilton to Spencer, 12 July
1884 AP KS 274

152 'This gentleman was supposed',
'The Dynamitards in Paris by
One Who Knows Them', *Echo*,
22 Apr. 1884

153 'a scare on a grand scale'
Jenkinson to Spencer, 15
Sep. 1884 AP KS 250

153 'illegitimate daughter of Prince
Albert' Davitt, 'Notes of an
Amateur Detective' Dav TCD
Ms 9551, p. 22

153 'dramatically escaping' Anon.,
*The Repeal of the Union
Conspiracy, Mr Parnell MP and
the IRB* (London, 1886)

154 'He behaved so badly' Jenkinson
to Harcourt, 21 Feb. 1885
WVH 103

154 'obtaining a conviction',
Jenkinson to Spencer, 28 July
1884 AP KS 250

154 'In England and also' Jenkinson
to Spencer, 4 Sep. 1884 AP KS
250

21

156 'A contemptible affair' Jenkinson
to Spencer, 3 Jan. 1885 AP KS
250

157 'Dynamite Saturday' *Brewer's
Dictionary of Phrase and Fable*
(1st ed., London, 1898)

157 'very reliable source' Jenkinson

to Monro, 26 Dec. 1884 AP KS
250

158 'glass buttons' M-MPS

158 'coaching witnesses' ibid.

158 For Commander McNeile *see*
Sackville-West to Pauncefote, 8
Apr. 1885 PRO FO 5/1931

159 'loaded with all the necessary',
Sackville-West to FO, 3 May
1886 PRO FO 5/1931

159 'I am dreadfully upset'
Jenkinson to Spencer, 10 Jan.
1885 AP KS 250

159 'England's invisible enemy'
United Irishman, 4 Apr. 1885;
reprint in PRO FO 97/475

159 FN 'the Russian may escape
hanging' William O'Brien, *The
Parnell of Real Life* (London,
1926), p. 92

160 'George Washington' *United
Irishman*, 4 Apr. 1885

22

163 'My Lord, I received a visit'
Carden to Granville, 29 Apr.
1885 PRO FO 5/1931

163 'Inform the chief clerk'
Pauncefote to Carden, 10 May
1885 PRO FO 5/1932

163 'Secret and urgent' FO to
Carden, 16 May 1885 PRO FO
5/1932

163 'Name of person General F. F.
Millen' Carden to FO, 17 May
1885 PRO FO 5/1932

164 'Private. Should you mind'
Plunkett to Currie, 11 May
1885 PRO FO 5/1932

165 'I have been taking advantage'
Jenkinson to Spencer, 1 Mar.
1885 AP KS 250

165 'It is monstrous that' Jenkinson
to Spencer, 21 May 1885, ibid.

165 'very sorry' 22 May 1885, ibid.

165 'come to France or Germany'
FO to Carden, 10 May 1885
PRO FO 5/1932

165 'Secret. If he comes' FO to Carden, 20 May 1885 PRO FO 5/1932
166 'to fetch papers from' Carden to FO, 22 May 1885 PRO FO 5/1932
166 'I have the honour to report' Carden to Granville, 23 May 1885 PRO FO 5/1932
167 'to supply the information' Harcourt to Spencer, 23 June 1885 AP KS 151
168 'cabinet of equals' Cross to Monro and Jenkinson, 7 July 1886 PRO HO 144/721

23

170 'The General will not be entitled' Jenkinson memo, 30 May 1885 PRO FO 5/1932
170 'daily interviews' Carden to Salisbury, 11 July 1885 PRO FO 5/1932
171 'Secret. My Lord . . .' ibid.
171 'The information now sent' Jenkinson to Pauncefote, 12 Aug. 1885 PRO FO 5/1932
172 'The Parnellites were not to be trusted', quoted in Roberts, *Salisbury*, p. 349
172 'any bargain with them', ibid.
172 'would hand over Ireland', Harcourt to Ponsonby, 1 July 1885 WVH 3 f. 151–4
173 'risky and devious' Roberts, op. cit., p. 351

24

174 'at the seaside' Jenkinson to Cross, 3 Sep. 1885 Carn-P PRO 30/6/62
174 'At present the situation' ibid.
174 'When you write to me' Carnarvon to Jenkinson, 17 Sep. 1885 Carn-B BL Add Mss 60829
174 'deficient in the detail' Carden to Salisbury, 3 Sep. 1885 PRO FO 5/1932
175 'He has given me to understand' ibid
175 'This report is' Jenkinson to Pauncefote, 17 Oct. 1885 PRO FO 5/1932
175 'If the hopes of' Jenkinson to Carnarvon, 26 Sep. 1885 Carn-P PRO 30/6/62
175 'It is therefore clear' ibid.
175 'secret dinner' ibid.
176 'we have no proof that' ibid.
176 'FO to Carden' 9 Oct. 1885 PRO FO 5/1932
176 'I would suggest forty pounds a month' Carden to Salisbury, 10 Oct. 1885 PRO FO 5/1932
176 'Start X at once' Salisbury to Carden, 12 Oct. 1885 PRO FO 5/1932
177 'XXX starts tonight' Carden to Salisbury, 15 Oct. 1885 PRO FO 5/1932
177 'I may have to go over' Jenkinson to Carnarvon, 2 Nov. 1885 Carn-P PRO 30/6/62
177 FN 'I had no idea you would send it' 6 Nov. 1885, ibid.
178 'Home Rule could not come' Jenkinson to Carnarvon, 6 Nov. 1885 Carn-B Add Mss 60829
178 'He thinks it must' ibid.
178 'leading Fenians in New York' ibid.
178 'The man from America' Jenkinson to Carnarvon, 11 Nov. 1885 Carn-P 30/6/62
179 FN Millen's expenses are in Carden to FO, 14 Oct. 1885 FO 5/1932

PART SIX: The Fall

25

183 FN 'I mean to hit back a stunner' 2 Nov. 1885, Katherine O'Shea, *Charles Stewart Parnell:*

His Love Story and Political Life (London, 1914), vol. ii, p. 90

184 'Secret and Private. I have to intimate' Jenkinson to Gladstone, 11 Dec. 1885 WEG BL Add Mss 44493

185 'Secret. I agree' Gladstone to Jenkinson, 12 Dec. 1885, ibid.

185 'The face of British politics' Roberts, op. cit., p. 362

185 'If five-sixths of the Irish people' *The Times*, 12 Dec. 1885

185 'GOM had a conversation' J. W. Flanagan, undated Parnell Box 4 TNL

185 'had evidence of the urgency' WEG BL Add Mss 49692/7

186 'I am very much disturbed' 17 Jan. 1885 AP KS 252

188 'Parnellism *Unmasked*' Windsor Castle was sent a copy. The Queen's private secretary told Lord Carnarvon: ' I have received a curious pamphlet called Parnellism...it probably came from Pigott who hates Parnell. Pigott when I was absent, asked the Queen for assistance and my deputy sent the usual answer – refusing. Ponsonby to Carnarvon. 15 Dec. 1885 PRO 30/6/54

189 'Mr Maurice Murphy' Pigott SC, 21 Feb. 1889, ii, pp. 345–8 and Soames SC, 1 Mar. 1889, ii, pp. 418–23

190 'liberty guaranteed' Sheridan to Thornton, 13 Mar. 1886 FO 5/1975

190 FN 'the lengths to which Parnell' Patrick Maume, 'Parnell and the IRB Oath', *Irish Historical Studies*, xxix, no. 116 (May 1995), p. 370

191 'Invincibles' see, for example, Warren to Jenkinson, 21 May 1886 PRO HO 144/721

192 'Gas and bunkum' Gosselin to

Jenkinson, 6 Mar. 1886 AP KS 252

193 'by orders of the members' Anon., *The Repeal of the Union Conspiracy*

193 'assuming him to be' Monro memo PRO HO 144/721 Dec. 1885

194 'school of private detectives' Monro memo PRO HO 144/721

194 'It is my duty' Jenkinson to Spencer, 13 June 1885 AP KS 252

26

196 'Five Irish-Americans' Pigott SC, 21 Feb. 1889, ii, pp. 345–8 and Soames SC, ii, 1 Mar. 1889, pp. 418–23

196 'I have no faith' Jenkinson to Spencer, 10 July 1886 AP KS 252

197 'I am afraid we shall' ibid.

197 'a suspicious looking bag' Elliot to FO, 10 July 1886 PRO FO 146/2844

197 'I have an agency' Jenkinson to Pauncefote, 17 July 1886 PRO FO 146/2820

198 'An exposé of my past' Jenkinson to Matthews, 22 July 1886 PRO HO 144/721

199 'had sent out emissaries' Jenkinson memo, 5 Aug. 1886 in AP KS 252

200 'We were escorted by a group' O'Brien, *Evening Memories*, p. 139

200 'From the start one personality' ibid., p. 142

201 'had an interview' Dav TCD Ms 9365

201 'Chicago Fenian' Cope to FO, 4 Sep. 1886 FO 5/1975

202 'supposed dynamitards' Monro to Matthews, 28 Sep. 1886 PRO FO 5/1975

202 'I don't know why' Jenkinson to
Matthews, 18 Oct. 1886 PRO
HO 144/721

202 'central political crime'
Jenkinson to Matthews (copy),
28 Oct. 1886 AP KS 252

202 'I regret that today' Matthews
to Jenkinson (copy), 11
Dec. 1886 AP KS 252

203 'I believe that from the moment'
Jenkinson to Spencer, 11
Dec. 1886 AP KS 252

203 'You have the ball at your feet'
Dav TCD Ms 9365

204 'I see in the papers' Annabella
Jenkinson to Spencer, 25
Dec. 1886 AP KS 250

27

205 'I had no wish to succeed'
Monro M-MPS

206 'for the private anti-Fenian
agents' Troup, 8 Apr. 1910
PRO HO/144/926/A49962/7

206 'assistant in the secret work' ibid.

206 'need not repay' Matthews
(undated) PRO HO/144/926/
A49962/1e

206 'Mr Monro came over'
Pauncefote to Lushington, 16
Feb. 1887 PRO FO 5/2044

207 'Inform Hicks-Beach' NY consul
to FO, 16 Feb. 1887 PRO FO
5/2044

207 'This telegram was sent' 18
Feb. 1887, ibid.

208 FN 'in the Council of the
Fenian', United Irishman
June-Jul. 1887

208 FN 'the police chief of New
York', ibid.

209 FN NAI Crime reports 5935
26–28 Jan. 1887

210 'escort her round town' minutes
of evidence taken before Select
Committee on House of
Commons (Admission of
Strangers) HMSO 1888, p. 37

211 'General Millen returned' Dillon
to Devoy NLI Ms 18003

210 FN 'It had come to this'
Salisbury to Cross, 12 Jan. 1887
RAC BL Add Mss 51263

214 'Many Irish fugitives' Elie de
Cyon, Mémoires et Souvenirs
1886–1894 (Paris, 1895),
pp. 274–6

214 'Shortly after the conversion'
Labour World, 1 Nov. 1890

215 FN 'SC came over' Dav TCD
Ms 9551

217 'attract 13,000 Irish' Tevis to
Duleep Singh, 15 May 1887
OIOC IOR R/1/1/66

218 'The F[enian] B[rotherhood]'
Michael Breslin to Devoy, 14
Mar. 1887 DPB, ii, p. 302. M.
Breslin was an ex-Dublin
policeman, the brother of
John J. Breslin, the prison
warder who sprang James
Stephens from prison in 1865.
Both became prominent
Clansmen.

218 'a cloud of detectives' Morier to
Salisbury PRO FO 65/1296

219 'to paralyse the foreign policy'
Le Voltaire, 22 Mar. 1887

220 'He went at once to Paris'
Monro, 4 Nov. 1887 PRO HO
144/1357

PART SEVEN: In the Year of
the Jubilee

28

223 'deliberately allying' The Times,
7 Mar. 1887

224 see Lyons Charles Stewart
Parnell p. 372 and gov. of
Limerick prison to Anderson 11
Nov. 1887 and PRO HO 144/
1538. Anderson was actively
working in support of the
'letters' from autumn 1887
onwards. The Times official
history states he examined the

Kilmainham letter the 'very month the Special Commission began its sittings,' that is, almost a year later.

224 'We place before our readers' *The Times*, 18 Apr. 1887

225 'Dear Anderson' Arnold-Forster to Anderson, 14 Apr. 1887 and PRO HO 144/1537

225 'I have seen Buckle' 19 Apr. 1887, ibid.

225 'quasi-constitutionalists' *The Times*, 13 May 1887

225 FN 'Mr Arnold-Forster pressed' *The Times*, 30 Apr. 1910

226 'Extreme nationalists' *New York Times*, 4 May 1887

226 'Mr Parnell should have no' *Morning Advertiser*, 28 May 1887

228 'It is definitely known that' *The Times*, 1 June 1887

228 FN 'J. Murphy, Ex-Detective Inspector' 22 Sep. 1888 TNL

229 'I send you a note' Monro to FO, 19 May 1887 PRO FO 5/2044

229 'There is no trace' Bernal to FO, 25 May 1887 PRO FO 5/2044

230 'Nothing of importance came to pass' Beach, op. cit., p. 250

230 FN 'inspired by the confidence' Anderson, *The Lighter Side . . .*, p. 295

230 FN 'We thought that Millen' M-MPS

29

231 'wrench India' 10 May 1887 Ganda Singh (ed.), *The Duleep Singh Correspondence* (Patiala, 1977), p. 374

231 'Your Highness, your business' 30 May 1887 DS-Secret OIOC

232 'had deputed Supt Thomson' M-MPS

232 'He was employed privately' minute from Henry to Troup,

28 Mar. 1910 PRO HO/144/926/A49962/5b

233 'Mr Thomson retired from the force' ibid.

233 FN 'Inspector Melville £25' Treasury to HO, 6 Feb. 1888 PRO HO 144/211/A48482. Agreeing payment the Treasury Secretary expressed certain doubts about the Jubilee plot: 'I am not of course in a position to form an accurate opinion of the amount of peril . . .'

234 'Gentle T called on Genl Z' Dav TCD Ms 9551

234 'I had no doubt' M-MPS

234 'like a Metropolitan Police man' M-MPS

234 'As you are aware' Monro to Matthews, 14 June 1887 PRO HO144/275/A60551

235 'His correspondence should be noted' ibid.

235 'It is also reported' ibid.

235 FN 'If any attempt' *St Louis Republican*, 2 June 1887

236 'In view of the 21st June', Matthews to Pauncefote 14 June 1887 PRO FO 5/2044

237 'I am directed' FO to Surplice, 14 June 1887 PRO FO 5/2044

237 'Millen. Description' 17 June 1887 PRO FO 5/2044

238 'Macadaras. Age 45' ibid.

238 'Have you any special information' *Morning Advertiser*, 17 June 1887

239 'We are assured' ibid.

239 For the 'Bluemantle' affair *see* PRO HO 144/190/A46470B

239 'What an opportunity' ibid.

239 'million Irish dead' *New York World*, 22 June 1887 in PRO FO 282/27

240 'Let us hope' ibid.

240 'I did not let my children' M-MPS

240 'Mr Gladstone' Buckle, *The*

Letters of Queen Victoria (third series, vol. i, p. 324)

240 'I never was in a more delicate' M-MPS

PART EIGHT: Delusion

30

245 'Drexel & Co.' PRO DPP 4/23
245 'many letters to London' Tournon to Surplice, 23 June 1887 PRO FO 5/2044
246 'The following information' Lyons to Pauncefote, 30 June 1887 PRO HO 144/275/
246 'His mission here' *New York World*, 12 Sep. 1887 in PRO FO 5/1987
248 'Parnell is the leader' Jenkinson to Spencer, 28 May 1887 AP KS 252
248 'The action of secret' printed memo, 4 June 1887 in AP KS 252
248 'When I got home' Jenkinson to Spencer, 12 July 1887 AP KS 252
248 'Fatal Accident' *The Times*, 12 July 1887
248 'after landing from central America', HoC (Strangers), 19 April 1888, p. 37
249 'They were taken to' ibid., p. 32

31

251 'letters or credentials' Beach, op. cit., p. 250
251 'Mr Anderson suggested' McIntyre, *Reynolds's Newspaper*, 25 May 1895
251 'The authorities learned' Beach, op. cit., p. 253
251 'Millen was joined by his daughters' M-MPS
251 'Gentle [Torpedo]' Dav TCD Ms 9551 f. 2r
251 'Private – No. 140 East 43rd

Street' And PRO HO 144/ 1358
252 'People at home' Millen to Pigott, 18 Sep. 1880 Dav TCD Ms 9441/3249
252 'Letters of Millen in Scotland Yard' undated misc. office notes (Parnell Box 1) TNL
252 FN 'Matter is being dealt' PRO HO 144/275/A60551
252 FN 'Suspected Dynamitard' ibid.
252 'I think it was in July' M-MPS
253 'Mr Joseph Melville, Astor House' HoC (Strangers), 19 Apr. 1888
255 'at the corner of St George's Circus' ibid.
255 'investigating frauds' ibid.
255 'About the 10th or 11th August' ibid.
256 'He told Melville' M-MPS
257 'Melville did not know' HoC (Strangers), 19 Apr. 1888
257 'she invested largely in lace' M-MPS

32

258 'I have already seen one' police and press reports in PRO DPP 4/23 and PRO CRIM 1/27/3
258 'being in America' ibid.
259 'dead but still warm' ibid.
259 'The police of "H"' M-MPS
259 'he had a friend in London' PRO DPP 4/23
259 'I must take you into custody' ibid.
260 'He had in his pocket' ibid.
260 'We went out together' ibid.

33

262 'Perhaps you will allow me' *Daily News*, 27 Oct. 1887 in PRO DPP 4/23
262 'You are taking as facts' ibid.
264 'Dynamite Plot Spoiled' *New York Times*, 27 Oct. 1887

265 'It was learned to-day' *New York Herald*, 28 Oct. 1887

266 'Several people in this city' ibid.

266 'working on a steamboat' ibid.

266 'had been designed to assist' ibid.

34

268 'took out some lime' police and committal reports in PRO DPP 4/23 and PRO CRIM/1/27/3

268 'a quiet, respectable' ibid.

268 'half a pailfull' ibid.

268 'President of the Clan-na-Gael' *The Times*, 27 Oct. 1887

268 'he really gone to Europe' interview in *Irish World and American Industrial Liberator*, 12 Nov. 1887

268 'Am I Melville?' ibid.

268 'SECRET. The Fenian agent' 4 Nov. 1887 And PRO HO 144/1357

269 'During the whole period' ibid.

271 'Millen forthwith' ibid.

271 'Two letters which came for' And PRO HO 144/1357

271 FN 'Now was the time' M-MPS

274 'Captain Melville in clover', *Penny Illustrated Paper*, 4 Nov. 1887

35

276 'found some white stuff' police and press reports in PRO DPP 4/23

276 'ill in the legs' ibid.

276 'man with broad shoulders' ibid.

277 'buying some boots' ibid.

277 'I had to do away with the tea' ibid.

278 'Harkins was brought up' M-MPS

278 'He had never seen' ibid.

278 'I have the tea' ibid.

279 'General Miller or Millen' ibid.

279 'an elderly dude' *New York Times*, 22 Nov. 1887

279 'It don't concern me' PRO DPP 4/23

279 'The name of any selected' Anderson to Governor Holloway Prison, 21 Nov. 1887, PRO HO 144/209 A 48131

279 'There is today *evidence*' Gosselin to Balfour, 22 Nov. 1887 AJB-SS PRO 30/60/13/ 21

280 'My dear Uncle Robert' Balfour to Salisbury, 27 Nov. 1887 Sals

280 'A "friend" of mine' Gosselin to Balfour, 15 Dec. 1887 AJB-SS PRO 30/60/13/21

281 'Another great grief' Jenkinson to Spencer, 22 Nov. 1887 AP KS 252
An index card in the OIOC reads 'Jenkinson, Edward John, b. Jhansi 1866, d. Deolali 21 Nov. 1887 Lt. 2nd West Yorks Regt.'

36

282 'conspiracy to injure persons' *Regina v. Callan and Harkins* PRO DPP 4/23

282 'It would be proved that the dynamite' ibid.

283 'I think you are a Member of Parliament' ibid.

283 'Callan and Harkins' *United Irishman*, 25 Feb. 1888

286 'We believe England's spies' ibid.

286 'There is a matter connected' Monro to Bradford, 10 Nov. 1891
PRO HO 144/209/A48131

287 'The convict made' Littlechild, 17 Dec., and Anderson cover to Matthews, 20 Dec. 1891, ibid.

37

289 'Salisbury suggests' W. H. Smith to Balfour, 17 Mar. 1888 AJB BL Add Mss 49698

289 'Monro as Secret Agent' PRO MEPO 4/487

289 'As to General Millen' HoC (Strangers), 19 Apr. 1888, p. 31

290 FN 'Jubilee gang' *The Times*, letters, 23 Apr. 1888

291 'never heard that the General' Commons-Strangers, op. cit., 19 Apr. 1888, p. 37

291 'What was the nature' ibid., 30 Apr. 1888, p. 48

292 '100,000 Irish' cutting in PRO ADM/1/8724/61

292 'I am informed that' Monro to Pauncefote, 18 May 1888 PRO FO 5/2044

292 Monro's mug-shot of Millen ended up in the files of the Royal Navy's West India station, where it lay for years. It was updated in 1914 when the long-dead Millen was presumed to be a 'German' agent – and returned to the Admiralty in London.

292 'The person about whom' St John to FO, 9 May 1888 PRO FO 5/2044

293 'The commission was set up' Hansard, 5 June 1888

293 'With reference to a letter' Pauncefote to Matthews, 5 June 1888 PRO FO 5/2044

294 'The result has been' PRO HO 144 190/A46721B

294 'time and energy' Warren to Matthews, 21 Apr. 1888 PRO HO 144/212/A548606/2

294 FN 'I have an uncomfortable feeling' Hamilton to Spencer, 25 July 1888 AP KS 276

295 'I must, in justice to myself' Monro to Matthews, 11 June 1888, PRO HO 144/212/A 548606

295 'Secret and confidential' St John to FO, 30 June 1888 PRO FO 5/2044

PART NINE: The Commission

38

299 'every assistance in my power' Jenkinson to Harcourt, 7 July 1888 WVH 216

300 'I am to request you to inform' Monro to FO, 4 July 1888 PRO FO 5/2044

300 'Inform X we are not' FO to St John, 5 July 1888 PRO FO 5/2044

300 'Could you let me see you' Buckle to Salisbury, 5 July 1888 Sals

301 'It was essential to show', *The History of the Times* (London, 1948), vol. iii, p. 67

301 'If we do not, it may get wasted' Balfour to Salisbury, 17 Aug. 1888 quoted in L. P. Curtis, *Coercion and Conciliation* (Princeton, 1963), p. 284

301 'There may be grounds' Salisbury to Balfour, 22 Aug. 1888, ibid.

302 'Grave differences of opinion' Monro to Matthews, 17 Aug. 1888 PRO HO 144/190/A464472C

302 'It is quite true' Jenkinson to Spencer, 24 Sept. 1888 AP KS 252

303 'exhaustion from overwork' Anderson, *The Lighter Side . . .*, p. 134

303 'Letters from Whitehall' ibid., p. 135

303 fn. 'I shall be' PRO HO 144/A49301C

39

305 'We know where the spies are' *Gaelic American*, 10 Jan. 1925

305 'malignant enemy' Le Caron, op. cit., p. 294

305 'Aleck is going to make' *Gaelic American*, 10 Jan. 1925

305 'a self-cocking revolver' ibid.

306 'the agent on the other side' *The Times*, 17 Dec. 1889 quoted in Beach, op. cit.

307 'My position as counsel' Curtis, op cit., pp. 281–2

307 'run away from the case' Salisbury to Smith, 4 Sep. 1888, ibid.

40

308 'P. S. Cassidy' Jenkinson to Spencer, 18 Oct. 1888 AP KS 252

310 'I am a welcome guest' Tevis Dav TCD Ms 9441/3219

310 'Interview with Z' Dav TCD Ms 9551 f. 15

310 FN 'What is this little' Dav TCD Ms 9441

311 'Millen in pay Hoare' Dav TCD Ms 9365/745/3

311 'Tevis, [Patrick] Casey' Dav TCD Ms 9441

312 'I had a long talk' Jenkinson to Spencer, 1 Oct. 1888 AP KS 252

312 'The feeling here is that' Beach to Anderson, 18 Sep. 1888 And PRO HO 144/1538

314 'The matter came about' SC, 15 Feb. 1889, ii, p. 282

315 'If the case is confined' Beach to Anderson, 30 Oct. 1888 And PRO HO 144/1538

315 FN 'All I can hear up to this' AB-SS PRO 30/60/13/2

316 'to see Sheridan' SC, 31 Oct. 1888, i, pp. 143–4

316 'professed dynamitard' ibid., p. 160

41

319 'Your Majesty is doubtless' Matthews to Queen Victoria, 24 Nov. 1888 MEPO 3/290

320 'Eugene Davis' misc. corres. files (Parnell Box 1) TNL

320 'Thomson, Supt. Bow St' ibid.

320 'General Millen 437 West' ibid.

320 'It is stated that' J. W. Flanagan undated misc. office notes (Parnell Box 1) TNL

321 'sgde hmzk' Har NLI Ms 8579 (typeset copy in Parnell case misc. TNL)

321 'The final decision' 13 Dec. 1888, ibid.

321 'Reply cable twelfth' 17 Dec. 1888, ibid.

321 'Am waiting final instructions' 20 Dec. 1888, ibid.

321 'With General, daily' 24 Dec. 1888, ibid.

322 'Counsel thinks Henry' 28 Dec. 1888, ibid.

323 'I have thought over' Beach to Anderson, 31 Dec. 1888 And PRO HO 144/1538

323 'I will come to you early' Macdonald to Anderson, 5 Jan. 1889 And PRO HO 144/1538

323 'Disclosures are now pressing' Macdonald to Anderson, 10 Jan. 1889, ibid.

42

325 'What is your name?' SC, 5 Feb. 1889, ii, p. 130

325 'I had learned that a "Colonel"' Davitt, op. cit. p. 609

326 'The doctor disobeyed' SC, 6 Feb. 1889, ii, p. 164

326 'Did you visit England' SC, 7 Feb. 1889, ii, p. 194

327 'I looked on myself' ibid.

328 'Do you want me to risk' 8 Feb. 1889 SC ii, p. 210

328 'Dr P. H. Cronin, one of'
     Chicago Tribune, 8 Feb. 1889
328 'An atmosphere of terror' *Gaelic
     American*, 14 Feb. 1925
329 'Have you been directed' SC, 14
     Feb. 1889, ii, p. 272–3
330 'What was his authority?' SC, 15
     Feb. 1889, ii, p. 282

43

332 'white-bearded, bald-headed' Sir
     Alfred Robbins, *Parnell: The
     Last Five Years* (London, 1926),
     p. 84
332 'five or six trips to Paris' SC, 21
     Feb. 1889, ii, p. 348
332 'the means to defeat' ibid.,
     pp. 363–9
333 'seemed to have disappeared'
     SC, 26 Feb. 1889, ii, p. 402
333 'It is suggested' Matthews to
     Anderson, 26 Feb. 1889 And
     PRO HO 144/1538
334 'I grieve to have to confess' SC,
     27 Feb. 1889, ii, p. 408
334 FN 'most scandalous books' Dav
     TCD Ms 9441
335 'My Lords . . . those who' ibid.,
     p. 409
335 'with the object of detaining'
     The Times 6 Mar. 1889
336 'I have just heard about Pigott'
     J. W. Flanagan misc. office notes
     (Parnell Box 1) TNL
336 '*The Times* has been stupid'
     Balfour to Ridgeway, 22
     Feb. 1889, quoted in Curtis, op.
     cit., p. 289
336 'Pigott was a thorough rogue'
     Salisbury to the Queen, 21 Feb.
     1889, in Curtis, op. cit., p. 290
336 'That was not with my
     cognisance' Hansard, 20
     Feb. 1889
336 'The Assistant Commissioner'
     ibid.
336 'A complete explanation' *The
     Times*, 21 Mar. 1889

337 'excessive ingestion' PRO T/
     164/62
338 'many strange things' Joyce NLI
     Ms 11119
338 'The whole system' ibid.
338 'I should be greatly' Balfour to
     Matthews, 24 Mar. 1889, Joyce
339 'sympathisers with opposite'
     Joyce
340 'Hoare, British Consul' 1 Apr.
     1889 Har NLI Ms 8579
340 'Hoare very civil' ibid.
340 'Give some reason' Currie to
     Hoare, 4 Apr. 1889 FO 5/2359
340 'Will leave on 13th' ibid.
340 'Sent to Monro' ibid.
341 'Yes: that will do' 6 Apr. 1889,
     ibid.
341 'Difficulties will be' 8 Apr. 1889
     Har NLI Ms 8579
341 'Sheridan met me yesterday'
     5 Apr. 1889, ibid.
342 'Question. Whether we' A. F.
     Walter, 11 Apr. 1889 AFW 3/
     3/3 TNL
343 'General Francis Millen' *The
     Times*, 12 Apr. 1889
343 'Considering the gravity' A. F.
     Walter, 12 Apr. 1889 AFW 3/
     3/3 TNL
343 'filing past the coffin' *New York
     Herald*, 13 Apr. 1889
343 'Across the foot' ibid.

44

345 'Were you aware' SC, 1 May
     1889, iii p. 722
345 'Until Le Caron's evidence' SC,
     2 May 1889, iii, p. 750
345 'Was Mr Nolan' ibid.
346 'Mr Jenkinson was' SC, 3 May
     1889, iii, p. 782
347 'reluctant to part' Joyce
347 'I think I may say' Sandars,
     5 May 1889 in Joyce
348 'For years past I have' Joyce
348 'Everyone knows the traitor'
     Chicago press

348 'Satisfied he will go' 20 Jun. 1889 Har NLI Ms 8579

349 'bound by an oath of secrecy' SC, 3 July 1889, iii, p. 594

349 'Was [Millen] a member' ibid., p. 592

350 'For the V in his name' Monro to Sandars, 4 July 1889 Sandars papers

350 'Who is Mr Thomson?' SC, 12 July 1889, iii, p. 712

350 'described as "M"?' ibid., p. 713

350 'a known associate' New York Times, 12 June 1889

350 'never been known since' ibid.

351 'There is no doubt that' The Times, 2 June 1889

351 'junta whose sole object' The Times, 17–28 Dec. 1889

352 'St John's Lodge' Littlechild report, 19 Nov. 1889 And PRO HO 144/1538

352 'As the O'Shea suit' Gosselin to Balfour, 1 Jan. 1890 AB-SS PRO 30/60/13/2

353 'We find that' SC, Report of the Judges, iv, pp. 475–89

353 'I'll prove a foul conspiracy' Hansard, Mar. 4 1890

353 'The final decision of FM' ibid.

45

355 'Don't mention Mexico' Egan to Davitt, 9 Feb. 1889 Dav TCD Ms 9368

356 'While this Mexican' Egan to Davitt, 13 Mar. 1889 Dav TCD Ms 9368

362 'All the original information' John T. Ennis, The Clan-na-Gael and the Murder of Dr Cronin (Chicago, 1889), p. 77

Epilogue

365 'Mr Monro..posed' Buckle op. cit. p. 615–616

365 'Forty insubordinate' ibid. p. 620

365 'contrary to the wishes' The Times, 13 June 1890p. 371

365 'evil practises' Lord Salisbury to the Queen, 20 July 1890 Buckle op. cit. p. 623

365 'against the abolition' Ruggles-Brise memo, 12 Dec 1890 Sals

366 'Brest, Finisterre' Foreign Office List, 1895

366 'The only circumstance' St John to Salisbury, 11 Jan. 1890 PRO FO 50/474

366 'The disinterment of' Luby to O'Leary, 1 Nov. 1889 Luby papers NLI Ms 5926

367 'an undertaking shrouded' Beach, op. cit., p. 255

367 'There is no use thinking' ibid., p. 276

367 'Inspector Littlechild formally' statement of Dr Macleod Yearsley, 6 Oct. 1924, pasted into the flyleaf of a copy of Beach's memoir bought that day for '1/– in the Farringdon Road' (Peter Bance, Duleep Singh collection). Yearsley attended Beach during his last illness – when he 'never slept without a loaded revolver under his pillow and the house was watched by four detectives. The body was so emaciated it weighed only 4st 8lbs. The large intestine was so kinked by adhesions as to appear as if pulled upon itself like a giant cracker.'

368 'An act of clemency' Gen. B. Butler to J. W. Foster, 26 Oct. 1892 PRO HO 144/209/A48131

369 'We had a ride in a brougham' Callan to 'Peter', 22 Sep. 1892, ibid.

369 FN Article by Zoe Lappin in WISE Words, newsletter of the Wales, Ireland, Scotland and England Family History Society, Jan.–June 2002, Denver, Colorado.

INDEX